Recognition of Belligerency and the Law of Armed Conflict

THE LIEBER STUDIES

The editors would like to thank the members of the Department of Law for their assistance making this publication possible. In addition, this publication would not have been possible without the efforts of Lieutenant Colonel Lakeyisa Harvin, LTC Thomas Oakley, MAJ Ronald Alcala, MAJ Phillip Dickerson, MAJ Trenton Powell, and CPT Robert Lawless.

The Lieber Studies is the flagship publication of the Lieber Institute for Law and Land Warfare. It is designed to provide scholars, practitioners, and students with in-depth and critical analysis of the most challenging legal issues related to warfare in the 21st Century. Established by the Department of Law of the United States Military Academy at West Point, the mission of the Lieber Institute is to foster a deeper understanding of the complex and evolving relationship between law and land warfare in order to educate and empower current and future combat leaders. It does so through global academic engagement and advanced interdisciplinary research. As such, it lies at the crossroads of scholarship and practice by bringing together scholars, military officers, government legal advisers, and members of civil society from around the world to collaboratively examine the role and application of the law of armed conflict in current and future armed conflicts, as well as that of other regimes of international law in situations threatening international peace and security.

Lieber Institute for Law and Land Warfare
The Lieber Studies

VOLUME 3

Recognition of Belligerency and the Law of Armed Conflict

General Editor

PROFESSOR MICHAEL N. SCHMITT

Managing Editors

LIEUTENANT COLONEL SHANE R. REEVES

LIEUTENANT COLONEL WINSTON S. WILLIAMS

Author

PROFESSOR ROBERT MCLAUGHLIN

OXFORD
UNIVERSITY PRESS

OXFORD
UNIVERSITY PRESS

Oxford University Press is a department of the University of Oxford. It furthers the University's objective of excellence in research, scholarship, and education by publishing worldwide. Oxford is a registered trademark of Oxford University Press in the UK and certain other countries.

Published in the United States of America by Oxford University Press
198 Madison Avenue, New York, NY 10016, United States of America.

Library of Congress Cataloging-in-Publication Data

Names: McLaughlin, Robert, 1964– author.
Title: Recognition of belligerency and the law of armed conflict / Robert McLaughlin.
Description: New York : Oxford University Press, 2020. | Series: The Lieber Studies series | Includes bibliographical references and index.
Identifiers: LCCN 2019038597 (print) | LCCN 2019038598 (ebook) | ISBN 9780197507056 (hardback) | ISBN 9780197507070 (epub) | ISBN 9780197507063 (updf) | ISBN 9780197507087 (online)
Subjects: LCSH: War (International law) | Belligerency. | Geneva Conventions (1949 August 12)
Classification: LCC KZ6355 .M397 2020 (print) | LCC KZ6355 (ebook) | DDC 341.6—dc23
LC record available at https://lccn.loc.gov/2019038597
LC ebook record available at https://lccn.loc.gov/2019038598

---

9 8 7 6 5 4 3 2 1

Printed by Integrated Books International, United States of America

Note to Readers
This publication is designed to provide accurate and authoritative information in regard to the subject matter covered. It is based upon sources believed to be accurate and reliable and is intended to be current as of the time it was written. It is sold with the understanding that the publisher is not engaged in rendering legal, accounting, or other professional services. If legal advice or other expert assistance is required, the services of a competent professional person should be sought. Also, to confirm that the information has not been affected or changed by recent developments, traditional legal research techniques should be used, including checking primary sources where appropriate.

(Based on the Declaration of Principles jointly adopted by a Committee of the American Bar Association and a Committee of Publishers and Associations.)

CONTENTS

PREFACE

In early 2012, I was invited by Mike Schmitt and James Farrant to join them, and other scholars of the law applicable to naval operations, at a roundtable in London. The topic was mine warfare, and I was asked to present a short introduction to the topic "Mine Warfare in Non-International Armed Conflict." My initial approach was to trace the relevant permissions and limitations by reference to three fundamental assertions: that hostilities conducted outside the territorial sea by a non-state actor will be inconsistent with the Law of the Sea and will in most cases amount to either piracy or a *Suppression of Unlawful Activities at Sea Convention* offense; as a general rule, only states get to exercise maritime belligerent rights; and characterization of rebel maritime operations inside the territorial sea will primarily be a matter of domestic law. However, as I drafted my piece for that roundtable, I recalled that I would need to make (for the sake of completeness) some introductory historical reference to the pre-1949 customary rules applicable in civil wars. The more I explored this historical background, the more I became convinced that in treating this customary rule set as "history" rather than operative "law," my analysis was actually overlooking a nuanced, relevant, and potentially *operative* rule set—the customary Law of War scheme relating to recognition of belligerency. I have now come to the view that—stand-fast a few notable exceptions—we, as a community of LOAC scholars, may unfortunately have lost sight of an intensely relevant customary rule set regarding formal recognition of belligerency and, to a lesser extent, the political-legal status of insurgency.

Thus began the intellectual journey distilled in this book. I began to delve more deeply into some of the often referenced but less frequently analyzed international law classics, and the wonderful compilations of documents and commentary by nineteenth- and early twentieth-century publicists: Smith, Hall, Lawrence, Wheaton, Dana, and so on. I looked at immediate post-World War II scholars as well—Lauterpacht, Chen, and McNair. It became increasingly clear (to me, at any rate) that all of these titans of the discipline had dealt with recognition of belligerency, and they had done so in terms that reflected an appreciation of the doctrine as an operative and extant legal framework for conflict analysis and the allocation of rights and obligations during civil wars. Indeed, fully one-third of Lauterpacht's *Recognition in International Law* was devoted to the topic—equal treatment with recognition of states and recognition of governments. Recognition of belligerency was not, for these scholars and advisers, merely an interesting legal anachronism. Yet while recognition of states and governments remains now, as then, a vibrant and vital field of practice and study, recognition of belligerency had—it seemed to me—been forgotten. It was, to draw a poor parallel with a very much more significant example, something like Stephen Greenblatt's description, in his book *The Swerve*, of the rediscovery on a monastery bookshelf in 1417 of Lucretius' Epicurean tract, *On the Nature of Things*. This very significant work—prized and lauded at the time of its publication more than a millennium earlier—had been thought lost. This rediscovery, wrote Greenblatt, was preceded by hints and possibilities, "But, neither debated nor disseminated, after each of these fugitive appearances it seemed to sink again beneath the waves."[1] This is how the doctrine on recognition of belligerency was presenting in my research—furtive post-World War II appearances, including by some of our discipline's most lauded scholars, but little sustained analysis and discussion. Why was this so? Why had recognition of belligerency, as appeared to be the case, fallen so (irredeemably? irrecoverably?) far to the wayside as an object of legal analysis and application?

Two years after the roundtable, I took the opportunity of another visit to the UK to spend some time at the National Archives—primarily to examine a file on the *Red Crusader* incident. However, while there, I thought to seek out anything I could find in relation to recognition of belligerency. I was most particularly interested to read official advices or discussions of the doctrine in governmental documents in the hope that these documents might tell me if recognition of belligerency had survived the Spanish Civil War—the conflict cited by many as the nadir, and then death, of the doctrine. The files were a goldmine. Over the course of the next five years, with many pilgrimages to the archives at Kew, days chasing single obscure footnotes in academic articles and monographs, and discussions with comrades who are very much smarter than me—I researched and wrote this book. Mike Schmitt, a lifelong mentor and friend, then agreed in conjunction with OUP (to whom also, my sincere thanks) to publish it in his Lieber series—it is an act of kindness for which I am deeply appreciative.

There are many people and organizations I must thank, for without their assistance and input, I would not have finally got to this point. First, I commenced this work while at ANU, and finished it at UNSW Canberra—I am deeply grateful to both institutions for the travel funding, library support, and research time they have happily provided. Second, I must thank the UK National Archives, which never failed to find a file and patiently showed me how to work the image capture system, and the Lieber Institute for their patient, painstaking, and greatly appreciated review and editing. I must also at this point acknowledge the unstinting comradeship of my friend and colleague David Letts, who was with me on many of these treks to Kew as he researched the *Belgrano* incident, and thus bore the brunt of many "hey Dave, look at this!" moments. Third, I am most thankful for the peer and student feedback I have received at conferences and discussion

1. Stephen Greenblatt, The Swerve: How the Renaissance Began 12–13 (London, Vintage Books 2011).

roundtables where I have talked about recognition of belligerency, for this has assisted me greatly in honing my drafts, avoiding mistakes (all that remain are mine alone), and ensuring that I never lost sight of the touchstone of relevance. Fourth, I am deeply indebted to the many colleagues and friends who discussed portions of this work and/or ideas with me, and who read drafts of chapters (and in some cases, the draft of the book in whole), providing me with exceptional feedback, corrections, and additional sources: Michael Schmitt, Shane Reeves, Winston Williams, Sandy Sivakumaran, Emily Crawford, Bruce Oswald, Hitoshi Nasu, David Letts, Don Rothwell, Marko Milanovic, Nigel White, Tim McCormack, Wolff Heintschel von Heinegg, Rain Liivoja, Anthea Roberts, Tristan Delroy, Tamsin Paige, Mitt Regan, Dominique Dalla-Pozza, Pete Pedrozo, Roger O'Keefe, Gerry Simpson, Dale Stephens, and Sarah Heathcote. I must also thank the many exceptional lawyers from the Office of International Law, the ADF Legal Service, and the Department of Foreign Affairs and Trade Legal Branch who very kindly took the time to talk with me about this and many associated topics.

Finally, my thanks—always—to my very patient and supportive family. This book is for F, A, N, and R.

Rob McLaughlin
Canberra, February 2018.

INTRODUCTION

In response to rumors of his death, Samuel Clemens, the great humorist, novelist, and social commentator who wrote under the pen name Mark Twain, was said to have quipped in 1897 that "The reports of my death are greatly exaggerated." At the time, he was in London and ill, but hardly on his deathbed.

The international law governing armed conflict, whether between States or between States and non-State actors, sometimes falls victim to the same dynamic, as it is not unusual for commentators to claim that aspects thereof have fallen into desuetude. Examples abound. For instance, it has been questioned whether the notion of debellatio, by which the spoils of war upon the total defeat of a vanquished adversary include the territory and sovereignty, has survived the law of occupation and the modern normative revulsion against annexation. Similarly, the doctrine of angary, which allows belligerent States in situations of necessity to use or destroy neutral property like merchant vessels or civil aircraft present on their territory (or on that which they occupy), subject to indemnification, appears to be fading away. Some commentators have even questioned whether the law of neutrality itself survives peace enforcement measures authorized or mandated by the UN Security Council under Chapter VII of the UN Charter.

Like its conceptual brethren, the doctrine of belligerency is oft characterized as having fallen into desuetude. Indeed, the concept is typically illustrated by reference to the U.S. Civil War, which ended over a century and a half ago. According to the traditional understanding of the doctrine, as exemplified by that conflict, a state of belligerency exists between a State and a non-State group when four cumulative conditions are fulfilled: hostilities of an intensity exceeding civil unrest; control of substantial territory by the non-State actor engaged in hostilities with the State; a significant degree of civil governance over that territory; and observance of the law of armed conflict by insurgent forces. Taken together, the situation must resemble a conflict between States.

The existence of a state of belligerency is further conditioned upon express or implied "recognition" of belligerency by either the State involved in the hostilities or by other States. In the former case, the *jus in bello* applicable in international armed conflicts applies, most significantly with regard to the treatment of captured soldiers on both sides as prisoners of war. Additionally, the law of neutrality applies as between the parties to the conflict and other States. In the latter, it governs relations between the State affording the recognition of belligerency and the parties to the conflict, including the requirement of impartiality, but does not affect the status of the hostilities between the parties or relations between other States and the parties.

An existential question regarding the doctrine is whether it has survived the twentieth-century treaty law (and any customary law analogue) that has been adopted to govern conflicts that are not international in character, in particular Common Article 3 to the 1949 Geneva Conventions and Additional Protocol II to those instruments. Additional Protocol II is noteworthy in this regard, for it incorporates criteria resembling those applicable to a belligerency in its reference to armed conflicts that "take place in the territory of a High Contracting Party between its armed forces and dissident armed forces or other organized armed groups which, under responsible command, exercise such control over a part of its territory as to enable them to carry out sustained and concerted military operations and to implement this Protocol."

In this important and thoughtful work, Professor Rob McLaughlin skillfully dissects the doctrine of belligerency. To accomplish this challenging task, he adopts a legal-historical approach to the doctrine, one in which he identifies its historical roots and application, asks whether doctrine effectively achieves its intended purpose(s), examines how it has fared in the face of various challenges, and assesses its contemporary utility in responding to the shortfalls in the characterization of a conflict as non-international. His is the most comprehensive and insightful consideration of the subject in many decades.

Professor McLaughlin is to be commended for taking on this complex subject. In an era where blog reactions to last night's events often masquerade as scholarship, there is a troublesome propensity for collective loss of memory in our field. The reality is that in this fast-paced, reactive environment, law of armed conflict norms that have not been recently implicated in a relatively direct fashion tend to lose traction. This dynamic is concerning because when it occurs, the law loses the granularity that can be instrumental in addressing conflict situations that do not mirror those currently underway but that might resemble those of the past. The consequence can be ignorance of useful normative lessons learned and the treatment of such situations as if they are cases of first impression.

I congratulate Professor McLaughlin on helping to fight this worrisome trend though this exceptional contribution to the Lieber Studies.

Michael N. Schmitt
Francis Lieber Distinguished Scholar
United States Military Academy at West Point

1

The Scope and Structure of This Book

> Of war I sing, war worse than civil, waged over the plains of Emathia, and of legality conferred on crime;
>
> I tell how an imperial people turned their victorious right hands against their own vitals;
>
> how kindred fought against kindred;
>
> how, when the compact of tyranny was shattered, all the forces of the shaken world contended to make mankind guilty;
>
> how standards confronted hostile standards, eagles were matched against each other, and pilum threatened pilum.
>
> What madness was this, my countrymen, what fierce orgy of slaughter?[1]
>
> —LUCAN, *The Civil War*

> It seems that civil war, like the poor, may always be with us . . . But civil war shouldn't also remain an impoverished area of inquiry. As many have noted, civil war has remained undertheorized and resistant to generalization . . . Our own time demands an unblinking encounter with civil war. The three hundred years between 1648 and 1945 constituted an era of war between states; the last sixty years appear to be an age of war within states.[2]
>
> —DAVID ARMITAGE, *Civil Wars: A History in Ideas*

1. LUCAN, THE CIVIL WAR (PHARSALIA) I.1–8 (Jeffrey Henderson ed., J. D. McDuff trans., Loeb Classical Library 1928).

2. DAVID ARMITAGE, CIVIL WARS: A HISTORY IN IDEAS 6–7 (2017).

A. INTRODUCTION

Most difficulties encountered in the application of the law of armed conflict (LOAC), or in proffering fixes for alleged lacunae in LOAC, are dealt with through exegetical analysis from modern rules and their underpinning principles. This is generally undertaken with a view toward progressive development of the law. Nowhere is this more currently apparent than in relation to grappling with the status and obligations of non-state armed groups (NSAG) in the context of non-international armed conflict (NIAC). It is often noted that this issue is notorious for thin legislation and fragile crystallization.[3] Indicatively, as the International Committee of the Red Cross's (ICRC) *Interpretive Guidance on the Notion of Direct Participation in Hostilities under International Humanitarian Law* noted,

> Derived from Article 3 common to the Geneva Conventions, the notion of taking a direct or active part in hostilities is found in many provisions of IHL. However, despite the serious legal consequences involved, neither the Conventions nor their additional Protocols provide a definition of direct participation in hostilities. The situation calls for the clarification of three questions under IHL.[4]

The three questions then formulated all revolve around the need to address a paucity of detailed rules on the legal status to be attributed to those taking a direct part in hostilities—whether as individuals ad hoc, or as members of NSAGs—as well as to their conduct, and their access to or loss of the civilian protections afforded under LOAC. Additionally, as many other writers have noted, it is becoming increasingly imperative (given the overwhelming current predominance of NIACs or mixed conflicts, as opposed to international armed conflicts (IAC)) that LOAC finds a suitable scheme for dealing with NSAGs as entities susceptible to some form of organizational legal obligation—at least as concerns their de facto (if not de jure) compliance with LOAC and certain human rights obligations.[5]

3. Commentary, I Geneva Convention for the Amelioration of the Condition of the Wounded and Sick in Armed Forces in the Field 39, 43–44, 60 (Jean S. Pictet ed., 1952); *see also* Lindsay Moir, The Law of Internal Armed Conflict chs. 1–3 (2002); Michael N. Schmitt, *The Status of Opposition Fighters in a Non-International Armed Conflict*, 88 Int'l L. Stud. 119 (2011).

4. Nils Melzer, Interpretive Guidance on the Notion of Direct Participation in Hostilities under International Humanitarian Law 12–13 (2009).

5. Antonio Cassese, *The Status of Rebels under the 1977 Geneva Protocol on Non-International Armed Conflicts*, 30 Int'l & Comp. L. Q. 416, 428–29; M. Cherif Bassiouni, *The New Wars and the Crisis of Compliance with the Law of Armed Conflict by Non-State Actors*, 98 J. Crim. L. & Criminology 711, 741, 750–58 (2008); Jann K. Kleffner, *The Applicability of International Humanitarian Law to Organized Armed Groups*, 93 Int'l Rev. Red Cross 443 (2011); Geneva Call, *Engaging with Armed Non-State Actors in the Broader Middle East on the Protection of Civilians* 6–9 (2012); Pascal Bongard, *Engaging Armed Non-State Actors on Humanitarian Norms: Reflections on Geneva Call's Experience*, Humanitarian Exchange, July 2013.

Richard Falk, in 1971, observed that "[t]he relevance of international law to civil-war situations needs to be rethought";[6] yet four decades and more later, Frédéric Mégret was still in a position to make what amounts to an almost identical appeal: "We clearly live in an age where it is becoming increasingly necessary to conceive of a sounder regime for NIAC."[7] Recognition of belligerency offers one well-tailored option to achieve just this, but its continued existence has been questioned,[8] and among other purposes, this book seeks to present sufficient background, case studies, and analysis so as to enable the reader to reach a view on this issue. In order to do so, however, it is my contention that we ought to be guided at the outset by three admonitions: legally, to be clear as to the threshold we are concerned with; doctrinally, to interrogate the almost forgotten experience of harmonization of IAC and NIAC LOAC represented by recognition of belligerency; and historically, to look to situations in which the doctrine on recognition of belligerency was actively canvassed as an analytical tool (i.e., not just those situations where recognition of belligerency was formally granted) in order to gain a proper appreciation of its interpretation, utility, and influence. Given the centrality of these three assumptions to the project manifested in this book, some further initial elaboration of each is warranted.

6. Richard A. Falk, *Introduction* to THE INTERNATIONAL LAW OF CIVIL WAR 1, 29 (1971).

7. *See* Claus Kreβ and Frédéric Mégret, *The Regulation of Non-International Armed Conflicts: Can a Privilege of Belligerency Be Envisioned in the Law of Non-International Armed Conflicts?*, 96 INT'L REV. RED CROSS 29, 45 (2015) (debating how international humanitarian law applicable to non-international armed conflict should develop).

8. Generally, the issue of the continued existence of the doctrine is simply not addressed. However, a number of scholars who have specifically addressed this doctrine have concluded that formal belligerency, although in "disuse," nevertheless remains "relevant." *See, e.g.*, Yoram Dinstein, *Concluding Remarks on Non-International Armed Conflicts*, 88 INT'L L. STUD. 399, 408–10; Marko Milanovic, *What Exactly Internationalises an Internal Armed Conflict?*, EJIL TALK!, May 7, 2010, *available at* http://www.ejiltalk.org/what-exactly-internationalizes-an-internal-armed-conflict/. For commentary on the historical scope of the doctrine, *see* inter alia EMER DE VATTEL, THE LAW OF NATIONS OR THE PRINCIPLES OF NATURAL LAW (Charles Ghequiere Fenwick trans., Oceana 1964) (1758), at bk. III, ch. XVIII; Robert R. Wilson, *Recognition of Insurgency and Belligerency*, *in* PROCEEDINGS OF THE AMERICAN SOCIETY OF INTERNATIONAL LAW AT ITS THIRTY-FIRST ANNUAL MEETING 136 (1937) [hereinafter PROCEEDINGS OF ASIL ANNUAL MEETING]; Fred K. Nielsen, *Insurgency and Maritime Law*, *in* PROCEEDINGS OF ASIL ANNUAL MEETING at 144; *Discussion*, *in* PROCEEDINGS OF ASIL ANNUAL MEETING at 153; Rogier Bartels, *Timelines, Borderlines and Conflicts*, 91 INT'L REV. RED CROSS 35 (2009); and Sasha Radin, *The Current Relevance of the Recognition of Belligerency*, *in* ARMED CONFLICT AND INTERNATIONAL LAW: IN SEARCH OF THE HUMAN FACE 115, 115–52 (Mariëlle Matthee et al. eds., 2013).

(i) The legal assumption—The threshold between civil war and IAC is not an exact correlate of that between NIAC and IAC

It is obvious, but bears repeating nevertheless, that determining the legal regime governing status and conduct in any situation of internal turmoil, conflict, or civil war is fundamentally beholden to the legal threshold between mere riot and civil unrest, and, in post-1949 LOAC terms, NIAC. The concept of internal armed conflict as a legally distinct form of "war" is not new,[9] although historically the priority was (as this book will describe) focused upon determining when a situation of internal unrest crossed a threshold that enlivened the "standard" Law of War—articulated most completely, as we shall see, in terms of the formal status of belligerency.[10] Since 1949, while law and practice has continued to entrench a legal differentiation between NIAC and IAC, the lower threshold—between civil disturbance not reaching the level of NIAC, and NIAC itself—has become significantly more nuanced as a legal concept and significantly more important as a political and operational threshold. Indeed, there are a range of treaty definitions describing the threshold between NIAC and less-than-NIAC situations, as opposed to the much cleaner, single, and simply articulated threshold between IAC and mere international tension.[11] The bivalent concept of "internationalized internal armed conflict"—which is perhaps better understood in terms of concurrent NIAC and IAC contexts within the same operational zone (as with Libya in 2011), than as a new status mixtus[12] between IAC and NIAC—offers challenges, but they are not insurmountable.

9. *See generally* ARMITAGE, CIVIL WARS: A HISTORY IN IDEAS, at 22–25 (citing as examples the Greek "satsis" or "emphylios polemos," Roman "bellum civile," Arabic "fitna," Japanese "naisen," and others).

10. *See generally* THEODOR MERON, HENRY'S WARS AND SHAKESPEARE'S LAWS (1993), at ch. 11.

11. *See, e.g.*, Geneva Convention Relative to the Treatment of Prisoners of War art. 3, Aug. 12, 1949, 6 U.S.T. 3316, 75 U.N.T.S. 135 (Common Article 3 to the Geneva Conventions of 1949); Protocol Additional to the Geneva Conventions of 12 August 1949, and Relating to the Protection of Victims of Non-International Armed Conflicts (Protocol II) art. 1(1), June 8, 1977, 1125 U.N.T.S. 609 [hereinafter APII] (providing a more exacting threshold); APII, art. 1(4) (describing the NIAC to IAC transferal regime). *See generally* INT'L INST. HUMANITARIAN L., THE MANUAL ON THE LAW OF NON-INTERNATIONAL ARMED CONFLICT para. 1.1.1 (Michael N. Schmitt, H.B. Garraway, and Yoram Dinstein eds., 2006).

12. In a 1943 article, Georg Schwarzenberger took the traditional, naturalist distinction between the law of war and the law of peace in international law to task, arguing that state practice evidenced a third paradigm of "status mixtus." Georg Schwarzenberger, *Jus Pacis Ac Belli? Prolegomena to a Sociology of International Law*, 37 AM. J. INT'L L. 460 (1943). Jessup, in a 1946 piece in *Foreign Affairs*, argued that there really ought to be a paradigm covering lesser uses of force than war. Phillip C. Jessup, *Force Under a Modern Law of Nations*, 25 FOREIGN AFFAIRS 90 (1946). In a 1954 editorial comment in the *American Journal of International Law*, Jessup again specifically asked, "Should International Law Recognise an Intermediate Status between Peace and War?" Phillip C. Jessup, *Should International Law Recognise an Intermediate Status between Peace and War?*, 48 AM. J. INT'L L. 98 (1954).

Consequently, in any conflict context involving internal armed conflict, exploring—and coming to a clear conclusion on—the legal characterization of the conflict (less-than-NIAC or NIAC; NIAC or IAC) is *the* fundamental first step in LOAC analysis. Of these thresholds, the most starkly drawn in terms of consequences for LOAC status, conduct, and treatment is (as noted) that between less-than-NIAC and NIAC. This is because in less-than-NIAC contexts, LOAC powers, obligations, and limitations simply do not apply de jure (standfast, of course, enduring obligations such as Common Article 1 of the 1949 *Geneva Conventions*, and Article 36 of 1977 *Additional Protocol* I). The applicable legal regime is the regular "peacetime" or "law enforcement" regime of criminal law and human rights law: search and seizure; arrest and prosecution; the full suite of human rights law checks and balances; and limitations on use of lethal force (generally) to situations of individual and unit self-defense, and defense of others.[13] When an internal unrest context spills across the threshold into NIAC, it triggers a radically different set of status allocations, powers, obligations, and limitations: Targeting operations in accordance with LOAC; detention operations that differentiate between mere criminality on one hand, and the criminality associated with direct participation in hostilities and membership of a NSAG on the other; as well as reduced availability of certain means and methods that are perfectly legitimate in a law enforcement context, but prohibited in a LOAC context (such as the use of certain ammunition types or riot control agents). This is the grist of myriad topical and operationally relevant debates: Where does law enforcement end and NIAC start? What human rights obligations and limitations

13. *See* the definitions for each type of self-defense in the *Sanremo Handbook on Rules of Engagement*. INT'L INST. HUMANITARIAN L., SANREMO HANDBOOK ON RULES OF ENGAGEMENT 3 (Dennis Mandsager et al. eds., 2009). "*Individual self-defence*. This refers to the right of an individual to defend himself or herself (and in some cases other individuals) from an *attack* or imminent *attack*. Some nations permit commanders to limit *individual self-defence* in the same way as for *unit self-defence*"; "*Unit self-defence*. Unit commanders have the right to defend their unit and other units from their nation in the face of an *attack* or imminent *attack*. For some nations, the concept of *unit self-defence* is both a right and an obligation; whereas for others the concept is only a right. Some nations permit the right of *unit self-defence* to be limited by orders from *higher authority*. *Unit self-defence* may be extended to units and individuals from other nations when authorised by the applicable ROE"; "Protection of Others. This refers to the right to defend specified persons (who are not part of the *Force*) against an *attack* or imminent *attack*. For some nations, the right of *individual self-defence* or *unit self-defence* may not include the right to use force to defend another nation's citizens." On the problems of mixing the concept of use of force in LOAC "attack" with the legally distinct concept of use of force in individual self-defense or defense of others, even if in an otherwise LOAC governed battle space, *see* Rob McLaughlin, *The Legal Regime Applicable to Use of Lethal Force When Operating under a United Nations Security Council Chapter VII Mandate Authorising "All Necessary Means*," 12 J. CONFLICT & SEC. L. 389 (2007); Rob McLaughlin, *The Use of Lethal Force by Military Forces on Law Enforcement Operations—Is There a "Lawful Authority"?*, 37 FED. L. REV. 441 (2009); Ian Henderson and Bryan Cavanagh, *Military Members Claiming Self-Defence during Armed Conflict: Often Misguided and Unhelpful*, *in* ACCOUNTABILITY FOR VIOLATIONS IN INTERNATIONAL HUMANITARIAN LAW: ESSAYS IN HONOUR OF TIM MCCORMACK 73–94 (Jadranka Petrovic ed., 2016).

permeate the threshold between less-than-NIAC and NIAC? How do we achieve interoperability in use of force where one force element views a context as less-than-NIAC, while a partner force views it as an NIAC or IAC?

As part of this paradigmatic squeeze on NIAC LOAC from below—from the 'less-than-NIAC' to NIAC threshold—it is this question as to the permeation of human rights law across that less-than-NIAC threshold into NIAC contexts that currently garners most attention. But this focus has perhaps temporarily obscured an equally important and operationally current debate that challenges us from the opposite direction: To what extent is NIAC LOAC being simultaneously colonized by its upper threshold neighbor, IAC LOAC? As shall become evident, although incidental reference to the less-than-NIAC and NIAC seam is impossible to avoid in relation to the pre-1949 legal contexts of rebellion and insurgency, it is actually this civil war and IAC LOAC dynamic and transition point that informs and animates the doctrine on recognition of belligerency. This is the primary reason why, apart from some brief references in Chapters 5 and 6, this book does not deal with 1977 *Additional Protocol II*. Recognition of belligerency was fundamentally concerned with application within civil wars of the Law of War, as if the conflict were international in nature. *Additional Protocol II*, by contrast, is necessarily bound by its purpose and provisions to the other side of this threshold—the less-than-NIAC to NIAC transition, and the law applicable in NIAC. Thus my first point is simply this: that while civil war and IAC differ legally, they do not necessarily differ in the same way as NIAC and IAC differ legally.

(ii) The doctrinal assumption—Harmonization of NIAC and IAC LOAC will never be total

The general tenor of legal debate regarding the application of conduct and status rules in NIAC contexts—conceptually relevant to, but not definitive of, discussions regarding the doctrine on recognition of belligerency—is heavily influenced by two intricately linked, thematic pressures concerning the place of NIAC LOAC within LOAC more generally: to humanize and to harmonize. It is essential that any consideration of the law relating to use of force in civil war contexts (as the generally accepted term of art employed prior to the development of the NIAC concept) recognize at the outset the influence and implications of these paradigmatic tensions, as the perspective of the analyst on these two thematic challenges will more often than not drive their interpretive choices. The thematic trend toward humanizing LOAC is, academically, well-tilled ground and centers upon the extent to which international human rights law and "humanitarian" interpretations—de jure and de facto—now permeate the NIAC (and, to a lesser extent IAC) LOAC regimes. As such, I do not propose to revisit this debate merely for the sake of a summative survey of what is already a well-illustrated and well-analyzed trend.[14]

14. *See, e.g.*, JAMES E. BOND, RULES OF RIOT: INTERNAL CONFLICT AND THE LAW OF WAR (1974) at chs. 2 and 3; Rogier Bartels, *Timelines, Borderlines and Conflicts: The Historical Evolution of*

As a response, however, to legion, long-term, and lingering difficulties in interpreting, developing, and applying LOAC to NIACs (and indeed to civil war), the second thematic tension—the push for harmonization of IAC and NIAC LOAC—is perhaps less well-tilled ground. As such it requires some brief introductory scoping because, as shall hopefully become evident, harmonization consciously underpinned the doctrine on recognition of belligerency. As Bruce Oswald has observed in a directly relevant indication of the granular challenges of the harmonization project,

> Two of the more controversial aspects of translating international armed conflict obligations to non-international armed conflicts are the principles governing combatant immunity—that is, immunity from prosecution for belligerent acts that do not violate the laws of war—and the treatment of captured belligerents.[15]

Perhaps the most striking and effective example of this thematic trend is the ICRC *Customary International Humanitarian Law* study,[16] which, as several commentators have noted, proceeds upon the assumption that much of IAC LOAC is directly transferable to, and obligatory within, NIAC contexts. In relation to the final stages of the NIAC between the government of Sri Lanka and the Liberation Tigers of Tamil Eelam (LTTE), for example, the UN Panel of Experts was in no doubt that the targeting law regime associated most generally with IAC was also applicable in all its granular detail within this NIAC. Citing the ICRC *Customary International Humanitarian Law* study, the Panel stated that the study's rules on targeting were "beyond dispute as rules of customary international humanitarian law" applicable in NIAC contexts.[17]

The harmonize trend is highly seductive. It holds forth the promise, for example, of application of the same sets of LOAC rules regardless of the context, presaging the stability and simplicity of a single code against which operational planning, conduct, and internal consequence assessment can be managed, and

the Legal Divide between International and Non-International Armed Conflicts, 91 Int'l Rev. Red Cross 35 (2009); Jelena Pejic, *Status of Armed Conflicts*, *in* Perspectives on the ICRC Study on Customary International Humanitarian Law 77–100 (Elizabeth Wilmshurst and Susan Breau eds., 2007).

15. Bruce "Ossie" Oswald, *The Harmonization Project: Improving Compliance with the Law of War in Non-International Armed Conflicts*, 53 Colum. J. Transnat'l L. 105, 110 (2014).

16. Jean-Marie Henckaerts and Louise Doswald-Beck, Customary International Humanitarian Law, Volume 1: Rules (2005).

17. Report of the Secretary-General's Panel of Experts on Accountability in Sri Lanka para. 183 (2011). *See also, e.g.*, *id.* para. 204 (on the precautions before and during attacks).

upon which scrutiny and accountability can be based.[18] It is also evident on many levels. The International Criminal Tribunal for the Former Yugoslavia's (ICTY) assertion in *Tadic* that the legal distinction between IAC and NIAC is now almost irrelevant, is oft cited.[19] But the tendency toward harmonization has also long been evident in jurisprudence and commentary much more broadly. In 2002, for example, Liesbeth Zegveld argued that it was by then "common practice for international bodies to read substantive norms of Protocol I and the Geneva Conventions into Common Article 3 and Protocol II."[20] A decade later, this trend continues to underpin detailed analyses of specific LOAC issues: Robin Geiβ and Michael Siegrist, for example, have asserted that, in the context of a NIAC,

> Protection of military objectives that cannot so readily be concealed may be sought by the use of human shields, thereby manipulating the enemy's proportionality assessment, in addition to violating the precautionary principle laid out in Article 58 of Additional Protocol I and part of customary IHL applicable in both international and non-international armed conflict.[21]

The reference point is clearly 1977 *Additional Protocol I* (*API*), and the equally clear assumption is that the detailed targeting law provisions of *API* are reflected in broad LOAC customary rules and therefore apply in NIAC contexts. Perhaps the most seductive allure of this trend is the very fact that it appears to promise a diminished, or even dissolved, need to tie ourselves in knots negotiating how NIAC and IAC can share a battlespace in order to establish which LOAC applies to what conduct. If the hard core of, in particular, "means and methods" LOAC is

18. Emily Crawford, *Unequal before the Law: The Case for the Elimination of the Distinction between International and Non-International Armed Conflicts*, 20 Leiden J. Int'l L. 441 (2007) (providing a strong, reasoned example that indicates the harmonization thematic trend).

19. Prosecutor v. Tadić, ICTY Case No. IT-94-1-AR72, Decision on the Defence Motion for Interlocutory Appeal on Jurisdiction, ¶¶ 97–98 (Int'l Crim. Trib. for the Former Yugoslavia Oct. 2, 1995).

20. Liesbeth Zegveld, The Accountability of Armed Opposition Groups in International Law 33 (2002).

21. Robin Geiβ and Michael Siegrist, *Has the Armed Conflict in Afghanistan Affected the Rules on the Conduct of Hostilities?*, 93 Int'l Rev. Red Cross 11, 19–20 (2011); *see also id.* at 29–32 (discussing the proportionality principle and proportionality assessments). The authors cite, as evidence of U.S. acceptance of this point, an official Collateral Damage Methodology document accessed via the Freedom of Information Act process, and submitted as evidence (Declaration of Jonathan Manes, dated 8 October 2010) in the U.S. District Court case of *Al-Aulaqi v. Obama*. Al-Aulaqi v. Obama, 727 F. Supp. 2d 1, 2010 U.S. Dist. LEXIS 129601 (D.D.C. 2010), *available at* http://www.ccrjustice.org/files/Declaration%20of%20Jonathan%20Manes%2010-08-2010.pdf. I respectfully disagree with this assessment; the document discloses a methodology and does not discuss the applicable law beyond generic terms. However, I do think it fair to say that the conclusion is correct: the United States does appear to apply the detail of their interpretation of targeting law under IAC LOAC rules within NIAC contexts.

the same for both contexts, then the characterization distinction becomes much less operationally significant.

To some extent this thematic trend toward harmonization between IAC and NIAC LOAC rules is indeed reflected in state practice, as will be discussed in Chapter 6 in relation to targeting operations. But this is not universally the case, and this trend is still opposed in some quarters. The U.S. response to the *Customary International Humanitarian Law* study is indicative of this critique, particularly in reaction to assertions "that certain rules contained in the Geneva Conventions and the Additional Protocols have become binding as a matter of customary international law in internal armed conflict, notwithstanding the fact that there is little evidence in support of those propositions."[22] Retaining some legal distinction, and indeed operational differentiation, between IAC and NIAC LOAC is for some advisers and analysts a point of principle: NIAC and IAC are fundamentally different in political—if not always in operational—character, and aspects of the applicable law reflect, and need to reflect, these differences.[23] This is perhaps most clearly evident in the issue of "status" and its associated consequences for detention operations in NIAC. As David Armitage observes in his history of the "idea" of civil war, "Civil war is not solely in the eye of the beholder, but the use of the term itself is often one source of strife among the combatants. Established governments will always view civil wars as rebellions or illegal uprisings against legitimate authority, particularly if they fail."[24] The drive to harmonize thus runs a significant risk of undermining one of the key legal, political, and operational distinctions between NIAC and IAC: the capacity to treat "the enemy" as a criminal.

In IAC, combatant status brings with it immunity from prosecution for acts done in operations against the adversary, so long as they were compliant with LOAC. In NIAC, a civilian taking a direct part in hostilities (CDPH) or (fighter) member of a NSAG who carries out operations against a military adversary—even when they do so in complete accord with the rules governing combatant conduct—is still liable to prosecution for those acts.[25] In modern NIAC LOAC, there is no CDPH or NSAG "combatant immunity" attaching to what would

22. *See, e.g.*, John B. Bellinger III and William J. Haynes II, *A US Government to the International Committee of the Red Cross Study* Customary International Humanitarian Law, 98 Int'l Rev. Red Cross 443, 448; *id.* at 447 ("[T]he United States long has stated that it will apply the rules in its manuals whether the conflict is characterized as international or non-international, but this clearly is not intended to indicate that it is bound to do so as a matter of law in non-international conflicts.").

23. *See, e.g.*, Pejic, *Status of Armed Conflicts*, at 77.

24. Armitage, Civil Wars: A History in Ideas, at 13.

25. Thus, for example, a civilian taking a direct part in hostilities (CDPH), or a fighter member of a NSAG, who shoots either a combatant member of the state military force, or a combatant member of the military force of an intervening state, has committed an unlawful killing—even if it was in all other respects a LOAC compliant killing. The killing of that CDPH or fighter member of an NSAG, by a combatant member of either state military force, in parallel circumstances, is not an unlawful killing; it is excused/permitted in accordance with LOAC.

otherwise be LOAC-compliant conduct against the adversary in a NIAC; the acts are definable at the discretion of the state as criminal acts, and the perpetrators enjoy no schematic immunity from prosecution in respect of them. Maintaining this criminal characterization of the adversary is of fundamental sovereign importance for many states engaged in a NIAC within their territory, and any trend to harmonize—which could, for example, lead to calls for members of NSAGs to be accorded de jure prisoner of war (PW) status—will likely be resisted.[26] As a matter of either reality or of perception, halting the informal but fundamental LOAC "status creep" of NSAGs is an important point of principle for many states, advisers, and analysts. And as shall hopefully become evident, one of the most significant achievements of the doctrine on recognition of belligerency and the three-level scheme was indeed that it incorporated a well calibrated, situationally nuanced, sovereignty-sensitive legal test for resolving precisely this issue.

(iii) The historical assumption—A true rendering of the utility and influence of a legal doctrine is born of an assessment of its use as an analytical tool, not just as a label for an outcome

As will no doubt already be clear, it is my argument that in our search for coherence and crystallization in modern LOAC, we sometimes ignore the hard-learned guidance offered by customary rule sets embodied in pre-1949 LOAC—or, more contextually correctly, the "Law of War." This is, it seems, the situation with the doctrine on recognition of belligerency: a coherent, well-practiced, customary scheme for characterizing the status of belligerent groups (the "NSAG") and their legal relationships with both the parent state against which they were rebelling (the "conflict state") and other states with which it was necessary to engage during the course of the armed conflict ("third states"). Indeed, as Herbert Smith noted in his 1932 treatise on *Great Britain and the Law of Nations*,

> The papers in the Record Office dealing with the problem of belligerent recognition are very numerous, particularly in the files which contain the opinions of the Law Officers. But from about 1825 onwards the general lines of policy appear to have been settled, and the questions which arise are simply those of applying recognised principles to varying states of fact.[27]

26. As James Stewart has noted, the idea that rebels have expanded "entitlements or liabilities" that alter "the humanitarian law applicable between State and internationalised insurgent" is anathema for many. James G. Stewart, *Towards a Single Definition of Armed Conflict in International Humanitarian Law: A Critique of Internationalised Armed Conflict*, 85 Int'l Rev. Red Cross 313, 343 (2003).

27. 1 Great Britain and the Law of Nations 261 (Herbert A. Smith ed., 1932). Indeed, a brief scan through the ninety-seven volumes of *Law Officers' Opinions to the Foreign Office, 1793–1860* illuminates the scope of issues: from the validity of commercial contracts with belligerent parties, through to decisions on compliance with rebel prize court judgments, and application of the U.K. *Foreign Enlistment Acts* of 1819 and 1870. Law Officers' Opinions

As these papers—and many other sources besides—clearly indicate, application of the international Law of War as between the contending parties in a civil war, and the law of neutrality as between each of these contending parties and third states, was the primary consequence of the recognition of belligerency. Indeed, the course of commentary on the doctrine in general international law treatises over the nineteenth and twentieth centuries was almost universal on this point: Von Martens (1829),[28] Halleck (1861),[29] Harcourt (1865),[30] Lorimer (1883),[31] Wheaton (and his editor, Dana, in 1866),[32] Hall (1890),[33] Lawrence (1900),[34] Taylor (1901),[35] Davis (1901),[36] Oppenheim

TO THE FOREIGN OFFICE, 1793–1860 (Clive Parry ed., 1970–73). It also discloses the range of situations addressed, including rebellions in the Spanish American colonies periodically from 1814; the Greek rebellion against the Ottoman Turkish Empire, and the Portuguese rebellion, in the 1820s and 1830s; the Venetian rebellion against the Austrian Hapsburgs in 1848; the Garibaldi revolution in Italy; and the American Civil War in the 1860s.

28. G. F. VON MARTENS, THE LAW OF NATIONS 79 (William Cobbett ed., 4th ed., 1829) ("[T]he dispute becomes the same as that which happens between two independent states.").

29. H. W. HALLECK, INTERNATIONAL LAW; OR RULES REGULATING THE INTERCOURSE OF STATES IN PEACE AND WAR 73 (1861) ("Both parties may be entitled to the rights of war toward each other, and consequently to the rights of belligerents with respect to foreign states as neutrals in the contest.").

30. W. Vernon Harcourt, *The Rights and Duties of Neutrals in Time of War*, 9 J. ROYAL UNITED SERV. INST. 313 (1865).

31. JAMES LORIMER, THE INSTITUTES OF THE LAW OF NATIONS 144 (London, Blackwood and Sons 1883) ("Belligerent recognition, then, confers all the rights of public war, and it binds the States which confer it to all the duties of neutrals.").

32. HENRY WHEATON, ELEMENTS OF INTERNATIONAL LAW: THE LITERAL REPRODUCTION OF THE EDITION OF 1866 BY RICHARD HENRY DANA, JR. §23 (photo. reprint 1964) (George Grafton Wilson ed., 1936) ("[T]reat the ancient government as sovereign, and the government de facto as a society entitled to the rights of war against its enemy.").

33. WILLIAM HALL, A TREATISE ON INTERNATIONAL LAW 32 (Oxford: Clarendon Press, 3rd ed., 1890) ("Frequently however [a belligerent community] is admitted, through what is called recognition as a belligerent, to the privileges of law for the purposes of the hostilities in which it has engaged in order to establish its legal independence.").

34. T. J. LAWRENCE, THE PRINCIPLES OF INTERNATIONAL LAW 78 (2nd ed., 1900) ("War exists as a fact, and interested states must open their eyes to it. This they do by according to the incipient political community what is known as Recognition of Belligerency. The effect of their action is to endow the community with all the rights and all the obligations of an independent state so far as the war is concerned, but no further.").

35. HANNIS TAYLOR, A TREATISE ON PUBLIC INTERNATIONAL LAW 457–58 (1901) ("Such action [recognition of belligerency] places the two sides upon an equality so far as actual warfare is concerned.").

36. CUSHMAN K. DAVIS, A TREATISE ON INTERNATIONAL LAW INCLUDING AMERICAN DIPLOMACY 107 n.4 (1901) ("Belligerent rights are accorded to a rebellious portion of a country that has thrown off its allegiance from the parent country, and organized armies for the purpose of maintaining its independence, in the interest of humanity, to make acts done by them in the

(1906),[37] Moore (1906),[38] Hyde (1922),[39] Brierly (1928),[40] Puente (1928),[41] Smith (1932),[42] and Hershey (1939),[43] all agreed that the primary consequence of recognition of belligerency was that the Law of War as applicable to a conflict between states would thenceforth apply as between the conflict state and the recognized rebel party (NSAG), and that the law of neutrality would apply as between each of those conflict parties and any third state that had recognized the belligerency. This consistent appreciation was itself underpinned by fairly consistent advice to the same effect in state legal opinions and correspondence,[44] and in case law.[45] It also

conduct of the war, when such acts are done in accordance with the recognized rules of war, legitimate, and to prevent cruelties of reprisal and retaliation.").

37. LASSA OPPENHEIM, INTERNATIONAL LAW: A TREATISE: DISPUTES, WAR AND NEUTRALITY 85–86 (1906) ("Whenever a case arises in which a State lacking the legal qualification to make war nevertheless actually makes war, such State is a belligerent, the contention a civil war, and all the rules of International Law respecting warfare apply to it.").

38. 1 JOHN BASSETT MOORE, A DIGEST OF INTERNATIONAL LAW §59 (1906).

39. 1 CHARLES CHENEY HYDE, INTERNATIONAL LAW CHIEFLY AS INTERPRETED AND APPLIED BY THE UNITED STATES §47 (1922) ("Recognition [of belligerency] thus presupposes the existence of what is equivalent to war between the parties in opposition, and serves to clothe each with such rights with respect to the outside State as might be fairly claimed were the conflict being waged between two independent powers.").

40. J. L. BRIERLY, THE LAW OF NATIONS 80 (1928) ("The effects of the recognition are purely provisional; it puts both belligerent parties in the position of states, but only for the purposes and for the duration of the war.").

41. JULIUS I. PUENTE, INTERNATIONAL LAW AS APPLIED TO FOREIGN STATES 34 (1928) ("[T]he recognition of belligerency, while not conferring all the rights of an independent State, concedes to the government so recognized, the rights, and imposes upon it the obligations of an independent State in matters relating to the war being waged.").

42. 1 GREAT BRITAIN AND THE LAW OF NATIONS, at 325 ("Once the decision has been taken to recognise an insurgent government as belligerent, the legal consequences of the decision are not limited to the concession of belligerent rights.").

43. AMOS S. HERSHEY, THE ESSENTIALS OF INTERNATIONAL PUBLIC LAW AND ORGANIZATION 204 (1939) ("The effect of a recognition of belligerency . . . is to admit the insurgents to all the rights and privileges, and to impose upon them all the duties of a State so far as the conduct of the war is concerned").

44. For example, *see* J.D. Harding to Lord Russell, "Opinion of the Queen's Advocate of 27 September 1861" (F.O. 83/2212): "The fact that the war now existing in North America, may in a certain sense, be viewed as a civil war, and that the President speaks of 'the insurrection' of the particular States named in the Proclamation, does not appear to me to make any very material or practical difference; more especially as Her Majesty's Govt and all other Governments have treated both parties as 'belligerentes inter se in justo bello,' and consider themselves as 'neutrals' internationally." HERSCH LAUTERPACHT, RECOGNITION IN INTERNATIONAL LAW 222–23 (1947); *see also* ARNOLD D. MCNAIR, INTERNATIONAL LAW OPINIONS: SELECTED AND ANNOTATED 358–59 (1956).

45. For example, in *The Prize Cases*, the U.S. Supreme Court pointedly found that the British declaration of neutrality on 13 May 1861, subsequent to President Lincoln's declaration closing

routinely appeared in codification proposals such as the extensive 1939 draft text for rules relating to *Rights and Duties of Neutral States in Naval and Aerial War*, as prepared by Philip Jessup and an extensive and expert team, wherein "belligerent" was precisely defined so as to cover situations of recognition of belligerency:

> Article 1(b) A 'belligerent' is a State or a politically organised group at war within a State or with a politically organised group.
>
> Comment: This explanation is included to bring out the fact that a belligerent may be a party to an international or a civil war provided, in the latter case, that belligerency has been recognised.[46]

Recognition of belligerency thus seems, at first blush, to have been an intensely useful and practical response to the challenges posed by what today would be a large-scale NIAC. But this utility did not reside solely, nor indeed primarily, in the provision of a label for an outcome, but was rather to be found in the doctrine's role as an analytical tool and legal frame of reference. Perhaps recognition of belligerency therefore warrants some renewed attention, and indeed that is the purpose of this book.

B. THE STRUCTURE OF THIS BOOK

(i) What is it that I am seeking to do?

My primary aim in this book is to explore and explain, in a legal-historical sense, the doctrine on recognition of belligerency. By examining and analyzing issues of conflict characterization, status, conduct, and treatment as they operated within the legal framework of recognition of belligerency and its attendant three-level scheme of characterization for internal conflicts, I seek to illustrate how and why this historically coherent, doctrinally nuanced, but relatively forgotten approach to navigating civil war as a LOAC venue was well calibrated to exactly this purpose. In doing so, my subordinate aim is to explore whether and how the doctrine on recognition of belligerency might be useful today, as an analytical tool, in relation to correlate NIAC contexts. Thus my purpose is first and foremost to act as a legal historian of the doctrine on recognition of belligerency. While, as will become abundantly clear, I am also an advocate for its narrow revival as a means of solving, in some contexts, the many legal challenges faced by NIAC LOAC, it is essential to note at this early juncture that this is a secondary purpose only.

Confederate ports—a blockade—was entirely legally sound, despite the U.S. governmental characterization of U.K. actions as an "unfriendly act." The Prize Cases, 67 U.S. (2 Black) 635 (1863).

46. *Rights and Duties of Neutral States in Naval and Aerial War*, 33 Am. J. Int'l L. (Supp.) 209.

(ii) Some methodological choices

It is important that I disclose at the very outset two methodological choices I have made in approaching this subject, so as to spare the reader potential frustration. The first such choice is that I have sought, where possible, to avoid traversing in detail ground that has been much more elegantly and eloquently traversed by other scholars who have dealt with this topic. Thus, I do not structure this book as an updated analysis of, or an addendum to, those parts of either Lauterpacht's seminal work on *Recognition in International Law* (1947) or Ti-Chiang Chen's *The International Law of Recognition* (1951), which were dedicated to recognition of insurgency and belligerency. Similarly, I have happily taken the opportunity presented by more recent work on recognition of belligerency and the law applicable to civil war by Erik Castren, Emily Crawford, Richard Falk, Jann Kleffner, Evan Luard, Konstantinos Mastorodimos, Lindsay Moir, John Norton Moore, Roscoe Oglesby, Sasha Radin, Sandy Sivakumaran, and many others, to avoid exhaustively revisiting each incidence of possible belligerency.

This leads to the second methodological choice I have made in structuring and writing this book: I have chosen to tackle the subject thematically, rather than chronologically or by reference to discrete issue focal points (such as piracy). My chapters therefore tend to center around illustrative themes (the scheme, its purposes, some challenges, and the "so what") rather than around a succession of iconic incidents and talismanic legal seams. I therefore apologize up front for the chronological diversity addressed under each heading; this is a function of my attempt to furnish, within each chapter, examples that demonstrate the thematic lefts and rights of arc, rather than necessarily as illustrations of chronological or conceptual progression. This said, the reader will nevertheless detect that at certain junctures in the narrative, I have digressed into more encapsulated vignettes on specific examples and incidents; my point, however, is that they are placed where I believe they offer the most coherent thematic sense, as opposed to conforming with any sub-narrative attempt at chronological discipline.

(iii) The questions I am seeking to answer

This book is informed by the four questions I asked as I embarked upon this project. I have, presumptuously, assumed that others interested in recognition of belligerency may therefore have similar questions, and I have broadly structured the book around them:

(1) What was recognition of belligerency, and where did it sit in the scheme for characterizing internal conflicts?
(2) Why was it useful and apparently well calibrated to its purposes?
(3) How did the doctrine fare in the face of challenges to its application as a matter of both practice and law?

(4) As a subsidiary question, does the doctrine still offer concepts, or a schematic 'flow-chart', that might be useful as we grapple with the legal challenges that currently bedevil the concept of NIAC?

(iv) Chapter outline

This book is structured around one introductory and five thematic chapters. This first, introductory, chapter sets out the methodological background to the project: why and how I will examine recognition of belligerency and, in the final section, some clarifications as to the terminology employed within this book.

Chapters 2 and 3 then delve into the broader scheme in which recognition of belligerency is located, seeking to provide an initial response to question one above. This three-level scheme—rebellion, insurgency, belligerency—is in many of its components intensely political and subjective. Thus, while the three-level scheme is in many ways characterizable as a spectrum, the thresholds between each level are intentionally and constructively permeable in the service of political purpose. This results in a clear and well-designed genuflection to subjective appreciation and application. This is not to say, by any means, that the entire scheme is so hopelessly instrumental that it cannot possibly form a coherent legal doctrine. Rather, the opposite is in fact true; the scheme is well endowed with objective elements and exhibits a range of clearly delineated and identified linkages and segues into other rule sets, such as neutrality, piracy, and responsibility. Indeed, the political and subjective elements within the scheme ultimately serve the same purpose—and in an almost identical fashion—as the conventional and customary requirement for third state recognition as the final element in state recognition.[47] International law is well adapted to and readily encompasses policy-based legal elements being incorporated within its multifarious schemes, tests, and doctrines. The three-level scheme, with recognition of belligerency at its pinnacle, is no orphan in this sense.

With the recognition of belligerency located within its broader schematic context, Chapter 4 then focuses upon the second question: that is, what exactly did the doctrine on recognition of belligerency achieve or deliver for those parties involved in or affected by the conflict? To this end, the chapter focuses upon the implications of recognition of belligerency for the three main parties to any conflict attended by this status: the conflict state, the adversary NSAG fighting against the conflict state, and third states affected in some way by this conflict (most usually in terms of trade and fiscal regulation, protection of nationals, treatment of parties, and submission of vessels to belligerent rights such as visit and search).

47. Montevideo Convention on the Rights and Duties of States arts. 1(d), 3, 6–7, Dec. 26, 1933, 49 Stat. 3097, 165 L.N.T.S. 19; *see, e.g.*, James Crawford, The Creation of States in International Law §3.6 (2nd ed., 2006) (on collective non-recognition); Thomas D Grant, *Defining Statehood: the Montevideo Convention and Its Discontents*, 37 Colum. J. Transnat'l L. 403 (1999).

This analysis of generally perceived purposes and utility will then inform the following chapter.

Chapter 5 hinges around an examination of the development and deployment of the doctrine by addressing four types of challenges that recognition of belligerency has faced and been required to accommodate. These challenges are of universality (was the doctrine a British-U.S. condominium, or of wider employment?), fact (how did the doctrine fare when applied to intensely complicated—both legally and politically—conflict situations such as the Spanish Civil War), legal exegesis (did the doctrine survive, for example, the *Geneva Conventions* 1949 and the *Additional Protocols* 1977), and relevance (such as whether the doctrine has fallen into desuetude). Chapter 5 therefore deals with question three (when and why was it applied, or not) but also in part with question four (have modern developments extinguished recognition of belligerency, radically reduced its potential field of application, or left it fundamentally unaltered but languishing far down the path to desuetude?). The ultimate aim of this chapter is, consequently, to determine whether the doctrine could be said to remain viable and operable.

Finally, in Chapter 6, I engage with the fourth question (and my subsidiary purpose): What challenges might the doctrine on recognition of belligerency help practitioners address in the interpretation and application of LOAC to certain NIAC situations today? I seek to contextualize this "so what?" by first describing some relevant challenges that currently attend the concept of NIAC in terms of lacunae and uncertainties in the interpretation and application of LOAC. I then elaborate how the doctrine on recognition of belligerency and its associated tripartite scheme of characterization has something historically useful and contemporarily relevant to say about these challenges. This chapter is by no means a complete accounting of the discontents within NIAC LOAC; that task has been finely and previously executed by others. Rather, this concluding chapter seeks only to address the subordinate aim of my inquiry—the "what might it mean for us now" question that partly informs the legal-historical methodology I have adopted.

C. SOME CAVEATS

(i) Sources and historical focus

An immediate and completely justifiable criticism of this book is that it is predominantly focused upon the development and practice of recognition of belligerency (and to a lesser extent insurgency) from U.S. and British perspectives. While I have sought out evidence of theory and practice from non-U.S. and non-British primary sources, this evidence has to some extent proven elusive (to me). While I have found snippets of independent practice in Austro-Hungarian, French, Portuguese, Prussian/German, Brazilian, Dutch, Spanish, Polish, Nigerian, Algerian, Indonesian, and other conflict contexts, and academic statements that recognize the existence and relevance of belligerency and insurgency among an even wider national pool, my research has been of necessity relatively limited with respect to these additional and alternative bodies of evidence. In part this is due to my own inadequacies in terms of the various languages required; in part it is because of my unfamiliarity with and inability to adequately navigate the relevant archives; in part it is because some of the twentieth-century incidents involving substantial non-U.S. and non-British practice and perspectives remain sensitive, and documents are difficult to obtain (as is the case, for example, with official French perspectives on belligerency with respect to the Algerian revolution); and in part it is due to my wish to keep this study within achievable bounds. To some extent, the broad employment of the doctrine will be patently evident from the protagonists involved in the incidents and issues canvased.

Nevertheless, I have made some attempt, in Chapter 5, to briefly note other indicators of non-U.S. and non-British analyses and practice. However, there is a wealth of relatively untapped material available in non-U.S. and non-British national archives, and I sincerely hope that other lawyer-historians might take up the challenge (and reward) that comes from following in the footsteps of those such as Dan O'Connell and Gerry Simpson—models for we who seek to study international law within its deep historical and "applied" context. Indeed, I suspect no international law book has exerted a more profound influence upon the way in which I have approached the research and writing for this book than O'Connell's *Influence of Law on Sea Power*,[48] itself a legally nuanced and practically grounded genuflection to Alfred Thayer Mahan's seminal work on naval strategy, *The Influence of Sea Power on History: 1660–1783*.

This said, however, my close focus upon U.S. and British practice and perspectives is the result of much more than linguistic inadequacy and the constraints of time and travel budgets. This is because it is an inescapable and unalterable fact that, when it comes to belligerency and insurgency, the doctrine and practice was in many respects a U.S.-British condominium. As will hopefully become evident for those tolerant and forgiving enough to read this book, the predominance of U.S. and British influence in the development, description, and practice of recognition of belligerency (and insurgency) was almost overwhelming. There are myriad reasons why this was the case; however, I shall briefly note but two.

The first reason flows from recognizing the simple geopolitical fact that both states spent the nineteenth century—the key period in the development and practice of the doctrine—engaged in or touched by their own and other peoples' rebellions, insurgencies, and civil wars. On one hand, the long influence of the Monroe Doctrine on U.S. foreign policy, for example, meant that the United States was a consistent and central player in a hemispheric century of decolonization conflicts in Central and South America, of necessity having to continually navigate an intensely practical engagement, and legally structured relationships, with both revolutionary entities and imperialist powers. And, of course, it was the American Civil War that provided the archetypal instance of recognition of belligerency. Britain, on the other hand, was continually faced with (or intervening in) internal, frontier, and competitor colonial challenges because of its empire, thus requiring

48. D. P. O'Connell, The Influence of Law on Sea Power (1975).

constant negotiation and characterization of relationships with fellow imperialist states, colonial entities, and rebellious subject groups. To some extent, these two different but deeply engaged perspectives may assist in explaining why it was that the United States was predominant in developing recognition of insurgency, for they most often took the role of an affected political bystander seeking to provide some succor (given their own history) to rebels seeking self-determination and freedom from imperialist overlords, while simultaneously avoiding the insult to fellow (imperialist) states that inevitably flowed from recognizing a rebel belligerency. Indeed, an interesting note in reporting by U.S. diplomats in Brazil, in relation to a request for recognition of belligerency by the Constitutionalist insurgents in 1932, refers to "modern North American doctrine, creator of recognition of insurrection."[49] For Britain, however, the option of employing the formal status of belligerency as a political and diplomatic tool in their ongoing struggle with other distant-water imperialist states—predominantly France, but also in terms of lingering frictions with Spain, Portugal, and The Netherlands as declining maritime powers, and Germany as a late starter—proved a useful tool. This perhaps provides some explanation as to how and why Britain played an arguably more significant role in the elucidation of the belligerency component of the doctrine.

A second partial explanation for the preponderance of U.S. and British influence in the development of the doctrine lays in the fact that both insurgency and belligerency, as discrete legal concepts, grew out of and in many respects were targeted at legal characterization and regulation of maritime communications in conflict contexts. It is thus no surprise that the (at that time) two predominant maritime powers, traders, and gunboat diplomatists played a disproportionately significant role in the development and practice of recognition of belligerency and insurgency; when rebellion touched upon third state interests at sea, third states took an interest, and no third states were more likely to be touched by maritime interference than the United States and Britain. In the nineteenth century, when it came to maritime matters, some states were most certainly more equal than others, and it is of little surprise that their interests and views played the major role in the emergence of the doctrine on recognition of belligerency. To some extent this also perhaps explains why a number of the other significant imperialist powers of the nineteenth century, particularly Austria-Hungary, Russia, and the Ottoman Empire had seemingly little influence on the development of the doctrine: their imperialist activity was mostly confined to territorially contiguous expansion. Although some of their activities did provoke significant crystallizing contexts (such as Austrian action in Hungary in the 1840s and Russian action in Poland in the 1860s), the relative absence of maritime dimensions, and the resultant territorially contained nature of these rebellions, was conspicuously cited at the time as one reason for denying recognition of belligerency.

49. Telegram from Chargé in Brazil (Thurston) to Secretary of State (Aug. 3, 1932), *in* 5 FOREIGN RELATIONS OF THE UNITED STATES DIPLOMATIC PAPERS, 1932, THE AMERICAN REPUBLICS 409–11 (1948), *available at* https://history.state.gov/historicaldocuments/frus1932v05/d438.

There is one further methodological matter that should be noted at this point: this topic necessarily entails some digression into the "foreign relations law" of the United States and Britain in relation to belligerency and insurgency.[50] As such, it neither presents nor reads as a purely international law-based analysis. To some extent, this is the inevitable consequence of the source material—state practice, domestic law cases, and expert commentary—given that there is very little by way of international case law or treaties dealing with the subject until well into the twentieth century, and even then such indicia remain very scant and scarce indeed.

(ii) Terminology

Prior to embarking upon any substantive discussion of recognition of belligerency, it is necessary to first define some of the central terms as they present through the course of the analysis. There are five terms that require some brief explanation as regards the manner in which they are employed in this book: Law of War, civil war, belligerency, NSAG, and IAC/NIAC.

The coming into force of the four *Geneva Conventions* of 1949 represented a significant development concerning the universal term of art employed for indicating and encapsulating the rules applicable between belligerents, and between belligerents and neutrals, in time of war. This was the introduction of the concept of "armed conflict" as an alternative trigger differentiated from the traditionally employed "declared war." However, during the formative stages of the development of the doctrine on recognition of belligerency, "Law of Armed Conflict" (LOAC) as a term was unknown. Consequently, I will employ the more historically correct umbrella term of "Law of War" when discussing pre-1949 contexts and practice; in discussing post-1949 developments, I will use both "Law of War" and "LOAC," but in each case I have attempted to make it contextually clear as to why I have favored one term over the other. I acknowledge that there is an often fuzzy but persisting debate regarding nuance between, and differentiated content of, "LOAC," "Law of War," and "international humanitarian law (IHL)," but it is of little significance for this study. I thus accept at the outset any criticism due for employing the term "Law of War" perhaps slightly more broadly than some may wish; however, it is a stylistic choice I have made in order to access a shorthand label for that interconnected body of rules on belligerent conduct, neutrality, and prize that form the backdrop to this analysis.

The concept of "civil war" will likewise recur throughout this study. This concept stands beside the Law of War and LOAC as a political or diplomatic fellow traveler but is not "of" the Law of War or LOAC in any meaningful legal sense. That is, the concept of civil war has no precisely defined legal content but is rather

50. In the sense of Campbell McLachlan's astute question and observation regarding "What is it about the conduct of the state in its external exercise of public power that provokes such controversy within contemporary Anglo-Commonwealth legal systems?," CAMPBELL MCLACHLAN, FOREIGN RELATIONS LAW 3 (2014).

a description of a state of affairs. This said, "civil war" nevertheless plays a major role in contextualizing the concept of belligerency, and while it both predates and has outlived the doctrine on recognition of belligerency—predominantly as a political term of art,[51] but occasionally masquerading as a legal concept—it is routinely encountered in writings and official correspondence as a description of situations to which application of the doctrine on recognition of belligerency was being assessed or considered. However, as noted above, it is incorrect to simply equate civil war with the post-1949 concept of NIAC; as will hopefully become evident, they are not direct correlates.

A similar problem is evoked by use of the term "belligerency." This is perhaps best illustrated with an example from the UN Security Council in the fulcrum of the 1967 Arab-Israel War, where Arab insistence on reference to "a state of belligerency" in one draft resolution caused confusion and consternation. This prompted the Soviet Legal Adviser to approach his British counterpart "to ask for clarification of the legal implications of this word in English." As British diplomatic reporting noted, "It is a fact that the word 'belligerency' has been used vaguely by a number of people in and around the U.N. without much differentiation between the technical legal aspect and actual hostilities."[52] In political parlance, belligerency is a term of similar meaning to "hostilities," albeit perhaps employed on a more strategic scale than the often "battlefield" and "use of force" focused concept of hostilities. In politico-legal terms, belligerency—as in a "state of belligerency"—is perhaps best described as a state of affairs by which legal analysis is both channeled and informed. In other words, it is a general politico-legal descriptor for a relationship between states that to a large extent (but not precisely) paralleled the concept of "war" before the concept of war became legally superfluous. However, it is a third form of the term—that which labels and describes a well-defined legal test and is then employed to indicate a clear legal status (recognized belligerent)—which is predominantly employed in, and indeed is the subject of, this book.

A fourth concept that is fundamental to this study is that of the NSAG. In dealing with belligerency and insurgency, however, we are faced with boxes within boxes in terms of NSAG. To this end, I will tend to use NSAG as the umbrella term for groups employing violence against their parent state. However, it will often be necessary to use doctrinally more precise labels when dealing with the three-level scheme, in that "rebels" are those whose actions are categorized as "rebellion"; "insurgents" are those whose fight has been afforded the political characterization (with some legal consequences) of "insurgency"; and "belligerent" is the appropriate label for a NSAG afforded formal recognition of belligerency. These subcategories of NSAG are important in the context of recognition of belligerency (and, in relation to piracy, to recognition of insurgency) because they portend—both for the relevant NSAG generally, but also for its members—a certain status in

51. *See, e.g.*, Christine Gray, *Bosnia and Herzegovina: Civil War or Inter-State Conflict? Characterization and Consequences*, 67 Brit. Y.B. Int'l L. 155 (1997).

52. Note in file, August 1967: "War and Belligerency: Middle East: Move Towards Termination," paras. 4–6, in U.K. Archives File: FCO 17/113.

relation to their parent (conflict) state and other states. These labels also presage certain entitlements to special treatment and to engage in specified forms of conduct—or, as with rebels, a denial of this entitlement.

Finally, in the pre-1949 components of this book, I will tend to avoid use of the terms IAC and NIAC because they did not exist at the time, and because they have no precisely defined correlates in the Law of War. Indeed, the whole point of applying the Law of War as applicable between states to a situation of "civil war" was to apply any "law" of "war" at all. Below this level, there was no "Law of War"; there was only the bloody and violent hand that the sovereign retained in suppressing internal rebellion, a hand considered doctrinally (albeit not always actually) free from direct interference by other sovereigns. As the concept of insurgency gathered momentum in the nineteenth century, this paradigmatic divide was subject to a degree of permeability as groups that were more than mere rebels, but less than recognized belligerents, were given some succor by "third" states (really, in legal terms at this paradigmatic point, merely "other" states). This predominantly took the form of a discretion in those other states to treat insurgents who came into their hands, and who had not interfered with third state shipping or territory, as something other than criminal rebels to be handed back to their parent state or dealt with by that other (third) state as pirates. In post-1949 LOAC, where IAC and NIAC are the predominant categorizations, it will be seen that situations of belligerency do not snuggly fit within what would logically and intuitively be the new relevant category genus: NIAC. Indeed, the whole purpose of recognition of belligerency was to apply the Law of War as applicable between states—that is, to apply what was prior to 1949 the only type of Law of War—to conflicts between a parent state and a rebel group that had been afforded formal belligerent status.

There is not, consequently, any simple analogy of belligerency to NIAC, nor of belligerency to IAC; rather, the traditional doctrine on recognition of belligerency straddles both characterizations. This does not, however, predestine any contemporary attempt to determine which parts of recognition of belligerency could be said to lie in IAC, and which in NIAC, to impossibility of performance; however, it is a fraught challenge. And it is made devilishly more complicated by the fact that such parallels are difficult to draw as a result of the almost complete disconnect since the 1950s between "standard" or "orthodox" post-1949 LOAC analysis, and the more sporadic instances of recognition of belligerency analysis. It is almost as if we, the community of practitioners and scholars who deal with LOAC, have carried on two separate dialogues on conflict characterization over the last seventy years: the dominant analytical discourse on IAC and NIAC, as carried out in the mainstream; and an underground, almost samizdat, parallel discussion in which some of the leading lights of the mainstream dialogue have also participated, but which has rarely (with a few notable exceptions) risen above the parapet.

2

The Customary Three-Level Scheme Part I

Rebellion and Insurgency

Let everyone be subject to the governing authorities, for there is no authority except that which God has established. The authorities that exist have been established by God. Consequently, whoever rebels against the authority is rebelling against what God has instituted, and those who do so will bring judgment on themselves.

—*The Epistle of St Paul to the Romans* 13:1–2

But if a prince, by violating the fundamental laws, gives his subjects a lawful cause for resisting him; if, by his insupportable tyranny, he brings on a national revolt against him, any foreign power may rightfully give assistance to an oppressed people who ask for its aid . . . Hence, whenever such dissension reaches a state of civil war, foreign nations may assist that one of the two parties which seems to have justice on its side. But to assist a detestable tyrant, or to come out in favour of an unjust and rebellious people, would certainly be a violation of duty. When, however, the political bonds between a sovereign and his people are broken, or at least suspended, they may be considered as two distinct parties, and since both are independent of all foreign authority, no one has the right to judge them . . . Hence, by virtue of the voluntary Law of Nations, the two parties must be allowed to act as if possessed of equal right, and to be treated accordingly, until the affair is decided.

But this principle should not be made use of so as to authorize criminal designs against the peace of Nations. It is a violation of the Law of Nations to call on subjects to revolt when they are actually obeying their sovereign, although complaining of his rule.[1]

—Emer de Vattel (1758)

1. Emerich de Vattel, The Laws of Nations or The Principles of Natural Law §56 (1844).

A. INTRODUCTION

Grotius did not like civil war as a legal concept. As Stephen Neff observes, "[t]hose who seek in Grotius an intellectual ancestor of Locke or Jefferson, as a supporter of a right of revolution against tyrannical rule, must look in vain."[2] Although Grotius admitted of William Barclay's analysis of the occasions when it was lawful for a segment of the population to rise against their sovereign, his strong preference was that, in most cases, it was better for malcontents to accept even death within the law, which was after all designed to manage generalities: "This is better than to live without a rule, or to suffer the rule to be left to everyone's discretion."[3]

> If sometimes under the influence of excessive fear or anger or other passions, rulers are turned aside so that they do not enter the straight road that leads to tranquillity, this after all must be reckoned among the things that less frequently happen; and such things . . . are offset by the interposition of better things. Laws, again count it sufficient to have in view what generally happens.[4]

Grotius was not alone.[5] As Wilson observes in relation to dynastic change in the Holy Roman Empire as early as the 1000s, "Rebellion ceased to be a personal dispute over status and became an affront to divine order. It was harder to forgive wrongdoers who were now considered sinners."[6] Some early modern theologians, such as Luther, generally considered rebels to have taken themselves outside of the law/grace of God and/or the sovereign, and thus deserve the harsh, generally extrajudicial treatment that followed.[7] Yet by the turn of the eighteenth-to-nineteenth century, under the influence of political and philosophical trends, and, it must be recognized, the legal innovation and influence of Emer de Vattel,[8] the previously dire consignment of all rebels to legal and spiritual damnation had

2. Hugo Grotius, On The Law of War and Peace p xxxi (Stephen Neff ed. and trans., Cambridge University Press, 5th ed., 1646).

3. *Id.* at 69.

4. *Id.*

5. *See, e.g.*, Leslie Green, *Low-Intensity Conflict and the Law*, 3 ILSA J. Int'l & Comp. L. 493, 493–97 (1997).

6. Peter Wilson, Heart of Europe: A History of the Holy Roman Empire 349 (2016).

7. *See, e.g., id.* at 6, 28, 349 (on further examples regarding rebellion and the Holy Roman Empire).

8. *See, e.g.*, David Armitage, Civil Wars: A History in Ideas, 128–34; Wyndham Walker, *Recognition of Belligerency and Grant of Belligerent Rights*, 23 Transactions Grotius Soc'y 177, 189–90 (1937) (on Vattel's influence on this transition).

radically shifted. This was, as David Armitage notes, in part attributable to an emerging political appreciation of differences between forms of rebellion: "Civil wars hark back to ancient grievances and deep-dyed divisions, while revolutions point the way toward an open and expansive future."[9] But it was also a legal appreciation, for Vattel asked whether sovereigns should treat their rebellious subjects in accordance with the Law of War as defined in the Law of Nations. His definitive answer (as evidenced in the opening quote) was that, in certain situations, they indeed should.[10] In arriving at this succinctly expressed conclusion, however, Vattel perpetrated, or perhaps crystallized, several important legal innovations. Two are of key significance in terms of the development of the doctrine on recognition of belligerency and the three-level scheme of rebellion-insurgency-belligerency.

First, Vattel briefly theorized and elaborated a typology of tumults, along with brief statements as to their varying degrees of lawfulness, laying important foundations for the evolution of a nuanced, structured, and legally coherent approach to different forms of rebellion—from mere civil unrest through to civil war. Second, and equally importantly, he elaborated a heretofore more limited legal justification for third state interference in a civil war and, as an adjunct to this, the application of the Law of War. Ultimately, and although not universally agreed,[11] these innovations—not solely the work of Vattel, but for which he arguably deserves significant credit—then became the stepping-off point for the development of a nuanced and substantive doctrine concerned with the legal effects of wide-scale internal conflict, and the legal consequences for both contesting parties and third states of that conflict.[12] By the first decades of the nineteenth

9. Armitage, Civil Wars: A History of Ideas, at 122.

10. *See generally* Simone Zurbuchen, *Emer de Vattel on the Society of Nations and the Political System of Europe, in* System, Order, and International Law: The Early History of International Legal Thought from Machiavelli to Hegel 263, 266–67 (Stefan Kadelbach, Thomas Kleinlein, and David Roth-Isigkeit eds., 2017) (for a general overview of Vattel's conception of the law of nations as it interacted with the European state system).

11. *See, e.g.*, Mountague Bernard, On The Principle of Non-Intervention: A Lecture 20–23 (1860) (on limiting Vattel's analysis to situations of civil war resulting from disputed succession or prolonged revolt (citing, with some disapproval, Lord Palmerston in 1834)—that is, only in situations where 'the social tie' of the state was broken, and thus the 'unity of the state' dissolved; at this point 'nations are entitled to regard the contending parties, while the war lasts, as distinct and independent powers'. Bernard, although he parsed differences between rebellion (aimed at change of government or dynasty) and revolt (an attempt to create two separate states from one), ultimately disagreed with even this proposition, concluding that as one of five purported exceptions to the rule against intervention, it failed and was inadmissible, proving that the rule as to non-intervention remained 'universally true').

12. *See, e.g.*, Walker, *Recognition of Belligerency and Grant of Belligerent Rights, at* 186 (stating 'Belligerency was accepted as a fact, dependent on the existence of an actual civil war, not a mere tumult or rising; and the doctrine of Vattel that a civil war to be treated as an actual war, in which third States might be allies or neutral, but the existence of which sooner or later could hardly be ignored, was in substance acted upon').

century, the tripartite conflict categorization scheme encompassing rebellion, insurrection, and belligerency was clearly discernible and being routinely applied.[13]

In order to come to grips with the detail of the three-level scheme, with a view to then assessing its purposes and current context, the next two chapters seek to describe the thresholds and, where applicable, the tests applied within this original three-level scheme that culminates in recognition of belligerency.[14] The membranes between the levels were to some extent permeable, and, as will become evident, the allocation of a particular conflict context to one or other level was as often slave to the political imperatives of a significant and engaged third state as it was to the factual circumstances attendant upon the conflict itself. This chapter will address the first two levels within the scheme, rebellion, and insurgency; the next chapter examines the third level, formally recognized belligerency.

B. REBELLION

> In the second place, they are starting a rebellion, and violently robbing and plundering monasteries and castles which are not theirs, by which they have a second time deserved death in body and soul, if only as highwaymen and murderers. Besides, any man against whom it can be proved that he is a maker of sedition is outside the law of God and Empire, so that the first who can slay him is doing right and well. For if a man is an open rebel every man is his judge and executioner, just as when a fire starts, the first to put it out is the best man. For rebellion is not simple murder, but is like a great fire, which attacks and lays waste a whole land. Thus rebellion brings with it a land full of murder and bloodshed, makes widows and orphans, and turns everything upside down, like the greatest disaster. Therefore let everyone who can, smite, slay and stab, secretly or openly, remembering that nothing can be more poisonous, hurtful or devilish than a rebel. It is just as when

13. It must be noted, however, that not all commentators agree on this point—Walker, for example, argues that the doctrine remained relatively inchoate until it was given more formalized expression ('harden[ed] into a legal doctrine') in response to the catalyst of the American Civil War. WALKER, *Recognition of Belligerency and Grant of Belligerent Rights, at* 177–86 (asserting, for example, that 'The Civil War in America caused the thrashing out of problems arising between parent state and the recognizing State'; and arguing that 'The outbreak of the American Civil War ushers in a new phase in the history of the subject, and brings with it, I believe, the new term "recognition of belligerency" ').

14. It is also important to recall, at this stage of analysis, that the key legal distinctions and thresholds that affected pre-1949 'internal conflict' were in large part driven by maritime concerns—particularly the triangular maritime and trade relationship between the conflict state, the NSAG, and third states—and often operationalized in maritime legal terminology and state practice. Thus, the preponderance of maritime-linked examples and concerns in any overview of the three-level scheme is as equally a genuflection to the applicable law and practice as it is to the author's naval predispositions.

> one must kill a mad dog; if you do not strike him, he will strike you, and a whole land with you.[15]
>
> *Martin Luther (1525)*

> The proper stand for a foreign State to take in case of domestic disturbance within another State can be none other than that of disinterestedness and non-intervention. It has no right either to aid or to suppress the rebellion.[16]
>
> *Ti-Chiang Chen (1951)*

The least legally significant form, for third states, of conflict categorization was that of "rebellion." "Text-books and treatises on international law do not as a rule," wrote Lauterpacht in 1928, "refer specifically to the question of state responsibility for revolutionary acts by private persons against foreign states."[17] This level of the customary conflict categorization scheme is not readily equated to less-than-NIAC civil unrest and riot, but was nevertheless assessed to be (then, as now) fundamentally a matter of domestic criminal law, with no alteration in either conflict state or third state rights and responsibilities.[18] The Duke of Parma, during the rebellion of the Dutch provinces against Spanish rule, refused to accept the surrender of Sichem in 1578, and hung or clubbed to death thousands of rebel soldiers.[19] Emperor Maximilian of Mexico, dealing with Constitutionalist rebels,

15. Martin Luther, Against the Robbing and Murdering Hordes of Peasants (1525) (relating to the German Peasants War/Rebellion of 1524–1525, during the suppression of which German princes executed more than 100,000); for analysis as to the context of Luther's exegesis, *see*, inter alia, Stephen Greenblatt, *Murdering Peasants: Status, Genre, and the Representation of Rebellion*, 1 Representations 1 (1983); Erik Midelfort, *The Revolution of 1525? Recent Studies of the Peasants' War*, 11 Central European History 189 (1978); Heiko Oberman, *The Gospel of Social Unrest: 450 Years after the So-Called "German Peasants' War" of 1525*, 69 Harvard Theological Review 103 (1976).

16. Ti-Chiang Chen, The International Law of Recognition 335 (1951).

17. Hersch Lauterpacht, *Revolutionary Activities by Private Persons Against Foreign States*, 22 Am. J. Int'l L. 105, 108 (1928); *see also*Charles King, *Revolutionary War, Guerrilla Warfare, and International Law*, 4 Case W. Res. J. Int'l L. 91, 103 (1971–1972) (stating that generally, "international law has not been concerned with internal or civil wars until they have assumed an international character, that is, until the insurgents have received recognition as a belligerent. Until such time as this status has been accorded, these wars have been considered to be a domestic matter for the States where they are being fought").

18. Richard A. Falk, *Introduction* to The international Law of Civil War 1, 11 (1971); G.I.A.D. Draper, *Humanitarian Law and Internal Armed Conflicts*, 13 Geo. J. Int'l L. 253, 254–55 (1983).

19. *See, e.g.*, Alexander Gillespie, A History of the Laws of War: Volume I 134–36 (2011); Neil Hanson, The Confident Hope of a Miracle 211–12 (2003).

ordered "the court-martial and summary execution of any rebel, regardless of his political principles or the nature of his organisation," including those who had previously surrendered as Prisoners of War (PWs).[20] Such brutality to rebels was common, legally justified, and according to some theologians, spiritually sanctioned. During the American War of Independence, Britain treated captured American fighters as criminals and refused them PW status, holding them in harsh conditions (it is reported that more American soldiers and sailors died in British captivity than on the battlefield), although, in a clear improvement in the fate of those historically categorized as rebels, they were ultimately released at the end of the war.[21] Nevertheless, the parlous legal status of rebels remained, albeit primarily as a municipal legal condition. As the Russian delegate to the 1912 International Red Cross Conference declared, "the Red Cross should have no duty towards insurgents or bands of revolutionaries whom the laws of my country regard as criminals."[22]

It is beyond the scope of this study to provide a comprehensive survey of domestic jurisdictions and the legal treatment of rebellion. However, it is possible to illustrate the general legal approach by examining one indicative jurisdiction. To this end, because the jurisprudence on rebellion as a distinct legal concept appears to have been most fully developed within a British context, I shall focus upon this jurisdiction as an exemplar of the category.

(i) Rebellion differentiated from riot

As a consequence of the purpose of rebellion when compared to mere riot, the form of domestic law used in response could alter. Indeed, the three-level scheme was not concerned with riot and only became relevant once riot had crossed the lower of the scheme's thresholds into rebellion. William Finlason, writing in 1868 on the use of martial law to suppress rebellion, described the difference between riot and rebellion in terms of the legal framework that could be employed to deal with each:

> And these words, riot and rebellion, indicated the scope of the powers of common law and of natural law respectively. Riot is, in its nature, casual, actual, and simple; and simple measures of resistance may suffice, and the simple powers of the common law may be sufficient. But rebellion, as it is more

20. Lester Nurick and Roger Barrett, *Legality of Guerrilla Forces under the Laws of War*, 40 Am. J. of Int'l L. 563, 571 (1946).

21. *See generally* Gillespie, A History of the Laws of War: Volume I, at 146.

22. James E. Bond, *Application of the Law of War to Internal Conflicts*, 3 Geo. J. Int'l L 345, 367–68 (1973); *see generally* Baron S.A. Korff, *The Ninth International Red Cross Conference* 6:4 Am. J. Int'l L. 858 (1912).

> dangerous and deep-seated, so it is necessarily more difficult to deal with, and may require not only full liberty of attack, but, as it may be passive as well as active, may follow a policy of exhaustion and devastation rather than one of aggression or attack, even full liberty of attack may be insufficient to subdue it, and deterrent measures may be necessary, and the power of speedy punishment . . . Rebellion is war: that is the cardinal principle. War requires measures of war.[23]

Charles Clode described the background to the "Six Mile Bridge" incident in County Clare, Ireland, in August 1852 as follows: forty soldiers were escorting eighteen voters into a village to cast their ballots in a contentious election; they were set upon with stones by a riotous group; the soldiers then responded with weapons fire that killed seven people. In terms of legal character, this was very clearly, Clode asserted, an instance of riot rather than a rebellion. The consequence was that "they [the soldiers] were prosecuted for homicide, and their conduct could be justified only under the law applicable to "ordinary persons."[24] Lord Campbell (as Attorney-General) during the treason trial of John Frost, one of the Chartist leaders of the Newport Uprising in Wales in November 1839, described the reason for this alteration in applicable law thus:

> Levying war against the King does not mean merely heading a force by a pretender to the Crown, as in the wars between the houses of York and Lancaster, or in 1745, but it is where there is an armed force seeking to supersede the law and to gain some public object.[25]

Thus while riot was mere criminality to be dealt with in accordance with the common law (and thus military forces were to act in compliance with the instructions of Magistrates, for the military was, in this situation, merely an adjunct to civil law enforcement),[26] as a matter of domestic law, rebellion was "always war against the Crown."[27] It could, therefore, be dealt with using martial law with

23. William Finlason, A Review of the Authorities as to the Repression of Riot or Rebellion: With Special Reference to Criminal or Civil Liability 47–48 (1868); *see also* William Finlason, Commentaries upon Martial Law with Special Reference to its Regulation and Restraint 81, 92–93, 130–31 (1867); Charles M. Clode, 2 The Military Forces of the Crown: Their Administration and Government 125–80 (1869).

24. Clode, 2 Military Forces of the Crown: Their Administration and Government, at 145–46.

25. *R. v. Frost and Eleven Others* (1939) 9 Carrington & Payne 129, 141.

26. Clode, 2 MILITARY FORCES OF THE CROWN: THEIR ADMINISTRATION AND GOVERNMENT, at 156–58 (quoting a dictum of Sir Edward Coke: 'I speak not of prosecution against a rebel, he may be slain in rebellion; but if he be taken, he cannot be put to death by Martial Law. When the courts are open, Martial Law cannot be executed').

27. Finlason, Commentaries upon Martial Law with Special Reference to its Regulation and Restraint, at 25.

its accompanying authorities to employ the Articles of War (including to attack as if fighting an enemy force),[28] under the military command's own initiative rather than subject to the overall control of a Magistrate,[29] and employing "the power of summary trial and execution of prisoners, who at common law would have to be simply handed to the civil power."[30] Rebellion, consequently, created a situation of necessity that permitted application of martial law as opposed to "routine law," and was thus narrowly construed. As James Macintosh, a Scottish philosopher, lawyer, and politician wrote in the early 1800s:

> Martial Law put in force against rebels can only be excused as a mode of more deliberately and equitably selecting the persons from whom quarter ought to be withheld, in a case where all have forfeited their claim to it. It is nothing more than a sort of better regulated decimation, founded upon choice, instead of chance, in order to provide for the safety of the conquerors without the horrors of undistinguished slaughter.[31]

However, this shift in internal legal paradigm from riot to rebellion did not also herald or indicate a shift in the applicable international law, for the situation remained, so far as third states were concerned, a purely internal matter. Echoing the analyses of Mackintosh and others that rebels had forfeited their claim to quarter from their sovereign, Lauterpacht summarized their legal position:

> In accepted theory, prior to the acknowledgment of a condition of insurgency, the rebellious bodies are in the eyes not only of their own state but also of foreign states law-breakers pure and simple. As it is often put, they are in the same category as robbers and pirates.[32]

This unsurprising conclusion drew its strength, in international law,[33] from the doctrine of sovereignty. As Vernon Harcourt elaborated:

28. *Id.* at 54; *see also* CLODE, 2 THE MILITARY FORCES OF THE CROWN: THEIR ADMINISTRATION AND GOVERNMENT, at 151–52.

29. FINLASON, COMMENTARIES UPON MARTIAL LAW WITH SPECIAL REFERENCE TO ITS REGULATION AND RESTRAINT, at 34–49.

30. *Id.* at 16–17.

31. CLODE, 2 THE MILITARY FORCES OF THE CROWN: THEIR ADMINISTRATION AND GOVERNMENT, at 162 (quoting Sir James Mackintosh). It is assumed that the 'decimation' referred to was the reported Roman punishment of execution of every tenth member of a military unit as a disciplinary and deterrent measure.

32. LAUTERPACHT, *Revolutionary Activities by Private Persons Against Foreign States*, at 278.

33. It is of note that in domestic law, the doctrine that rebellion could be dealt with via application of martial law was expressed not in these terms, but rather more in terms of the actuality of the rebels being an opposing quasi-military force, and thus characterizable as 'soldiers' to whom the more severe Articles of War, and martial law, could thus be applied; *see, e.g.*, FINLASON,

> The general principle which underlies and forms the sub-stratum of the whole discussion is the fundamental doctrine of the respect exacted by International Law for the independence of sovereign States. Each State is bound in its international relations to observe and respect the sovereignty, however symbolised, of every other State. Sovereignty, by the very definition of the term, implies a right to the obedience of subjects, whether the Sovereign be a despot, a monarch, or a republic. A breach of this obedience is a violation of this right. Revolution must always be a violation of Right, though it may sometimes be the consummation of Justice. No political sect I know of, except the Red Republicans, have ever maintained the doctrine of the prima facie legitimacy of Rebellion.[34]

The consequence was that should a maritime rebel, for example, fall into the power of a third state, it was expected that they would be treated in accordance with the status allocated them by their parent state—generally that of pirate.[35]

(ii) British legal approaches to colonial rebellions

Unsurprisingly, statements referencing international law in respect of rebellions taking place ashore (the lowest threshold in the three-level scheme of rebellion-insurgency-belligerency) are rare. This is because, as noted, rebellion that did not extend to the seas was considered a purely internal matter upon which—so long as it did not rise to the level of insurgency—international law had little to say, and from which flowed very few substantive international law consequences. Rebels were criminals liable to the domestic legal consequences due unto rebellion—such as the application of martial law. Only where rebels crossed land borders or put to sea were international interests potentially engaged. At that point, maritime rebels could then be treated as pirates by all, and rebels falling into the custody of a third state could be returned to the conflict state for ordinary criminal prosecution. Otherwise, the premier international law doctrine at play in situations of rebellion was that of non-interference.

Consequently, it is more fruitful to look to domestic legal treatises to find examples of the legal treatment of rebellion. To this end, writers such as Finlason and Clode, dealing with martial law and the discipline and administration of the military forces of the British Crown, offer some insight into the characterization of conflicts as rebellions below the level of insurgency. Finlason dedicates

Commentaries upon Martial Law with Special Reference to its Regulation and Restraint, at 94–95, 104–108.

34. Sir William Vernon Harcourt, Letters by Historicus on Some Questions of International Law 3 (Kraus Reprint Co. 1971) (1863).

35. *See, e.g.*, Christopher Robinson *To the Marquis of Londonderry and the Lords Justices, 4 October 1821, in* Law Officers' Opinions to the Foreign Office 1793–1860, Volume 88 318–20 (Vol. 88); Henry Wheaton, Elements of International Law, §23 n15 (29–32 at 30–31 in particular) (Richard Henry Dana ed., 1866); Philip Jessup, A Modern Law of Nations: An Introduction 53 (1968). This issue will be dealt with a little later.

significant attention to the way courts and Parliament dealt with governors and military commanders for potentially excessive conduct while employing martial law in the suppression of rebellions. For example, after the Irish Rebellion of 1798, Bills of Indemnity were passed by the Parliament in Ireland to regularize—as described by Finlason—"the excesses which took place in the exercise of martial law . . . excesses, be it observed, owing not to the nature of martial law itself, so much as to the fierce passions of the country and the utter absence of due control over its exercise."[36] During a further Irish rebellion (the "Tithe War"—a campaign of civil disobedience and occasional violence between 1831–1836 protesting against the levying of tithes upon the predominantly Catholic population in support of the Protestant Church of Ireland), a series of Irish Coercion Bills formalized martial law in some areas (with some limitations),[37] albeit with significant ongoing debate in Westminster.[38]

Similarly, after the suppression of a rebellion in Jamaica in 1865, reports of excesses during the period of martial law were the subject of a Commission of Inquiry. Recognizing that "the evils of martial law must be very great" when dealing with rebellion, the Commissioners were still driven to ask whether martial law had remained in force beyond the point of necessity.[39] The Governor (Eyre) was criticized in a number of quarters for both the severity in implementation of martial law, and the length of time for which it was continued, permitting some detainees to be dealt with summarily under martial law well after the violence had subsided, and at a time when the ordinary courts were again available for the dispensation of justice.

> Her Majesty's Government cannot but agree with the conclusion of your report, 'that by the continuance of martial law in its full force to the extreme limit of its statutory operation, the people were deprived for longer than the necessary period of the great constitutional privileges by which the security of life and property is provided for.'[40]

Other situations of local rebellion that did not rise to the level of insurgency were also dealt with under martial law. This practice facilitated the execution of many

36. Finlason, Commentaries upon Martial Law with Special Reference to its Regulation and Restraint, at 130–32.

37. *Id.* at 223; Clode, 2 Military Forces of the Crown: Their Adminitration and Government, at 174–75.

38. *See, e.g.*, The Earl of Roden speech to the House of Lords, 16 Parl. Deb., H.L. (3rd ser.) (1833) 196–98; *see also* 16 Parl. Deb., H.C. (3rd ser.) (1833) 1236–83, *available at* http://hansard.millbanksystems.com/bills/irish-coercion-bill.

39. Finlason, Commentaries upon Martial Law with Special Reference to its Regulation and Restraint, at 192–203; Clode, 2 Military Forces of the Crown: Their Administration and Government, at 490–97.

40. Finlason, Commentaries upon Martial Law with Special Reference to its Regulation and Restraint, at 202.

rebels, but entailed no apparent recognition by third states of any insurgency—for example: Barbados (1805 and 1815);[41] Lower Canada (1837–1838);[42] and Ceylon (1848).[43] In each case, the rebellions, ranging in size from mostly hundreds or some thousands, although, in the case of the Indian Army mutiny (1857–1858) the rebel force was many tens of thousands, were dealt with as domestic colonial matters with no international consequences beyond the requirement for non-interference from third states. There were, however, a limited number of primarily maritime situations in which international law did have something to say about third states and rebellion. A case study of how such an instance was dealt with in terms of British legal appreciations will illustrate this nexus.

(iii) Confederate privateering and British plans for dealing with the Confederate warship *Shenandoah* after the conclusion of the American Civil War (1865)

In an open letter addressed to Senator Ira Harris, dated 21 December 1861, and published in the *New York Tribune* on 3 January 1862, Judge Charles Daly of the NY Court of Common Pleas asked, "Are the Southern Privateersmen Pirates?" This letter gained significant attention in both the United States and in Britain,[44] and was informed by the conviction on charges of piracy, in a U.S. court, of some crew members of the Confederate privateer *Jefferson Davis*. Judge Daly's ultimate conclusion was that Confederate privateersmen "should be regarded as prisoners of war and not as pirates."[45] He based this conclusion on three interrelated grounds. The first was that the law was clear:

> [P]rivateersmen act under and are subject to the authority of the nation or power by whom they are commissioned . . . A privateer does no more than is done by a man-of-war, namely seize the vessel of the enemy, the prize or booty being distributed as a reward among the captors. The only difference between them is, that the vessel of war is the property of the Government, manned and maintained by it, while the other is a private enterprise, undertaken for

41. Clode, 2 Military Forces of the Crown: Their Administation and Government, at 481–82.

42. *Id.* at 497–500.

43. Finlason, Commentaries upon Martial Law with Special Reference to its Regulation and Restraint, at 135; Clode, 2 Military Forces of the Crown: Their Administation and Government, at 501–502.

44. *See* Letter from Lord Lyon to Earl Russell (Jan. 4, 1862) (on file in U.K. Archives File: FO 881/1048, item 18 and enclosure) (enclosing a copy of the letter and hoping that it might assist in bringing the U.S. government to 'perceive the advantage and propriety of dealing with the facts of the present civil war as they exist in reality').

45. Letter from Charles Daly, *Are the Southern Privateersmen Pirates?* (Dec. 21, 1861), (on file in in U.K. Archives File: FO 881/1048, Item 18 Enclosure).

> the same general purpose, and giving guarantees that it will be conducted according to the established usages of war.[46]

Daly's second point was that the interests of the U.S. reputation for legality and consistency in international conduct surely dictated that the government act in compliance with this finding—not only because it was law that other nations recognized, but also because the United States had itself previously relied upon exactly these rights:

> The principal nations of Europe, recognizing this state of things, have conceded to the rebellious States the rights of belligerents—a course of which we have no reason to complain, as we did precisely the same thing towards the States of South America in their revolt against the Government of Spain.[47]

Daly's third point was that the dictates of logic and humanity mandated that this be so:

> Is the Government prepared to say that every man in arms against the United States upon the land or upon the water is to be tried and executed as a traitor or pirate, either upon the ground that it is right, or upon the supposition that it will prove an effective means for suppressing the rebellion? That policy was tried by the Duke of Alva in the revolt of the seven Provinces of the Netherlands, and 18,000 persons by his order suffered death upon the scaffold; the result being a more desperate resistance, the sympathy of surrounding nations, and the ultimate independence of the Dutch.[48]

The context of this letter is critical, and two aspects deign brief elaboration prior to dealing with the *Shenandoah* as an incidence of the characterization of international law obligations relevant for third states in situations of rebellion. The first contextual note is that Daly's letter was not merely that of a disinterested legal observer—indeed, it was sanctioned by the U.S. administration as part of a public affairs campaign aimed at shaping opinion toward a possible prisoner swap with the Confederacy. The Confederate Government, in response to the death sentences imposed upon, but not yet carried out on the *Jefferson Davis* crew, threatened to hang in retaliation a group of Union officers held as a PW by the Confederate authorities. This group of prisoners included a close friend of Judge Daly, Colonel Michael Corcoran. Daly approached President Lincoln with an offer to negotiate a prisoner swap, and the Cabinet agreed. The first step in this plan was for Daly to address an open letter to Senator Harris describing why the *Jefferson Davis* crew ought to be treated as PW and not as pirates, thus placing them within the ambit

46. *Id.*

47. *Id.*

48. *Id.*

of a Law of War governed prisoner exchange. On 3 February 1862, affording a respectable month for due consideration of the situation, the U.S. Government subsequently resolved to treat Confederate privateers as PW.[49] Ultimately, none of the executions were carried out; however, Corcoran refused the Confederate offer of parole as he intended to return to fighting duties as soon as he was released. Corcoran was promoted to Brigadier General in July 1862, while still in captivity, and was ultimately exchanged in August 1862.[50] He died, still in uniform, because of a riding accident in December 1863.

The second point to note is that while privateering was by this point illegal for British subjects (as a consequence of the *Paris Declaration* of 1856—"Privateering is, and remains, abolished"), it remained a valid legal option for U.S. nationals and was understood as such by the British. Despite some initial indications in mid-1861 of U.S. "readiness to sign a convention embracing the four points of the Declaration of Paris,"[51] the United States remained outside the *Paris Declaration*:

> The Government of the United States declined to become a party to the International Treaty of Paris in 1856, and therefore the whole of the people of the United States, as well those who are maintaining the Government as those who are in rebellion against it, have never agreed to dispense with privateering.[52]

Consequently, it was the British position that

> Privateers, duly commissioned as such by the Government of the Confederate States, acting under the authority and using the flag of that Government, and capturing and taking into port, for adjudication as 'prize of war', vessels either sailing under the flag of the United States, or even British or other neutral vessels, having goods on board belonging to citizens of the United States, or to persons (of whatever origin) domiciled in those states, or strongly suspected of having such, cannot be considered or treated as pirates, either in British waters or elsewhere, by British Colonial authorities or naval Officers; nor will

49. Aidan O'Hara, *Judge Charles Daly and the New York Irish in the Era of the Civil War, in* Fighting Irish in the American Civil War and the Invasion of Mexico: Essays 147 (Arthur H. Mitchell ed., 2017); *see also* Ford v. Surget, 97 U.S. 594 (1878).

50. Michael Corcoran, The captivity of General Corcoran (1862).

51. Letter from the Duke of Newcastle to Governor Hincks (Windward Islands) and relayed to other Colonial Governors Nov. 30, 1861 (on file in U.K. Archives File: FO 881/2068, Item 5 Enclosure 1) responding to a request for instructions regarding 'the course which should be taken by the British authorities in regard to privateers carrying the flag of the so-styled Confederate States'); *see also* Roscoe R. Oglesby, Internal War and the Search for Normative Order 93–95 (1971).

52. Letter from Charles Daly.

> their being so considered by the United States' Government or laws make any difference in this respect.[53]

This important distinction between Confederate privateer and mere pirate was assiduously maintained by the UK in relation to U.S. requests to deliver up "pirates" found within British jurisdiction. One example, upon which the Law Officers of the Crown—at this time, Roundell Palmer, Robert Collier, and Robert Phillimore—provided advice on 15 January 1864, concerned a request for instructions from Nova Scotia as to U.S. demands for extradition for prosecution of a group of passengers on board the U.S. vessel *Chesapeake*, who had seized the vessel at sea (killing a crew member in the process) and taken it to Nova Scotia in the name of the Confederacy. If the seizure was by pirates, then the proper course of action would be to extradite the felons and return the vessel to the United States. However, if the capture had been effected by properly authorized Confederate privateers, then it was good in law and the vessel need not be returned to the United States, nor the privateers extradited to the United States. This is, indeed, what the Law Officers advised:

> [S]eizure of a United States' merchant-vessel, and the homicide of one of her officers by persons who came on board her as ordinary passengers at New York, is prima facie piracy and murder. But we find it stated in some of the papers . . . that Lieutenant Braine, who commanded the capturing party, represented himself to be a Confederate officer, and professed to have acted in this transaction not only under a commission or letters of marque from Mr. Jefferson Davis, but also under express instructions from the Confederate Government to capture this particular steamer. Should these representations prove to be correct, we apprehend that the acts in question would not properly be within the category of piracy or murder, but ought rather to be deemed by neutral nations to be acts of war; however unjustifiable the stratagem resorted to obtain possession of the 'Chesapeake' may be considered to be.[54]

It was within this general legal background that the Confederate vessel *Shenandoah* caused significant concern for British colonial governors at the conclusion of the American Civil War. On 16 August 1865, the Foreign Office noted that "reports have reached Her Majesty's Government from Washington, that the 'Shenandoah' has continued her depredations, although informed that General Lee had surrendered and the war was virtually over."[55] Instructions sent to the colonies from Downing Street on 7 September 1865, detailed that *Shenandoah*, still operating as if war was ongoing, should be detained "by force if necessary, supposing

53. Letter from the Duke of Newcastle to Governor Hincks.

54. Legal Advice from Roundell Palmer, Robert Collier, and Robert Phillimore, to Earl Russell, Jan. 15, 1864 (on file in U.K. Archives File: FO 881/2068, Item12 Enclosure 1).

55. Foreign Office Letter (Aug. 16, 1865) (on file in U.K. Archives File: FO 881/2068, Item 21 Enclosure).

that you have on the spot a sufficient force to command obedience," and the vessel and armament surrendered to the colonial authorities for subsequent disposition by the British government.[56] The legal position was that the vessel could no longer claim a Confederate commission, nor could she claim the status of privateer as legal cover for her acts of war, for the Confederate flag (and ability to even issue a letter of marque) "has for some time ceased to be recognised by all nations." The vessel was thus required to comply with the directions of the U.S. Government. *Shenandoah's* refusal to do so, compounded by her recalcitrance in "sailing and acting without a commission" from the now reunified U.S. Government, resulted in legal advice from Palmer, Collier, and Phillimore to the effect that "We think that, prima facie, such a vessel would be liable to be treated in a British Court as a pirate."[57] Instructions for *Shenandoah*'s capture if encountered by the Royal Navy on the high seas, or seizure if she entered a British or British colony port, were subsequently promulgated on 11 October 1865, albeit with the caveat that "It is the pleasure of Her Majesty's Government, however, that the crew should not be given up to the United States' authorities, but allowed to go free in such a manner as may at the time be most convenient."[58] *Shenandoah* ultimately surrendered to the Royal Navy at Liverpool on 6 November 1865.[59]

(iv) The *Huascar* (1877)

On 6 May 1877, in the midst of a rebellion against the Peruvian government led by Nicholas Pierola, the crew of the Peruvian naval vessel *Huascar* mutinied and declared for the rebels, sailing from Lima to escape governmental control. The government declared the vessel mutinied and asked for assistance to return her to government authority. During her voyage as a rebel vessel, *Huascar* stopped two British mail steamers at sea, seeking to seize official Peruvian mail, and then boarded a third British vessel and abducted two Peruvian officials. *Huascar* then commandeered coal from a fourth British vessel and abducted a British national to be their engineer. The Royal Navy squadron in the area then interdicted the

56. Letter from Downing Street (Sept. 7, 1865) (on file in U.K. Archives File: FO 881/2068, Item 21).

57. Legal Advice from Law Officers to Earl Russell (Sept. 21, 1865) (on file in U.K. Archives File: FO 881/2068, Item 23 Enclosure 2); Legal Advice from Palmer, Collier, and Phillimore, to Earl of Clarendon (Jan. 9, 1866), *in* ARNOLD MCNAIR, INTERNATIONAL LAW OPINIONS VOLUME II 361–65 (1956).

58. Letter from Downing Street (Oct. 11, 1865) (on file in U.K. Archives File: FO 881/2068, Item 22).

59. *Details of the surrender; reported change of crew; the crew of the Shenandoah*, N.Y. TIMES, Nov. 21, 1865 *available at* http://www.nytimes.com/1865/11/21/news/details-of-the-surrender-reported-change-of-crew-the-crew-of-the-shenandoah.html. Many Confederate warships were built in Liverpool, exploiting both legal ambiguity in the U.K. *Foreign Enlistment Act*, and political hesitancy in applying the law—*see, e.g.*, Nir Arielli et al., *The Foreign Enlistment Act, International Law, and British Politics, 1819–2014*, 38 INT'L HIST. REV. 636, 642–45 (2016).

Huascar and engaged her at sea, causing significant damage such that *Huascar* shortly thereafter surrendered to Peruvian authorities.[60] Outraged at the damage inflicted upon their warship, the Peruvian government asserted in June 1877 that the British action had been excessive, and that *Huascar* did not, "on account of having refused to recognise the authority of Government, cease to belong to Peru. And, although the supreme decree of 8th May last was issued to bring about her apprehension, foreign ships of war were not thereby entitled to attack her. "[61] In an advice to Lord Derby, dated 21 July 1877, Holker, Giffard, and Deane observed that as the Peruvian government "had disavowed all liability for the acts" of the warship while under rebel control, the *Huascar*'s interference with British shipping on the high seas was, consequently, not attributable to Peru. As *Huascar* was "sailing under no national flag," the conduct of the Royal Navy was lawful; although unstated, it is implicit that the legal advisers considered *Huascar*'s conduct against British vessels to have been piratical and unmitigated by any national or belligerent status.[62]

C. INSURGENCY

> Fully aware of the inconveniences and inconsistences inherent in non-recognition when war actually prevails, third Powers have made it a practice in the past to distinguish between belligerency and insurgency, between war in the legal sense and war in the material sense, between war *de jure* and war *de facto*. As a consequence, insurgents gained the right to carry on limited naval operations within the territorial waters under their actual control without running the risk of being treated as pirates by foreign States.[63]
>
> *Vernon O'Rourke (1936)*

Insurgency is a half-way house between essentially ephemeral, or spasmodic or unorganised civil disorders and the conduct of an organised war between contending factions within a State. It is a shadowy condition, there being no well-defined conditions to be satisfied for its existence, and neither giving rise to any clearly recognisable consequences, nor conferring upon the insurgents any legal personality in international law. Insurgency is not

60. Thomas Walker, A Manual of Public International Law 57–58 (1895); Lauterpacht, *Revolutionary Activities by Private Persons Against Foreign States*, at ch. XVIII.

61. Walker, A Manual of Public International Law, at 58.

62. Lauterpacht, *Revolutionary Activities by Private Persons Against Foreign States*, at 313 (citing John Holker, Hardinge Giffard, and Parker Deane, Advice to Lord Derby, July 21, 1877).

63. Vernon A. O'Rourke, *Recognition of Belligerency and the Spanish War*, 31 Am. J. Int'l L. 398, 403 (1937).

> a special status with special rights and duties of its own. All that can be said is that a condition of insurgency will exist when there is within a State an armed conflict which has reached proportions necessitating outside States taking cognizance of it, but not yet fulfilling the conditions calling for the recognition of a state of belligerency.[64]
>
> *McNair and Watts (1966)*

The second level in the three-level scheme was "insurrection" or "insurgency." This category was the most legally problematic of the three, as it was generally considered to be a political characterization with some legal consequences for third states recognizing the situation as such. Whereas "belligerency gives rise to definite rights, insurgency has certain important consequences lacking in any conflict characterised as a rebellion."[65] David Eldar described the situation thus: "The traditional law, though there is less consensus on its content or effects, included a doctrine of 'recognition of insurgency,' whereby the recognizing state could deal with the insurgents in practical matters of mutual importance, while not recognizing their legal status as belligerent or as the de jure government."[66] Evidencing the limited legal definitions available, Thomas Franck and Nigel Rodley described insurgency as "inclu[ding] all movements that are more general than rebellion but less pervasive than belligerency."[67] Discussing an instance of insurgency related to the "Venezuela Affair"—a complicated 1902–1903 web of Venezuelan civil war-related British and German claims in relation to their citizens, investments, and a rejected (ineffective and non-belligerent) blockade[68]—Amos Hershey cited with approval the conclusions of the Institut de Droit International in 1900 to the effect that insurgency below the belligerency threshold "imposes upon third powers . . . certain obligations towards established or recognised governments," including, most importantly, that "it is interdicted to every third power to permit the organisation within its domains of military expeditions hostile to established or recognised governments."[69] That is, in cases

64. Arnold McNair and Arthur Watts, The Legal Effects of War 30–31 (1966).

65. Christopher Quaye, Liberation Struggles in International Law 29–30 (1991).

66. David Elder, *The Historical Background of Common Article 3 of the Geneva Convention of 1949*, 11 Case W. Res. J. Int'l L. 37, 40 (1979).

67. Thomas Frank and Nigel Rodley, *Legitimacy and Legal Rights of Revolutionary Movements with Special Reference to the Peoples' Revolutionary Government of South Viet Nam*, 45 N.Y.U. L. Rev. 679, 680 (1970).

68. *See generally* Amos Hershey, *The Venezuelan Affair in the Light of International Law*, 51 Am. L. Reg. 249 (1903); Benjamin Coates, Legalist Empire: International Law and American Foreign Relations in the Early Twentieth Century 111–25 (2016).

69. *Id.* at 253–54.

of insurgency, the third state was not relieved of its normal duties to deny support to a rebellion against a fellow state, and indeed must act in support of that fellow state to the extent of curtailing within its own jurisdiction any action in support of the insurgency. Stowell, who did not necessarily agree, argued that atrocity-fueled insurgency required third states to refrain from support of either party and that interference should only be considered as an impartial humanitarian intervention. However, he nevertheless accepted that "since unrecognised insurrectionists have no legal standing, any appeal they make must be considered solely from a political or moral viewpoint."[70]

McNair and Watts have argued that the distinction between belligerency and insurgency was a "relatively recent development," emerging in the latter half of the nineteenth century.[71] There is certainly an argument that this concept was in part a "legal" development addressing a conflicted U.S. perspective on belligerency, necessitating a middle path between long-standing U.S. advocacy of the 1823 "Monroe Doctrine" as a diplomatic article of faith,[72] and the related but often contradictory policy of "non-entanglement."[73] To some degree, it is evident that the status of insurgency allowed the United States to afford some limited succor to independence movements in South America (in support of the Monroe Doctrine), while complying, as a matter of the letter of the law, with "non-entanglement" through avoiding the clearly interventionary step of recognizing belligerency. As at 1947, however, Lauterpacht was readily able to summarize the orthodox position on insurgency, as a quasi-legal concept, as follows:

> Insurgency, so far as foreign states are concerned, results, on the one hand, from the determination of those states not to recognize the rebellious party as a belligerent on the ground that there are absent one or more of the requirements of belligerency. On the other hand, recognition of insurgency is the outcome both of the unwillingness of foreign states to treat the rebels as mere law-breakers and the desire of those states to put their relations with the insurgents on a regular, although clearly provisional, basis.[74]

One commentator, writing at the time, described the negotiation of draft Article 1 of *Additional Protocol II* as specifically addressing the "previously illusive" concept of insurgency, noting that it "may come closer to legal definition in this draft

70. Ellery Stowell, Intervention in International Law 352 (1921).

71. McNair and Watts, The Legal Effects of War, at 30.

72. *See generally* Coates, Legalist Empire: International Law and American Foreign Relations in the Early Twentieth Century, at 25 (stating that 'The American continents, by the free and independent condition which they have assumed and maintain, are henceforth not to be considered as subjects for colonization by any European powers').

73. Hershey, *The Venezuelan Affair in the Light of International Law*, at 44.

74. Lauterpacht, *Revolutionary Activities by Private Persons Against Foreign States*, at 270; *see also* Thomas Grassey, *Some Perspectives on Revolution*, 62 Int'l L. Stud. 66 (1980).

article, and both incumbents and insurgents may find less latitude in the future to parry the application of Article 3 semantically to internal conflicts."[75] Another argued that Common Article 3 indeed bound insurgents below the recognized belligerency threshold, but explicitly noted that, as distinct from recognized belligerents, such "an insurgent force has no authority under international law to convene courts to try captives or Convention violators."[76]

(i) Purpose of the status

Certainly, the traditional approach to insurgency was focused upon third state responses to situations more serious and widespread than mere rebellion, but yet below the threshold of recognized belligerency. As Padelford noted, recognition of insurgency did not "alter the legal status of the insurgents within their own state . . . They remain, as previously, engaged in an unlawful attempt to overthrow the established government, and their legal status can be altered only by an amnesty or by successfully establishing themselves as *the* government of the state."[77] Rather, the legal ambiguity of this status was of particular utility to third states who wished to retain a free hand to assist the conflicted parent state without the legal complications that would accompany breaches of neutrality should they first recognize the rebel NSAG as a belligerent. Whether the status carried with it actual (albeit very narrow) legal consequences, or merely political repercussions, has remained a topic of debate;[78] but this argument is to some extent irrelevant because the status presaged both outcomes—it was legally irrelevant to the conflict state, but carried discretionary legal consequences for third states.

One expression of the legally informed political calculus that defined the status of "insurgent" is found in a UK Foreign Office memorandum on "United States Military Aid in Indo-China: Question of Belligerency," dated May 1954. Subsequent to a brief discussion of the fact that "furnishing of military supplies . . . is not in itself an act of belligerency, particularly where there has been no recognition of the rebels as belligerents themselves," the memorandum concludes that

> The fact that American military aircraft have been transporting French troops to Indo-China is more equivocal; but in view of the fact that the Viet Minh have never been recognised either by H.M.G. or by the United States Government as belligerents it can hardly be argued that the United States Government has been guilty of un-neutral service or breach of

75. Eugene Fryer, *Applicability of International Law to Internal Armed Conflicts: Old Problems, Current Endeavors,* 11 Int'l Law. 567, 571 (1977).

76. King, *Revolutionary War, Guerrilla Warfare, and International Law*, at110.

77. Norman Padelford, International Law and Diplomacy in the Spanish Civil Strife 196 (1939).

78. *See, e.g.*, Ann van Wynen and A.J. Thomas Jr., *International Legal Aspects of the Civil War in Spain, in* The International Law of Civil War, 142–43 (Richard Falk ed., 1971).

> neutrality by affording direct military aid of this kind to the French Government.[79]

The classic example of a clear and consciously expressed recognition of insurgency, but not of belligerency, is President Cleveland's several proclamations in relation to the Cuban insurgency of 1895–1898.[80] Although this denial of belligerent rights to the Cuban insurgents was at the time roundly criticized by (among others) Amos Hershey,[81] this lesser status was nevertheless given a degree of legal effect by the U.S. Supreme Court in a series of decisions including *The Three Friends* (1897). This case concerned the application of the U.S. *Neutrality Act* in relation to a vessel being fitted out in Florida for Cuban rebels,[82] and must be narrowly understood as a case about the application and interpretation of a U.S. statute, rather than as an indicator of the general position at international law. In fact, the recognition of the political status of insurgency did not, de jure, bring international law on neutrality into play. Nevertheless, the case evidenced a detailed judicial appreciation of the customary scheme.[83]

Similarly, it is clear from the language used in a wide range of British diplomatic reporting of insurgency contexts, that the use of the terms "insurgency" and "insurgent" was as often fastidiously calibrated as it was hortatory (albeit legally

79. Memorandum from the U.K. Delegation to the Geneva Conference to the Foreign Office on United States Military Aid in Indo-China: Question of Belligerency (May 17, 1954) (on file in U.K. Archives File: FO 371/112062).

80. John Bassett Moore, A Digest of International Law: Volume I, §74 (1906).

81. Amos S. Hershey, *The Recognition of Cuban Belligerency*, 7 Annals Am. Acad. Pol. & Soc. Sci. 450 (1896).

82. *The Three Friends* 166 U.S. 1, 2 (1897) (stating 'The word "people," as used in Rev. Stat. § 5283, forbidding the fitting out or arming of vessels with intent that they shall be employed in the service of any foreign people, or to cruise or commit hostilities against the subjects, citizens, or property of any foreign people with whom the United States are at peace, covers any insurgent or insurrectionary body conducting hostilities, although its belligerency has not been recognized.

Although the political department of the government has not recognized the existence of a de facto belligerent power, engaged in hostility with Spain, it has recognized the existence of insurrectionary warfare, prevailing before, at the time, and since the forfeiture sought to be enforced in this case was incurred, and the case sharply illustrates the distinction between recognition of belligerency and recognition of a condition of political revolt—between recognition of the existence of war in a material sense and of war in a legal sense.

The courts of the United States having been informed by the political department of the existence of an actual conflict of arms, in resistance of the authority of a government with which the United States are on terms of peace and amity, although acknowledgment of the insurgents as belligerents has not taken place, the statute is applicable to the case.

The order for the release of the vessel was improvidently made, as it should not have been released'.).

83. Oglesby, Internal War and the Search for Normative Order 102–104.

careless). This was particularly evident in three situations: first, where a possible recognition of belligerency was being mooted by Britain; second, where belligerent rights were (in the view of British authorities) being incorrectly applied by another state; and third, where a decision had been made by Britain not to afford recognition. One example of the fastidiousness applied in terms of the first situation is the care taken by the British government during the Polish Rebellion in 1863 to clearly refer to the Polish NSAG as insurgents and their rebellion as an insurgency.[84] A second example is the clear distinction drawn by Britain between insurgent and belligerent rights in the context of the Chinese Revolution in 1949, concerning the bombing of a British vessel, *Anchises*, by Chinese Nationalist aircraft in June 1949 in purported enforcement of a blockade. In a cable from the Foreign Office to the Washington Embassy dated 22 June 1949, the position was succinctly expressed:

> A lawful government is entitled to proclaim a blockade of the coast occupied by insurgents. The existence of the blockade, however, constitutes an admission by the government instituting it that a state of belligerency exists . . . It follows from the fact that the declaration of a blockade implies a state of belligerency that the blockade must be conducted in accordance with the internationally accepted rules of war.[85]

Handwritten legal advice, dated 23 June 1949, was even more succinct:

> The proper way to deal with unrecognised insurgents is by decree; or in other words unless your adversary has belligerent status you deal with him like a policeman. On the other hand . . . if your adversary has belligerent status, you may not proceed against him by municipal law or decree or police action, but must blockade him or deal with him by means of other belligerent rights.[86]

However, as the British government informed the U.S. government on 24 June 1949, Britain had "received no indication from the Chinese Nationalist government that they recognise, or are about to recognise, the Chinese Communists as having belligerent status," and also remained unconvinced that the Nationalists had "at their disposal armed forces which will enable them to exercise a real and effective blockade." Consequently, "Her Majesty's Government cannot accept the announcement . . . as a valid proclamation of blockade in international law."[87]

84. *See, e.g.*, the drafts of, and letters between, various senior British politicians and diplomats where this care was clearly taken—for example, the letters and drafts of April–July 1863 in U.K. Archives File: PRO 30/22/14F, and in U.K. Archives File: FO 417/311; this case is discussed in greater detail in Chapter 4.

85. Secret Cable No. 6405, ¶3 (June 22, 1949) (on file in U.K. Archives File: ADM 116/5713).

86. Legal Advice (June 23, 1949) (on file in U.K. Archives File: ADM 116/5713).

87. Secret Cable No. 6508, ¶ 2–4 (June 24, 1949) (on file in U.K. Archives File: ADM 116/5713); Secret Message 211933A/June (June 21, 1949) (on file in U.K. Archives File: ADM 116/

France made a similar determination.[88] Instructions to Her Majesty's Ships on how to respond to the Nationalist-claimed blockade were promptly promulgated on 24 June 1949, stressing that Royal Navy (RN) warships could act to assist, and if necessary use force to defend, British vessels being subjected to blockade enforcement or visit and search outside the limits of Chinese territorial waters (assessed to be three nautical miles).[89] British merchant shipping was likewise advised to ignore challenges by Nationalist warships.[90] By September 1949, this advice had extended even to non-recognition of Nationalist Chinese regulations relating to the territorial waters around (Communist) insurgent held ports: "We think it is established that when the de jure Government has completely lost control of a considerable part of the country, a mere paper edict by the de jure Government purporting to close ports, with no force behind it to secure its observance, would be insufficient and of no effect."[91] But, as Hartley Shawcross made clear, this did not mean that British warships could or should now escort British merchant vessels through contested territorial seas into Shanghai for, regardless of the contested claims, this would not be in accordance with "the so-called right of innocent passage."[92]

An example of the second context (belligerent rights being incorrectly applied by another state) is evident in the issue of British instructions dated 24 March 1864, in relation to British vessels (in particular, the vessel *Julia*) seized and condemned in prize by Spain for allegedly contravening a blockade of insurgent ports in San Domingo.[93] The first point of concern was that the blockade, if it were to have any prospect of legality, must be "of the most effective nature" lest it be no blockade at all, a direct genuflection to the *Paris Declaration*'s crystallization of the requirement for a blockade to be effective if it was to be lawful. If it was not effective, then the condemnations as prize were likewise ineffective in

5713) (mirroring the reasoning of the Admiralty, which considered both visit and search and blockade).

88. Confidential Cable No. 715 (June 30, 1949) (on file in U.K. Archives File: ADM 116/5713).

89. Admiralty Message 241630Z/June (June 24, 1949) (on file in U.K. Archives File: ADM 116/5713).

90. Admiralty Letter M.01669/49, ¶5(Aug. 25, 1949) (on file in U.K. Archives File: ADM 116/5713).

91. Law Officers' Opinion, *Chinese Closure of Ports and Territorial Waters in Insurgent Hands*, ¶4 (Sept. 9, 1949) (on file in U.K. Archives File: ADM 116/5713).

92. Law Officers' Opinion, ¶4 (Sept. 5, 1949) (on file in U.K. Archives File: ADM 116/5713).

93. British authorities had been monitoring the effects of the Dominican rebellion from May 1861, particularly as it related to trade and interference with British merchant shipping in the region: *See, e.g.*, Letter from Consul Hood to Lord Russell (May 20, 1861) (on file in U.K. Archives File: FO 881/1012, Item 30); Colonial Office Letter (Aug. 5, 1865) (on file in U.K. Archives File: FO 72/1302 (indicating that the British authorities should 'hold out no prospect of the interference of Her Majesty's Government in a case where the [British] parties complaining have willfully and knowingly run the risks of trading with blockaded ports'.).

law.[94] The second issue, however, was whether the blockade could be claimed at all if the Spanish insisted on describing the Haitian rebels as "insurgents" as opposed to "belligerents." A letter dated 22 June 1864, from the Foreign Office to the Admiralty, provided legal advice from the Law Officers of the Crown as to the rectitude or otherwise of instructions given by the local RN authority (Admiral Sir James Hope) for British warships to "convoy British ships trading with St Domingo and to prevent the exercise of any belligerent rights by Spain against such vessels being at a distance of more than three miles from shore."[95] The legal advice ultimately concluded that the instructions were incorrect in law, and that British vessels must submit to both the enforcement of the blockade on the high seas and also to the separate municipal regulation as to interdictions within three miles of insurgent held ports. The key legal reasoning behind the advice, however, was that the blockade, if effective, was to be respected by neutrals because it was a de facto recognition of belligerent rights by Spain, which held good even in the face of express Spanish denials of belligerency status for the San Domingo insurgents. "A blockade necessarily implies a state of war, is an incident of it—and cannot exist without it—and on these grounds the Law Officers are of opinion that Admiral Hope's instructions are founded on an erroneous principle."[96]

An example of the third situation (a British decision not to grant recognition of belligerency) is found in the November 1883 Colonial Office correspondence attending a request for guidance from the British authorities in Barbados concerning a Haitian government communication requesting that the Barbados authorities seize a cargo of arms and ammunition destined for Haitian insurgents. The file note, "Cargo of arms and ammunition for Haitian insurgents, asks authority to seize," is accompanied by handwritten Foreign Office legal advice to the effect that there was no international, British, or relevant colonial law that authorized such an act against insurgents. The legal advice ultimately concluded that, "the Haitian Govt must seek their remedy by stopping the ship on its way to the rebel port in accordance with belligerent rights where a state of war exists."[97] Indeed, six years later, on 11 July 1889, Britain specifically withdrew recognition of a subsequent Haitian blockade because it "had plainly ceased to be effective and that . . . in consequence . . . it could no longer be respected by Her Majesty's Government." As a result, the Haitian authorities were informed that "British

94. Foreign Office letter (Mar. 24, 1864) (on file in U.K. Archives File: ADM 128/47).

95. Foreign Office letter (June 22, 1864) (on file in U.K. Archive File: ADM 128/47).

96. *Id.*

97. File No. 18890, Barbados (Nov. 1883) (on file in U.K. Archive File: CO 321/62); *see also* the publication of the Haitian claimed blockade notice for the port of Miragoane, in the *The London Gazette*, 22 May 1883, in U.K. Archives File: FO 881/4854X.

vessels entering or leaving ports in the possession of the insurgents must not be molested by the cruisers of the Haitian government."[98]

(ii) Consequences of recognition of insurgency

The primary consequence of recognition of insurgency was actually a negative inference—that is, that the recognizing third state was not bound to observe neutrality, and thus it remained lawful for such states to support the recognized government, although they could not support the insurgent NSAG.[99] McNair and Watts summarized the situation thus: "Recognition of a state of insurgency does not bring the laws of war and neutrality into operation; at the same time, the situation is not in all respects the same as in a normal state of peace."[100] Two such legal implications, dealt with in more detail in Chapter 4, are that "the provisions of the *Foreign Enlistment Act*, 1870, become effective, [and] 'war risks' clauses in insurance contracts will usually apply."[101] Nevertheless, as McNair and Watts continued, it is "probable, but not entirely clear, that insurgents may be regarded as a 'Party to the conflict' for purposes of the application" of Common Article 3 of the *Geneva Conventions*.[102] A further incident of legal consequence flowing from this quasi-status was that although remaining unrecognized as a belligerent, an insurgent who actually controlled ports was "probably to be acknowledged as having the same powers as the lawful government of closing by decree the ports in their possession and of enforcing such closure within territorial waters in any manner compatible with the non-possession of belligerent rights."[103] That is, the insurgent could close ports by instituting a regime limited to the territorial sea (provided they actually could enforce this closure), so long as it did not claim to implement a blockade (an incident of the Law of War that could be enforced on adjacent high seas but which, because it had not received recognition as a belligerent, an insurgent was not entitled to implement).

The second major consequence of "recognition of insurgency" was that custom did not require third states to honor the conflict state's declaration that insurgent naval forces who fell into the hands of third states were to be treated as pirates in terms of their dealings with the conflict state's forces. Jessup summarized the position: "The principal consequence of a recognition of insurgency is to protect the insurgents from having their warlike activities, especially on the high seas, from being regarded as lawless acts of violence which, in the absence of recognition,

98. Notice published in *The London Gazette*, 12 July 1889, in U.K. Archives File: FO 881/5799X; on the U.S. position with regard to recognition of belligerency in the Haitian context in 1889, *see* MOORE, A DIGEST OF INTERNATIONAL LAW: VOLUME I, §69.

99. MCNAIR and WATTS, THE LEGAL EFFECTS OF WAR, at 31.

100. *Id.* at 53.

101. *Id.*

102. Id at 31.

103. *Id.* at 32.

might subject them to treatment as pirates."[104] However, as was made clear by the U.S. Supreme Court in *The Ambrose Light*, if the insurgent naval force interfered with third state shipping, they were then liable to characterization as pirates. Judge Addison Brown, of the United States District Court for the Southern District of New York, cited Hall extensively on this point:

> The practice is stated by Hall as follows: 'When, however, piratical acts have a political object, and are directed solely against a particular state, it is not the practice for states other than that attacked to seize, and still less to punish, the persons committing them. It would be otherwise, so far as seizure is concerned, with respect to vessels manned by persons acting with a political object, if the crew, in the course of carrying out their object, committed acts of violence against ships of other states than that against which their political operation was aimed; and the mode in which the crew were dealt with would probably depend on the circumstances of the case.'[105]

This approach was routinely employed by the United States in the latter part of the nineteenth century. In an operation almost contemporaneous with the situation in Cuba, Admiral Benham—commanding the U.S. Navy flotilla stationed in Brazilian waters during the Brazilian Naval Revolt in 1894, particularly in the vicinity of the port of Rio de Janeiro—was tasked with ensuring that U.S. shipping remained unmolested. To this end, he informed the rebelling Brazilian Admiral (da Gama) that

> In no case have I interfered in the slightest way with the military operations of either side in the contest now going on. . . . American vessels must not be interfered with in any way in their movements in going to the wharves or about the harbour, it being understood, however, that they must take the consequences of getting in the line of fire where legitimate hostilities are actually in progress . . . Until belligerent rights are accorded you, you have no right to exercise any authority whatever over American ships or property of any kind. You can not search neutral vessels or seize any portion of their cargos, even they be within the class which may be clearly defined as contraband of war, during hostilities between two independent governments. The forcible seizure of any such articles by those under your command would be, in your present status, an act of piracy.[106]

104. Jessup, A Modern Law of Nations: An Introduction, at 53.

105. *The Ambrose Light*, 25 Fed. 408, 442 (1885) (quoting with approval William Hall, International Law § 81 (1880)).

106. *Admiral Benham to Admiral da Gama, in* Moore, A Digest of International Law: Volume I, at 204.

It was, in fact, the issue of piracy around which most state practice on insurgency coalesced. In the 1928 *Havana Convention on the Rights and Duties of States in Event of Civil Strife*, the applicable law was expressed as follows:

> Article 2: The declaration of piracy against vessels which have risen in arms, emanating from a government, is not binding upon the other states. The state that may be injured by depredations originating from insurgent vessels is entitled to adopt the following punitive measures against them:
>
> Should the authors of the damages be warships, it may capture and return them to the government of the state to which they belong, for their trial; should the damage originate with merchantmen, the injured state may capture and subject them to the appropriate penal laws.
>
> The insurgent vessel, whether a warship or a merchantman, which flies the flag of a foreign country to shield its actions, may also be captured and tried by the state of said flag.
>
> Article 3: The insurgent vessel, whether a warship or a merchantman, equipped by the rebels, which arrives at a foreign country or seeks refuge therein, shall be delivered by the government of the latter to the constituted government of the state in civil strife, and the members of the crew shall be considered as political refugees.[107]

Lauterpacht conducted a thorough analysis of state practice, iconic incidents, and cases in respect of the interplay between the political condition of insurgency and the legal condition of piracy: *The Maparari* (a Venezuelan insurgent vessel that fired upon and damaged the British merchant vessel *Clemencia* in 1870); the *Montezuma* (a Spanish vessel violently taken over by Cuban insurgents, who murdered a number of the crew, in 1877); and the *Huascar* (as noted earlier, a Peruvian warship taken over by insurgents in 1877, who then boarded British merchant vessels, kidnapped a British engineer, forcing him to serve in *Huascar*, and engaged two RN warships in battle at sea). He also referenced U.S. practice in relation to the Spanish-Venezuelan conflict in 1823, the Argentine rebellion in 1832, the Haitian insurrection of 1869, *The Ambrose Light* (1885),[108] and the

107. *Inter-American Convention on the Rights and Duties of States in Event of Civil Strife*, 134 LNTS 45 (1928).

108. *The Ambrose Light*, 25 Fed. at 412–13 (stating 'From these principles it necessarily follows that in the absence of recognition by any government of their belligerent rights, insurgents that send out vessels of war are, in legal contemplation, merely combinations of private persons engaged in unlawful depredations on the high seas; that they are civilly and criminally responsible in the tribunals for all their acts of violence; that in blockading ports which all nations are entitled to enter, they attack the rights of all mankind, and menace with destruction the lives and property of all who resist their unlawful acts; that such acts are therefore piratical, and entitle the ships and tribunals of every nation whose interests are attacked or menaced, to suppress, at their discretion, such unauthorized warfare by the seizure and confiscation of the vessels engaged in it. The right of seizure by other nations arises in such cases, ex necessitate, from the very nature of the case. There is no other remedy except open war; and nations are not

Brazilian Naval Revolt in 1893.[109] His conclusions clearly indicate that this appreciation of an insurgency caveat upon the concept of piracy was generally accepted.[110] Ultimately, his analysis yielded the following three conclusions, all of which are consistent with the 1928 *Havana Convention*:

> (1) So long as unrecognized insurgents refrain from interfering with the ships of neutral States, the weight of practice and the principle of non-interference seem to favour the view that third States have no occasion to treat their activities as piratical. Domestic treason is not an international crime.
> (2) When unrecognized insurgents molest the ships of third States they may be treated as pirates, although even in this case the political motives of the act and the absence of an *animus furandi* suggest punishment less severe and drastic than that ordinarily meted out to pirates.
> (3) When to the illegality of the insurgent depredations upon shipping of third States there is added criminal and callous ruthlessness resulting in actual loss of life, the perpetrators of the piratical act, if they fall into the hands of the injured State, may justly be subjected to the customary penalties which the law of nations reserves for pirates *jure gentium*.[111]

This appreciation that third states could lawfully choose not to treat apprehended maritime rebels participating in an insurrection as pirates, so long as their attacks had only been upon conflict state vessels, arguably remains in general accord with the current state of LOAC. Analyzing the possible applicability of insurgency

required to declare war against individual rebels whom they are unwilling and are not required to recognize as a belligerent power. Nor are other nations required, for their own security, in such a case, to make any alliance with the parent state. By the right of self-defense, they may simply seize such law-breakers as come in their way and menace them with injury. Without this right, insurgents, though recognition were rightly refused them, and however insignificant their cause, or unworthy their conduct, might violate the rights of all other nations, harass their commerce, and capture or sink their ships with impunity. The whole significance and importance of the doctrine of recognition of belligerency would be gone, since the absence of recognition could be safely disregarded; the distinction between lawful and unlawful war would be practically abolished; and the most unworthy revolt would have the same immunities for acts of violence on the high seas, without any recognition of belligerent rights, as the most justifiable revolt would have with it. The right to treat unlawful and unauthorized warfare as piratical, seems to me, therefore, clearly imbedded in the very roots of international law.').

109. Lauterpacht, *Revolutionary Activities by Private Persons Against Foreign States*, at 295–328.

110. It should be noted, however, that his views on this matter in 1957 represented a shift from his earlier views on political piracy expressed in 1939 in the wake of the *Nyon Agreement* 1937 in the context of the Spanish Civil War, of which more in subsequent chapters. *See generally* Walter Rech, *Rightless Enemies: Schmitt and Lauterpacht on Political Piracy* 32 Oxford J. Legal Stud. 235, 255–56 (2012).

111. Lauterpacht, *Revolutionary Activities by Private Persons Against Foreign States*, at 310.

status in the Vietnam War as at 1971, Percy Corbett, citing Padelford, considered it settled law that recognition of insurgency meant "conceding to the insurgents the right to take military action on the land and in the ports under their control, as well as in the corresponding territorial waters, though not on the high seas, that might damage interests of the recognizing state."[112] Correspondingly, there is nothing in modern NIAC LOAC that mandates that third states must prosecute as criminals any insurgents who happen to fall into that third state's hands, where those insurgents have engaged only in LOAC compliant attacks upon the parent conflict state's forces. However, it is vital to simultaneously recall that insurgency still did not enliven the entirety of neutrality law. UK Foreign Office legal advice in relation to a Venezuelan decree closing certain ports occupied by insurgents who had not been recognized by the UK as belligerents, was that the Venezuelan government was entitled to employ "municipal regulation, which Venezuela would have the right to enforce as part of her revenue laws within a marine league from her coast."[113] In further advice, Travers Twiss observed that because the Venezuelan government "refuses to recognize any state of war between him [Hernandez's 'so-called Government'] and the Government of the Republic, which would entitle him [Hernandez] to establish a belligerent blockade of the three ports," the UK ought to instruct British shipping to comply with the government regulation closing the ports.[114]

(iii) *R v. Tunkoo Mahomed Saad and Others* (1840)

It is difficult to find a better, more clearly expressed, instance of distinction between a vessel acting on behalf of rebels, as compared to a vessel acting on behalf of insurgents or belligerents, than that which arose out of a judgment rendered in the Straits Settlements in 1840. The defendants claimed to be subjects of the Principality of Kedah, which had been independent until conquered by Siam in 1821; indeed, Tunkoo Mohamed Saad claimed to be the heir to the throne of Kedah. The British East India Company had formerly treated the Prince of Kedah as an independent sovereign at the time in question (1840). Kedah was, however, rebelling against Siamese rule, and the RN was assisting Siam in suppressing the rebellion, in part through the imposition of a blockade across the Kedah River. The defendants had previously taken part in operations on land and at sea, including taking a British vessel in "prize." When captured by the RN, the rebels were prosecuted for piracy.[115]

112. P.E. Corbett, *The Vietnam Struggle and International Law*, *in* The International Law of Civil War 371 (Richard Falk ed., 1971).

113. Lauterpacht, *Revolutionary Activities by Private Persons Against Foreign States*, at 217 (citing Travers Twiss, Opinion, 1 July 1870 (F.O. 83/2403).

114. Lauterpacht, *Revolutionary Activities by Private Persons Against Foreign States*, at 220–21 (citing Travers Twiss to Earl Granville, 13 August 1870 (F.O. 83/2403).

115. *R v. Tunkoo Mahomed Saad and Others), in* Clive Parry and J. Hopkins, Commonwealth International Law Cases: Vol I 31–34 (Clive Parry and J.A. Hopkins eds., 1974).

The argument posed by Tunkoo Mohamed Saad's advocate was that Kedah was justified in its rebellion and that the conduct of the defendants must thus take the legal hue ascribed to rightful insurgents, not pirates:

> My Lord, if ever this right and obligation of individuals to war upon their own impulses against the common enemy existed in any nation, it does in Qedah. All history cannot shew an instance of a country that more loudly and imperatively required its sons each for himself to draw the sword and fight for his fatherland.[116]

As the defense counsel argued, in making a treaty with Siam—in compliance with which the British were involved in suppressing the Kedah rebellion—Britain was in fact acting at odds with a preexisting treaty by which they had recognized the sovereignty of Kedah.[117] In judgment, however, the court noted that

> [E]ven admitting the truth of the facts stated in the plea, it would not necessarily follow that the act imputed should not be piracy, inasmuch as for ought that appears, on the face of the indictment, the persons alleged to have been robbed may be neither British subjects nor Siamese, but subjects of some other European or native Government.[118]

The law, the Judge continued, was as explained by Hume:

> Any adventurer . . . who sails on a voluntary and unlicensed warfare against the enemy, and who condemns, distributes, or disposes of his prizes at sea, or elsewhere, by his own authority, is no other than a pirate, and if taken by the enemy may be lawfully be dealt with as such.[119]

In this case however, the Judge concluded that the defendant "had no need of a licence or commission from any higher authority than himself" as he had been exercising the government of the Prince. Further, because his attacks had been only against Siamese and British vessels, "nor could a capture of enemies" property at sea under such circumstances be, with any reason or justice, called predonious or piratical.[120] Consequently, Tunkoo Mahomed Saad and his followers were found not guilty of piracy; the "others" were released, but Tunkoo Mahomed Saad, as the chief rebel and thus an adversary of Britain in its character as an ally of Siam, was

116. *Id.* at 47.

117. *Id.* at 58–59.

118. *Id.* at 65.

119. *Id.* at 72.

120. *Id.*

to be retained on the proviso that "he will not again be remanded to the common gaol to be associated with felons, but will go into a kind of honourable captivity."[121]

(iv) *The Ambrose Light* (1885)

The case of *The Ambrose Light* arose out of the seizure in 1885 of a vessel acting in support of an insurgent force at that time fighting against its parent state of Columbia. It is a complicated and much criticized case: Alfred Rubin, and many others, have noted that the judgment does not deal with the orthodox understanding of insurgency, and confuses the legal consequences of rebellion with those of insurgency.[122] The problem, arguably, is that the judgment fails to make clear the differing treatment to be afforded (on one hand) to a rebel vessel that has been engaged in operations against either or both adversary conflict state shipping and/or third state shipping via blockade, and (on the other hand) an insurgent vessel that has engaged only in attacks on adversary conflict state shipping. In *The Ambrose Light*, the situation was argued by the U.S. government's counsel to have been that insurgents had indeed attacked U.S. (third state) shipping, and thus, in the absence of recognition of belligerency, had deprived themselves of the ability to claim the narrowly prescribed insurgent's immunity from characterization as a pirate.

During the rebellion in Columbia, insurgents held a number of ports, and *The Ambrose Light* had been engaged in blockading the Columbian government-held port of Cartagena.[123] *The Ambrose Light* was later captured by a U.S. warship (*Alliance*) and taken to New York for adjudication because the master had produced papers purporting to prove her a Columbian warship, but which the Captain of the *Alliance* considered of doubtful provenance. In fact, as became clear, *The Ambrose Light* was an insurgent commissioned vessel. In the resulting case, much hinged around the legal characterization of the rebels. If the rebels were recognized belligerents, then their commission, if in order, should be respected and their conduct could not be defined as piratical. If, on the other hand, the insurgents were not recognized as belligerents, then their conduct at sea was amenable to the label of piracy.[124] Judge Brown, rendering his decision in the case in 1885, summarized the law:

> The consideration that I have been able to give to the subject leads me to the conclusion that the liability of the vessel to seizure, as piratical, turns wholly

121. *Id.* at 74.

122. Alfred Rubin, *Is Piracy Illegal?* 70 Am. J. Int'l L. 92 (1976); Charles Cheney Hyde, International Law Chiefly as Interpreted and Applied by The United States: Vol I §233 (1922).

123. *The Ambrose Light*, 25 Fed. at 410–11; *The Ambrose Light*, N.Y. Times, June 8, 1885 *available at* https://timesmachine.nytimes.com/timesmachine/1885/06/08/103021995.pdf

124. *The Ambrose Light*, 25 Fed. at 412–14.

> upon the question whether the insurgents had or had not obtained any previous recognition of belligerent rights, either from their own government or from the political or executive department of any other nation; and that, in the absence of recognition by any government whatever, the tribunals of other nations must hold such expeditions as this to be technically piratical. This result follows logically and necessarily, both from the definition of piracy in the view of international law and from a few well-settled principles.[125]

Ultimately, as to the law, he concluded that

> The insurgent leaders, in sending out the *Ambrose Light* to blockade Cartagena, were, so far as this court can recognize, in the position of seeking some political revolution or usurpation by means that were unlawful as respects foreign nations. They could not, by merely commissioning their own vessels, without any recognition by the executive or political departments of any other government, make themselves lawful belligerents, or become entitled to exercise acts of constraint or of violence towards the vessels of other nations. They knew that, with this lack of legal authority, they took the risk of having the vessel treated as piratical. They knew that, until recognition, their position in the courts, both at home and abroad, was that of mere usurpers who, in addition to treason against their own country, were threatening, by their attempted blockade, the lives and property of the subjects of all other commercial nations. They took all the risks of being treated as criminals, or as piratical cruisers, until they secured recognition of belligerent rights from abroad.[126]

Thus, if the insurgents were not recognized belligerents, then the fact that their conduct against foreign vessels was for a belligerent purpose, rather than intended as a common "robbery," made no difference to the ultimately piratical character of their conduct: "if the warfare be unlawful, the *animus belligerandi* becomes felonious."[127] Nor was it permissible for the courts to deem a situation one of belligerency if the political organs had not yet furnished this status by word or deed.[128]

This was the law. However, the decision ultimately settled was that the U.S. government had indeed impliedly recognized the insurgents' belligerent status, and thus the vessel's conduct was not piratical. As Judge Brown concluded,

> Upon these considerations and on these authorities I cannot doubt that in thus notifying the Colombian government, in effect, that the United States would recognize no right in Colombia to close the insurgent ports by virtue

125. *Id.* at 412.

126. *Id.* at 428.

127. *Id.* at 435.

128. *Id.* at 438.

> of her own sovereignty, but only through the exercise of the belligerent right of blockade, i.e., by war, our government recognized, by necessary implication, the existing insurrection as a state of war, and the insurgent forces as a de facto power, having the counter-rights of a belligerent. From this indirect and implied recognition of the belligerency of the insurgents, the conclusion of law follows that their vessels of war cannot be regarded as piratical.[129]

The U.S. Supreme Court thus considered it abundantly clear in law that all maritime attacks by rebels in situations that had not risen to the level of insurgency were to be treated as piracy, regardless of whether they targeted only adversary conflict state vessels, or third state vessels as well. Additionally, if the insurgents were recognized belligerents, their conduct for recognizing states could not be characterized as piratical. That is, while recognized maritime belligerents were not pirates, and only some maritime insurgents were pirates, all maritime rebels were pirates.

(v) Report of the League of Nations Committee of Experts (1927) and the Harvard Draft Articles on Piracy (1932)

As a Rapporteur of the League of Nations appointed Committee of Experts in relation to possible codification of international law concerning piracy, Ambassador Michikazu Matsuda's 1927 draft codification made explicit reference to the settled state of the law as regards piracy and insurgency:

> Article 4. Where, during a civil war, warships of insurgents who are not recognised as belligerents are regarded by the regular Government as pirates, third Powers are not thereby obliged to treat them as such.
>
> Insurgents committing acts of the kind mentioned in Article 1 [piracy defined as depredations for private ends; acts committed with a purely political object are not piracy] must be considered as pirates, unless such acts are inspired by purely political motives.[130]

129. *Id.* at 446–47.

130. *Report of the League of Nations Committee of Experts*, League of Nations Doc. C.196.M.70.1927.V, 119 (1927), *available at* https://search.un.org/results.php?tpl=lon&SS=&lang=en&query=League+of+Nations+Document+C.196.M.70.1927.V&Submit=Search&__utma=114554307.100145107.1476506528.1476506528.1476508393.2&__utmz=114554307.1476508393.2.2.utmcsr%3Dgoogle%7Cutmccn%3D%28organic%29%7Cutmcmd%3Dorganic%7Cutmctr%3D%28not+provided%29&_ga=GA1.2.100145107.1476506528&_gat=1&NSC_j_xg-bqbdif_iuuq_mc_wt=ffffffff09f2003445525d5f4f58455e445a4a423660; *see also* Committee of Experts for the Progressive Codification of International Law, *Report to the Council of the League of Nations on the Questions which Appear Ripe for International Regulation*, 22 Am. J. Int'l L. 4, 25–33 (Supplement: Codification of International Law 1928).

The *Harvard Research Draft Articles on Piracy* (1932), and associated commentary and research, provided even clearer recognition of the need to distinguish piracy from certain insurgent conduct at sea.[131] Article Three of the draft provided that:

> Piracy is any of the following acts, committed in a place not within the territorial jurisdiction of any state:
>
> 1. Any act of violence or of depredation committed with intent to rob, rape, wound, enslave, imprison or kill a person or with intent to steal or destroy property, for private ends without bona fide purpose of asserting a claim of right, provided that the act is connected with an attack on or from the sea or in or from the air. If the act is connected with an attack which starts from or on board ship, either that ship or another ship which is involved must be a pirate ship or a ship without national character . . .

The learned commentary on the draft article then outlined fifteen separate points of analysis in relation to acts within and outside this definition. Points twelve to fourteen dealt with the intersection of piracy and insurgency, focusing upon the issue of whether insurgent action at sea met the "private ends" requirement of piracy.[132] The commentary notes, for example, that "the draft convention excludes from its definition of piracy all cases of wrongful attacks on persons or property for political ends, whether they are made on behalf of states, or of recognised belligerent organisations, or of unrecognised revolutionary bands [insurgents]."[133] Consequently,

> Although states at times have claimed the right to treat as pirates unrecognised insurgents against a foreign government who have pretended to exercise belligerent rights on the sea against neutral commerce, or privateers whose commissions violated the announced policy of the captor, and although there is authority for subjecting some cases of these types to the common jurisdiction of all states, it seems best to confine the common jurisdiction to offenders acting for private ends only.[134]

The rationale was that a pirate, as *hostis humani generis*, "preys on the world at large," while insurgents, so long as they limited their attacks to the adversary conflict state, were not a threat to all. Indeed, the commentary observed, "all states have not a common interest in preventing attacks which purposely are confined to the commerce of a single state."[135] Citing Halleck, Oppenheim, Wheaton, Calvao,

131. *Part IV—Piracy* 26 AM. J. INT'L L. 739, 743 (Supplement: Research in International Law 1932).

132. *Id.* at 777–79.

133. *Id.* at 786.

134. *Id.* at 798.

135. *Id.* at 803.

and the League of Nations Report, the commentary thus supported a summative analysis along the following lines:

1. An insurgent privateer always remains characteriseable by the adversary conflict state as a pirate, whereas (as shall be dealt with in the next chapter) a formal belligerent privateer must be treated as a PW by the adversary conflict state;
2. An insurgent privateer may also be treated as a pirate by his or her own state of nationality (where that nationality is of a third state) as a matter of that third state's own domestic law, regardless of whether that privateer has restricted their attacks only to adversary conflict state shipping or not;
3. An insurgent privateer who attacks only adversary conflict state shipping 'ought not' be treated as a pirate by third states (but, of course, if the privateer is merely a rebel rather than an insurgent, they may still be treated as a pirate by all states regardless of whether they have attacked third state shipping or not); and
4. An insurgent privateer who, in addition to attacking adversary conflict state vessels, also attacks third state shipping, may be treated as a pirate by the wronged third state and, depending upon the position in their domestic law, by any other third state which has not recognised that NSAG's formal belligerency.

This analytical framework for distinguishing between piracy and some limited forms of insurgency clearly informed the *SS Falke* incident in 1929. This involved twenty-two Venezuelan insurgents boarding the German flagged *Falke* in Gdansk with a "mystery" cargo (of arms) and "secret orders." Upon sailing from the port on 28 July 1929, the insurgents subverted the crew into joining the insurgency. The ship had been recently sold by her German owners to a new owner, who, as became evident, was in league with the Venezuelan insurgents. The ship's Captain took "an oath on the rebel flag" and became "an 'admiral' of the insurgent forces," allegedly forcing his crew, at gunpoint, to join him in this new loyalty.[136] The vessel then took on further fighters and equipment from a "rebel sloop," and was employed in support of an ultimately failed insurgent landing at Cumana on 11 August 1929.[137] *Falke* was declared "piratical" by the Venezuelan government the

136. *Falke with "Admiral" Stuck at Trinidad: Skipper Tells of Rank Conferred by Venezuelan Rebels and of Flying "Liberation Colors,"* N.Y. Times, Aug. 17, 1929, at 2; Samuel Menefee, *Piracy, Terrorism, and the Insurgent Passenger: A Historical and Legal Perspective*, *in* Maritime Terrorism and International Law 55–56 (Natalino Ronzitti ed., 1990).

137. *Venezuelan Rebels Rout Federal Force: Hold Cumana Against Attack of Troops and Plane—Junta Ridicules Falke Report*, N.Y. Times, Aug. 21, 1929, at 7.

following day.[138] The United States, however, refused to publicly endorse this characterization, explaining that

> The question whether a vessel in the hands of insurgents is piratical depends upon its actions, that is, whether it confines itself to depredations against its own country or commits depredations against vessels of other countries . . . The weight of opinion is clearly to the effect that an insurgent vessel cannot be treated as piratical merely because the insurgents have not been recognized as belligerents.[139]

Britain similarly refused to treat the vessel and the insurgents as pirates when they came within British colonial jurisdiction while seeking to coal at Port of Spain in Trinidad.[140]

This appreciation of the discrete legal character of maritime insurgency continued to enjoy currency into the post-World War II legal context.[141] Volume Four (1965) of *Whiteman's Digest of International Law*, for example, devotes several pages of extracts and comments to the distinction between piracy and insurgency.[142] Similarly, Telfer writing in 1981, felt safe in asserting that

> An analysis of maritime insurgency as piracy should consider three factors: (1) the interrelated duality of piracy as both a domestic crime and as an offense against the law of nations; (2) the 'private ends' requirement; and (3) intent as evidenced by selectivity of victims. The first factor, as developed through history to codification in the Law of the Sea Convention, is important as a gradual limitation of municipal jurisdiction. The other factors serve to delineate the limited arena within which acts may be insurgency, but beyond which are piracy.[143]

138. Leslie Green, *The Santa Maria: Rebels or Pirates*, 37 Brit. Y.B. Int'l L. 496, 502 (1961); Green Haywood Hackworth, Digest of International Law: Vol 2 698–99 (1940); Menefee, *Piracy, Terrorism, and the Insurgent Passenger: A Historical and Legal Perspective* 55–56.

139. Menefee, *Piracy, Terrorism, and the Insurgent Passenger: A Historical and Legal Perspective*, at 56.

140. *Id.*; *British Isolate Falke Filibusters: Trinidad Authorities Forbid Supplying of Venezuelan Rebel Ship at Port of Spain*, N.Y. Times, Aug. 16 1929, at 10.

141. *See* D.H.N. Johnson, *Piracy in Modern International Law*, 43 Transactions Grotius Soc'y 63 (1953) (summarizing the issues as at 1953).

142. Marjorie M. Whiteman, Digest of International Law: Vol 4 652–54 (1965).

143. Grant Richard Telfer, *Maritime Insurgency and the Law of the Sea: An Analysis using the Doctrine of Distress*, 20 San Diego L. Rev. 625, 640–41 (1983).

(vi) The *Santa Maria* incident (1961)

This policy-based legal consequence—the distinction between maritime insurgents and pirates—was also still evident, at least in the background, in the 1961 *Santa Maria* incident.[144] Over the course of 21–22 January 1961, the Portuguese flagged *Santa Maria*, carrying approximately three hundred crew and six hundred passengers en route from Curacao to La Guaira, was taken over from within by Henrique Galvao and a team of twenty-three men,[145] although Portuguese authorities erroneously claimed at the time that the party had numbered seventy.[146] They had boarded the ship in disguise at various previous ports of call[147] and then,

> At one thirty in the morning of the 21st of January they attacked the strategic points in the ship using revolvers and light machine guns. The Commander was relieved of his command and arrested. The third pilot, who was on duty on the bridge was killed. Other officers were gravely beaten and wounded.[148]

144. Ferenc Vali, *The Santa Maria Case*, 56 Nw. U. L. Rev. 168 (1962); Green, 496; Whiteman, Digest of International Law: Vol 4, at 665–66; Clyde Crockett, *Toward a Revision of the International Law of Piracy*, 26 DePaul L. Rev. 78, 94–96; Thomas Franck, *To Define and Punish Piracies—The Lesson of the Santa Maria: A Comment*, 36 N.Y.U. L. Rev. 839 (1961); C. John Colombos, The International Law of the Sea 459–59A (6th ed., 1967); for an excellent pre-1961 summary of the debate on 'private ends' *See generally* Johnson, *Piracy in Modern International Law*, at 63.

145. Letter from the British Embassy Lisbon to the Foreign Office, ¶4 (Apr. 5, 1961) (on file in U.K. Archives File: FO 371/160755) (confirming this number subsequently in a Portuguese police investigation).

146. Thirteen Portuguese, ten Spaniards, and one Venezuelan—Rhea Smith, *Book Review: Santa Maria: My Crusade for Portugal, by Henrique Galavao*, 42 Hisp. Am. Hist. Rev. 578, 579 (1962); Statement by Government of Portugal (on file in U.K. Archives File: FO 179/585) (stating that 'the gang numbered 70 people of several nationalities—Spaniards, Cubans, Venezuelans—and only five Portuguese'.).

147. Whiteman, Digest of International Law: Vol 4, at 665; apparently, Galvao had boarded disguised as a passenger in a wheelchair: Vali, *The Santa Maria Case*, at168.

148. *See, e.g.*, Official Note Issued by the Office of the President of the Council on the Santa Maria Incident, ¶2 (on file in U.K. Archives File: FO 179/585). The subsequent return to Lisbon of the *Santa Maria* on 16 February, and her passengers and crew prior, as well as the funeral of the Third Officer, Nascimento Costa, were exploited by the Salazar regime as opportunities to buttress domestic support: As Sir Archibald Ross reported to London from Lisbon on 22 February 1961, 'my impression now is that in Portugal the pendulum has swung in favour of the regime . . . and that the immediate effect, due partly to successful stage-management of the *Santa Maria's* return, has been to rally the nation as a whole in support of their leader Dr. Salazar. The Ministry of Foreign Affairs now take the line that Galvao in fact did the Government here a very good turn': Confidential Memorandum 10110/121/61 No. 15, British Embassy Lisbon 4 (Feb. 22 1961) (on file in U.K. Archives File: FO 179/585). This was a different assessment from that provided by Ross in the more immediate aftermath of the incident, on 8 February 1961, where he assessed that 'there is no doubt that the general atmosphere has changed here as a result of then *Santa Maria* affair . . . There is a mood for change, but so far no leader to exploit

Galvao claimed to be acting in the name of "the Independent Junta of Liberation" (also described as the "National Independence Movement") led by General Humberto Delgado, a failed presidential candidate in the 1958 election who had been granted political asylum in Brazil.[149] The vessel was renamed *Santa Libertade*, and the wounded and those crew who refused to join the insurgent cause were put ashore in St Lucia.[150] Galvao, a former colonial administrator and Army officer, had been in prison since 1952 for counter-Salazar activities (escaping in 1959),[151] and may have intended to take the ship to Angola to raise a force with which to embark on operations in Portugal.[152] General Delgado sent a telegram to the British Embassy in Rio de Janeiro on the morning of 24 January 1961, asking that the Ambassador "inform your Government immediately that the *Santa Maria* case is neither piracy nor mutiny but appropriation of Portuguese vessel by Portuguese persons for Portuguese political ends. Demand emphatically that your Government should not interfere in the matter."[153] He similarly informed the U.S. Government that this was a "purely political act of democratic insurrectional force against a tyrannical dictatorship."[154]

Speculation as to any wider "plot" was rife.[155] As the UK representative in Portugal, Sir Archibald Ross, explained in a summative account of the affair dated 8 February 1961:

it': Memorandum from Archibald Ross to Lord Home, *The Santa Maria Affair: Its Implications for Portuguese Policies at Home and Abroad*, ¶9 (Feb. 8, 1961) (on file in U.K. Archives File: FO 179/585).

149. Although, as was clarified over the course of 1961–1962, it became increasingly evident that both men were vying for leadership of the anti-Salazar movement in exile, and that they had very different objectives in mind despite a general agreement upon the insurrectionary plan to overthrow Salazar: *See, e.g.*, David Raby, *Transatlantic intrigues: Humberto Delgado, Henrique Galvao and the Portuguese exiles in Brazil and Morocco*, 3 PORT. J. SOC. SCI. 143 (2004).

150. Vali, *The Santa Maria Case*, at 169; according to the Administrator on St Lucia, Galvao threatened to scuttle *Santa Maria* if he was approached by any British warship—*See* Report from the Administrator, St. Lucia to the Secretary of State for Colonies, *Factual Report on the "Santa Maria" incident so far as St. Lucia*, ¶2 (Jan. 27 1961) (on file in U.K. Archives File: FO 371/160248).

151. Smith, *Book Review: Santa Maria: My Crusade for Portugal, by Henrique Galavao*, at 578–79; *see also* Letter from John Wicks to the MP John Biggs-Davidson (Jul. 10 1961) (regarding Galvao's background); *see also* Letter, from Joseph Godber (Jul. 26, 1961) (on file in U.K. Archives File: FO 371/160755) (responding to the Letter from John Wicks).

152. This was the reported initial assumption: Cable No. 34, British Embassy Lisbon to Foreign Office (Jan. 24, 1961), ¶2 (on file in U.K. Archives File: FO371/160248).

153. Cable No. 16, British Embassy Rio de Janeiro (Jan. 24, 1961) (on file in U.K. Archives File: FO371/160248).

154. Cable No. 147, British Embassy Washington to Foreign Office, ¶4 (Jan. 25, 1961) (on file in U.K. Archives File: FO 371/160248).

155. *See, e.g.*, Cable No. 34, British Embassy Lisbon to Foreign Office, ¶3 (Jan. 24, 1961) (on file in U.K. Archives File: FO371/160248) (Portuguese authorities immediately alerting *Santa Maria's* sister ship, *Vera Cruz*, which had recently sailed from Lisbon).

> Many theories have been advanced: a pure publicity stunt designed only to focus world attention on Spain and Portugal; or a widespread plot involving the seizure of the liner *Vera Cruz* as well as the *Santa Maria*, with synchronised uprisings in Portuguese Africa, if not also in Metropolitan Portugal, and the capture of Sal Island as a base for provisional 'democratic' Governments of Spain and Portugal by armed men from Brazil who would first have commandeered in mid-air a Transportes Aereos Portugeses airliner en route to Sal from Brazil.[156]

Indeed, as late as 3 February 1961, almost two weeks after the seizure of the *Santa Maria*, the British Embassy in Lisbon informed the Foreign Office that "It is not yet absolutely clear here that there is no possibility of Galvao contriving to sail the *Santa Maria* once more from Brazil for an unknown destination."[157] The Foreign Office Legal Advisers remained unsure as to the definitive legal position to be adopted if this occurred, particularly as British assistance to continue pursuit and apprehension in such circumstances had been requested.[158] Spain was concerned that "insurgents may endeavour to set up in [an] African state an opposition Government which might be recognised by the Soviet Union and thus open the way to a Spanish coup of like nature."[159] Although initially concerned about the prospect of Galvao making for Africa to set up a base of operations,[160] the ultimate U.S. view was that "Galvao's primary intention was publicity."[161]

The Netherlands, UK, and United States were requested by Portuguese authorities (the Salazar government) to help recapture *Santa Maria*.[162] The United States initially agreed, noting its authority under the "well-defined terms of international law governing piracy and insurrection on board ship."[163] However, it soon became clear that the vessel had been taken over from within, and that there had not been two ships involved (as required for piracy per Article 15 of the 1958

156. Ross The Santa Maria Affair: Its Implications for Portuguese Policies at Home and Abroad, ¶5.

157. Confidential Telegram No.75, Lisbon to Foreign Office Feb. 3, 1961) (on file in U.K. Archives File: FO 179/585).

158. File note RB1651/19 (1 Feb. 1, 1961) (on file in U.K. Archives File: FO 371/160249).

159. Cable No. 56, British Embassy Madrid to Foreign Office, ¶4 (Jan. 28, 1961) (on file in U.K. Archives File: FO 371/160248).

160. Cable No. 210, British Embassy Washington to Foreign Office, ¶2 (Jan. 31, 1961) (on file in U.K. Archives File: PREM 11/3472).

161. Letter from British Embassy Washington to Foreign Office, ¶2 (Feb. 16, 1961) (on file in U.K. Archives File: FO 371/160249).

162. *See, e.g.*, the Portuguese 'Official Note Issued by the Office of the President of the Council on the Santa Maria Incident', ¶5; Cable from British Embassy Lisbon to Foreign Office ¶3–4 (Jan. 23, 1961) (on file in U.K. Archives File: FO 371/160248).

163. Cable No. 447, Foreign Office to British Embassy Washington, ¶1 (Jan. 25, 1961) (on file in U.K. Archives File: FO 371/160248).

Geneva Convention on the High Seas).[164] The U.S. position subsequently evolved. The U.S. State Department legal adviser explained to British counterparts that the public U.S. position had been based in an assessment that there were "reasonable grounds for suspicion of piracy" and a valid Portuguese request, although his personal view was that "there was little chance that piracy could be established."[165] This opacity is in part likely explained by the fact that the United States was required to trod both a more robust and a more circumspect path than Britain, given that there were an estimated fifty U.S. citizens on board *Santa Maria*.[166] Britain also agreed to assist Portugal, and immediately dispatched *HMS Rothesay* to assist in locating *Santa Maria*;[167] *HMS Scorpion* was also dispatched to assist soon thereafter.[168]

As an aside, it is interesting to observe that initial British instructions had been to the effect that RN warships could participate in the capture of *Santa Maria*, based on the request of the Portuguese government. Subsequently, Anna van Zwanenberg, then at the University of Bristol, wrote several times to the Assistant Legal Adviser, Bushell, seeking clarification as to the legal reasoning.[169] Two government lawyers, Barnes and Vallet, had given the relevant advice "orally at fairly short notice" to the Civil Lord of the Admiralty, and while secure in their advice, Barnes was not sure "if there is any authority in international law which we can quote in support of this position." Lush agreed that the reply should be to the effect that they could not answer van Zwanenberg's question without disclosing confidential advice to Ministers. Barnes, however, argued that "although we do not want to encourage Miss van Zwanenberg to ask awkward questions, can we not do a bit better than this? Can we not, for example, refer to some suitable passage in Oppenheim or the report of the International Law Commission and then say that this is as far as we can go without disclosing the confidential advice given to Ministers?"[170] The response ultimately provided to van Zwanenberg did indeed note the confidentiality of legal advice to Ministers, but attempted to assuage her curiosity by reference to Article 6 of the *High Seas Convention*, the capacity of a flag state to request assistance, and a general invocation of both "police

164. Whiteman, Digest of International Law: Vol 4, at 666.

165. Cable No. 147, British Embassy Washington to Foreign Office, ¶3 (Jan. 25, 1961) (on file in U.K. Archives File: FO 371/160248).

166. *See Factual Report on the "Santa Maria" incident so far as St. Lucia was concerned*, ¶2 (Jan. 27, 196) (on file in U.K. Archives File: FO 371/160248).

167. Cable No.137, Foreign Office to Lisbon, ¶4 (Jan. 31, 1961) (on file in U.K. Archives File: FO 179/585).

168. Cable No. 548, Foreign Office to Washington, ¶7 (Jan. 31, 1961) (on file in U.K. Archives File: FO 371/160249).

169. *See, e.g.*, Letter from Anna van Zwanenberg to JCW Bushell (June 17, 1961) (on file in U.K. Archives File: FO 371/160755).

170. *See* File Minute and notes, CP1651/4 (June 29–Jul. 6, 1961) (on file in U.K. Archives File: FO 371/160755).

cooperation" through Interpol, and of extradition law, "both of which enable the requesting State to exercise its jurisdiction effectively."[171]

Behind closed doors, however, the British assessed that the *Santa Maria* situation placed them on the horns of a dilemma. Instructions from London to the Ambassador in Washington observed that

> I share the American desire not to become ostensibly involved in Portuguese internal politics and we should be faced with some very awkward decisions if Galvao and his friends and the ship fall into our hands. On the other hand, it seems important (with Jordan and Lebanon in mind) to maintain the right to respond to the request of a friendly government. We certainly do not want to appear to condone the violent seizure of merchant vessels at sea, even if it is not piracy.[172]

The final, considered, British position on the issue of characterizing *Santa Maria's* conduct was twofold.[173] First, it was clear from the outset, to the British at least, that the act could not be considered piracy. As a confidential cable from the Foreign Office to the Embassy in Lisbon made abundantly clear, on 31 January 1961,

> [I]f an act is to be regarded as piracy in International Law it must among other things involve action by one ship against another. In this case no second ship was involved . . . On these grounds alone we were forced to conclude that this was legally not an act of piracy and to act accordingly . . . It was therefore superfluous trying to reach a determination whether or not [the] act was committed for private ends. It is unjustified and indeed absurd for the Portuguese to suggest we were trying to make a political judgement or to prepare the way for recognising some other Portuguese Government.
>
> This position was adopted after full consideration of the legal factors and it was on this basis that the Portuguese Government were asked . . . not to base their request for our help on an allegation that piracy had taken place since this could only serve to tie our hands.[174]

171. Letter from Foreign Office to Anna van Zwanenberg (Jul. 13, 1961) (on file in U.K. Archives File: FO 371/160755); *see also* Cable No. 75, Foreign Office to British Embassy Lisbon, ¶1 (January 24, 1961) (on file in U.K. Archive File: FO 371/160248) (describing the early elucidation of this legal basis).

172. Cable No. 548, Foreign Office to Washington, ¶6 (Jan. 31, 1961) (on file in U.K. Archives File: FO 371/160249).

173. There was some to and fro initially, as the legal implications of piracy were balanced against the 'humanitarian' imperative of rescuing the passengers: *See, e.g.*, File Note to RP1651/3 (Jan. 26, 1961) (on file in U.K. Archives File: FO 371/160248).

174. Cable No.137, Foreign Office to Lisbon, ¶2–3 (Jan. 31, 1961) (on file in U.K. Archives File: FO 179/585); *See also* Ross, The Santa Maria Affair: Its Implications for Portuguese Policies at Home and Abroad, ¶¶2, 4.

However, the undoubtedly legally correct British refusal to use the term "piracy" in relation to the incident was nevertheless initially interpreted as a pointed diplomatic slight by Portugal. The impression of the Portuguese Government appeared to have been that "legal quibbles,"[175] including disquiet as to this issue of "private ends,"[176] were being employed by Britain as an excuse to provide generalized help, but no actual assistance, in terms of interdicting *Santa Maria*. This position was "greatly resented" by the Portuguese.[177] Indeed, the chairman of the British Chamber of Commerce in Portugal wrote to the British ambassador on 8 February 1961, to explain that "the prevailing opinion in Portuguese business circles is that Great Britain avoided her obligations as an ally of Portugal, and rendered little or no assistance during the course of the operations at sea . . . Unless some effort is made to correct the existing impression, the result upon British exports to Portugal could be serious."[178] Portugal further claimed that Britain had exerted pressure on the United States to alter its initial characterization of the incident as piracy, although the British position is that the United States had reached a new and "different decision" along the same lines as the British assessment prior to Britain informing the United States of its own legal view.[179] Interestingly, just as Portugal was most concerned at British attitudes, the U.S. position was targeted by Spain. As the British Embassy in Madrid reported on 3 February 1961, "The United States Government . . . has been criticized on the score of having entered into negotiations with pirates [most likely a reference to U.S. Navy communications with Galvao and the offer of escort to a Brazilian port[180]] rather than presumably hanging them from the most accessible yard-arm. Indeed, the American Ambassador has been informed officially that it is inexplicable to the Spanish

175. Cable No. 41, British Embassy Lisbon to Foreign Office (Jan. 25, 1961) (on file in U.K. Archives File: PREM 11/3472).

176. Cable No. 48, British Embassy Lisbon to Foreign Office, ¶3 (Jan. 27, 1961) (on file in U.K. Archives File: PREM 11/3472).

177. British Foreign Office, *The Santa Maria affair: its implications to Portuguese policies at home and abroad—Summary* (on file in U.K. Archives File: FO371/160249); *see also* Letter from British Embassy Washington to Foreign Office, ¶4 (Feb. 16, 1961) (on file in U.K. Archives File: FO 271/160249) (reporting of the U.S. view on Portuguese resentment being based on not understanding that *HMS Rothesay* was withdrawn with U.S. agreement because the U.S. had taken over the 'chase' in that area).

178. Letter from Michael Stilwell, Chairman of the British Chamber of Commerce in Portugal, to British Ambassador to Portugal, Sir Archibald Ross (Feb. 8, 1961) (on file in U.K. Archives File: FO 179/585).

179. Cable No.137, Foreign Office to Lisbon, ¶4 (Jan. 31, 1961) (on file in U.K. Archives File: FO 179/585); Cable No. 48, British Embassy Lisbon to Foreign Office, ¶5 (Jan. 27, 1961) (on file in U.K. Archives File: PREM 11/3472).

180. *See, e.g.*, Cable No. 23, British Embassy Rio de Janeiro to Foreign Office, ¶4 (Jan. 29, 1961).

Government that the United States Fleet has not arrested the 'Santa Maria' on the high seas."[181]

The second legal dimension to the British response is more ambiguous, in that the British government was clearly uncomfortable at being seen to support Salazar.[182] In debate in the House of Commons on 24 January 1961, the demarcation between insurgency and piracy was expressly raised:

> Mr. Paget: May I ask the Civil Lord [of the Admiralty] a further question? Is not the position that we have no obligation, either by custom or anything else, to interfere where there is a case of political rebellion against a sovereign country? If we have to intervene here, it is because it is piracy and, in the light of piracy, possibly for humanitarian reasons. In neither of those events are we under any obligation—indeed, it is quite contrary to our duty—to hand over anybody we arrest to the Government of Portugal. If they are pirates, we have jurisdiction. If they are not pirates, we have no business.
>
> Mr. Orr-Ewing: I think, as I have said, that the hon. and learned Gentleman has made a perfectly valid point, and I have also said that the Law Officers of the Crown will be consulted about this complicated matter of international law, and will certainly bear in mind the point that he has made.[183]

A cable from the Foreign Office to the British Embassy in Washington specifically mooted Galvao's likely claim to "insurgent status" as the basis of a "call for

181. Letter from British Embassy Madrid to Foreign Office, ¶4 (Feb. 3, 1961) (on file in U.K. Archives File: FO 271/160249).

182. 'There is a tendency in this country, because people do not like Dr Salazar, to jump to the conclusion that Galvao and his gang are a noble band of patriots and democrats': Handwritten file note to RP1651/11 (Feb. 1, 1961) (on file in U.K. Archives File: FO 371/160249); *see also* Green, *The Santa Maria: Rebels or Pirates*, at 496; The Civil Lord of the Admiralty (Mr. C. Ian Orr-Ewing) 633 Parl. Deb., H.C. (5th ser.) (1961) 32–35 (stating 'The full facts concerning the seizure of this vessel are not clear, but Her Majesty's Government and the United States Government were asked by the Portuguese Government for any information on the "Santa Maria's" whereabouts and for all possible help in securing the restoration of the vessel and her cargo to the rightful owners. Acting on this request, instructions were issued to the Senior Naval Officer, West Indies, to attempt to arrest the ship provided contact was gained outside territorial waters and provided this could be done by peaceful means without loss of life or risk of scuttling. If, however, this was impracticable the Senior Naval Officer was instructed to shadow the "Santa Maria" and report. I am advised that Her Majesty's Government are fully entitled, in accordance with international law, to take this action to meet this request'; 'As I explained at the beginning of my statement, the full facts of this case are not known. We do not know whether the ship was boarded, or whether those who took over took passage at Curacao, which was the last place of call. Until the full facts are known I think that it would be wrong to pronounce on it. I give the undertaking to the House that the Law Officers of the Crown and other legal advisers will carefully consider the legal implications before any action is taken'), *available at* http://hansard.millbanksystems.com/commons/1961/jan/24/.

183. *Id.*

non-intervention by foreign powers."[184] A piece in *The Guardian* on 25 January 1961, by that paper's "legal correspondent," clearly asserted that "insurrection is not piracy."[185] Ultimately, it does not appear that the British government made a definitive statement as to this issue in relation to the *Santa Maria*.

The U.S. Navy located *Santa Maria* on 26 January 1961, shadowing her and then contacting the vessel to ascertain Galvao's intentions. He indicated a willingness to offload the passengers either at sea or in a neutral port, but maintained that he and his associates' status was as "political insurgents." Indeed, in an exchange of telegrams over the period 28–29 January 1961 between Galvao and the Brazilian President-elect Janio Quadros (who took office on 31 January 1961), Galvao specifically requested recognition of belligerency status from Brazil. As a British diplomatic cable reporting the exchange outlined:

> Galvao asked for right not only to land passengers in a Brazilian port but also to refuel *Santa Maria* and for recognition as 'belligerent' . . . [the response] explained that although right of asylum in Brazil could be guaranteed no decision on belligerent status or provision of fuel could be taken until President elect had taken office.[186]

The Brazilian President-elect offered Galvao and his men asylum on 29 January 1961, responding to a telegram from Galvao by confirming that "within the exercise of my constitutional powers, the right of asylum on our soil will be conceded to you and to those who desire it together with whatever further facilities existing laws and treaties may permit."[187] The official Brazilian position, clearly illustrating a nuanced and considered legal view on the interaction of insurgency and piracy, was that

> If the vessel puts in at a Brazilian port or enters Brazilian territorial waters, she will be liable to seizure for restitution to her lawful owners. . . .
>
> As for the insurgents under Henrique Galvao, it only remains to intern them in Brazil in conformity with Brazil's long-standing diplomatic tradition which precludes her from accepting the classification of piracy.[188]

184. Cable No. 548, Foreign Office to Washington, ¶3 (Jan. 31, 1961) (on file in U.K. Archives File: FO 371/160249).

185. *Insurrection is not piracy: Doubts about right to intervene*, GUARDIAN, Jan. 25, 1961 (on file in U.K. Archives File: FO 371/160248).

186. British Foreign Office communication, Rio de Janeiro to Lisbon, Telegram No. 9 (Jan. 30, 1961) (on file in U.K. Archives File: FO 179/585).

187. British Foreign Office communication, Rio de Janeiro to Lisbon, Telegram No.14 (Feb. 1, 1961) (on file in U.K. Archives File: FO 179/585) (containing translation).

188. Text of Brazilian Diplomatic note delivered to Government of Portugal (Jan. 29, 1961) (on file in U.K. Archives File: FO 179/585) (in British file note RP1651/15, dated Jan. 30, 1961).

Brazilian Ministry of Foreign Affairs legal advice, as communicated to the British Embassy in Rio de Janeiro, was that "the events on board *Santa Maria* did not amount to piracy, but were rather a combination of mutiny and insurrection."[189] Venezuela also asserted that Galvao's conduct did not amount to piracy.[190] The "Portuguese Patriotic Junta" similarly wrote to the British Ambassador in Caracas on 25 January 1961 to explain the political and national character of Galvao's actions,[191] and the "Committee for the Defence of Portuguese Democratic Freedoms in Paris" telegrammed the British Prime Minister in the same terms on the same day.[192]

Ultimately, on 31 January 1961, U.S. warships formally offered to escort *Santa Maria* to an appropriate port so that the passengers could be disembarked, assuring Galvao that they would not interfere with the vessel otherwise.[193] *Santa Maria* entered the Brazilian port of Recife on 2 February 1961, where the passengers and remaining crew were landed, Galvao and his men were given political asylum, and the vessel was turned over to Brazilian authorities the following day (being eventually returned by Brazil to her owners).[194] Although the Portuguese authorities steadfastly "repudiat[ed] completely the alleged political character of this criminal adventure,"[195] and signaled an intention to request extradition of Galvao and a number of others from Brazil in order to face prosecution,[196] they did not ultimately insist upon this measure:[197]

> During all this incident the Government, without forgetting the question of safeguarding lives and property, could not ignore the general problem which interests all maritime countries, namely the safety of maritime vessels on the high seas against acts of piracy. The Government brought this repeatedly to the attention of other powers. The Government were not influenced, however,

189. Letter from British Embassy Rio de Janeiro to Foreign Office (Jan. 27, 1961) (on file in U.K. Archives File: FO 371/160249).

190. Letter from British Embassy Caracas to Foreign Office, ¶6 (Feb. 10, 1961) (on filein U.K. Archives File: FO 371/160249).

191. Letter from Portuguese Patriotic Junta to British Ambassador Caracas (Jan. 25, 1961) (on file in U.K. Archives File: FO 371/160248).

192. Telegram BPL1544 Paris 308047 91 25 0120 (on file in U.K. Archives File: FO 371/160248).

193. Vali, *The Santa Maria Case*, at 169–70.

194. *See* Anna van Zwanenberg, *Interference with Ships on the High Seas*, 10 INT'L COMP. L. QUARTERLY 785, 799–801 (1961); Vali, *The Santa Maria Case*, at 170.

195. Statement by Government of Portugal.

196. Letter from British Embassy Lisbon to the Foreign Office, ¶7 (Apr. 5, 1961) (on file in U.K. Archives File: FO 371/160755).

197. Cable No. 565 from Foreign Office to Washington (Jan. 31, 1961) (on file in U.K. Archives File: PREM 11/3472) (stating (at ¶3) that the 'Portuguese Embassy here have said, for what it is worth, that the Portuguese Government do not want the "rebels" to be handed over to them, but are very anxious for the return of the ship').

> by political considerations which some people invoked and wished to detect behind events. The Government always considered such aspects to be secondary except to the extent in which they confirmed the support given to the attackers by forces dedicated to the destruction of the West and the collusion of the attackers with these forces. In accordance with this attitude the Portuguese Government has not insisted on the return of those responsible for crimes of robbery, murder, corporal assault, falsification of passports, smuggling of arms and depriving hundreds of people of their liberty. The Government rely completely on the judgement and conscience of the international community, and in particular on the appreciation, on the part of those countries which are in a position to translate their sympathy into effective action, of the policy followed by the Portuguese Government in harmony with the law governing such cases as the *Santa Maria*.[198]

This is a most interesting and revealing position statement. On one reading, the legal difficulty alluded to could be the issue of the "two ship rule" in piracy, the first and most clearly elucidated stumbling block for Britain in characterizing the action as piracy. However, the clear political context and the centrality of references to political motivations and debate as to "private ends" tend to indicate that the ultimately settled Portuguese view was one that tacitly recognized and affirmed the law of maritime insurgency. However, the British assessed that behind this legal view, as ever, stood a bald political calculation: "the Portuguese are, we think, too anxious at the moment to obtain Brazilian support for Portuguese policy in Africa to be willing to risk affronting the Quadros Government by raising such a delicate issue as the extradition of Galvao and Delgado."[199] Ultimately, Galvao went on to lead other insurgent/rebel acts, most notably the hijacking of a TAP airliner on 10 November 1961 while en route from Casablanca to Lisbon, which also involved the dropping of anti-Salazar propaganda leaflets over Lisbon[200] (an act that exhausted the patience of the Moroccan authorities in terms of his presence on their territory[201]). He was also a central figure in a subsequent plan

198. Portuguese Official Note Issued by the Office of the President of the Council on the Santa Maria Incident, ¶5.

199. Letter from British Embassy Lisbon to the Foreign Office, ¶7 (Apr. 5, 1961) (on file in U.K. Archives File: FO 371/160755).

200. Telegram from Rabat to Foreign Office, No. 430 (Nov. 11, 1961) (on file in U.K. Archives File: FO 371/160755) (stating that Galvao by this time was estranged from Delgado); Telegram from Lisbon to Foreign Office, No. 603, ¶2 (Nov. 10, 1961) (on file in U.K. Archives File: FO 371/160755) (stating that Galvao was not himself one of the hijackers (four men and one woman) but met them on arrival at Tangier).

201. Cable No. 32, Tangier to Foreign Office (Nov. 14, 1961) (on file in U.K. Archives File: FO 371/160755); Letter from John Sanders, British Embassy Rabat, to JWR Shakespeare, Foreign Office (Nov. 21, 1961 (on file in U.K. Archives File: FO 371/160755).

to clandestinely enter Portugal to raise further insurrection.[202] As David Raby concludes of Galvao's attempts in conjunction with exile insurrection movements, "Certainly it was a significant attempt to spark a revolt, although Galvao could claim that the *Santa Maria* affair amounted to an act of armed revolt, technically on Portuguese territory."[203]

Citing Oppenheim, Ferenc Vali observed that the *Santa Maria* incident provided a textbook instance of the dictum that insurgents who had not interfered with third state shipping should not be treated by third states as pirates. There had been "no evidence that these acts were committed 'for private ends,' both the intent to rob (*animus furandi*) and the intent to take private vengeance being notably absent."[204] Although he described the attempted "coup" as "theatrical" and "hardly effective to jeopardize in any degree the Lisbon government," he concluded that the "political motivation of this action seems to be beyond doubt."[205] Fenwick, however, observed of both the incident and Galvao's claims, that "The status of insurgency is not one to be conceded to any and every citizen who believes that the government of his country is tyrannical and should be overthrown."[206] Nevertheless, as Green responded, "Neither mutiny nor insurrection at sea is an offence which by international law is within the jurisdiction of any State other than the flag State."[207] Yet, despite different assessments as to the claim of insurgency, both Fenwick and Green, along with almost all other commentators who addressed the incident, agreed that the distinction remained extant and legally important. Thus Green, among others, specifically noted that the application of the label "pirate" by the national state of the insurgents to both them and their vessel, "imposes no obligation upon any other State to treat them in this way."[208] He cited as conclusive Lushington's famous analysis in *The Magellan Pirates*:[209]

> It is true, that where the subjects of one country may rebel against the ruling power, and commit divers acts of violence in regard to that ruling power, that other nations may not think fit to consider them as acts of piracy . . . I think it does not follow that, because persons who are rebels or insurgents may commit against the ruling power of their own country acts of violence, they may not be, as well as insurgents and rebels, pirates also; pirates for other acts committed towards other powers. It does not follow that rebels or insurgents may

202. Raby, *Transatlantic intrigues: Humberto Delgado, Henrique Galvao and the Portuguese exiles in Brazil and Morocco*, at 146, 148.

203. *Id.* at 153.

204. Vali, *The Santa Maria Case*, at 170–71.

205. *Id.* at 172.

206. Charles Fenwick, *Piracy in the Caribbean*, 55 Am. J. Int'l L. 426 (1961).

207. Green, *The Santa Maria: Rebels or Pirates*, at 497.

208. *Id.* at 499.

209. *The Magellan Pirates* [1853] 1 Sap Ecc & Ad 81 July 26 1853.

> not commit piratical acts against the subjects of other states, especially if such acts were in no degree connected with the insurrection or rebellion.

In line with this dictum, noting that his actions were limited to a Portuguese vessel, and were for Portuguese insurrectionary purposes, Galvao's actions, Green concluded, "cannot . . . be regarded as piracy."[210]

Whether this was an overt and correct application of the quasi-law on insurgent status, perhaps with a partially sympathetic eye upon Galvao in comparison to the Salazar regime, is ultimately not the point. What is significant is that the "insurgency" status language used by Galvao and others throughout this incident was schematically and legally consequential. It also appears that it was understood as such by the United States and Britain and it was most certainly analyzed as such within contemporaneous and subsequent commentary. A similar situation, and outcome, was evident in the near simultaneous case of *The Anzoategui* (1963).[211] In this incident, a group of Venezuelan rebels who had hijacked *The Anzoategui* were later "processed" through Czechoslovak territory (as part of "Operation Manuel," during which Prague was utilized by communist sympathizer groups as a "transit hub" for their personnel[212]) and given asylum.[213] Again, they were treated, as Galvao and his team were treated, as insurgents rather than pirates.

210. Green, *The Santa Maria: Rebels or Pirates*, at 503.

211. Whiteman, Digest of International Law: Vol 4, at 666–67.

212. Michal Zourek, *Operation MANUEL: When Prague was a Key Transit Hub for International Terrorism*, 3 Cent. Eur. J. Int'l & Sec. Stud. 78, 87–88 (2015).

213. Haro Van Panhuys, *Aircraft Hijacking and International Law*, 9 Colum. J. Transnat'l L. 1, 13–14 (1970).

3

The Customary Three-Level Scheme Part II

Belligerency

> It is undoubtedly true that the notion of belligerency is inseparable from the existence of war, and all the rules of international law regulating the conduct of belligerents are primarily concerned with the relations arising out of the conduct of hostilities . . . There is, therefore, a large measure of truth in referring to a belligerent community as a military organisation. But that truth is only a part-truth; it over-emphasises the military character of a belligerent community and neglects its capacity as a civil government. Indeed, the aim of a belligerent body is military success. Yet, to achieve such military success it must be able to maintain law and order in the territory under its control, exploit resources, raise men and supply-materials.[1]
>
> —Ti-Chiang Chen, *The International Law of Recognition*

> The hostilities within a State may reach such proportions that the situation can no longer be regarded as one of mere insurgency. Where there exists within a State an armed conflict of a general (as distinguished from purely local) character, where the insurgents occupy and administer a substantial portion of national territory, and where they conduct the hostilities in accordance with the rules of war and through organised armed forces acting under a responsible authority, it can be said that the situation has grown beyond one of insurgency and deserves to be considered one of belligerency.[2]
>
> —McNair and Watts, *The Legal Effect of War*

1. Ti-Chiang Chen, The International Law of Recognition 307 (L.C. Green ed., 1951).
2. Lord McNair and A.D. Watts, The Legal Effects of War 32 (4th ed., 1966).

> According to traditional principles of international law, international war occurs between sovereign states or in the case of a revolutionary war, where the insurgents have attained belligerent status.[3]
>
> —Charles King, *Revolutionary War, Guerrilla Warfare, and International Law*

A. INTRODUCTION

Belligerency, under the customary three-level scheme, was a formal legal status.[4] Eugene Fryer expressed the position thus: "Principal Western commentators on traditional international law do not admit of any form of formally cognizable international conflict other than declared war or a sub-war contest between formally recognized belligerents."[5] Once the conflict state accorded an adversary NSAG formal belligerency status—either directly or by implication (most routinely through the declaration of a blockade over rebel held ports)—both parties were bound by the Law of War as applicable to conflicts between states. As Justice Brown noted in *The Ambrose Light* (1885): "The recognition by foreign states of a state of war in civil strife, or, what is the same thing, a recognition of the belligerent rights of the insurgents, authorizes courts of law to treat the insurgents as lawful combatants."[6] This recognition did not bind third states, who were entitled to make their own determination based upon a part objective, part political test. As a matter of practicality however, once the conflict state afforded the NSAG belligerency status, third states directly affected by the conflict (generally in terms of maritime communications and commercial intercourse) usually acted in accordance with

3. Charles R. King, *Revolutionary War, Guerrilla Warfare, and International Law*, 4 Case W. Res. J. of Int'l L. 91, 114 (1972).

4. Debate remains as to when the first "formal" recognition of belligerency occurred; although there is no doubt that the doctrine was operative by the 1820s, Francois Bugnion and others have opined that the earlier American War of Independence was also an instance of formally recognized belligerency. Francois Bugnion, *Jus ad Bellum, Jus in Bello and Non-International Armed Conflicts, in* 6 Yearbook of International Humanitarian Law 167, 178 (Avril McDonald and Timothy McCormack eds., 2003): "The first recorded case of recognition of belligerency occurred during the American War of Independence. Sir James Robertson, appointed to take command of the British forces in America, informed General George Washington of his determination to comply with the laws and customs of war and proposed that the two supreme commanders agree that such rules be respected and enforced on either side."

5. Eugene D. Fryer, *Applicability of International Law to Internal Armed Conflicts: Old Problems, Current Endeavors, in* 11 The International Lawyer 569 (1977).

6. U.S. v. The Ambrose Light, 25 F. 408, 418 (S.D.N.Y. 1885).

this recognition.[7] They then instructed their vessels to submit to both conflict state and belligerent status NSAG visit and search operations as necessary:

> Official notice of such a proclamation makes it the duty of foreign nations to conform to the international rules of war in that regard . . . [such nations] may assist the government de jure as an independent power, or it may assist the insurgents, in either of which cases it becomes a party to the war, or it may remain impartial, still continuing to treat the government de jure as an independent power whilst it treats the insurgents as a community entitled to the rights of war against its adversary.[8]

This was also the British legal view in declaring, on 13 May 1861, its neutrality as between the contending parties in the American Civil War. President Lincoln's declaration of a blockade against the Confederate States[9] acted as evidence, in the British view, of an implied recognition of belligerency, although it was stated that Britain's declaration of neutrality followed as a practical consequence of an independent assessment of the situation rather than a result of the Union declaration.[10] Similarly, as Amos Hershey argued—in support of the United States granting recognition of Cuban belligerency against Spain in 1896—such recognition, "Implies to the Cubans no aid or support other than moral, nor would it give them any special advantage over Spain. We on the contrary bind ourselves to the observance of a stricter neutrality . . . and we accord both parties certain rights which only one of the parties in this contest (Spain) is in a position to take advantage of."[11]

B. BELLIGERENCY—THE TEST

"Once an insurrection acquires sufficient force and permanency, and the interest of third Powers are affected thereby," asserted Vernon O'Rourke in the fulcrum of the Spanish Civil War, "recognition of belligerency is perfectly justifiable in the eyes of international law." "It would be futile," he continued, "to attack the propriety of this principle."[12] In 1865, during the American Civil War, Vernon Harcourt

7. *See, e.g.*, McNair and Watts, The Legal Effects of War, at 33; Vernon O'Rourke, *Recognition of Belligerency and the Spanish War*, 3 Am J. of Int'l Law 398, 402 (1937).

8. Ford v Surget, 97 U.S. 594, 610 (1878).

9. President Abraham Lincoln, "Declaration of Blockade," April 19, 1891, *in* Mountague Bernard, A Historical Account of the Neutrality of Great Britain during the American Civil War 79–80 (1870).

10. *See, e.g.*, Charles C. Hyde, 1 International Law Chiefly as Interpreted and Applied by The United States 2, §49 (1922).

11. Amos S. Hershey, The Recognition of Cuban Belligerency, 450–51 (1896).

12. O'Rourke, *Recognition of Belligerency and the Spanish War*, at 399.

similarly observed that, the distinction between insurgency and belligerency, "is a question upon which, fortunately, there may be found a very great amount of authority."[13] One animating attribute of the test, he asserted, was its recognition that the characterization at stake was "clearly a question of degree and a question of amount."[14] Another, he continued, was that

> belligerency is a question of fact, and it is a question of fact which is to be determined by the neutral Governments upon their own responsibility. They will form their judgment of what is the condition of things, whether it deserves the name of a local insurrection, or whether it has reached the proportions of a civil war.[15]

As evidence of the centrality of discretion to the test, Vernon Harcourt elsewhere described how the fact that Britain may have recognized Confederate belligerency (13 May 1861) prior to having been formally informed of the Union's declaration of blockade (19 May 1861)[16] was immaterial, stating that "Our [Britain's] proclamation of neutrality was founded upon our conviction that a state of war had arisen. We came to that conclusion on May 13th."[17] Indeed, it is evident that the British Government had determined to take this course of action before even this date—as a letter forwarded from Downing Street to colonial governors, dated 11 May 1861,[18] makes clear.

A third attribute of the test is that although it maintained a strikingly coherent and consistent form and shape as it evolved, some of the articulated elements within the test have been iteratively subject to limited interpretive dispute. In describing the test for recognition of belligerency just prior to World War II, Wilson traced two extremes within this interpretive tussle. At one end of the spectrum was the view that the belligerent must be attributed with analogies of statehood, "when the regime to be recognized fulfills the basic conditions as to territory, free communication; organization of government and forces, and political objectives consistent with moral principle." The other end of the spectrum, however, reflected an assessment that recognition was simply a matter of political policy for the recognizing state, implying some degree of organization and

13. Vernon Harcourt, *The Rights and Duties of Neutrals in Time of War: Part I*, 9 Royal United Services Institution J. 313, 316 (1865).

14. *Id.*

15. *Id.* at 319.

16. Abraham Lincoln, *Proclamation 81—Declaring a Blockade of Ports in Rebellious States* (Apr. 19, 1861), The Am. Presidency Project, https://www.presidency.ucsb.edu/documents/proclamation-81-declaring-blockade-ports-rebellious-states.

17. Vernon Harcourt, *The Rights and Duties of Neutrals in Time of War: Part II*, 9 Royal United Services Institution J. 329, 330 (1866); Harcourt, *The Rights and Duties of Neutrals in Time of War: Part I*, at 320.

18. Letter, Downing Street, May 11, 1861, *in* UK Archives File: FO 881/2068, Item No.2.

capability ("capacity to be a responsible person"). It could not be, as stated by President Grant, a "gratuitous demonstration of moral support to the rebellion," but nor did this status necessarily require the full accessories of quasi-statehood.[19] Hyde asserted as late as 1922 that the test was not capable of "nice statement," but this was arguably a minority view,[20] for the test appears to have been much more settled than either Wilson or Hyde suggested. Justice Grier of the U.S. Supreme Court, in *The Prize Cases* (1862), described the test succinctly as follows:

> Insurrection against a government may or may not culminate in an organized rebellion, but a civil war always begins by insurrection against the lawful authority of the Government. A civil war is never solemnly declared; it becomes such by its accidents—the number, power, and organization of the persons who originate and carry it on. When the party in rebellion occupy and hold in a hostile manner a certain portion of territory, have declared their independence, have cast off their allegiance, have organized armies, have commenced hostilities against their former sovereign, the world acknowledges them as belligerents, and the contest a war. They claim to be in arms to establish their liberty and independence, in order to become a sovereign State, while the sovereign party treats them as insurgents and rebels who owe allegiance, and who should be punished with death for their treason. The laws of war, as established among nations, have their foundation in reason, and all tend to mitigate the cruelties and misery produced by the scourge of war. Hence the parties to a civil war usually concede to each other belligerent rights. They exchange prisoners, and adopt the other courtesies and rules common to public or national wars.[21]

Similarly, the Institute of International Law's 1900 resolution on the Rights and Duties of Foreign Powers as Regards the Established and Recognized Governments in Case of Insurrection, at article 8, set out a three-element test and an additional permission—at articles 4 and 9—for third states to make their own independent determinations, free of any requirement to comply with the conflict state's own views (whether that be the granting of, or refusal of, belligerent

19. Robert R. Wilson, *Recognition of Belligerency and Insurgency*, 31 Am. Soc'y of Int'l L., 136, 139–40 (1937); *see also* Fred K. Nielsen, *Insurgency and Maritime Law*, 31 Am. Soc'y of Int'l L., 136, 146 (1937); Yair Lootsteen, *The Concept of Belligerency in International Law*, 166 Mil. L. Rev. 109, 109–114 (2000) (discussing the first step as requiring that "[c]ertain conditions of fact" arise, including: "the existence of civil war within a state, beyond the scope of mere local unrest; occupation by insurgents of a substantial part of the territory of the state; a measure of orderly administration by that group in the area it controls; and observance of the laws of war by the rebel forces, acting under responsible authority.").

20. Hyde, 1 International Law Chiefly as Interpreted and Applied by The United States 2, §47.

21. The Prize Cases, 67 U.S. (2 Black) 635, 666–67 (1863).

status).[22] The test[23] (here summarized by Higgins) is thus generally considered to involve the following features:

> [F]irst, the existence within a state of a widely spread armed conflict; second, the occupation and administration by rebels of a substantial portion of territory; thirdly, the conduct of hostilities in accordance with the rules of war and through armed forces responsible to an identifiable authority; and fourth, the existence of circumstances which make it necessary for third parties to define their attitude by acknowledging the status of belligerency.[24]

Similarly, legal advice to the British Cabinet in light of questions surrounding the nature of the conflict in the Formosa Strait in 1957 set out the test as follows:

> (i) There must exist an armed conflict of a general (as distinguished from a purely local) character.
> (ii) The contesting party which is not the legitimate government must occupy and administer a substantial portion of the national territory.
> (iii) The above-named contesting party must conduct the hostilities in accordance with the rules of war and through organised armed forces acting under a responsible authority.
> (iv) There must exist circumstances which make it necessary for outside states to define their attitude by means of recognition of belligerency.[25]

As will become apparent, the marked coherence and consistency of the test across time, context, and national assessment, tend to speak quite favorably as to its utility.

22. Institute of International Law, *Resolution on Rights and Duties of Foreign Powers as Regards the Established and Recognized Governments in Case of Insurrection*, Neuchatel meeting, September 8, 1900, *in* RESOLUTIONS OF THE INST. OF INT'L L., 158–59 (James Brown Scott ed., Oxford University Press 1916).

23. *See, e.g.*, Joseph Beale Jr., *The Recognition of Cuban Belligerency*, 9 HARV. L. REV. 406, 407 (1895–1896); CHEN, THE INTERNATIONAL LAW OF RECOGNITION, at 364–68; G.I.A.D Draper, Humanitarian Law and Internal Armed Conflicts, 13 GA. J. INT'L & COMP. L. 253, 257 (1983).

24. Rosalyn Higgins, *International Law and Civil Conflict*, *in* THE INTERNATIONAL REGULATION OF CIVIL WARS, 170–71 (Evan Luard ed., Thames & Hudson, London, 1972) (Higgins's view was that neither the Biafran party in Nigeria, nor the Communist Vietnamese party in Vietnam, could be recognized belligerents as they did not meet the third criteria.).

25. Cabinet Paper—Belligerency in the Formosa Strait: Memorandum by the Foreign Office, Annex A, *in* U. Archives File: FO 371/120939.

C. APPLICATION OF THE TEST

The first cumulative step in the test, as noted, hinged around three factual criteria that collectively expressed an overall requirement that the NSAG and its activities reach a relatively high threshold in terms of scale, organization, and control. For the conflict state itself, the test essentially comprised these three elements. However, for a concerned third state, a further step required a political assessment by that third state as to the necessity of recognizing belligerency. Understanding the test, however, requires a closer assessment of each of these discrete elements and the elaboration of a case study as an example of application.

(i) Element one: Conflict

The first factual element focused upon the scale and scope of the armed conflict. At the upper end of the spectrum, the exemplar is the American Civil War, a conflict in which more than three million people served under arms and single battles involved casualties in the tens of thousands.[26] The United States did not, however, grant belligerency status to Cuban insurgents in 1895–1898 even though their force numbered, on some estimates 20,000–50,000 men and had effectively tied down a Spanish force of more than 120,000.[27] Similarly, during the Spanish Civil War, hundreds of thousands of fighters were engaged in operations (including "4,000 Soviet advisers, some 35,000 volunteers from over 53 countries [in] . . . the 'International Brigades' . . . [and, on the Nationalist side] almost 50,000 Italian, 12,000 German and 8,000 Portuguese 'volunteers'"[28]), yet belligerent status was never accorded to the Nationalists by either Britain or the United States. This was regardless of the fact that it was widely accepted that the test had been met and that withholding this status from Franco and the Nationalists in particular was a political bargaining tactic, not the result of an impartial legal assessment.

(A) Relevance of force size

During the Polish rebellion, the insurgent forces (which adopted guerrilla tactics) were much smaller (outnumbered ten to one) and far less organized than the adversary Imperial Russian Army: "The insurgents were on the whole meagrely armed, 'raw and undisciplined levies, no more conversant with war than are English yeomen and shopkeepers.'"[29] Indeed, the insurgent force never numbered,

26. *Civil War Facts: 1861–1865*, Nat'l Park Serv., https://www.nps.gov/civilwar/facts.htm (last visited Jan. 3, 2019).

27. Hershey, The Recognition of Cuban Belligerency, at 460–61; Ellery Cory Stowell, Intervention in International Law 120–23 (2018) (describes the subsequent U.S. "humanitarian" intervention in Cuba as part of the 1898 Spanish-American War (consequent on the sinking of *USS Maine* in Havana Harbor, and a U.S. recognition of Cuban independence from Spain)).

28. Alexander Gillespie, A History of the Laws of War Volume I 60 (2011).

29. Walter Laqueur, Guerrilla Warfare: A Historical and Critical Study 66 (1976).

at any given time, more than around "20,000 ill-equipped men dispersed in bands of between fifty and five hundred," had no artillery, and could not capture towns or deploy against large Russian formations.[30] Yet, the insurgency was widespread—generating sympathetic uprisings in Polish areas of Lithuania, for example—albeit primarily carried out via ambush and small-scale attacks as opposed to large-scale pitched battles.[31] As a British officer (Colonel Edward Stanton) tasked with reporting on the insurgency to Earl Russell explained, the insurgents had learned to avoid pitched battles against formed bodies of Imperial Russian troops, as the consequent defeats had "a most depressing effect on other insurgent bands, and show[ed] them the folly of attempting with a half-armed mob to resist the attack of regular troops supplied with artillery."[32] Yet, even though the logical subsequent adoption, with much success, of "partisan" tactics nevertheless enabled the Polish insurgents to tie down a Russian force of 80,000–100,000 troops,[33] belligerency was never ultimately recognized.

The size of the fighting force carrying on the insurgency, in this particular case, should not be read as indicative of a situation falling below the threshold required for element one of the test. This is because the factor of scale does not appear to have been cited in British or French consideration as militating *against* recognition of Polish belligerency. Indeed, it was clearly an issue that militated toward recognition, given that the insurgency was considered to have "succeeded in maintaining itself in every part of the kingdom, if not in gaining advantage over the Imperial troops."[34] Rather, as will come to be seen, it was the factors of control over a substantial portion of territory and, ultimately, the political inclinations and interest of third states that quashed recognition of belligerency in this case. It is, consequently, neither consistent nor coherent with the test that some minimum threshold of NSAG fighting force numbers must be achieved. Rather, what is necessary is that the force be contextually sufficient to allow it to carry on operations over a wide territorial scale as opposed to being restricted to a territorially localized and isolated operation.

(B) RELEVANCE OF RESORT TO GUERRILLA TACTICS

This said, however, state practice appears to evidence a concern with the characterization to be given to an insurgency carried on predominantly through guerrilla tactics,[35] and the subsequent effect of this assessment upon this first element of the

30. ADAM ZAMOYSKI, POLAND: A HISTORY 24 (William Collins ed., 2009)

31. *Id.*

32. Report of Colonel Stanton to Earl Russell, dated 6 February 1863, *in Correspondence Respecting the Insurrection in Poland: January to April 1863*, in UK Archives File: FO 417/311.

33. Report of Colonel Stanton to Earl Russell, dated 4 March 1863, in *Correspondence Respecting the Insurrection in Poland: January to April 1863*, in UK Archives File: FO 417/311.

34. *Id.*

35. *See generally* BRIAN CROZIER, THE REBELS—A STUDY OF POST-WAR INSURRECTIONS 127–29 (1960); King, *Revolutionary War, Guerrilla Warfare, and International Law*, at 91.

test (and of relevance for the second element). During the 1846–1848 Mexican-American War, Mexican forces who resorted to guerrilla tactics were informed by some American commanders that they would be executed on capture.[36] President Grant's response to the claims of Cuban insurgents to recognition of belligerency in 1870 included the following assessment, as reported in the press at the time:

> 'Fighting', the President truly says, 'though fierce and protracted, does not alone constitute war'. War must be invested with a certain pomp and circumstance; it must have passed beyond the stage of mere guerrilla contest. 'There must be military forces, acting in accordance with the rules and customs of war, flags of truce, cartels, exchange of prisoners'.[37]

The classic Clausewitzian conditions for successful guerrilla warfare—while in no way defined in international law—do tend to identify points of intersection with recognition of belligerency:

1. The war must be fought in the interior of the country.
2. It must not be decided by a single stroke.
3. The theatre of operations must be fairly large.
4. The national character must be suited to that type of war.
5. The country must be rough and inaccessible, because of mountains, or forests, marshes or the local methods of cultivation.[38]

A similar assessment as to the scale of the conflict, and an indicator of the relevance of guerrilla tactics to this assessment, was evident in British and U.S. considerations regarding whether to grant recognition of belligerency to Indonesian insurgents in 1958. In a minute from the British Deputy Chief of the General Staff to his Minister, outlining discussions with Sir Patrick Dean (Foreign Office legal adviser, and later British Permanent Representative to the UN and then Ambassador to the United States) on "the question of according belligerent rights to the rebels in Indonesia," it was recorded that:

> I understand from him [Dean] that this question has been under continual consideration in the Foreign Office and that it has been discussed between the Foreign Secretary and Mr. Dulles. It is agreed both by the Foreign Office and the State Department that it would not be feasible to do so if the rebels were reduced to Guerrilla activities and could indeed only be regarded as a

36. Justin Smith, The War with Mexico: Volume II 168–70 (1919).

37. *President Grant on Belligerency*, The Daily Evening Telegraph—Philadelphia, July 25, 1879, at 2, https://chroniclingamerica.loc.gov/lccn/sn83025925/1870-07-25/ed-1/seq-2.pdf.

38. Carl von Clausewitz, On War 480 (Michael Howards and Peter Paret, trans., Princeton University Press 1976).

possibility if the invasion of western Sumatra had been effectively repulsed with loss.[39]

Falk also appeared to consider the existence of secure rebel "base areas" as almost a precondition for recognition.[40] Perhaps the best that can be said is that while the adoption by insurgents of guerrilla tactics was not, as a practical matter, a definitive indication that the scale and territorial control elements of the test were not met—as with both the Polish insurgency in 1863, and the Indonesian insurgency in 1958—it was nevertheless considered to be an indicator weighing in that direction.

(ii) Element two: Territory

The second factual element—"occupation and administration by rebels of a substantial portion of territory"—seems to have generally been interpreted as requiring indications of scale, stability, endurance, and governance. The necessary prerequisites were evident, for example, in the relative stability of the rebellious Buenos Ayres entity (and then the "United Provinces of Rio de la Plata"[41]). The finding was considered less assured in the case of the Artigan Banda Oriental entity, which contracted in size over the course of a meandering three-front conflict with both Brazil and Portugal on its northern border, the United Provinces to the south, and the Spanish and Portuguese fleets at sea.[42] The Polish "Revolution" of 1830–1831, and the Hungarian "War of Independence" of 1848–1849 were considered to have been of significant scale, but the insurrectionist forces were not granted recognition of belligerency status.[43] However, recognition of belligerency was consciously considered in both situations. Indeed, U.S. President Taylor's emissary sent to investigate the Hungarian insurrection (Mann) was despatched there "absolutely invested . . . with authority to recognise the insurgents at his

39. Minute, "Indonesia," DCGS to the Minister, dated 29 April 1958, in UK Archives File: FO 371/135884.

40. Richard Falk, *The International Law of Internal War*, *in* International Aspects of Civil Strife 223 (James Rosenau ed., 1964).

41. *E.g.*, Tyson Reeder, *Sovereign Lords and Dependent Administrators: Artigan Privateers, Atlantic Borderwaters, and State Building in the early Nineteenth Century*, J. of Am. Hist. 323, 325–26 (2016); Enoch Resnick, *Spain's Reaction to Portugal's Invasion of the Banda Oriental in 1816*, 73(74) Revista de Historia de Am. 131, 133 (1972); Kevin Arlyck, *Plaintiffs v Privateers: Litigation and Foreign Affairs in the Federal Courts 1816–1822*, 30 Law and Hist. Rev. 245, 252, 261 (2012).

42. *E.g.*, Joel Samuels, *The Full Story of United States v Smith, America's most Important Piracy Case*, 1(2) Penn State J. of L. and Int'l Aff. 320, 336–39 (2012); Resnick, *Spain's Reaction to Portugal's Invasion of the Banda Oriental in* 1816, at 134.

43. *See, e.g.*, Roscoe Ralph Oglesby, Internal War and the Search for Normative Order 24–25 (1971).

discretion"—an "indefensible transaction" against Austria, by Harcourt's reckoning.[44] Despite clear public sympathy, the United States refused to recognize Cuban insurgents as belligerents during the period 1866–1879 mainly because, as Walker notes, "there was no organised insurgent Government which could be dealt with as an independent political authority."[45] As one news report of President Grant's assessment recorded, "He objects against the claim of the insurgents, that they hold no town or city, have no established seat of government, no prize courts, no revenue organisation, no seaports, no recognised legislature representing any popular constituency, no civil authorities."[46] And, although the United States did not ultimately recognize Cuban belligerency, Hershey in 1896 clinically and contemporaneously applied each of the elements of the recognition of belligerency test to the insurgency in Cuba, and concluded the existence of a rebel administrative structure. This was based on prefectures and central ministries, the existence of a President and other high offices of state, and a "Declaration of Independence and Provisional Constitution." Hershey argued this certainly met the requirements of this element of the test.[47] The validity of this denial of Cuban belligerency remained an intensely debated issue for several years to come, often informed by closely argued contextual correlations between the American Civil War, Cuba in 1870, Cuba in 1898, and the Philippines in 1901.[48]

In 1932, the Paulistas / Constitutionalists, rebelling against the junta in Brazil, argued that they met this component of the test on the following grounds:

> [Sao Paulo] possesses an organised and established government in authority and control over a very large territory embracing a population of 8,000,000 persons. That government is affording protection to the persons and property of nationals and foreigners, and with its armed forces is waging war according to the rules of warfare. It possesses in abundance the necessary economic, material and moral equipment to prolong the war indefinitely until final victory is achieved.[49]

44. Sir William V. Harcourt, Letters by Historicus on Some Questions of International Law 21 (London & Cambridge, Macmillan & Co. 1863).

45. Wyndham L. Walker, *Recognition of Belligerency and Grant of Belligerent Rights*, 23 Transactions of the Grotius Soc'y 177, 188 (1937).

46. *President Grant on Belligerency*, 35.

47. Hershey, The Recognition of Cuban Belligerency, at 458–59 (this matter was widely discussed in the press at the time, with argument for and against recognition based on the facts as reported from time to time) *See, e.g., Cuba*, The Wichita Daily Eagle, December 7, 1897, at 2, https://chroniclingamerica.loc.gov/lccn/sn82014635/1897-12-07/ed-1/seq-2.pdf.

48. *See, e.g., War Legislation of the Senate*, The Natl. Tr., July 30, 1903, at 1, https://chroniclingamerica.loc.gov/lccn/sn82016187/1903-07-30/ed-1/seq-1.pdf.

49. Telegram File No: 832.00 Revolutions/298, The Charge in Brazil (Thurston) to the Secretary of State, August 3, 1932, 409–411, para 2.

Thurston concluded his report by observing that the Naval Attaché believed that "there is no doubt as to the ability" of the Brazilian government to make its declared blockade effective, yet it would be best to await "similar announcements"—of a likely refusal to recognize belligerency—by "other important governments" so as to "avoid the resentment the definitive announcement of our attitude" was likely to engender.[50]

Similarly, the French government considered, but ultimately did not extend recognition of belligerency to the Polish rebels in 1863. France ultimately subordinated its self-interest in recognizing Polish belligerency,[51] and offers of assistance from Sweden should France choose to commit troops in support of the insurgents,[52] to its contending self-interest in maintaining existing structures for managing the broader European balance of power.[53] Indeed, it was the view of Austria, for example, that the "main-springs of the insurrection are at Paris," as France anticipated benefits accruing if Prussia was drawn into supporting Russia in Poland, freeing France to seize German territory on the Rhine (and, as an Austrian concern, perhaps jeopardizing Austrian possession of Galicia through an expanding Polish nationalist movement).[54] Britain, records Stowell, was still haunted by "recollections of the Crimean war" and was deeply animated by "distrust of France," and therefore was hesitant to "pick up the gauntlet" on behalf of the Polish insurgency.[55] Indeed, the contemporaneous willingness of Britain to recognize Confederate belligerency, but to refuse Polish belligerency was pointedly noted by the United States. As Seward observed to the U.S. Minister in London on 14 July 1863: "The European states suffer long and forbear much with a nation that falls under the affliction of civil war, if it be only near home. They are very intolerant of a nation, on this continent, that suffers its domestic wrangles to break the peace of the world."[56]

50. *Id.* at para 6.

51. *See* the report, dated September 3, provided to the British government and purporting to contain a record of the outcomes of two French Council of Ministers meetings in late August, at which the Polish question was discussed and, coincidentally, French recognition of Confederate belligerency, was approved, in UK Archives File: PRO 30/22/14F.

52. Earl Cowley reported to Earl Russell on March 26, 1863 that he had it "on good authority that about a week ago the [French] Emperor received a letter from the King of Sweden, in which His Swedish Majesty, adverting to the Polish question, said that he had 100,000 as good troops as could be brought into the field, and that he was ready to employ them in helping to restore the independence of Poland." UK Archives File: FO 417/311.

53. *See, e.g.*, John Kutolowski, *Mid-Victorian Public Opinion, Polish Propaganda, and the Uprising of 1863*, 8(2) J. of British Stud. 86, 90, 103 (1969); Laurence Orzell, *A "Favourable Interval": The Polish Insurrection in Civil War Diplomacy, 1863* 24(4) Civil War Hist. 332, 335–38 (1978).

54. Lord Bloomfield to Earl Russel, 12 March 1863, in *Correspondence Respecting the Insurrection in Poland: January to April 1863*, UK Archives File: FO 417/311.

55. Stowell, Intervention in International Law, at 98.

56. *Id.* at 71.

Nevertheless, even in the face of evidence of settled Polish insurgent governance and administration,[57] and of insurgent operations in the major centers of Cracow, Warsaw, and Lemberg,[58] "The French Government refused to recognize the insurgents after the Senate noted that they did not control a clearly defined territory."[59] Zorgbibe quotes French President Stourm as explaining to the Senate that:

> The Poles have no government, nor even a de facto government, for one cannot accord this title to an assembly of a few men whose names are a mystery and whose location is unknown. Neither is it possible to regard as an army those bands and parties who fight, sometimes in one place and sometimes in another, always courageously but without common direction, under a variety of chiefs who do not recognize a single superior. As for territory, we must recognize that these unhappy Poles have none, except for the places where they temporarily find themselves, places which change every day as they are forced to move, either to seek out or escape from their enemy.[60]

Behind the scenes, however, it would appear that French Minister Drouyn de Lhuys had indirectly suggested to Britain a plan that would see France and Britain "absolved from all recognition of the right of Russia to that Duchy [the Duchy of Warsaw]; that consequently they should cease to look upon the Polish movement as an insurrection, and should treat both Russians and Poles as belligerents."[61]

(A) The Influence of a Maritime Dimension to the Conflict

On 17 October 1818, John Quincy Adams recorded in his diary a conversation with the Portuguese Minister in the United States, Jose Correia de Serra (also known as the Abbe Correa). The conversation concerned the involvement of U.S. nationals in privateering on rebellious Artigan Banda Oriental commissions against Portuguese vessels. Correia's argument was, Adams records, that as the Artigan Banda Oriental entity had no seaports, such commissions were "mere

57. *See, e.g.*, "Proclamation of the Central National Committee as a national Government," dated 22 January 1863, in UK Archives File: FO 417/311; "Order of the Day of the Chief of the Town of Warsaw," dated 4 February 1863, in UK Archives File: FO 417/311; Report of Mr. Mounsey to Lord Bloomfield, dated 7 April 1863, in UK Archives File: FO 417/311.

58. *Events in Poland*, Fremden Blatt, 19 March 1863, extracted and forwarded by Lord Bloomfield to Earl Russell, in UK Archives File: FO 417/311; Report of Mr. Mounsey to Lord Bloomfield, dated 7 April 1863, in UK Archives File: FO 417/311.

59. *Remigiusz Bierzanek, Humanitarian Law in Armed Conflicts: The Doctrine and Practice of Polish Insurgents in the 19th Century*, 17(192) Int'l Rev. of the Red Cross 128, 131 (1977).

60. Charles Zorgbibe, *Sources of the recognition of belligerent status*, 17(192) Int'l Rev. of the Red Cross 111, 121–22 (1977).

61. Earl Cowley to Earl Russell, 7 May 1863, in UK Archives File: FO 417/311.

absurdities."[62] In part, the ultimate non-recognition of belligerency in both the Polish and Hungarian situations was attributable to the tendency, as is understandable given its significant maritime trade-based consequences, to overlay the recognition of belligerency test with an "additional" (but certainly not doctrinal) caveat to the effect that recognition of belligerency was only relevant for a third state where there was either an adjoining border with the conflict state and/or the rebel entity, or where ports and coasts were involved.[63] Hence, as was noted by Zorgbibe, and others, "Non-recognition of the insurgents in the Polish and Hungarian revolts of 1830 and 1848 can certainly be explained in part by the fact that these wars were carried out on land."[64] Along the same lines was a similar occasionally voiced argument deployed against recognition of Polish belligerency in 1863. This argument proposed that because the Tsar's Polish dominion was effectively landlocked, the conflict engaged no maritime dimension or concerns.[65] Similar assessments of other "landlocked" rebellion contexts reinforce that they tended to play a limited role in the evolution of the doctrine, not least because they did not involve significant disruption to maritime communications, which was the surest way to directly engage third state concerns.[66]

The overall effect was that in many situations where it could be argued that the rebels held a significant portion of territory (for example, the Hungarian War of Independence, where elements of the Austrian-approved Hungarian government joined the revolt), recognition of belligerency was nevertheless denied. As noted, one argument deployed by the Portuguese Consul in the United States during discussions in 1850 regarding compensation claims relating to privateer actions against Portuguese vessels between 1816 and 1828, was that recognition of the Artigan Banda Oriental as a belligerent NSAG could not have been

62. JOHN Q. ADAMS, MEMOIRS OF JOHN QUINCY ADAMS VOL IV 133–35 (Charles Adams ed., Philadelphia, Lippincott & Co. 1875).

63. *See, e.g.*, HENRY WHEATON, ELEMENTS OF INTERNATIONAL LAW §23:16 (Richard H. Dana Jr., ed., London, Sampson Low, Son & Co. 1866) (p39) (as Dana observed, although the other, at the time perhaps more inchoate, elements of the test were arguably satisfied, the fact that the civil war was taking place in central Europe in a state with no ports, certainly militated against recognition of belligerency).

64. Zorgbibe, *Sources of the recognition of belligerent status*, at 125.

65. *See, e.g.*, Henryk Wereszycki, *Great Britain and the Polish Question in 1863*, 50(197) THE ENG. HIST. REV. 78, 108 (1935).

66. *See, e.g.*, THE EARL OF BIRKENHEAD, INTERNATIONAL LAW 201 (Ron Moelwyn-Hughes ed., London, J.M Dent & Sons, 6th ed., 1927) ("it becomes necessary to distinguish between cases when the civil hostilities are confined to land, and those when they extend to the sea. In the first case the neutral has little to gain by an early recognition of belligerency; in the second, such a recognition need not be delayed a moment after it has become clear that an organised struggle is in progress."); AMOS S. HERSHEY, THE ESSENTIALS OF INTERNATIONAL PUBLIC LAW AND ORGANIZATION 206, n. 22 (1927) (analyzing Hall, asserts that "[I]n the case of maritime warfare, the presumption is in favour of recognition"); *see also* Pieter Kuyper, *Recognition: Netherlands Theory and State Practice*, *in* H.F. van Panhuys et al. eds., INTERNATIONAL LAW IN THE NETHERLANDS: VOLUME I, TMC ASSER, The Hague, 371, 384 (1978).

warranted because that insurgent entity controlled no coast and had no naval resources apart from U.S. nationals and vessels acting as privateers under Artigan Letters of Marque.[67] As a landlocked rebellious province, the Portuguese argument concluded that the Banda Oriental should not have been considered able to even commission privateers. Harcourt records that an early Union argument against recognition of Confederate belligerency was that "the Confederate States had no naval resources."[68] Certainly, as discussed previously, the United States initially condemned Confederate naval and privateer crews as pirates, ultimately recanting from this view in February 1862.[69] However, to say that there is a bias toward recognition of belligerency where there is both occupation of territory *and* a maritime dimension, is not to mandate this requirement. Rather, it provides recognition of the fact that where the insurgent force has access to coasts, consequences for third states—in terms of their vessels and maritime trade—are much more likely to manifest. In the case of the Brazilian Naval Revolt, for example, the rebellion certainly had a significant maritime dimension and involved the port of Rio de Janeiro. However, the very fact that it was limited to the Navy was cited as a reason to exclude recognition of belligerency on the grounds that no other substantial territory was under rebel control.[70] O'Rourke neatly summarized the orthodox view in his analysis of recognition of belligerency and the Spanish Civil War, stating:

> First, if the insurgents are isolated in the midst of loyal provinces, the question of recognition hardly arises, since the interests of third states are not likely to be affected. Second, if the rebels control territories contiguous to a neutral Power, the problem, at least as far as that State is concerned, may have to be faced. Third, in cases where internecine disputes involve maritime warfare, the presumption is in favour of recognition.[71]

(iii) Element three: Organization

The third factual element centered upon the NSAG controlling and employing a rough facsimile of state military forces. Thus, as was the case with many of the South American colonies in their wars of independence from Spain and Portugal in the first quarter of the nineteenth century, while Spain and Portugal

67. Sir William Harcourt, The Rights and Duties of Neutrals in Time of War: Part II 339 (London & Cambridge, Macmillan & Co. 1863).

68. *Id.* at 331.

69. O'Hara, *The Daly Letter (1861)*, *in* Judge Charles Daly and the New York Irish in the Era of the Civil War 147 (Arthur H. Mitchell ed., 1936).

70. John B. Moore, A Digest of International Law: Volume I 204, n. a (1906).

71. O'Rourke, *Recognition of Belligerency and the Spanish War*, at 400.

(the conflict states) deployed navies, the belligerent entities deployed privateers.[72] More recently, it was Higgins's view that neither the Biafran party in Nigeria, nor the Communist Vietnamese party in Vietnam, could be afforded recognized belligerency status as they did not meet this third criteria.[73] However, given the scale of these insurgent forces (the Biafran force employed airpower as equally as the Nigerian Air Force, for example[74]), the territory they controlled (even if the precise limits waxed and waned with military operations), and their organization and capabilities, this analysis is, at the very least, arguable. Similarly, it was the settled U.S. view from 1965 that the Vietnam conflict was governed by the LOAC applicable in IAC—including Prisoner of War (PW) status—and that North Vietnam was a belligerent. Conversely, the North Vietnamese authorities consistently maintained that the conflict was an internal matter, and that captured U.S. pilots were "pirates" who were not entitled to PW status, although the North Vietnamese authorities publicly stated that such captives would be treated "humanely."[75]

72. *See, e.g.*, Tyson Reeder, *"Sovereign Lords" and "Dependent Administrators": Artigan Privateers, Atlantic Borderwaters, and State Building in the early Nineteenth Century*, 103 J. OF AM. HIST. 2, 323–46 (2016); Samuels, *The Full Story of United States v Smith, America's most Important Piracy Case*; Fred Hopkins, *For Freedom and Profit: Baltimore Privateers in the Wars of South American Independence* XVIII: 3–4 THE NORTHERN MARINER 93 (2008).

73. Higgins, *International Law and Civil Conflict*, at 170–71.

74. TOYIN FALOLA, HISTORY OF NIGERIA 124 (Westport, Greenwood Press 1999) (The Biafran forces gained arms including aircraft from a variety of sources: A UK cabinet meeting on 30 July 1969, for example, noted "the continued activities of Count von Rosen, the Swedish soldier of fortune who was conducting air attacks on targets in federal territory with light aircraft flown by mercenary pilots and armed in France. . . . The Swedish Government had banned the export of aircraft to Count von Rosen and to the insurgents, but he had been able to obtain aircraft and armaments in France. The Swedish Government had also attempted to curb Count von Rosen's activities, but had been unable to find any legal basis for doing so."): *Conclusions of a Meeting of the Cabinet held at 10 Downing Street, S.W.1, on Wednesday, 30th July, 1969, at 10.30 a.m.*, UK National Archives File CAB/128/44; (The UK government later noted that although they had "supplied the Federal Military Government (FMG) with anti-aircraft weapons . . . the FMG were having difficulty in finding personnel to operate them effectively."): *Conclusions of a Meeting of the Cabinet held at 10 Downing Street, S.W.1, on Thursday, 6th November, 1969, at 10 a.m.*, UK National Archives File CAB/128/44.

75. *See, e.g.*, *Application of Geneva Conventions in Viet-Nam: Letter of Democratic Republic Of Viet-Nam*, 5 INT'L. LEGAL MATERIALS 124 (1966); Major General George Prugh, *Law at War: Vietnam 1964–1973* 652–63 (Washington, D.C., Department of the Army 1975); *see also* SANDESH SIVAKUMARAN, THE LAW OF NON-INTERNATIONAL ARMED CONFLICT 562–64 (Oxford University Press 2012); GILLESPIE, A HISTORY OF THE LAWS OF WAR VOLUME I, at 224; legal advice attached to note (F1071/485(D)) from the UK Delegation Geneva to Foreign Office South-East Asia Department, dated 17 May 1954, para 2 ("There has been no recognition by the United States Government, express or implied, of the belligerency of the Viet Minh rebels. Strictly therefore there is no duty of impartiality and neutrality imposed upon the United States Government."); UK National Archives File: FO 371/112062.

(iv) Element four: Political discretion

Insofar as the conflict state itself was concerned, these three limbs of the test were open to it as assessment criteria, although it was generally appreciated that the conflict state would ultimately make a recognition decision based upon its own naked self-interest, as opposed to the rigid application of a set of general legal criteria.[76] The second step, element four in the test, was that the relevant third state—that is, any nonparticipant state considering how to respond to a particular conflict situation—must ultimately make a political determination as to the need to afford this legal characterization to the situation, and thus to the NSAG. This was a subjective and nakedly instrumental aspect of the test, yet it was also functionally essential and specifically defined. Further, this element presents as much more than a mere background political consideration informing the third state's analysis of the first three elements.[77] States clearly treated this element of the test as an independent and explicitly sanctioned invitation to apply a final gloss of political judgment, allowing them, if necessary, to leverage this opportunity to avoid a legally sound but politically illiterate outcome. This opportunity was clearly and consciously taken, for example, in the hope of avoiding a Europe-wide war that Austria and Britain in particular feared would be the inevitable consequence of a strictly legal—but practically problematic—appreciation and application of the recognition of belligerency test to the Polish insurgency in 1863.[78] Most commentators appear relatively certain and agreed, however, that this element nevertheless required a degree of necessity. That is, that the civil war had become such that the third state in question could no longer simply remain aloof from the direct effects of the conflict. This was most often a consequence of the dictates of trade, taxation, and obligations in relation to the protection of nationals. As Halleck recorded in 1861, "a foreign state should remain a passive spectator, or, if its own relations require diplomatic intercourse with the revolted society, it

76. For example, Sri Lanka's willingness to negotiate with, but persistent refusal to countenance any formal international recognition for, the Liberation Tigers of Tamil Eelam (LTTE) during the Civil War; *see* Peter Layton, *How Sri Lanka Won the War*, The Diplomat, April 9, 2015, https://thediplomat.com/2015/04/how-sri-lanka-won-the-war/ ("In mid-2006, sensing victory was in its grasp, the LTTE deliberately ended the Norwegian-brokered ceasefire and initiated the so-called Eelam War IV. In response, the Sri Lankan government finally decided to change its strategic objective, from negotiating with the LTTE to annihilating it."); *see* Rob McLaughlin, *Legal-Policy Considerations and Conflict Characterisation at the Threshold Between Law Enforcement and Non-International Armed Conflict* 13(1) Melbourne J. of Int'l. L. 94 (2012) (during "The Troubles" in Northern Ireland, the British government refused to recognize the situation even as one of armed conflict, which deprived the IRA of any capacity whatsoever to claim either insurgent status, or be accorded belligerent status by any third state. Indeed, under the customary three-level scheme, the British approach to characterizing the situation was as criminality—a rebellion—which did not even enliven the application of LOAC).

77. *See generally* Hersch Lauterpacht, Recognition in International Law 175–76, 184–85 (Cambridge University Press 2012).

78. Lord Bloomfield to Earl Russel, 27 April 1863, in UK Archives File: FO 417/311; Sir Buchanan to Earl Russell, 27 April 1863, in UK Archives File: FO 417/311.

should treat such revolted society as a de facto government only."[79] Similarly, forty years later, Hannis Taylor observed that

> If the disturbance is in the interior and of local importance, it should not be officially noticed except for the purpose of holding the general government liable for all damages to foreigners and their interests. If the revolt reaches the border, especially a seaport, the case is altered. Foreign interests, particularly of the neighboring state, are apt to be so involved as to force the sending of warships by different states for the protection of their citizens. In that event, if the insurrection is formidable and so organized and continued as to effect such interests, a recognition of belligerency should follow.[80]

State practice also endorsed this view. In responding to a request by the Sao Paulo (Paulistan, or Constitutionalist) insurgents for U.S. (and other third state) recognition of their belligerency against the Brazilian government in 1932, the U.S. State Department advised its Consul in Sao Paulo that

> in present state of things between the parent State and the Sao Paulo insurgents it would not be justified in giving consideration to a request for recognition of belligerency. Neither the extent of the hostilities which have thus far taken place nor the effects of these hostilities on the rights and interests of the United States appear to require any definition of our relation to the two parties to the conflict.[81]

Largely, this element of the test for recognition of belligerency is neither surprising nor unique. It is not surprising because, as will be discussed in the next chapter, one of the fundamental purposes of the doctrine, as far as third states were concerned, was to provide a politically useful middle option for characterizing their

79. Henry Halleck, International Law; Or, Rules Regulating the Intercourse of States in Peace and War 74 (Sir Shelton Baker ed., London, Kegan Paul, Trench, Trubner & Co. 1893); *see also* Wheaton, Elements of International Law, at 29–32; William E. Hall, A Treatise on International Law 35 (3rd ed., Oxford University Press 1890) (describing recognition as "a reasonable measure of self-protection" by a third state); Lassa Oppenheim, International Law: A Treatise, Volume II Disputes, War and Neutrality §76 (1906) ("Without the latter requirement [a practical necessity for third states to define their attitude to the civil war] recognition of belligerency might be open to abuse for the purpose of a gratuitous manifestation of sympathy with the cause of the insurgents."); *see also* Vidya Dhar Mahajan, Public International Law 210 (5th ed., Lucknow, Eastern Book Co. 1974); Jorge Coquia and Miriam Defensor Santiago, Public International Law 83 (Philippine Jurisprudence Project, Quezon City 1984).

80. Haniss Taylor, A Teatise on Public International Law 457 (1901).

81. Telegram File No: 832.00 Revolutions/292, "Acting Secretary of State to the Consul General at Sao Paulo (Cameron), 2 August 1932," *in Foreign Relations of the United States Diplomatic Papers, 1932,* The Am. Republics, V. V, U.S. Dep't of State, Washington, D.C., document 436, at https://history.state.gov/historicaldocuments/frus1932v05.

relationship with the conflict state and the NSAG. This necessity arose most clearly in relation to political discourse in the United States and Britain, as leading democratic states, in which public opinion tended toward support for rebels fighting for independence from repressive overlords, like the South American colonies from Spain in the first quarter of the nineteenth century, or Poland from Russia in the early 1860s.[82] In order to find a legally and politically "meaningful" middle ground between this public sympathy for independence-seeking rebels, and the need to maintain a broader policy of non-intervention in support of the post-Congress of Vienna "balance of power," which clearly favored the European imperialist states,[83] recognition of belligerency navigated a useful middle course between these two destabilizing options. Similarly, the overt political discretion built into the doctrine on recognition of belligerency is not unique, as it is in many ways reflective of, and analogous to, the political test required for recognition of states—that the entity has sufficient international recognition from other states so as to meet the requirement that it possess the "capacity to enter into relations with the other states."[84]

(v) Case study of application of the test: Formosa Strait 1956

On 1 January 1956, a Nationalist Chinese F-86 Sabre jet fighter entered Communist Chinese controlled airspace over Fukien and Kwantung Provinces and was engaged by Chinese Peoples' Liberation Army aircraft. The Nationalist jet fled Chinese airspace and landed at Hong Kong's Kai Tak airfield. The Peoples Republic of China (PRC) immediately communicated to the Hong Kong authorities its expectation that the pilot and aircraft be detained, and followed up with a formal diplomatic note on 4 February 1956.[85] In response to the incident, Britain was required to assess the nature of the Nationalist-Communist conflict to divine the legally correct course of action. Ultimately, and much to the PRC's annoyance, Britain returned the pilot to Taiwan on 12 March 1956, despite PRC protest. Britain subsequently

82. "The sufferings of Poland have excited general sympathy among the nations of Europe": draft letter dated April 1863, in UK Archives File: PRO 30/22/14F.

83. *See generally* Adam Zamoyski, Rites of Peace: The Fall of Napoleon and the Congress of Vienna Ch. 34 (London, Harper Press 2007).

84. As encapsulated in Article 1 of the *Convention on Rights and Duties of States (Montevideo Convention)* 1933 ("The state as a person of international law should possess the following qualifications: a) a permanent population; b) a defined territory; c) government; and d) capacity to enter into relations with the other states.").

85. *See* the timeline and details of diplomatic correspondence on this incident as summarized in the P.R.C *Foreign Ministry Note to Britain: New China News Agency, Peking, 22 June 1957* (Document 18-3), in Jerome Cohen and Hungdah Chiu, People's China and International Law: A Documentary Study, Volume I 595–96 (Princeton University Press 1974); *see generally* Gary Catron, *Hong Kong and Chinese Foreign Policy, 1955–60*, 51 China Q. 405, 413 (1972).

returned the aircraft to Taiwan in June 1957, again subject to strong PRC protest.[86]

In order, however, to reach a settled legal view on the proper course of action, Britain was required to undertake an explicit assessment of the conflict situation. If Britain recognized the belligerency of the Nationalists, then the law of neutrality would apply de jure, and Britain would be required to detain for the duration of the conflict any combatant forces of either party found in British (Hong Kong) territory. This included, for example, the Nationalist fighter aircraft and its pilot. On the other hand, if Britain did not recognize the belligerency of the Nationalists, then the law of neutrality was irrelevant, and the normal course of events would dictate that the pilot and aircraft be returned to Taiwan. The matter came up for Cabinet consideration in February 1956, in order to resolve the quandary and to determine the appropriate next steps. The Foreign Office described the conundrum thus:

> In connexion [*sic*] with the recent incident involving a Chinese Nationalist military aircraft in Hong Kong the Colonial Secretary has asked his colleagues to consider whether it would not be to our advantage to recognize a state of belligerency between the Peking Government and the Chinese Nationalists, to enable Hong Kong to maintain a strictly neutral position between the two parties and to enable us in the future to prevent combatants from either side from using Hong Kong as a haven or refuge.[87]

After reference to, and a summary of, legal advice on the test for recognition of belligerency, the Foreign Office concluded that the legal core of the issue, as the Cabinet Paper observed, was that

> If we recognised a state of belligerency we should merely be saying that the hostilities waged were of such a character and scope as to entitle the parties to be treated as belligerents engaged in a war in a sense ordinarily attached to the term in international law. Our action would not involve recognizing the nationalists as a Government.[88]

As the legal advice annexed to the paper made clear, it did not matter that Britain did not recognize nationalist China as a sovereign state as recognition of their belligerency in the "civil war" would merely mean, "the contesting parties are legally entitled to be treated as if they were engaged in a war between sovereign states." Furthermore, Britain was not under any obligation to recognize

86. P.R.C., *Foreign Ministry Note to Britain: New China News Agency, Peking, 22 June 1957*, 595–96.

87. *Belligerency in the Formosa Strait. Memorandum by the Foreign Office*, February 1956, para 1, *in* UK Archives File: FO 371/120939.

88. *Id.* at para 3.

Nationalist belligerency even if the application of the test (the "conditions") justified recognition.[89]

Ultimately, the Cabinet Paper was settled on 22 February 1956 and sent to Cabinet on 24 February 1956, having been agreed upon by the Foreign Office, the Colonial Office,[90] the Admiralty,[91] and the Ministry of Transport and Civil Aviation.[92] Noting that while the legality of returning the pilot and aircraft could be resolved through a decision not to recognize belligerency, the issue of "ensuring the Governor of Hong Kong is in a position to prevent the use of Hong Kong as a refuge for aircraft or ships in furtherance of military operations" was characterized as "a different problem." This issue would "no doubt be decided by Ministers in the context of the present incident."[93] The overall recommendation was as follows:

> Our view has hitherto been that the disadvantages of recognizing a state of belligerency in the Formosa Strait heavily outweighed the advantages. These views have been confirmed by the re-examination which we have now carried out of both the legal and practical aspects.[94]

Although not set out as a formulaic and sequential assessment of the recognition of belligerency test elements as against the relevant facts and considerations, the Foreign Office Memorandum on the matter of "Belligerency in the Formosa Strait" reveals a clear engagement with the test. On the first element—the existence of a civil war of a general character—the assessment concluded that "the present hostilities could hardly be described as an armed conflict of a general character" because military activity was now limited to "reconnaissance flights over the mainland, artillery duels in the area of Quemoy and Matsu, and attacks by both sides on coastal shipping." Thus, "On strictly legal grounds . . . there is no very good case, on the facts as they exist to-day, for the according of belligerent rights to the Nationalists."[95]

As to the second element of the recognition of belligerency test—that the rebels / insurgents "occupy and administer a substantial portion of the national

89. *The Legal Aspects of the Recognition of Belligerency*, para 1 (Annex A to "Belligerency in the Formosa Strait. Memorandum by the Foreign Office"), in UK Archives File: FO 371/120939.

90. *Colonial Office Letter to Foreign Office*, dated 15 February 1956, in UK Archives File: FO 371/120939.

91. *Admiralty Letter* M.358/2/56, to Foreign Office, dated 17 February 1956, in UK Archives File: FO 371/120939.

92. *Ministry of Civil Aviation and Transport letter* FSR 6/3/001 Pt.4, to Foreign Office, dated 20 February 1956, in UK Archives File: FO 371/120939.

93. *Recognition of a State of Belligerency in the Formosa Strait*, dated 22 February 1956, para 3, in UK Archives File: FO 371/120939.

94. *Id.* at para 2.

95. *Id.* at para 4.

territory"—it was assessed that the Nationalists held only Formosa ("the status of which is in our view undetermined"), and of Chinese territory controlled "only a few small islands." Interestingly, and as noted previously, the British analysis of this aspect of the test did include an assessment that the Nationalists had "no visible prospect of reasserting their position as the Government of China."[96]

Although the third element of the test—that the contesting parties conduct operations "in accordance with the rules of war and through organised armed forces acting under a responsible authority"—was not specifically addressed, there is reason to discern that this element was found fulfilled. Indeed, the clear desire to be able to return the pilot and aircraft to Nationalist authorities, to warn both parties against further incursions into Hong Kong airspace, and to indicate that forces from both sides would be "detained" (indicating an appreciation of the availability of a status other than "criminal"), tend to point toward a belief that Nationalist forces were sufficiently organized. Additionally, the discussion around the fact that recognition of belligerency would allow the Hong Kong authorities to "intern" forces, and to apply the 24-hour rule to warships of both parties,[97] tends to presuppose the requisite level of organization and compliance.[98] Similarly, an appreciation that Nationalist naval forces operating in the Formosa Strait were attempting to apply something akin to visit and search rules—even though their right to do so was denied by Britain—along with the British response to such assertions being to "protest . . . to the Nationalist authorities in Formosa,"[99] tend to evidence a belief that Nationalist forces met the necessary organization and compliance requirements.

Assessment as to the final element of the test—the need for Britain to define her relationship with the contesting parties in this way—provides a clear illustration of how the political context properly informed the application of the recognition of belligerency test. On the "recognize" side of the assessment, the memorandum outlined the benefits of formal neutrality in terms of rights to demand respect for that neutrality, and to intern forces that came within Hong Kong jurisdiction.[100]

96. *Id.*

97. *Convention Concerning the Rights and Duties of Neutral Powers in Naval War*, Oct. 18, 1907, 36 Stat. 2415, 1 Bevans 723, art. 12 ("In the absence of special provisions to the contrary in the legislation of a neutral Power, belligerent war-ships are not permitted to remain in the ports, roadsteads, or territorial waters of the said Power for more than twenty-four hours, except in the cases covered by the present Convention."); *Id* at art. 16 ("When war-ships belonging to both belligerents are present simultaneously in a neutral port or roadstead, a period of not less than twenty-four hours must elapse between the departure of the ship belonging to one belligerent and the departure of the ship belonging to the other.

The order of departure is determined by the order of arrival, unless the ship which arrived first is so circumstanced that an extension of its stay is permissible. A belligerent war-ship may not leave a neutral port or roadstead until twenty-four hours after the departure of a merchant ship flying the flag of its adversary.")

98. *Recognition of a State of Belligerency in the Formosa Strait*, at paras. 7, 9.

99. *Id.* at para. 6.

100. *Id.* at para 7.

Such benefits, however, were clearly outweighed by the "don't recognize" side. First, recognition of belligerency would confirm the right of Nationalist forces to "stop and search our ships and perhaps to capture them and condemn them in prize."[101] Second, difficulties in trade with mainland China would "greatly increase"[102] (presumably because the Nationalists would gain blockade and visit and search rights that would hamper British trade with the PRC). Finally, such a concession to the Nationalists "would be widely interpreted as meaning that we were ready to adopt a 'two-Chinas' policy by recognizing the Nationalists as the Government of Formosa," it being "not desirable to commit ourselves now to any step of this kind."[103] Furthermore, there were regulatory mechanisms available to the governor of Hong Kong (such as the issuing of a warning that infringing aircraft would be "liable to be detained until he is satisfied that they are not being used and will not be used to commit acts prejudicial to the security of the territory"[104]) that would allow Britain to strike a firm line with both parties in relation to any movement by their forces into or through Hong Kong territory. These mechanisms did not require the preliminary step of recognizing Nationalist belligerency.[105] The Foreign Office concluded, consequently, that "Our view is therefore that even assuming recognition to be legally justifiable, the disadvantages of recognizing a state of belligerency heavily outweigh the advantages."[106]

D. INDICATORS

Although there was strong, coherent, and consistent general agreement as to the elements of the recognition of belligerency test, there was greater debate and uncertainty as to the weight to be given to certain indicators that tended to promote or detract from the application of the test. The case study of the Formosa Strait illuminates some of the factors considered relevant in the assessment. This next section will discuss several illustrative additional factors that have often intruded into the assessment process. Some have consistently carried significant weight, while others appear to have been of highly variable and inconsistent effect. These factors are (1) the relatively low weight given to the NSAG's ultimate likelihood of success in the conflict with the parent state; (2) whether satisfaction of the test elicited an obligation to recognize belligerency, or merely furnished a discretion to do so; (3) the modes of tacit recognition of belligerency and the significant weight given to inferences from conduct; (4) the relative insignificance

101. *Id.* at para 6.

102. *Id.*

103. *Id.* at paras 5–6.

104. *Id.* at para 9.

105. *Id.* at paras 7, 9–10.

106. *Id.* at para 8.

of inconsistent domestic judicial decisions; and (5) the relevance of treating captured fighters as PW.

(i) Likelihood of NSAG success not an element of the test

There is a minor degree of uncertainty around whether the likelihood of ultimate success of the rebel NSAG was a relevant factor to be considered in applying the tests.[107] However, the preponderance of opinion seems to have been that while this concern may subsist in the political background to a recognition of belligerency decision, it was not an objective element of the test.[108]

(ii) Recognition as obligation or discretion?

Likewise, there is some lingering debate[109] as to whether the test elicits an obligation to recognize, or merely a legal right to make a manifestly and overtly political decision to recognize, although the trend is probably for the latter reading. This debate is distinguishable from the fourth element of the test. That element concerned the discretionary question of whether the third state was sufficiently affected by the situation as to have to make a decision. The debate regarding obligatory or discretionary recognition, however, took as its start point that all four elements of the test had been fulfilled, including that the third state was sufficiently affected by the conflict to be required to decide on belligerency. The question then became whether, if all the conditions were met, the third state was consequently obliged to recognize the NSAG's belligerency, or alternatively whether—even after having assessed that the elements of the test were met—the third state could nevertheless still decline to afford the status. Harris,[110]

107. Noting, however, that it was a factor in the consideration of element one of the test in relation to the Formosa Strait case study.

108. *See, e.g.*, FRANCIS WHARTON, A DIGEST OF THE INTERNATIONAL LAW OF THE UNITED STATES 515 (U.S. Government Printing Office, Washington, D.C., 1887) (quoting President Monroe's assessment that "As soon as the movement assumes such a steady and consistent form as to make the success of the provinces probable, the rights to which they were entitled by the law of nations as equal parties to the civil war, have been extended to them"). This statement is criticized by, inter alia, Woolsey, whom Wharton cites thus, "The probability is a creature of the mind, something merely subjective, and ought not to enter into a definition of what a nation ought to do . . . If you make probability of success the criterion of right in the case, you have to weigh other circumstances before being able to judge which is most probable, success or defeat. Would you, if you conceded belligerent rights, withdraw the concession whenever success ceased to be probable?" *Id.*

109. *See, e.g.*, COQUIA and SANTIAGO, PUBLIC INTERNATIONAL LAW, at 83. An example is the 1946 assessment made as to the unlikelihood of the Nationalist Chinese ever regaining control of mainland China, as a component of the decision to withhold recognition of belligerency form the nationalists in relation to the Formosa Strait. *Id.*

110. THOMAS HARRIS, THE TRENT AFFAIR, INCLUDING A REVIEW OF ENGLISH AND AMERICAN RELATIONS AT THE BEGINNING OF THE CIVIL WAR 41, ch. XIX (Indianapolis, Bobbs-Merrill Co.

O'Rourke,[111] and Walker,[112] among others, appear to have held the "obligatory consequence" view, but it is Lauterpacht who remains the strongest proponent of this interpretation, arguing, "There is only slender support in the practice of States for the view that governments regard recognition of belligerency as an act of grace or of political convenience."[113] The latter view, discretionary recognition, is however evident in twentieth-century British applications of the recognition of belligerency test. One example is the Spanish Civil War; another is the case of Formosa, where the Foreign Office Legal Advisers expressly stated in 1956, that "there is no duty on outside states to accord recognition whatever the circumstances."[114] The discretionary approach has also been the relatively consistent U.S. approach,[115] evident for example in the proposition put by then U.S. Secretary of State Fish to the United States Minister to England, Mr. Motley, on 15 May 1869:

> The President recognizes the right of every power, when a civil conflict has arisen within another state, and has attained a sufficient complexity, magnitude, and completeness, to define its own relations and those of its citizens and subjects toward the parties to the conflict, so far as their rights and interests are necessarily affected by the conflict.[116]

1896) The "Trent Affair" concerned the stopping and boarding at sea of a British merchant vessel (*Trent*) by a U.S. Warship on 8 November 1861, in order to arrest two Confederate commissioners (James Mason, a former Chairman of the U.S. Senate Foreign Relations Committee, and John Sidell, a New Orleans lawyer, both appointed by CSA President Davis) who had taken passage to Europe on the vessel from Havana in an attempt to travel to avoid the Union blockade. Harris, The Trent Affair, Including a Review of English and American Relations at the Beginning of the Civil War, at ch IX; Office of the Historian, *The Trent Affair, 1861*, U.S. Dep't of State, at https://history.state.gov/milestones/1861-1865/trent-affair. Their mission was to present the case to British and French governments for full recognition of the CSA as a state. The Captain of the *Trent* protested strongly, but ultimately the commissioners and their secretaries were taken, some by force. They were subsequently handed to Union authorities ashore. Protests as to the violation of British neutrality followed, and the men were all released. The key issue in terms of British neutrality was that the proper course of action for the U.S. commander to have taken would have been to have seized the *Trent* and allowed a court to assess the propriety of having taken the prisoners—technically, as contraband.

111. O'Rourke, *Recognition of Belligerency and the Spanish War*, at 399, 402–403, 407, 412.

112. Walker, *Recognition of Belligerency and Grant of Belligerent Rights*, at 177.

113. Lauterpacht, Recognition in International Law, at 186.

114. "Legal Aspects of the Recognition of Belligerency," Annex A to "Belligerency in the Formosa Strait," February 1957, in UK Archives File: FO 371/120939.

115. *See, e.g.*, Oglesby, Internal War and the Search for Normative Order, at 62–69.

116. Moore, A Digest of International Law: Volume I, at 192; *see also* Wharton, A Digest of the International Law of the United States, at n. 45, 51. (Mr. Fish to Mr. Motley, 25 September 1869—"The President does not deny, on the contrary he maintains, that every sovereign power decides for itself, on its responsibility, the question whether or not it will, at a given time, accord the status of belligerency to the insurgent subjects of another power,").

In either case, however, the sensitivity of this element is obvious. The dilemma, as expressed by President Grant in his special message of 13 June 1870 and relating to an earlier iteration of the Cuban insurrection, is often quoted as an example: "It is a well-established principle of public law that a recognition by a foreign State of belligerent rights to insurgents under circumstances such as now exist in Cuba, if not justified by necessity, is a gratuitous demonstration of moral support to the rebellion."[117] Falk concisely summarizes the ultimate political consequences of this element of the test stating, "naturally the formal recognition of the 'belligerency' of a rebel force was in practice an act of calculated hostility to the ruling government."[118] That said, however, it was equally recognized in some situations—most particularly where the conflict trespassed upon a maritime trade relationship—that recognition could become a necessary act by a third state wishing to impart some degree of regulation and predictability to that relationship. This is because "When the war extends to the sea," as Brierly and others noted, "it is almost inevitable that any state which possesses a mercantile marine will be compelled to make a decision for or against the recognition of the insurgents."[119]

(iii) Inferences from conduct and tacit acts of recognition

There also remains some debate as to whether recognition of belligerency could be "inferred by conduct," or needed to be explicit.[120] It was quickly accepted that the declaration of a blockade by the conflict state was an "admission" of belligerency: "The manner in which the proclamation of blockade becomes material is this, that it is an admission upon the part of the belligerent

117. Moore, A Digest of International Law: Volume I, at 194–96. There was some very detailed press reporting on this message, accompanied by quite nuanced discussion of the significance and application of the various elements of the test in relation to the situation in Cuba. *President Grant on Belligerency*, The Daily Evening Telegraph—Philadelphia, July 25, 1879, at 2, https://chroniclingamerica.loc.gov/lccn/sn83025925/1870-07-25/ed-1/seq-2.pdf.

118. Evan Luard, "Civil Conflicts in Modern International Relations," *in The International Regulation of Civil Wars* (Evan Luard ed., New York University Press 1972, p20; *see also* Julius I. Puente, International Law as Applied to Foreign States 35 (Chicago, Burdette J. Smith & Co. 1928), 34: "Unless justified by necessity, it [recognition of belligerency] is always—and justly—regarded as an unfriendly act, and a gratuitous demonstration of moral support of the rebellion."

119. J.L. Brierly, The Law of Nations 79 (1928); Oglesby, Internal War and the Search for Normative Order, at 58 ("The single most important test of the presence of a true civil war, as distinguished from an insurrection, is the existence of war-like measures on the high seas.").

120. *See generally* Chen, The International Law of Recognition, at 369–94 (concerning "modes" of recognition).

Government itself that a condition of legitimate war has arisen."[121] Puente in 1928, observed that

> Recognition of belligerency may be accorded in various ways: (1) tacitly, as when there is long acquiescence in belligerent acts affecting another nation's interests, without protest or objection, such as the blockade of ports, or the use of a nation's ports as a harbour for prizes; (2) impliedly, as by a declaration of blockade; and, (3) expressly, as when made by a proclamation of neutrality.[122]

Wilson was of the view that by the end of the nineteenth century the state of the law was such that it permitted conduct by the conflict / imperiled state—such as the declaration of a blockade—to afford sufficient evidence of recognition of belligerency of the adversary NSAG, but that recognition by a third state would require an explicit statement to that effect.[123] Others asserted that recognition of belligerency by the parent / conflict state "compels acquiescence in the new order on the part of foreign nations."[124] Yet other writers indicated that the acceptance of a blockade regime by a third state was sufficient to, at the very least, entitle that third state to deal with the rebels as if they could legitimately impose such a measure.[125] *The Ambrose Light* (1885), for all its flaws as a precedent concerning insurgency, also offered a concise and clearly expressed triptych for recognition of belligerency: "Recognition of belligerency may be express, as by proclamation; implied by acts of war, such as blockade; or tacit, by acquiescence in the exercise of belligerent rights."[126]

121. Harcourt, The Rights and Duties of Neutrals in Time of War: Part II, at 330; *see also* McNair and Watts, The Legal Effects of War, at 31–33 ("[T]he imposition of a blockade would transform the insurgency into a state of belligerency.").

122. Julius I. Puente, International Law as Applied to Foreign States 35 (Chicago, Burdette J. Smith & Co. 1928) (citing Hawkins v Filkins, 24 Ark. 286, 315 (1866)) (This case concerned the validity of a debt judgment delivered by an Arkansas court during the Civil War); *see also* Daoud Khairallah, Insurrection under International Law with Emphasis on the Rights and Duties of Insurgents 20–26 (Beurit, Lebanese University 1973) (describing the options as express recognition and tacit recognition, with his category of indicators as to tacit recognition including: the proclamation of a blockade by the conflict state; "interference with foreign merchant ships on the high seas," which assimilates, in its practice, to blockade or visit and search; and treaties entered into between the conflict state and the NSAG, although (he notes) there is some debate around whether agreements requiring "observance of the laws of war for humanitarian reasons," and "arrangements for the exchange of prisoners or war," constitute arrangements that create a tacit recognition of belligerency.).

123. Wilson, 141–42.

124. *See, e.g.*, O'Rourke, *Recognition of Belligerency and the Spanish War*, at 402, 412.

125. *See, e.g.*, T.S. Woolsey, *The Consequences of Cuban Belligerency*, 5 Yale L. J. 182 (1892–1896); O'Rourke, *Recognition of Belligerency and the Spanish War*, at 408.

126. U.S. v. The Ambrose Light, 409.

State practice is also clearly to the effect that a declaration of neutrality simultaneously furnished recognition of belligerency. President Monroe's message of 2 December 1817 provided an early indication of this approach:

> It was anticipated at an early stage that the contest between Spain and the colonies would become highly interesting to the United States . . . Through every stage of the conflict the United States has maintained an impartial neutrality, giving aid to neither of the parties in men, money, ships, or munitions of war. They have regarded the contest not in the light of an ordinary insurrection or rebellion, but as a civil war between parties nearly equal, having as to neutral powers equal rights. Our ports have been open to both.[127]

It was, however, the declaration of a blockade that is most often cited as evidence of tacit recognition of belligerency. This was certainly the understanding of the Nationalist Chinese government, which agreed in 1945 to "recognition of the Communists as a political party in China but declines to recognize them as an armed belligerent or insurrectionary group."[128] This conscious appreciation of the doctrine on recognition of belligerency was still evident in 1949, as the Nationalist government considered its military options as Communist forces invested Shanghai. When the Minister-Counsellor at the United States Embassy in Canton cabled the State Department on 6 June 1949, he reported that the Vice Minister of the Nationalist Foreign Office had indicated that the impending restrictions placed around Shanghai would be legally nuanced, stating, "As belligerency of Communists unrecognized, Chinese would carefully avoid use of word blockade."[129] Given the scale of U.S. military and other support to the Nationalist government,[130] it can be safely assumed that a formal recognition of Communist belligerency by the Nationalist government, thus requiring formal neutrality of the United States, would have created major practical and political challenges.

Advices provided to the British government, separated by almost a century, are remarkably consistent on this point. In June 1864, in relation to the Spanish

127. Moore, A Digest of International Law: Volume I, at 173; *see also* Hershey, The Essentials of International Public Law and Organization, at 204, n. 16 (observing that "The recognition of the belligerency of [several South American colonies in rebellion with Spain] . . . was tacitly recognized by the admission of their vessels to the ports of the United States on equal terms with those of Spain.").

128. Cable 893.00/6-2345, Ambassador in China (Hurley) to the Secretary of State, dated 23 June, 1945, at https://history.state.gov/historicaldocuments/frus1945v07/d286.

129. Cable 893.801/6-649, Minister-Counselor of Embassy in China (Clark) to the Secretary of State, dated 6 June 1949, at https://history.state.gov/historicaldocuments/frus1949v09/d1058.

130. "Foreign aid authorised for the Chinese Government since V-J Day [by 3 April 1949] had amounted to approximately 2,254 million dollars," in U.S. Department of State, *United States Relations with China, with Special Reference to the Period 1944–1949*, U.S. Government Printing Office, Washington, D.C., 1949, p 405.

blockade over insurgent ports in San Domingo, the Law Officers' opinion was that instructions issued by the Royal Navy to ignore the blockade were erroneous in that they appeared to assume that such a blockade could not be declared by Spain, unless Spain had first accorded formal recognition of belligerency to the insurgents. This, the Law Officers confirmed, was not correct, as the declaration of a blockade "necessarily implies" this outcome.[131] Indeed, while clearly on notice that it was an outcome the government assiduously wished to avoid, the Law Officers expressly confirmed,

> That we think Her Majesty's Government cannot, consistently with the principles and practice of International Law, refuse to recognize the Dominican Insurgents as belligerents, inasmuch as Her Majesty's Government has already accorded to the Spanish Government the rights of a belligerent power—that is rights [such as blockade] incident, and only incident, to a State of War.[132]

Spain, although arguing against recognition of belligerency for the Dominican insurgents, apparently accepted that its declaration of a blockade nevertheless had legal consequences such that Spanish authorities (according to British correspondence) "acquiesc[ed] in the proposed limitation of their rights of search etc. to the territorial waters of the coast occupied by the Insurgents."[133] The Foreign Office provided similarly cast legal advice to Lord Stanley, dated 14 August 1867, in relation to Ottoman actions in the context of the Cretan rebellion writing,

> We do not, however, know whether this be the case or not: but if the Ottoman Government does require from Foreign States the recognition of what is, strictly speaking, a Blockade, and not merely a right incident to every Independent State, of closing the ports of any part of its Dominions against Foreign Vessels;—if, in fact, the Ottoman Government has declared a formal Blockade, it would have no reason to complain if Foreign States simply recognized the Rebels as Belligerents: because a Blockade implies the existence of War and of two Belligerents at least, bound to respect the rights of Neutral States.[134]

Subsequently, in relation to China in 1949, the Law Officers were again explicit that declaration of a blockade amounted to a recognition of belligerency stating,

131. Foreign Office Letter, dated 22 June 1864, in UK Archives File: FO 881/1012.

132. Law Officer's opinion, 22 November 1864, extracted in Smith, Great Britain and the Law of Nations, Vol 1, pp 317–19 at p 318; for a further discussion on the San Domingo case, *see* inter alia, Walker, *Recognition of Belligerency and Grant of Belligerent Rights*, at 200–201.

133. Law Officer's opinion 22 August 1864 (FO 83/2372) extracted in Smith, GREAT BRITAIN AND THE LAW OF NATIONS, pp 313–17, at p 315.

134. John Karslake, Charles Selwyn, and Robert Phillimore, to Lord Stanley, 14 August 1867 (FO 83/2396), extracted in Smith, GREAT BRITAIN AND THE LAW OF NATIONS, pp 262–65 at 264.

> The position in international law is that a lawful government is entitled to proclaim a blockade of the coast occupied by insurgents. The existence of the blockade, however, constitutes an admission by the government instituting it that a state of belligerency exists. Other governments are then required to recognize a blockade, duly notified, provided that it is real and effective and not a mere paper blockade. It follows from the fact that the declaration of a blockade implies a state of belligerency that the blockade must be conducted in accordance with the internationally accepted rules of war.[135]

The Nigeria-Biafra conflict also provides a case study of continuing cognizance of the effect of a declaration of blockade as a tacit recognition of belligerency. It also speaks to the issue of political calculation as part of the fourth element of the belligerency test. Higgins was of the view that the Biafran-Nigerian conflict was certainly a "civil war." However, she focused upon the issue of non-intervention rather than of recognition of belligerency, which, she indicated, had not been forthcoming because of "the outmoded nature of the traditional law."[136] Mastorodimos, by contrast, argues "the conflict in Nigeria / Biafra was the last recorded recognition of belligerency by the incumbent government," citing the blockade as the "indication."[137] Kuyper records that,

> The Dutch Government declined [in 1969–1970] to recognize Biafra as a belligerent, because such recognition was deemed to be meaningless coming from a country lying far distant from the theatre of war and practically out of touch with the conflict.[138]

135. Cable No. 6405, dated 22 June 1949, Foreign Office to Washington, para 3, and Cable No. 101, dated 1 July 1949, British Embassy Canton to Foreign Office, both in UK Archives File: ADM 116/5713.

136. Higgins, *International Law and Civil Conflict*, at 172; Georg Schwarzenberger, *Human Rights and Guerrilla Warfare*, 1 Is. Y.B. Hum. Rts. 246, 255 (1971) (Schwarzenberger records that four states recognised Biafran independence in 1968, and thus characterized the war as an IAC—Gabon, Ivory Coast, Tanzania, and Zambia.).

137. Konstantinos Mastorodimos, *Belligerency Recognition: Past, Present and Future*, 29 Conn. J. of Int'l L. 301, 311 (2014).

138. Kuyper, *Recognition: Netherlands Theory and State Practice*, at 387; Chris Okeke, Controversial Subjects of Contemporary International Law 142–57, 158–77 (Rotterdam, Rotterdam University Press, 1974).On Biafra/Nigeria, and the East Pakistan/Bangladesh conflict, Okeke specifically raises the question of British compliance with the customary law on recognition of belligerency in relation to "forbidding her subjects to pay royalties to the de facto authority of Biafra," as well as the implied—but, in accordance with the customary doctrine of recognition of belligerency, effective and perfected—Nigerian recognition of belligerency of Biafra via its declaration of a blockade over Biafran controlled ports. *Id.* at 172–74. He also questions the motives behind the Dutch declaration, arguing that it may have been legal cover for a decision to support the Nigerian government whilst avoiding any allegation of unneutral engagement with one party. *Id.*

The Swedish government similarly did not recognize Biafran belligerency, and as a result "had been unable to find any legal basis"—something neutrality would have provided—to "curb" the activities of "Count von Rosen, the Swedish soldier of fortune who was conducting air attacks on targets in Federal territory with light aircraft flown by mercenary pilots and armed in France."[139] Canada—concerned at the intersecting issues of Quebec, federalism, French influence in Nigeria, and the law relating to intervention—provided humanitarian aid and observers, but did not characterize the conflict.[140] With the aim of achieving a more thorough and mutually reinforcing contextualization of this situation, both the broader political, and the more specific blockade, aspects will be dealt with at this point.

The British government quite evidently considered the Biafran situation in relation to the legal framework for a possible recognition of belligerency. Noting that one consequence of recognition of belligerency was that it was defensible at international law to pay tariffs and duties to the belligerent status NSAG, and that this was in most situations a defense to claims by the recognized government for double payment, the cabinet specifically noted that, "We shall also shortly have to consider whether to agree to the payment of oil royalties to the Government of the eastern region, or whether they should continue to be paid to the Federal Government."[141] Other options included that such royalties be paid into a "suspense account pending clarification of the situation in respect of the declaration of independence by the Government of the Eastern Region."[142] This decision was complicated by the fact that Shell / British Petroleum had given the Biafran leader (Ojukwu) "a letter of intent, by which they undertook to make an advance payment of royalties in respect of oil shipments"—one of the reasons behind the Federal declaration of a blockade.[143] Awaiting "developments," the Cabinet also deferred any decisions "as regards recognition of a separate State in the East,"[144] ultimately deciding against this move.

It is quite plain that the British government clearly considered the recognition of belligerency as something to be avoided, choosing—for a range of political

139. "Conclusions of a Meeting of the Cabinet held at 10 Downing Street, S.W.1, on Wednesday, 30th July, 1967, at 10.30 a.m.," in UK Archives File: CAB/128/42; *see also* "Conclusions of a Meeting of the Cabinet held at 10 Downing Street, S.W.1, on Thursday, 6th July, 1967, at 9.30 a.m.," in UK Archives File: CAB/128/42.

140. Stephanie Bangarth, *The Politics of African Intervention: Canada and Biafra, 1967–70, in* From Kinshasa to Kandahar: Canada and Fragile States in Historical Perspective 53–72 (Michael K. Carroll and Greg Donaghy eds., Calgary, University of Calgary Press, 2016).

141. "Conclusions of a Meeting of the Cabinet held at 10 Downing Street, S.W.1, on Tuesday, 30th May, 1967, at 10 a.m.," in UK Archives File: CAB/128/42.

142. "Conclusions of a Meeting of the Cabinet held at 10 Downing Street, S.W.1, on Thursday, 15th June, 1967, at 11 a.m.," in UK Archives File: CAB/128/42.

143. "Conclusions of a Meeting of the Cabinet held at 10 Downing Street, S.W.1, on Thursday, 6th July, 1967, at 9.30 a.m.," in U. Archives File: CAB/128/42.

144. "Conclusions of a Meeting of the Cabinet held at 10 Downing Street, S.W.1, on Thursday, 1st June, 1967, at 10 a.m.," in UK Archives File: CAB/128/42.

reasons—not to recognize Biafran belligerency. One factor was that "there were some 17,000 British lives at stake in Federal controlled territory."[145] Another was to protect British investments (estimated at 150–175 million pounds) and export trade (about 90 million pounds a year).[146] Third, it was asserted that "we were supplying arms to the Federal authorities not for commercial reasons but because they were the legitimate government of Nigeria, and because if we failed to do so we should have been unable to achieve even the present progress in regard to the establishment of a "mercy corridor" and the acceptance of observers."[147] A fourth justification was that it was "undoubtedly right to help a former colony and fellow Commonwealth country when it faced secession," noting that this was a wider problem in Africa as a whole, and that the French and Soviets would step into any vacuum if Britain walked back from this policy in Nigeria.[148] Finally, as starvation took hold, it entered British calculations that continued support of the Federal Military government would hopefully bring the protracted conflict to a swifter end, allowing relief operations to then come to the fore.[149] Collectively, this array of political and humanitarian concerns clearly militated against, in the British view, any recognition of Biafran belligerency. Additionally, it was also vital to ensure that the British policy of ongoing arms sales to the Nigerian government[150]—a point of concern noting that "public sympathy for Biafra was widespread in the

145. "Conclusions of a Meeting of the Cabinet held at 10 Downing Street, S.W.1, on Thursday, 7th September, 1967, at 10 a.m.," in UK Archives File: CAB/128/42.

146. "Cabinet Memorandum by the Secretary of State for Foreign and Commonwealth Affairs: Nigeria," dated 9 December 1968, para 2, in UK Archives File: CAB/129/139.

147. These arguments were often reiterated by the British Cabinet. *See, e.g.*, "Cabinet Memorandum by the Secretary of State for Foreign and Commonwealth Affairs: Oversea Policy: Nigeria," dated 10 March 1969, para 7, in UK Archives File: CAB/129/140; "Conclusions of a Meeting of the Cabinet held at 10 Downing Street, S.W.1, on Tuesday, 10th December, 1968, at 10 a.m.," in UK Archives File: CAB/128/43.

148. "Cabinet Memorandum by the Secretary of State for Foreign and Commonwealth Affairs: Oversea Policy: Nigeria," dated 10 March 1969, para 15(3), in UK Archives File: CAB/129/140; "Conclusions of a Meeting of the Cabinet held at 10 Downing Street, S.W.1, on Tuesday, 10th December, 1968, at 10 a.m.," paras 4–7, in UK Archives File: CAB/128/43.

149. *See, e.g.*, "Note for Cabinet by Secretary of State for Foreign and Commonwealth Affairs: Nigeria; Relief for Biafra," 17 December 1969, in UK Archives File: CAB/129/146.

150. *See also* KEESING'S RECORD OF WORLD EVENTS: *Volume 14*, Issue No. 12, 22875 (London, Longman, December 1968) (quoting a record of a House of Commons debate on 12 June 1968, "The House, Sir Alec continued, must give weight to the Government's argument that if arms shipments ceased Britain would lose all influence with the Federal Government; although he did not completely accept its validity in certain circumstances, he was not much attracted by the sort of unilateral gesture where Britain was always asked to give a moral lead which no one else followed. That did not really make much of a contribution to peace. There was a strong feeling, which perhaps the Government had not previously appreciated, that a final and terrible massacre of the Ibos would be intolerable, particularly if it came about with the support of British arms.").

country"[151]—could not be characterized as a breach of neutrality. As Mr. Stanley Henig noted during a House of Commons debate on 27 August 1968,

> The British Government have said that we have relations with the Nigerian Government and must sell them arms. Could we not have granted de facto recognition or the right of insurgency or belligerency in all these things? But we did nothing, for political reasons. We made a political choice when we should have declared our neutrality. My right hon. Friend said twelve months ago that, in effect, we would not take sides but he said today that it was impossible to be neutral. Why is it impossible? Why is it impossible for us, a thousand miles away or more, to be neutral in a conflict which does not concern us save from the humanitarian point of view in that we would like to see as little suffering as possible?[152]

There would, however, be no weakening of this policy. Indeed, as soon as the civil war had ended, the Foreign Secretary wrote to the British Prime Minister stating,

> As you know, we limited our supplies of weapons during the civil war to types which we had traditionally supplied. This excluded all aircraft with military capability, bombs and some types of advanced heavy weapons. With the end of the fighting I consider there is no longer any justification for maintaining this general restriction.[153]

As the Foreign Secretary continued, not only was there a commercial interest in again ramping up arms sales to Nigeria, but it was important that the growing dependence of the Nigerian Air Force on Soviet influence be countered.[154]

Considering the specific issue of blockade and tacit recognition of belligerency, it has been argued that the Nigerian Federal government did in fact tacitly recognize Biafran belligerency through the declaration of the blockade over Biafran-controlled coastal areas,[155] notably Port

151. "Conclusions of a Meeting of the Cabinet held at 10 Downing Street, S.W.1, on Thursday, 20th June, 1967, at 10 a.m.," in UK Archives File: CAB/128/42.

152. HC Deb 27 August 1968 vol 769 cc1433–1534, p 1488.

153. Letter PM/70/25, Foreign Secretary to Prime Minister, dated 16 February 1970, in UK Archives File: FCO 65/780.

154. *Id.*

155. KEESING'S RECORD OF WORLD EVENTS: *Volume 13*, Issue No. 6, 22087 (June 1967) The contemporary *Kessing's Archive* states that: "Mr. P. C. Asiodu, Permanent Secretary of the Federal Ministry of Industry, said at a press conference in London on June 14 [1967] that a total and complete blockade of the secessionist Eastern Region was in operation, as the Nigerian Navy was patrolling the coast and had not met any blockade runners; the Cameroon Republic had closed the frontier, and British shipping and other firms were co-operating fully with the Federal Government . . . The United Kingdom/West African Lines Joint Service had announced on May 31 that its vessels—comprising those of Eider Dempster, Guinea Gulf, the Palm Line (a

Harcourt.[156] This act was explicitly understood within the customary three-level scheme to equate to recognition of belligerency. Zorgbibe additionally interpreted the 12 August 1967 radio statement by the Federal Military government of Nigeria as a "declaration of war . . . prior to which time the federal authorities had admitted to nothing more serious than a "police operation."[157] It is unclear, however, whether the blockade was a non-LOAC "closure of ports within the territorial sea"—this issue is discussed in more detail in Chapter 4 in relation to the Formosa Strait in 1956; however, it is important to note at this point that such action was generally accepted to be a municipal act, not a LOAC-governed law of naval warfare measure. On this basis alone, it is difficult to assert without reservation that the Federal Nigerian authorities tacitly recognized Biafran belligerency, although it is notable that they separately indicated an intention to treat all Biafran fighters as PW.[158] However, blockade was not the only means by which it was understood that tacit recognition of belligerency could be accorded. In the non-maritime context of Poland in 1863, for example, Earl Cowley reported to Earl Russell that Austria held deep concerns with proposals to request of Russia an armistice in Poland because "to ask Russia to consent to an armistice, was to ask her to recognize the

Unilever subsidiary), the Nigerian National Shipping Line, and the Black Star Line of Ghana—would not call at Port Harcourt, Calabar, and Abonnema." *Id.*

156. "Conclusions of a Meeting of the Cabinet held at 10 Downing Street, S.W.1, on Thursday, 1st June, 1967, at 10 a.m.," in UK Archives File: CAB/128/42.

157. Zorgbibe, *Sources of the recognition of belligerent status*, at 114; Mastorodimos, *Belligerency Recognition: Past, Present and Future*, at 311 (stating that "the conflict in Nigeria/Biafra was the last recorded recognition of belligerency by the incumbent government"); Heather Wilson, International Law and the Use of Force by National Liberation Movements 154–55 (Oxford, Clarendon Press 1990) (noting the Nigerian government instruction to its forces to treat captured Biafran forces as PWs); Michael Bothe, *Article 3 and Protocol II: Case Studies of Nigeria and El Salvador (1982)*, 31 Am. Univ. L.R. 899, 902 (1982) (indicating that, "My own view is that Biafra was a local de facto regime and that the four Geneva Conventions as well as certain customary rules relating to the protection of the civilian population were applicable as a matter of law."). Other scholars are less certain. *See, e.g.*, James E Bond, *Internal Conflict and Article Three of the Geneva Conventions*, 48 Denver L. J. 263, 271 (1971–1972) (stating that despite the fact that the Nigerian government "permitted the ICRC to perform certain humanitarian functions and itself vowed to conduct military operations humanely," it never made a clear statement as to the applicability, de jure, of common article 3); David Ijalaye, *Was "Biafra" at any Time a State in International Law?*, 65(3) Am. J. of Int'l L. 551, 555 (asserting that "[N]o country (including those that recognized Biafra) formally granted the status of belligerency to either side in the Nigerian Civil War. The reason would appear to be that the warfare was in the main on land, and foreign states were not sufficiently affected by it to induce them to take this course.").

158. *See* "Operational Code of Conduct for the Nigerian Army," July 1967, para 4(e), *in* AHM Kirk-Greene, Crisis and Conflict in Nigeria: A Documentary Sourcebook, 1966–70 Vol. I, 455–56 (Oxford, Oxford University Press 1971); Sivakumaran, The Law of Non-International Armed Conflict, at 524; Emily Crawford, The Treatment of Combatants and Insurgents under the Law of Armed Conflict 28–39 (Oxford, Oxford University Press 2010).

belligerent rights of her insurgent subjects."[159] This clearly indicates that it was Austria's considered view that the conflict state, through the act of agreeing an armistice with insurgents, in effect furnished a tacit recognition of belligerency, as armistices are a function of the law of war rather than of domestic law.

(iv) The relative insignificance of inconsistent domestic judicial decisions

A more problematic form of tacit recognition of belligerency was a municipal law-sourced statement as to "neutrality" by a third state, but only for domestic legal purposes. In the ordinary course of events,[160] such a declaration at international law constituted a clear recognition of belligerency. On one hand, as will be discussed in the next chapter, the adoption of neutral rights and obligations by third states in such situations was indeed a definitive aspect of the doctrine. However, a specific but municipally based determination that the UK *Foreign Enlistment Act* or the equivalent U.S. *Neutrality Acts* were to be applied for the purposes of domestic legal process was, on the other hand, not considered to be a tacit recognition of belligerency.[161] In the UK situation, this was because the definition of "foreign state" in section 30 of the *Foreign Enlistment Act* was quite broad:

> 'Foreign state' includes any foreign prince, colony, province, or part of any province or people, or any person or persons exercising or assuming to exercise the powers of government in or over any foreign country, colony, province, or part of any province or people.[162]

Thus, an unrecognized insurgent NSAG could be characterized, for the purposes of domestic application of the *Foreign Enlistment Act*, as a "foreign state." In turn, this brought into play domestic legal obligations for British subjects, such as prohibitions on enlisting in the service of that NSAG (section 4 of the 1870 Act) or "build[ing] or agree[ing] to build, or caus[ing] to be built any ship with intent or knowledge, or having reasonable cause to believe that the same shall or will be employed in the military or naval service of any foreign state at war with any friendly state" (section 8(1) of the 1870 Act). That this was the clear intention of the drafters was never in doubt, as the "Diplock Report" noted in 1976:

> It is, and was no doubt intended by the draftsman to be, broad enough to make it an offence to enlist in armed forces raised by rival governments in a civil war

159. Earl Cowley to Earl Russell, 12 May 1863, in UK Archives File: FO 417/311.

160. McNair and Watts, The Legal Effects of War, at 33–34, n. 6.

161. *Id.* at 33 n. 6, 448–53. For a short general political history of the UK *Foreign Enlistment Act, see* Arielli, Frei, and Van Hulle, *The Foreign Enlistment Act, International Law, and British Politics, 1819–2014*, 38(4) The Int'l Hist. Rev. 1–21 (Dec. 2015).

162. *Foreign Enlistment Act* (1870) c. 90 (Regnal. 33 and 34 Vict), section 30, at http://www.legislation.gov.uk/ukpga/Vict/33-34/90/contents.

> such as that which had been waged in the United States of America, or forces such as those which had been raised by insurgents in the Spanish American colonies in their recent struggles for independence.[163]

This domestic legal device, however, was specifically understood as not implying any recognition of the relevant insurgents as belligerents for the purposes of international law,[164] although it is equally clear that one political purpose of the legislation was nevertheless to bolster the "international legal order, especially in the fields of recognition, non-intervention, and neutrality."[165]

This leads to further incidences of municipal law application, which were similarly considered to be delinked from the separate issue of tacit recognition of belligerency. These included, for example, the "blockade" and "war risks" related clauses in a range of commercial, carriage, and marine insurance contracts.[166] It is not possible to assert definitively that characterization for the purposes of interpretation and application of such clauses was describable in all circumstances as either consistent or inconsistent with the parallel application or non-application of the doctrine on recognition of belligerency. But, it is safe to observe that the recognition of insurgency or belligerency as a matter of international law was largely irrelevant to this consistency or inconsistency. In *Republic of Bolivia v. Indemnity Mutual Marine Assurance Co Ltd* (1909), the Court of Appeal upheld a decision at first instance (in the Kings Bench Division) that the term "piracy" as used in a contract of marine insurance was not necessarily the same as the term when used in international law. The context for the case was the loss of cargo belonging to the Bolivian government from the vessel *Labrea*, which had been seized by forces operating under the banner of the breakaway government of the Free Republic of El Acre. The argument before the Court of Appeal drew heavily upon the issue of whether the forces of the "Free Republic" were entitled to insurgent or belligerent status, and thus to have their visit and search regime respected, or at the least to have their conduct—targeted only at the conflict state, Bolivia—deemed other than piratical.[167]

Similarly, in *Eastern Carrying Insurance Company v. National Benefit Life and Property Insurance Co Ltd* (1919), it was held that regardless of the international

163. *Report of the Committee of Privy Counsellors appointed to inquire into the recruitment of mercenaries, Cmnd. 6569, August 1976* ("Diplock Report"), para 34.

164. *See, e.g.*, Law Officers Opinion dated 10 October 1876, *in* Lord McNair, International Law Opinions, Vol I 368–69 (Cambridge, Cambridge University Press 1956); McNair and Watts, The Legal Effects of War, at 448–53; Lauterpacht, Recognition in International Law, at 266–68, and the additional Law Officers' Opinions both refer to therein.

165. Arielli, Frei, and Van Hulle, *The Foreign Enlistment Act, International Law, and British Politics, 1819*-2014, at 637–39.

166. *See generally* McNair and Watts, The Legal Effects of War at 53–54.

167. Republic of Bolivia v Indemnity Mutual Marine Assurance Co. Ltd. (1909) 1 KB 785; *see, e.g.*, the submissions of counsel at *id.* at 793–96.

law status of active British support (including troops) for the recognized White Russian government against the unrecognized Bolshevik party, this held no implications for the purposes of a commercial arrangement, that a Petrograd registered insurance company nominally under Bolshevik governance, was an "enemy alien."[168] The fact of recognition or non-recognition of Bolshevik insurgency or belligerency was simply irrelevant.

The case of *Luther v. James Sagor and Company* (1921)[169] concerned a factory and materials seized by the Soviet government in 1919 in pursuance of a decree that nationalized, *inter alia*, mechanical sawmills and woodworking establishments. The immunity of the act from suit in British courts was an issue in the case, and the key evidence was a Foreign Office communication that asserted that the British government had recognized the Soviet government in 1921. Furthermore, in 1917, it was the British view that "the Soviet authorities expelled the previous government recognized by His Majesty."[170] Consequently, the seizure, which took place before formal British recognition of the Soviet government, but after British acceptance that the old Provisional government no longer held authority, was to "be treated by the Courts of this country with all the respect due to the acts of a duly recognized foreign sovereign state."[171] Thus, despite reference to de jure and de facto governments and to international law publicists such as Wheaton and Bernard, the parsing of insurgency and belligerency, although clearly applicable to the situation for other purposes, was irrelevant.

Similarly, in *Curtis and Sons v Mathews* (1919),[172] the claim related to payment under an insurance policy for destruction of a building and contents in Dublin during the Easter Uprising in April 1916. The rebels (approximately two thousand) occupied a number of buildings, including the General Post Office, and declared the formation of a Provisional government. Subsequently, a fire broke out during a British artillery bombardment of the General Post Office. This fire then destroyed Curtis's building.[173] At issue was the insurance clause that covered loss and damage "directly caused by war, bombardment, military or usurped power . . . and fire . . . directly caused by any of the foregoing," along with a proviso relating to "destruction by the Government of the country in which the property is situated." Although the key distinction in the case was between riot and civil commotion on one hand, and "usurped power" on the other (such "usurped power" being considered rebellion as it was "something more than the action of

168. Eastern Carrying Insurance Company v National Benefit Life and Property Insurance Co Ltd (1919) 35 TLR 292.

169. Luther v James Sagor & Co. [1921] 3 KB 532.

170. *Id.* at 543 (per Bankes L.J.); *id.* at 551 (Warrington L.J.); *id.* at 556 (Scrutton LJ).

171. *See, e.g., id.* at 543 (per Bankes L.J.).

172. Curtis and Sons v Mathews [1919] 1 KB 425.

173. *Id.* at 426–27.

an unorganized rabble"[174]), it was nevertheless determined that the event was one of "civil strife amounting to warfare." Thus, a clear invitation to assess the facts in the light of the civil disturbance-rebellion-insurrection scheme, and any applicable Law of War and martial law, was ignored and the matter decided solely on the basis of interpretation of contractual terms. Ultimately, it was determined that as the destruction was not intentional, the proviso did not apply and the claim was upheld.[175]

In *Spanish Government v The North of England Steamship Company* (1938),[176] the owners of the *SS Hartbridge* had accepted a charter party to take cargo to one of six named ports in Spain in December 1937 during the Spanish Civil War. The owners ultimately refused to allow the vessel to enter the chosen port of Barcelona because the Nationalist forces had declared a blockade over the port. The charterers, the Spanish Republican government, disagreed and demanded the vessel proceed into port. Ultimately, the parties accepted that the vessel would proceed to a different port and unload the cargo for on-forwarding at the charterer's expense. The charter party contract included a standard clause relating to "blockaded" ports as part of the war risks conditions. The Spanish government then sought to recover costs from the vessel owners on the basis that the blockaded port clause should never have been invoked as the blockade around Barcelona was one in name only and had never been effective.[177] The owners argued that "reference to a blockaded port in the clauses did not mean a blockade in its strict legal sense." The court disagreed and said that this was precisely what it meant, although, the court referred to an Admiralty and marine insurance publicist rather than an international law publicist for the substance of the term. However, given that the Spanish government had denounced the blockade, that it was not effective, and that Barcelona "was not at any material time a blockaded port," the court upheld the charterer's claim for redress.[178] Once again, the international legal regime relating to insurgency and belligerency in relation to the closure of ports, blockade, and tacit acceptance of blockade, did not enter into the court's assessment.

A final example is furnished by *Luigi Monta of Genoa v. Cechofracht Co. Ltd.* (1956),[179] a case involving an Italian flagged vessel chartered by a Czech company for a passage to Europe from a Communist Chinese port. The vessel was interdicted by Nationalist warships and ordered into a Formosan port where its cargo was discharged. The charter party was subject to English law, and included a provision that permitted the vessel to comply with directions given "by the government of the nation under whose flag the vessel sails . . . or any

174. *Id.* at 429 (per Bankes L.J.).

175. *Id.* at 431 (per Bankes L.J. and Scrutton L.J.).

176. Spanish Government v, The North of England Steamship Company (1938) 54 TLR 852.

177. *Id.* at 853-56 (per Lewis J.).

178. *Id.* at 857 (per Lewis J.).

179. Luigi Monta of Genoa v Cechofracht Co. Ltd. [1956] 2 All ER 769.

other government." At the time, Italy recognized the Nationalist government, but Britain recognized the Communist government and "did not recognize that any government was located in Formosa."[180] In deciding the case, Justice Sellers had no cause to look to the meanings or implications of the status of insurgency or to the details of Britain's complicated legal relationship with Nationalist naval activity and claims, stating that

> As a matter of construction of the charter party, an ordinary trading or commercial contract, there would seem to me to be no ground for saying that the authority giving the orders or directions has to be a government recognized as such by Her Majesty's government here.[181]

Indeed, Sellers J went on to determine that the Foreign Office statement as to the nature of its (non)recognition of the Nationalist authorities "was not conclusive as the words were to be interpreted in the sense in which an ordinary commercial man would use them." For the purposes of the charter party, the act was thus one by a "government" and the ship owners were entitled to the freight costs.

In the United States legal system, executive statements as to the nature of a conflict, and the status of parties to it, generally appear to have had a more decisive influence upon the interpretation of such clauses. This is because these courts had to deal, very directly, with the legal aftermath of an indigenous instance of recognition of belligerency at the conclusion of the American Civil War. Consequently, the status of the Confederacy as a recognized belligerent in international law appears to have asserted significant contextual influence over U.S. courts dealing with post-Civil War claims. As the syllabus for the United States Supreme Court case of *Mauran v. Insurance Company*, (1867),[182] for example, notes,

> 1. A taking of a vessel by the naval forces of a now extinct rebellious confederation, whose authority was unlawful and whose proceedings in overthrowing the former government were wholly illegal and void, and which confederation has never been recognized as one of the family of nations, is a 'capture' within the meaning of a warranty on a policy of insurance having a marginal warranty 'free from loss or expense by capture,' if such rebellious confederation was at the time sufficiently in possession of the attributes of government to be regarded as in fact the ruling or supreme power of the country over which its pretended jurisdiction extended.
> 2. Accordingly, a seizure by a vessel of the late so-called Confederate States of America for their benefit was a 'capture' within the terms of such a warranty.[183]

180. *Id.* at 769.

181. *Id.* at 733 (per Sellers J.).

182. Mauran v Insurance Company 73 US (6 Wall.) 1 (1867).

183. *Id.*

Justice Nelson in that case observed that "In the case of a capture under a commission from an organized government against an enemy, jure belli, to bring the capture within the policy, it is not necessary that the commission should issue from a perfectly lawful government any more than that the capture itself should be lawful."[184] The key influence on his findings, however, was U.S. practice from the time of the South American revolts against Spain in the 1820s, which he asserted was clearly to the effect that

> from the time the revolt had reached the dimensions of a civil war, the government had recognized the war and conceded equal belligerent rights to the respective parties, and the capture of the vessels of Spain by a commander under a commission by one of the colonies in the exercise of this right was recognized as legal as if it had occurred in open public war, and, as a matter of course, would have been within the marginal warranty clause of the insured in a policy of insurance.[185]

As this, and other cases such as *The Three Friends* (1897) attest, U.S. courts—cognizant in particular of recent U.S. history—appear to have treated U.S. governmental determinations in relation to belligerency and insurgency as significantly more authoritative in maritime and Admiralty cases than was the practice of their counterpart British courts.

(v) The relevance of treatment of captives as PW

A final, quite problematic possible indicator of implied recognition of belligerency, is a third state demand that those detained on the battlefield or in the course of naval operations be treated as PW, and / or a conflict state declaration that it will treat detained insurgents in accordance with the PW regime. The former appears to have been the situation in relation to British demands during the Malagasay rebellion that French authorities treat captured British nationals fighting for the insurgents as PW. This situation will be dealt with in more detail in the next chapter. An example of the latter situation is the assertion by some commentators that the Nigerian Federal government declaration that it would treat captured Biafran forces as PW similarly represented a tacit recognition of Biafran belligerency by that government. However, this contentious potential indicator is often combined with the more clear-cut indicator of a Nigerian "blockade" (as noted previously) in order to arrive at this conclusion.

At this point, as a brief aside, it is perhaps appropriate to place on record my own view regarding the legal effect of a policy of treating battlefield captives in accordance with the PW regime as a tacit recognition of belligerency. It is my view that it is legally consistent that demands by a third state that the forces of

184. *Id.* at 11 (per Nelson J.).

185. *Id.* at 12.

either contesting party in an insurgency, who are detained on the battlefield or at sea, should be treated as PW does indeed constitute implied recognition of belligerency by that third state. However, it is not as equally obvious or certain that a *policy* decision by the conflict state itself, to treat captured insurgents as if they were PW, necessarily leads to the *legal* consequence of implied recognition of the belligerency of that NSAG. In the former case, the expectation by the third state can only be that a legally enforceable obligation to treat, as a minimum, that third state's citizens as PW, not as rebels, is the aim of the assertion. This would of course then place an obligation of neutrality upon that third state in return. In the latter situation, however, the conflict state could rightly and fairly claim that it had determined upon that course of action based on purely humanitarian motives. Thus, this sovereign concession to humanity (that is, treating the insurgents as if they were PW rather than as criminals to be prosecuted) should not be abused by external states. Such abuse, from the perspective of the conflict state, could be manifested in the form of assertions that the conflict state has recognized the insurgents' belligerency, and that these third states must now act as neutrals (although generally, this would be to the detriment of the conflict state in terms of the freedom of third states to continue all manner of trade and support to the conflict state).

Noting that the issues of blockade and application of the law of neutrality will be dealt with in more detail in the next chapter, the key indicators of belligerency can at this point be briefly summarized as follows:

(1) Expressly, through a statement of recognition of belligerency by the conflict state, which then bound that state and the adversary NSAG, and was considered—for practical reasons—highly influential upon third states, which often then acted in accordance with that status;
(2) Implicitly, through the declaration of a blockade over NSAG controlled ports, coasts, and waters by the conflict state, which was likewise considered—for practical reasons—highly influential upon third states, which often then acted in accordance with the declared blockade, applying the law of neutrality as between the two contending parties;
(3) Expressly, through a statement of recognition of belligerency of the NSAG by a third state, which bound only that third state and did not bind the conflict state, but which also required that third state to act in accordance with the law of neutrality as between the contending parties;
(4) Implicitly, through acquiescence by the third state to a blockade declared by either the conflict state or the NSAG, most obviously through instructions to vessels flying that third state's flag to submit to visit and search by both contending parties, and by thus applying the law of neutrality as between them in the process.

E. CONCLUSION—THE THREE-LEVEL SCHEME

The three-level scheme for legally conceptualizing and defining conflict relationships was, and arguably remains, a practical, useful, and readily deployable legal framework. Its particular strengths lay in its utility for analyzing and navigating political and operational responses to the myriad relationship and characterization challenges that present whenever a conflict state, its adversary NSAG, and third states are required to seek out and legally express the accommodations they have made with each other. This applies to both routine rights and intercourse, and the disruptions that can be caused to this when a rebellion rises to the level of insurgency or belligerency. Further, within this scheme, as the politically useful and convenient legal doctrine at its apex, recognition of belligerency has evidenced a remarkable degree of consistency in terms of the elucidation of its constitutive elements. The first three elements bear some similarity to the elements articulating the threshold for those conflicts countenanced by Additional Protocol II, Article 1,[186] and for the affording of certain militias and other organized armed groups with Geneva Convention III, Article 4A[187] and Additional Protocol I Article 44(3) PW status.[188] The fourth element—political

186. Protocol Additional to the Geneva Conventions of 12 August 1949, and Relating to the Protection of Victims of Non-International Armed Conflict, Jun. 8, 1977, 1125 U.N.T.S. 609:

> Art 1—(1) This Protocol, which develops and supplements Article 3 common to the Geneva Conventions of 12 August 1949 without modifying its existing conditions of application, shall apply to all armed conflicts which are not covered by Article 1 of the Protocol Additional to the Geneva Conventions of 12 August 1949, and relating to the Protection of Victims of International Armed Conflicts (Protocol I) and which take place in the territory of a High Contracting Party between its armed forces and dissident armed forces or other organized armed groups which, under responsible command, exercise such control over a part of its territory as to enable them to carry out sustained and concerted military operations and to implement this Protocol. (2) This Protocol shall not apply to situations of internal disturbances and tensions, such as riots, isolated and sporadic acts of violence and other acts of a similar nature, as not being armed conflicts.

187. Geneva Convention relative to the Treatment of Prisoners of War, art. 4(A)(2)(3), Aug. 12, 1949, 75 U.N.T.S. 135:

> (2) Members of other militias and members of other volunteer corps, including those of organized resistance movements, belonging to a Party to the conflict and operating in or outside their own territory, even if this territory is occupied, provided that such militias or volunteer corps, including such organized resistance movements, fulfil the following conditions: (a) that of being commanded by a person responsible for his subordinates; (b) that of having a fixed distinctive sign recognizable at a distance; (c) that of carrying arms openly; (d) that of conducting their operations in accordance with the laws and customs of war. (3) Members of regular armed forces who profess allegiance to a government or an authority not recognized by the Detaining Power.

188. Protocol Additional to the Geneva Conventions of 12 August 1949, and Relating to the Protection of Victims of International Armed Conflict (Protocol I) art. 44(3), June 8, 1977, 1125 U.N.T.S. 609):

> In order to promote the protection of the civilian population from the effects of hostilities, combatants are obliged to distinguish themselves from the civilian population while they

necessity, or political discretion—as an explicit rather than tacit threshold element is perhaps rare, but not unique. This level of internal doctrinal coherence and broad practical acceptance must, therefore, have been underpinned by a high degree of utility and "fitness for purpose." This inquiry is the subject of the next chapter.

are engaged in an attack or in a military operation preparatory to an attack. Recognizing, however, that there are situations in armed conflicts where, owing to the nature of the hostilities an armed combatant cannot so distinguish himself, he shall retain his status as a combatant, provided that, in such situations, he carries his arms openly: (a) during each military engagement, and (b) during such time as he is visible to the adversary while he is engaged in a military deployment preceding the launching of an attack in which he is to participate. Acts which comply with the requirements of this paragraph shall not be considered as perfidious within the meaning of Article 37, paragraph 1(c).

4

The Purposes of Recognition of Belligerency

> [T]he Government of the United states, having recognized the existence of a civil war between Spain and her colonies but remaining neutral, the courts of the Union are bound to consider as lawful those acts which war authorizes and which the new governments in South America may direct against their enemy.[1]
>
> —Divina Pastora (1819)

> The government of the United States has recognized the existence of a civil war between Spain and her colonies, and has avowed a determination to remain neutral between the parties, and to allow to each the same rights of asylum and hospitality and intercourse. Each party is therefore deemed by us a belligerent nation, having, so far as concerns us, the sovereign rights of war, and entitled to be respected in the exercise of those rights. We cannot interfere to the prejudice of either belligerent without making ourselves a party to the contest, and departing from the posture of neutrality. All captures made by each must be considered as having the same validity, and all the immunities which may be claimed by public ships in our ports under the law of nations must be considered as equally the right of each, and as such must be recognized by our courts of justice, until Congress shall prescribe a different rule.[2]
>
> —The Santissima Trinidad (1822)

A. INTRODUCTION

As a framework for assessing the legal nature and consequences of a conflict situation involving a state and an adversary Non-State Armed Group (NSAG),

1. The Divina Pastora, 17 U.S. 52, 63 (1819).

2. The Santissima Trinidad, 20 U.S. 283, 337 (1822).

the doctrine on recognition of belligerency has provided a clear test with defined elements. The doctrine is also coherently located within a scheme that provides thresholds both above (state against state "war") and below (insurgency) the strata of formal belligerency in which the test has been understood to be applicable, and thus applied. It next becomes salient to ask why recognition of belligerency took on such central importance in the legal characterization of, in particular, nineteenth- and twentieth-century civil wars.[3] Clearly, one answer is that it was well-calibrated as a legal analytical framework for such situations—that is, it was considered well-fitted for its purpose and thus routinely used. Given this fit with its context, it is instructive to interrogate the purposes the doctrine served. Such inquiry will help to illuminate why it was a well-utilized analytical framework. Furthermore, the distillation of this set of purposes may also point toward useful avenues of examination in the quest to find whether, or not, recognition of belligerency may still have continuing relevance and utility.

This chapter, consequently, seeks to analyze the purposes—humanitarian, political, operational, and fiscal—which were traditionally served by the customary Law of War doctrine on recognition of belligerency. In order to engage with the historical record, and the views of commentators over the two hundred years during which the doctrine has evolved, I approach this component of the analysis by first noting the shared interest of all parties in the imposition of some humanity over an otherwise almost extralegal form of conflict. Following this, I examine the separate interests and purposes served in relation to each of the three core parties affected by the doctrine: the conflict (or parent) state; the belligerent-status NSAG; and neutral third states that recognized the NSAG's formal belligerency.

B. THE HUMANITARIAN IMPERATIVE

While the perceived purposes served by recognition of belligerency differed as between the interested parties, the primary interest of the international community as a whole was humanitarianism. This was most clearly and eloquently expressed in Lord Canning's December 1824 letter to Lord Wellesley, at that time the British Minister in Vienna, concerning Austrian refusals to treat the Greek rebels fighting against the Ottoman Empire as full belligerents:

3. Although, it must be said, Wyndham Walker argued in 1937 that the doctrine did not crystallize into a coherent, coordinated test until the American Civil War. He cites Harcourt as a publicist of the doctrine in its immediate pre-pivot to formality guise, and Hall as a publicist of the post-American Civil War doctrine. Wyndham Walker, Recognition of Belligerency and Grant of Belligerent Rights 177–86 (1938). As will become evident, I respectfully disagree with Walker on this point, and would argue that there was indeed clear recognition of a coherent doctrine prior to the American Civil War.

> The doctrine of Prince Metternich, that the Greeks, as rebels, are not entitled to the same rights of war, as legitimate belligerents, is one, of which, we think His Highness would do well to weigh all the consequences, before he promulgates it to the world. The practical enforcement of that doctrine could have no other effect than to convert the contest which has been brought, in a great measure by our exertions, into one of a regular and civilized character, into one of indiscriminate rapine and massacre.[4]

Although there was, during the initial stages of the American Civil War, an apparent distinction between treating Confederate soldiers as Prisoners of War (PWs), and Confederate sailors and privateers as pirates, the absurdity of this position on humanitarian grounds was quickly pointed out:

> Let us take counsel of our common sense. These men are treated as criminals because, while we give to the Southern soldier the rights of war (for numerous exchanges of soldiers have taken place), we convict the Southern mariner of a crime punishable with death. Is there any reason, even upon the grounds of policy, for making this distinction?[5]

The author of this letter, the New York Judge Charles Daly, continued, "We have the fruitful experience of history to admonish us that in such acts are sown the seeds of the dissolution of nations, and especially of Republics."[6]

Similarly, the U.S. Supreme Court in, inter alia, *Ford v. Surget* was of the view that the application of the international Law of War during the American Civil War was "conceded, in the interest of humanity, and to prevent the cruelties of reprisals and retaliations."[7] The Court further stated that "[s]hould the sovereign conceive that he has the right to hand up his prisoners as rebels, the opposite party will make reprisals. . . . Should he burn and ravage, they will follow his example and the war will become cruel, horrible, and every day more destructive to the nation."[8] Mountague Bernard, in his influential 1870 treatise *A Historical Account of the Neutrality of Great Britain during the American Civil War*, asserted that

> It is generally expedient that the ordinary rules of war should extend, as far as possible, to civil wars. The restraints which they impose are wholesome, their

4. Letter from Lord Canning to Lord Wellesley (Dec. 31, 1824), *in* GREAT BRITAIN AND THE LAW OF NATIONS 294, 296 (H. A. Smith ed., 1932).

5. Charles Daly, "Are the Southern Privateersmen Pirates?," dated 21 December 1861, extracted in UK Archives File: FO 881/1048, Item 18 Enclosure ("The Daly Letter (1861)"). This issue will be discussed further a little later.

6. *Id.*

7. Ford v. Surget, 97 U.S. 594, 605 (1878).

8. *Id.*

> influence in making war regular and humane and in confining its range are as useful; all the reasons of convenience on which they repose apply to these wars with as much force as others.[9]

The issue was also certain enough for Hall, writing in 1890, to assess that it was the dictates of humanity that ultimately underscored the purpose of recognition of belligerency:

> As soon, it is said, as a considerable population is arrayed in arms with the professed object of attaining political ends . . . it would be inhuman for the enemy to execute his prisoners; it would be still more inhuman for foreign states to capture and hang the crews of war-ships as pirates; humanity requires that the members of such a community shall be treated as belligerents.[10]

Ellery Stowell, writing in 1921, argued that the failure to recognize belligerency in relation to Poland in 1863 was a humanitarian catastrophe, although he tended to analyze the situation as one of failed "humanitarian intervention."[11] Lauterpacht, although describing the humanitarian argument

9. Mountague Bernard, A Historical Account of the Neutrality of Great Britain during the American Civil War 115 (1870). As noted previously, the traditional understanding of the effects of formal belligerency on the validity of a blockade are well summarized in, for example, Instructions sent to the Governor of Victoria relative to the Reception of Belligerent Cruizers and then Observance of Neutrality during the Civil War in the United States (Feb. 1872), *in* UK Archives File: FO 881/2068. *See also in the same file* Letter from Downing Street (May 11, 1861) (requiring that "nothing should be done by the naval forces which would indicate any partiality or preference of either party in the contest which may ensue."); Letter from Downing Street (Jan. 16, 1862) (reiterating "the determination of Her Majesty's Government to maintain the strictest neutrality."); Letter from Downing Street (June 2, 1864) (regarding "the decisions at which Her Majesty's Government have arrived on certain questions which have arisen respecting the treatment of prizes captured by Federal or Confederate cruizers, if brought into British waters"). For further reading, *see* Correspondence Relative to the Civil War in North America (Jan. 8–Feb. 1, 1862), *reprinted in* UK Archives File: FO 881/1048; Letter from Earl Russel to the Lords Commissioners of the Admiralty (Jan. 31, 1862), *reprinted in* UK Archives File: FO 881/996 (setting out four rules for the Admiralty, and British colonial governments, to follow); Joseph H. Beale Jr., *The Recognition of Cuban Belligerency*, 9 Harvard L. Rev. 406 (1896); Dispatch from Lord Lyons, *in* UK Archives File: FO 800/924 (giving account of an interview with Mr. Seward on 29 April 1861, stating that "Secretary of the Navy . . . said the 'Blockade will be conducted as strictly according to the recognised rules of public law, and with as much liberality towards Neutrals, as any blockade ever was by a belligerent'"); T. S. Woolsey, *The Consequences of Cuban Belligerency*, 5 Yale L. J. 182 (1896); Edwin D. Dickinson, *The Closure of Ports in Control of Insurgents*, 24 Am. J. Int'l L. 69 (1930); Norman Padelford, *Foreign Shipping During the Spanish Civil War*, 32 Am. J. Int'l L. 264 (1938).

10. William E. Hall, A Treatise on International Law 33–34 (1895); *see also* Ellery C. Stowell, Intervention in International Law 120–22 (1921) (discussing the humanitarian imperatives publicly placed at the forefront of the U.S. intervention in support of Cuban insurgents in 1898).

11. Stowell, Intervention in International Law, 89–120.

as "to a large extent deceptive," nevertheless noted in his 1947 analysis that "[i]t is often maintained that recognition of belligerency by outside States is an important factor in securing compliance with rules of warfare and in helping to infuse into an otherwise savage and irregular combat an indispensable measure of restraint and humanity."[12] Charles King records that North Vietnam "desisted from trying captured American pilots as war criminals in response to the world public outcry against such action."[13] However, as Lauterpacht's perceptive statement clearly indicates, while humanitarianism may have been a driving force, it was to some extent the "spin"—a salable guise—for the decision to recognize belligerency. It is not, however, a sufficient argument for the doctrine's utility; states being states, there must have been other more concrete, interest-based reasons for supporting and utilizing the doctrine. It is to these more instrumental purposes that recognition of belligerency served that I now turn.

C. THE CONFLICT STATE PERSPECTIVE

For the conflict (or parent) state, there was a range of benefits in recognizing the formal belligerency of an adversary rebel group, quite apart from the actual or chimerical humanization of conduct within the conflict implicit in following the rules encapsulated in the international Law of War. As Wheaton (Dana) noted, the benefit of recognition of belligerency was "not solely to the advantage of the insurgents."[14] Indeed, as Hershey commented, while belligerency gave the insurgents "moral comfort" as well as actionable rights, they may well not have been "in as good a position to take advantage of these opportunities as the parent State, which also acquires these same rights and privileges."[15] I shall examine the consequence of recognition of belligerency from the perspective of the conflict state by reference to three aspects of the relevant law: the law applicable to means and methods of warfare, through the example of the law of blockade; the issue of state responsibility for the acts of a recognized belligerent NSAG; and the application of the law of neutrality.

(i) Means and methods: Blockade

The first additional benefit for the conflict state was, of course, that it gained the legal ability to employ international Law of War rules on means and methods of

12. Hersch Lauterpacht, Recognition in International Law 227 (1947).

13. Charles R. King, *Revolutionary War, Guerrilla Warfare, and International Law*, 4 Case W. Res. J. Int'l L. 91, 106 (1972).

14. Henry Wheaton, Elements of International Law § 23 (Richard Henry Dana Jr. ed., 8th ed., 1866).

15. Amos Hershey, The Essentials of International Public Law and Organization 204 (1912).

warfare against the NSAG, and to call upon the law of neutrality in relation to the activities of third states as they touched upon that conflict. McNair and Watts, citing Oppenheim, have argued that recognition of belligerency certainly brings the conflict within Common Article 3 of the *Geneva Conventions* (CA3), and most probably within Common Article 2 (CA2).[16] In an advice dated 8 February 1956 by Joyce Gutteridge, a senior Foreign Office legal adviser, it was noted specifically—in the context of British Cabinet discussions as to whether Britain ought to recognize "belligerency in the Formosa Strait"—that the list of entitlements accruing to both the belligerent parties, once recognition of belligerency was afforded, included the rights of blockade, visit and search, capture and prize, and the right of angary, "i.e.[,] the right to destroy or use, in case of necessity, for the purpose of offence and defence, neutral property on their territory, or on enemy territory or on the open sea."[17] During the heyday of the doctrine's influence and application, this benefit was most routinely understood in maritime terms, opening up to the conflict state the unimpeachable right to declare and enforce a blockade against insurgent-held coasts and ports, and to validly exercise visit and search rights in respect of neutral shipping destined for rebel ports.[18] Four vignettes will serve to illustrate this point.

The first vignette is found in diplomatic reporting concerning the case of the British barque *Saxon*, a vessel carrying a cargo (mainly wool) that was taken in prize on 28 October 1863 by the Union warship *Vanderbilt* approximately 400 miles north of the Cape of Good Hope. The correspondence discloses a British assessment as to the possible unlawful seizure of the vessel on the grounds of compliance with the applicable law on capture of neutral vessels (and particularly the contentious doctrine of "continuous voyage"[19]), but not on the grounds

16. Arnold McNair and A. D. Watts, The Legal Effects of War 33 (1966) (citing 2 Lassa Oppenheim, International Law: A Treatise § 126 (Hersch Lauterpacht ed., 7th ed. 1952). This matter is dealt with in greater detail in Chapter 5.

17. Joyce Gutteridge, Consequences of the Recognition of Belligerency ¶ 2 (1957), *reprinted in* UK Archives File: FO 371/120939 (F.C. 1092/1).

18. *See, e.g.*, W. Vernon Harcourt, The Rights and Duties of Neutrals in Time of War: Part I, *in* 9 Royal United Serv. Institution J. 313, 323–24 (1865).

19. This highly contested legal device asserted that "the doctrine of continuous voyage is applicable whenever an intermediate port is fraudulently interjected into a voyage which, if direct, would by the law of nations be illegal. In practice, as is well known, the theory of continuous voyages has been applied chiefly in four sorts of cases: where subjects of a belligerent trade with the enemy; where subjects of a neutral carry on the coastwise or colonial trade of a belligerent contrary to the rule of the war of 1756; where a neutral carries contraband to a belligerent port; where a neutral intends ultimately to break a blockade." Lester Woolsey, *Early Cases on the Doctrine of Continuous Voyages*, 4 Am. J. Int'l L. 823 (1910); *see also* Charles Gregory, *Doctrine of Continuous Voyage*, 24 Harv. L. Rev. 167 (1910); Orby Mootham, *The Doctrine of Continuous Voyage, 1756–1815*, 8 Brit. Y.B. Int'l L. 62 (1927).

that this body of law did not de jure apply.[20] A British Foreign Office memorandum, titled "History of the Negotiations between the British Government and the United States Government in Regard to the Restrictions Placed on British Trade by the Latter 1862–1864," notes that in the course of correspondence between the British Foreign Office and the U.S. Department of State concerning the taking of bonds against certain British vessels by the New York Collector of Customs,

> Lord Russell instructs Mr Stuart [the British representative in the United States] to lodge a further protest on the ground that British subjects have a right to trade with the Southern States, subject to the rules of blockade recognised by international law, and that the only method by which the United States can legitimately prevent such trade is by capture on the high seas.[21]

Sometime after the war, in criticizing the (misplaced) outrage of Union officials in relation to British neutrality with respect to both the Union and Confederate blockades, Lorimer tartly observed that "[a]ny one acquainted with the law of nations knew perfectly well that although a country might put down an insurrection against its authority, it had no power or right to interfere with neutral commerce without giving the insurgents a belligerent character."[22]

The second vignette concerns the British schooner *Three Bells*, which was detained by Dominican authorities in 1904 for attempting to run the blockade declared around the insurgent—or impliedly, because of the blockade, the belligerent-status—rebel-held port of "Monti Cristy." The vessel was condemned in a Dominican prize court, but later released ("apparently by an oversight"[23]) with part of her cargo. The owners requested British intervention, through the authorities in Jamaica, to approach the Dominican authorities in order to recover losses. However, in view of the lawful right of the Dominican authorities to impose the blockade, and the consequent obligation upon neutral shipping to respect it, the Colonial Office was informed that the Foreign Secretary, Sir Edward Grey was "of the opinion that there is no evidence before His Majesty's Government which would justify them impressing the claim further on the Dominican Government."[24]

20. Correspondence Respecting the Capture of the "Saxon" by the United States Ship "Vanderbilt" (Feb. 16, 1864), American Civil War 1862–64: Continuous Voyage, etc., *reprinted in* UK Archives File: FO 800/924 (particularly at encls. 2, 5, 6).

21. History of the Negotiations between the British Government and the United States Government in Regard to the Restrictions Placed on British Trade by the Latter 1862–1864, American Civil War 1862–64: Continuous Voyage, etc., *reprinted in* UK Archives File: FO 800/924.

22. James Lorimer, The Institutes of the Law of Nations 148 (1883).

23. Letter 37365/07 from Foreign Office to Under Secretary of State, Colonial Office (Nov. 26, 1907), *in* UK Archives File: C.O. 137/661.

24. *Id.*

A third vignette is significant—and requires longer treatment—because it raises both a simple associated issue (effectiveness), but also the substantially more vexing associated matter of the interaction between (or indeed the separation to be maintained between) Law of War blockade as a measure of belligerency, and the municipally based right to close ports and territorial waters as a police measure while dealing with rebellion. Both of these issues arose—not for the first time, but in a sufficiently clear manner to act as an illustration—during the Spanish blockade declared over several insurgent-held ports in San Domingo during 1864–1865. A series of British vessels taken in prize for breaching the blockade—*Rapid* and *Thomas Pearson* are specifically referred to in correspondence—sought British government assistance in challenging their condemnation. The position of Her Majesty's Government, however, was that they would not interfere in any case "where the parties complaining have wilfully and knowingly run the risks of trading with blockaded ports,"[25] and that in the absence of any "proper defence to offer . . . H.M. Govt cannot be called upon to interfere."[26] The first associated matter, as already noted, was that the effectiveness of the Spanish blockade—a central concern in the legal validity of a Law of War blockade—was ultimately questioned by British authorities.[27] This close adherence to the requirements for a valid blockade was a consistent feature of British legal assessment of belligerent blockades in insurgency and belligerency contexts. On 11 July 1889, for example, the British government decreed (published in *The London Gazette* the following day) that a previously accepted Haitian blockade around insurgent-held ports was no longer to be respected by British vessels as it "had plainly ceased to be effective."[28] Similarly, Britain steadfastly refused to recognize the Chinese Nationalist government blockade in 1949 on the basis that the Chinese Nationalist government "have not (repeat not) at their disposal armed forces which will enable them to exercise a real and effective blockade."[29]

This San Domingo context, however, also furnished legal advice in relation to the distinction to be maintained between a Law of War blockade—which was an incident of, and could not exist outside of, "a state of war," including situations of both tacitly or expressly recognized belligerency—and lawfully imposed restrictions within the three miles of territorial waters around rebel-held ports. This latter form of regulation of shipping, the advice affirmed, was a matter of municipal law and was separate from the de jure application of the Law of War. The advice appears, logically enough, to be based around a distinction between

25. Colonial Secretary Letter (Aug. 3, 1865), *in* UK Archives File: FO 72/1302.

26. Foreign Office Letter (Apr. 29, 1864), *in* UK Archives File: A.D.M. 128/47.

27. *Id.*

28. *Notice*, The London Gazette, July 12, 1889, *reprinted in* UK Archives File: FO 881/5799. On the criterion of "effectiveness," *see generally* Robert Tucker, The Law of War and Neutrality at Sea 288–89 (1955).

29. Cable No. 6508 from Foreign Office to London (June 24, 1949), *in* UK Archives File: A.D.M. 116/5713.

blockade enforcement beyond the territorial sea, and the concurrent, coexistent, but legally distinct right of innocent shipping to operate within the territorial sea. Confusingly, however, the advice then continues by stating that (presumably innocent) British nationals onboard vessels captured within the three mile zone "cannot lawfully be detained or treated as criminals or prisoners of war nor as participating with the insurgents in acts of rebellion."[30] This advice was most curious for there was evidently quite clear advice from as early as 1783 in relation to a French counter-rebellion blockade of the Barbary Coast that indicated a firm British appreciation of the difference between blockade as "a war measure made by a belligerent against an enemy, or a simple measure of municipal police . . . interdicting for a time all intercourse with a possession belonging to the French Crown."[31] The best that can be said of this aspect of the 1889 San Domingo advice is that it is confusing. While raising the important distinction between the Law of War based right of blockade, and the municipal, non-Law of War based right of a state to regulate, and even prohibit, shipping within three miles of rebel-held ports while fighting a rebellion or insurgency (which has no legal implications of blockade, and does not constitute tacit recognition of belligerency), the concurrent advice regarding criminality or the characterization of support to insurgents, when delivered within the territorial sea, is very opaque.

The fourth vignette deals with a similar context in 1949, in that it concerned the closure of territorial waters by Chinese Nationalist authorities (at that time, for the UK, still the recognized Chinese government) in relation to Communist-held ports. By this point, the clear distinction between territorial waters restrictions as a municipal act (a "closure order"), and blockade as a Law of War act, in terms of both legal basis and legal consequences, was better elaborated and more legally nuanced,[32] but still attended by some uncertainty:

> His Majesty's Government are . . . unable to recognise the right of a Government to claim to close by a general order territorial waters and ports in de facto

30. *Id.*

31. Undated Appendix, Two early cases on the right to close ports, *in* UK Archives File: A.D.M. 116/5713.

32. For an example of this nuance, *see* the Foreign Office and Admiralty message traffic concerning the detention of the British vessel *Edith Moller* on August 23, 1949, and again on September 21, 1949, by Nationalist forces in the vicinity of Shanghai. *E.g.*, Admiralty Letter to Foreign Office (Aug. 31 1949), *in* UK Archives File: A.D.M. 116/5752; Admiralty Message 061012Z/September 1949, *in* UK Archives File: A.D.M. 116/5752; Admiralty Message 210823Z/September 1959, *in* U.K. Archives File: A.D.M. 116/5752. It was the view of British authorities that the seizure of *Edith Moller* was "illegal having been made outside Territorial waters." Message 210823Z/September 1949, ¶ 3. The clear implication is that while the British government recognized the regulations and closure regime within the three mile limit—that is, territorial waters—it did not recognize any blockade regime outside territorial waters, and thus any interference outside of three miles was unlawful. This series of incidents provides an interesting case study of interaction between British official and commercial interests in terms of using the vessel as a test case of Nationalist intentions and resolve. For example, in relation to a request

> control of forces in open rebellion against the recognised government of a country . . . a decree purporting to have this effect cannot be regarded as valid, inasmuch as it constitutes an attempt to secure results which it is only legitimate in international law to obtain by the proclamation and effective maintenance of a blockade.[33]

This differentiation between the right of a government to close a port it controls, as distinct from one that is in the hands of insurgents and which it does not control, outside of the Law of War regime of blockade, was itself of significant provenance.[34] Yet, even this appreciation of the issue apparently required further clarification, given that it did not differentiate between blockade and visit and search. On 21 June 1949, for example, the Admiralty felt it necessary to remind authorities that

> [i]f contending sides had belligerent rights, they would have right of visit and search both on high seas and in territorial waters, and right of seizure if contraband were found. But they have not been formally recognised as having belligerent rights. Nor have they attempted to carry out other prerequisites such as defining contraband, establishing Prize Courts etc. . . . Blockade is a separate question. Like visit and search it also cannot be imposed without belligerent rights. In addition blockade to be legal must be effective; so called Nationalist blockade of Shanghai is clearly not effective.[35]

Ultimately, the Admiralty promulgated specific instructions for the Royal Navy in relation to both high seas and territorial waters responses to any attempts to enforce the Nationalist "blockade."[36] These instructions were, in essence, to ignore it in all forms. However, these instructions were then followed by a much

for advice as to whether British authorities ought to prevent *Louise Moller* from attempting to run the blockade (Admiralty Message 060641Z/September 1949, *in* UK Archives File: A.D.M. 116/5752) the official Admiralty response was unequivocal: "Mollers [the shipping company] should not repetition not be dissuaded." Admiralty Message/September 1949, *in* UK Archives File: A.D.M. 116/5752. This situation persisted for some time. In November 1950, the *Shun Lee* was similarly arrested by Nationalist naval forces outside territorial waters. Britain protested the arrest as illegal. The Nationalists claimed that while the arrest had been effected outside three miles, this was because the vessel had been ordered to heave to within three miles but then fled, and it was not until the Nationalist warship was able to catch her, outside three miles, that the arrest could be effected. *See HMS Cardigan Bay*, Report of Proceedings (Dec. 21, 1950), excerpts & enclosures, *in* UK Archive File: A.D.M. 116/5862.

33. Cable No. 763 from Foreign Office to Nanking (July 6, 1949), ¶¶ 1–2, *in* UK Archive File: A.D.M. 116/5713.

34. Two Early Cases on the Right to Close Ports, *in* UK Archives File: A.D.M. 116/5713.

35. Message 211933A/June 1949, ¶¶ 1, 3, *in* UK Archives File: A.D.M. 116/5713.

36. Admiralty Message 241630Z/June 1949, *in* UK Archives File: A.D.M. 116/5713; Admiralty Letter "China" (Aug. 25, 1949), *in* UK Archives File: A.D.M. 116/5713.

disputed Law Officers' opinion (signed by Sir Hartley Shawcross), which appeared to indicate that "it would not be lawful for British warships to connive at breaches of legitimate Chinese regulations."[37] The basis of this view was the Law Officers' conclusion that

> [w]e think that it is established in general that a Government recognised, as is the present Chinese Government, as an existing de jure Government, is entitled as a domestic measure to take steps on territory or within territorial waters under its jurisdiction to deny access to all or any of its ports to foreign shipping for reasons of security or for purposes connected with its own municipal laws such as customs law. . . .
>
> . . . [O]n balance we prefer the view that the de jure Government retains its right, if it can, by force used within its territorial waters to prevent access to ports which have passed into the possession and under the control of insurgents. In our view it cannot be said in the prevailing state of the authorities that if British ships were intercepted and turned back by Chinese National men of war within Chinese territorial waters, there would be any claim for redress against the Chinese Government.[38]

A subsequent, quite excoriating, file note from a senior Admiralty official noted that "it is indeed much to be hoped that we can eventually get the legal position properly stated on [this] narrow point," observing that the Law Officers' position appeared to fly in the face of the "theory of marginal seas" (requiring an ability to exercise effective control from the land).[39] Nevertheless, the view expressed in the Law Officers' opinion appears to have held, and Admiralty instructions were amended. It had only taken between 1783 and 1949 to sort it out.

(ii) State responsibility

A second benefit that accrued to the conflict State from recognizing the formal belligerency of the rebel group, was to be excused from state responsibility, and liability, for damage inflicted upon the nationals, property, and—very importantly—shipping of neutral third states.[40] During the 1821–1825 Greek rebellion against the Ottoman Empire, Britain's formal adoption of neutrality as between the parties was explicitly understood to have immunized The Porte from British claims for damages inflicted by the rebellious Greek party. In a legal advice of 29 May 1823,

37. Admiralty minute, Chinese Closure of Ports and Territorial Waters in Insurgent Hands, (Sept. 9, 1949), ¶ 2, *in* UK Archives File: A.D.M. 116/5713.

38. Hartley Shawcross, Law Officers' Opinion (Sept. 5, 1949), *in* UK Archives File: A.D.M. 116/5713.

39. *Id.*

40. Georg Schwarzenberger, *Human Rights and Guerrilla Warfare*, 1 Israel Y.B. Hum. Rts. 246, 253–54 (1971).

Lushington was clear that "Great-Britain would not, under present circumstances, be justified in demanding from the Turkish Government any reparation or indemnity for any losses British subjects might sustain from the Greeks, though the general rule undoubtedly is, that every state is responsible to foreigners for the acts of its own subjects, though in rebellion."[41] Gary Bass describes the background to this policy thus:

> Canning began tilting toward the Greeks. Officially, he declared Britain to be neutral. This was in itself a slap to the Ottoman government, putting insurgents on the same level as the empire. Then, in March 1823, Canning went a step further: he formally recognised the Greek revolutionaries as belligerents, giving them the protections of the laws and customs of war. Thus British ships now respected the Greeks' naval blockade, rather than treating them as pirates; British merchant vessels were searched by Greek cruisers, who could confiscate enemy property, since Britain was ostensibly neutral.[42]

Jenner's advice to Palmerston—in the context of the conflict in Portugal (1828–1832) between Queen Donna Maria and her uncle Don Miguel (the Regent)[43]—was also uncompromising on this issue. He advised of the liability for "confiscation of the property of British subjects, engaged in transactions, held to be illegal by the Law of Nations, and their liability to be considered, personally as enemies of the Government against which they had taken up Arms; and, as such, to be treated, in the same manner as the subjects of the power under whose banner they had enlisted."[44] Similarly, in 1874, the British Consul in Carthagena requested advice on a call from British subjects that the British government intervene with the government in Madrid in relation to damage to their property sustained during a bombardment of the town. Richard Baggallay, John Holker, and Parker Deane advised that

> As a matter of international right and a subject for diplomatic interference, a government cannot be held responsible for injuries inflicted on the property or persons of foreigners resident in the country by insurgents engaged in armed

41. Dr. Lushington, Legal Advice (May 29, 1823), *in* GREAT BRITAIN AND THE LAW OF NATIONS, 292–93. This particular advice does not appear in the relevant volume (88) of THE LAW OFFICERS' OPINIONS TO THE FOREIGN OFFICE 1793–1860. For a general account of British policy with respect to the Greek rebellion, *see* GARY BASS, FREEDOM'S BATTLE: THE ORIGINS OF HUMANITARIAN INTERVENTION 45–151 (2008).

42. BASS, FREEDOM'S BATTLE: THE ORIGINS OF HUMANITARIAN INTERVENTION, 114.

43. For a brief description of British maritime and other interests at play in this situation, and the "thin-ness" of British neutrality, *see* ANDREW LAMBERT, ADMIRALS 214–21 (2008) (discussing Admiral William Parker, who commanded the Royal Naval force stationed in and around Portugal during this period).

44. Letter from Herbert Jenner to Viscount Palmerston (FO 83/2367) (Aug. 21, 1832), *in* 81 LAW OFFICERS' OPINIONS TO THE FOREIGN OFFICE 1793–1860 277 (Clive Parry ed., 1971).

> hostility to the government, and which injuries the Government had not the power to prevent.[45]

A learned article reporting on U.S. Senate debates regarding "war legislation" in *The National Tribune*, dated 30 July 1903, advised readers that recognition of belligerency would not only "give rise to countless vexations," but also had the effect of "releas[ing] the parent Government from responsibility for acts done by the insurgents."[46] In a series of cases subsequent to the American Civil War, and in analyses by jurists including Wilson and O'Rourke, it was further asserted that even if a recognized belligerent NSAG ultimately failed to establish itself, and the territory and populace at one time under their control reverted to that of the parent state, "the recognising [third] state can hold no one responsible for acts of the revolting community subsequent to the date of recognition of belligerency."[47]

British practice on this point, however, was more inconsistent. McNair, for example, interprets this immunization of the parent state from claims as also arising in cases of insurgency that had not yet been recognized as belligerency. Foreign Office legal opinions on this point, he continues, are characterized by "a marked degree of consistency," allowing him to summarize the basic rule as follows:

> (i) A State on whose territory an insurrection occurs is not responsible for loss or damage sustained by a foreigner unless it can be shown that the Government of that State was negligent in the use of, or in the failure to use, the forces at its disposal for the prevention or suppression of the insurrection.[48]

However, Vernon Harcourt ("Historicus"), writing in 1863, argued that it was only "recognition of insurgents as belligerents [that] gives them quite a sufficient personality to enable foreign powers to address to them remonstrance, and to receive at their hands satisfaction."[49] The Institute of International Law's resolution on damages suffered by aliens in case of riot, insurrection, or civil war, neatly summarized the customary law as understood at 1900:

> certain demands for indemnity may be set aside when they rest on acts occurring after the government of the State to which the injured person

45. Letter from Richard Baggallay, John Holker, and Parker Deane to Earl Derby (FO 83/2379) (May 9, 1874), *in* LAUTERPACHT, RECOGNITION IN INTERNATIONAL LAW, 259.

46. *War Legislation of the Senate*, THE NATIONAL TRIBUNE, July 30, 1903, at 1.

47. Vernon A. O'Rourke, *Recognition of Belligerency and the Spanish War*, 31 AM. J. INT'L L. 398, 401–402 (1937).

48. 2 INTERNATIONAL LAW OPINIONS 244–45 (Lord McNair ed., 1956); *see also* JAMES L. BRIERLY, THE LAW OF NATIONS 80 (1963) ("Further, the act is also advantageous to the state against whom the rebellion is made, since it is relieved thereby of responsibility for the acts of its own insurgents towards other states.").

49. WILLIAM VERNON HARCOURT, LETTERS BY HISTORICUS ON SOME QUESTIONS OF INTERNATIONAL LAW 13 (1863).

> belongs has recognised the insurrectionary government as a belligerent power, and when the injured person has continued to keep his domicile or his habitation on the territory of the insurrectionary government.
>
> As long as the latter is considered as a belligerent power by the government of the person alleged to be injured, the demands may only be addressed . . . to the insurrectionary government and not to the legitimate government.[50]

The same view was consistently taken by the U.S. government. The American minister in London (Adams), for example, noted of the British recognition of Confederate belligerency in May 1861: "At any rate there was one compensation; the act had released the Government of the United States from responsibility for any misdeeds of the rebels towards Great Britain."[51]

At this point, a short case study is warranted, for it assists in grasping the nuance of this rule. In 1950, the British government sent a note to the Spanish government "concerning damages suffered by British subjects during the Spanish Civil War." The Spanish government (of the successful insurgent, Franco) roundly rejected this application, observing that all learned opinion on this issue was to "deny the responsibility of the State and the obligation to compensate the damages suffered by foreign nationals in the course of a civil war"—a legal conclusion "precisely the opposite of that set out in the Embassy's note dated May 6th 1950."[52] DHN Johnson provided a summary of his legal advice on this issue, dated 19 February 1952, and his parsing is valuable for its detail. Warning the reader that "the international law on this subject is far from clear," Johnson advised thus:

> My conclusion is that the Franco Government is responsible for damage caused to British subjects and property by acts done by the Franco forces contrary to the accepted rules of war (eg wanton destruction, pillage) and in certain cases by acts done by the Franco forces in accordance with these rules (eg cases of compensation for lawful requisition); but the Franco Government is not responsible for acts, lawful or unlawful, done by the forces of the Spanish Republican Government, nor for damage caused by the inevitable destruction of war.[53]

50. Resolutions of the Institute of International Law 159–61, (James Brown Scott ed., 1916).

51. *See* Lorimer, The Institutes of the Law of Nations, 150 (quoting Adams's note (June 14, 1861); *see also* Francis Wharton, A Digest of the International Law of the United States 511 (1887).

52. Note Verbale No.190, Spanish Ministry of Foreign Affairs to British Embassy Madrid (Jan. 23, 1951), *in* UK Archives File: FO 371—W.S. 1483/1.

53. Advice by D.H.N. Johnson (Feb. 19, 1952) *in* UK Archives File: FO 371—WS 1483/1. The full 15-page legal advice is found in *Responsibility of the Franco Government for Damage to British Property Occurring during the Spanish Civil War* (Feb. 18, 1952), *in* UK Archives File: FO 371—W.S. 1483/6. The key portion of the legal advice is located in *id.* at 6–11, ¶ 3(iv).

While at least one senior Foreign Office official was concerned that this not be interpreted as "exempt[ing] successful insurgents from liability for the requisitions, wanton destruction or pillage committed by the original government, which the insurgents replace," it was agreed that there was "no reasonable alternative to reviewing the whole corpus of claims, in order to eliminate those which are, as a matter of law, not sustainable and those in which the available evidence is insufficient to justify their renewed presentation."[54]

(iii) Invoking the law of neutrality

A third important benefit accruing to the conflict state as a result of recognizing the belligerency of its adversary NSAG was the ability, as already noted, to deal with neutral third states in accordance with the law of neutrality. During the American Civil War, for example, the U.S. government made a series of representations to Britain regarding the use of Canadian territory as a base for Confederate operational planning and force concentration, and the fitting out of Confederate privateers, characterizing this as "yeild[ing] to them [the Confederates] extraordinary facilities for the abuse of the neutrality adopted by Great Britain."[55]

For some scholars, this was in fact the most important driving force behind the evolution of the doctrine.[56] As the U.S. Supreme Court observed in the 1822 case of *The Santissima Trinidad and the St Sander*,

> The government of the United States has recognized the existence of a civil war between Spain and her colonies, and has avowed a determination to remain neutral between the parties, and to allow to each the same rights of asylum and hospitality and intercourse. Each party is therefore deemed by us a belligerent nation, having, so far as concerns us, the sovereign rights of war, and entitled to be respected in the exercise of those rights. We cannot interfere to the prejudice of either belligerent without making ourselves a party to the contest, and departing from the posture of neutrality. All captures made by each

54. Note from R.S.B. Best to Sir Eric Beckett (Feb. 27, 1952), ¶¶ 3, 6, *in* UK Archives File: FO 371—W.S. 1483/1. Sir Beckett was not keen to invest the staff time required and proposed that the matters be dropped. *See* Note (Feb. 28, 1952), *in* UK Archives File: FO 371—W.S. 1483/1. Ultimately, discussions as to the appropriate course of action continued for some time. *See*, inter alia, the options and policy discussion papers put forward and discussed during 1952, found in UK Archives File: FO 371—W.S. 1483/6.

55. Letter from Mr. Adams (Legation of the United States in London) to Earl Russell (Feb. 12, 1864), *in* A CENTURY OF LAWMAKING FOR A NEW NATION: U.S. CONGRESSIONAL DOCUMENTS AND DEBATES, 1774–1875, U.S. Serial Set, No. 1395, Senate Executive Document 11, 41st Congress, 1st Session, https://memory.loc.gov/cgi-bin/ampage?collId=llss&fileName=1300/1395/llss1395.db&recNum=82.

56. *See, e.g.*, Thomas Franck and Nigel Rodley, *Legitimacy and Legal Rights of Revolutionary Movements with Special Reference to the Peoples' Revolutionary Government of South Viet Nam*, 45 N.Y.U. L. REV. 679, 682 (1970) ("the status of belligerency was developed, not primarily to sanction aid to the forces of change but to permit other states to proclaim their neutrality.").

> must be considered as having the same validity, and all the immunities which may be claimed by public ships in our ports under the law of nations must be considered as equally the right of each, and as such must be recognized by our courts of justice, until Congress shall prescribe a different rule.[57]

Thus international law and domestic law relating to arms sales and other support given to the NSAG by neutral states, and by private citizens of those neutral states, could be called into play by the conflict state.[58] Indeed, the 1871 *Treaty of Washington*, summarizing (at Article VI) the international law rules that the "Alabama Arbitration" was required to apply, established as its first rule that:

> A neutral Government is bound—
>
> First, to use due diligence to prevent the fitting out, arming, or equipping, within its jurisdiction, of any vessel which it has reasonable ground to believe is intended to cruise or to carry on war against a Power with which it is at peace; and also to use like diligence to prevent the departure from its jurisdiction of any vessel intended to cruise or carry on war as above, such vessel having been specially adapted, in whole or in part, within such jurisdiction, to warlike use.[59]

As will be noted in the final section of this chapter, this intersection between neutrality at international law, and domestic laws supposedly imposing "neutrality" obligations upon citizens in their private relations with the belligerents, did not always fully align. The early U.S. privateer cases applying the U.S. Neutrality Act of 1817 (which was shortly thereafter amended in 1818), determined that the legislation at that time only rendered it unlawful, *in the territory of the United States*, to enter into the service of a foreign colony, district, or people. Many privateers employed this loophole to sail as merchants, but to then—once outside the United States—transact to acquire belligerent-entity "nationality" and Letters of Marque.[60] However, the law—after amendment in 1818—thereafter provided grounds for Portuguese and Spanish nationals who had lost vessels and cargo to

57. *The Santissima Trinidad*, 337.

58. *See, e.g.*, McNair, International Law Opinions: Vol. II, 367; Smith, Great Britain and the Law of Nations, 275.

59. Treaty of Washington: Treaty between Her Majesty and the United States of America, UK-U.S., May 8, 1871, https://archive.org/details/cihm_16272.

60. *See*, for example, the case of Captain John Danels, a U.S. national of Baltimore, who sailed as a merchant down to South America, whereupon he then took on Banda Oriental and Buenos Ayres "nationality" and Letters of Marque. He also "sold" his ship *Irresistible* into the Artigan (Banda Oriental) "navy" in order to avoid application of the U.S. Neutrality Act. Fred Hopkins, *For Flag and Profit: The Life of Commodore John Daniel Danels of Baltimore*, 80 Maryland Historical Magazine 392 (1985). A "letter of marque" was the "commission" given to a private vessel and her master, by a recognized authority, which transformed the vessel and her crew into "privateers." *See generally* David Bederman, *Privateering*, Max Planck Encyclopedia of Public International Law, http://opil.ouplaw.com/view/10.1093/law:epil/9780199231690/law-9780199231690-e382?rskey=g5gbiW&result=3&prd=OPIL (updated Oct. 2008).

legitimate prize action by belligerent privateers bearing these Letters of Marque, to later recover some of their losses. This was enabled by virtue of the fact that in undertaking such seizures—which was lawful with respect to the law of nations—these privateers of U.S. citizenship had nevertheless breached U.S. domestic law by taking up belligerent commissions in the first place. Consequently, restitution of the otherwise lawful prize was achievable via a domestic U.S. law and remedy. Reminding the United States of its invocation of neutrality thus ultimately served a useful post facto commercial purpose for these claimants.

The invocation of neutrality also served as a useful political tool for the conflict state, for it was generally agreed that once the conflict state itself recognized the belligerency of its adversary NSAG, it was difficult for third states that had dealings with the NSAG, or with both parties, not to quickly follow suit.[61] As a consequence, the conflict state could employ recognition of belligerency as a way to taint third state support for the NSAG with the legal opprobrium of un-neutral conduct, as opposed to the merely political label of interference.[62]

On this point, and as an aside already prefigured, there are clear indications in British and U.S. practice—in relation to the UK Foreign Enlistment Act[63] and its close U.S. counterpart, the Neutrality Act[64]—that courts in both jurisdictions sometimes struggled with the positions of their governments as third states concerned with insurgencies and belligerencies.[65] As noted earlier in relation to McNair's assessment regarding the point on the insurgency-belligerency spectrum at which the conflict state could disclaim responsibility, this was occasionally crystallized by a politically and practically favorable recognition of the rights of the conflict state under a facsimile of neutrality in insurgency situations near to, but still below the threshold of, recognized belligerencies.[66] Indeed, the debates

61. This was the case for Britain in relation to the American Civil War once the Union had declared a blockade on the Confederacy. *See, e.g.*, Charles Chaney Hyde, 1 International Law Chiefly as Interpreted and Applied by The United States § 49 (1922).

62. This is what, in essence, the United States achieved via the Alabama Claims Arbitration, whereby Britain was required to pay damages of U.S. $15.5 million in respect of what was effectively un-neutral service in relation to the construction, fitting out, and partial crewing of three Confederate warships: *Alabama, Florida*, and *Shenandoah*. *See, e.g.*, Tom Bingham, *The* Alabama *Claims Arbitration*, 54 Int'l Comp. L. Q. 1, 22 (2005). *See also*, as discussed previously, the view of the Republican Spanish Government with respect to discussions around a proposed recognition of Nationalist (Franco) rebel belligerency during the Spanish Civil War.

63. For a contemporaneous comparison of the U.S. and British Foreign Enlistment Acts, *see* James Kent, Kent's Commentary on International Law 268–97 (J. Abdy ed., 2nd ed., 1878). The updated 1870 version of the U.K. Act is at http://www.legislation.gov.uk/ukpga/Vict/33-34/90/contents.

64. On the later history of the U.S. Neutrality Acts, *see* https://history.state.gov/milestones/1921-1936/neutrality-acts.

65. *See generally* G.J. Wheeler, Foreign Enlistment Act, 1870, 33 & 34 Vict. C. 90: with notes of the leading cases on this and the American Act, 33–34 (1896).

66. The U.S. Congress passed many versions of its Neutrality Acts (*see* 18 U.S.C. §§ 956 et seq).

surrounding the passing or updating of both Acts clearly included strong critiques founded upon them being the opposite of "neutrality," in that both Acts applied, it was argued, to in fact limit support to rebels against the Spanish crown by using a corpus of law—neutrality law—that would only otherwise have applied de jure once belligerency was recognized.[67] A series of both prize and piracy trials arising out of the conduct of U.S. (mainly Baltimore-based) privateers sailing under commission of the insurgent entities in South America over the period 1815–1825 was clearly informed by the delicate background fact that public opinion tended to be on the side of the insurgents rather than Spain.[68] In the penumbra around the key piracy case of *United States v. Smith* (1820)[69]—which arose from the South American privateering context, but in which the explicit absence of an insurgent commission after a mutiny led to the case being treated as piracy—sixteen death sentences were at the last opportunity commuted by Secretary of State Adams, with the approval of President Monroe. In part, the sentences were commuted on the basis that there was a high level of sympathy with both the plight of the men in trying to return to the United States after being misled into a mutiny with no subsequent insurgent commission actually in place, and in part because U.S. public opinion was sensitive to the cause of the insurgent republics in the first place, and the men had all previously been serving in duly commissioned insurgent privateer vessels.[70] It is illustrative to refer briefly to some U.S. and British examples.

U.S. courts were particularly sensitive to the intensely political nature of executive decisions to recognize belligerency, accepting them as a legal fact not susceptible to review. However, where the executive was silent, the courts appeared willing to engage in an independent "fact finding" process in order to assess belligerent status for the purposes of determining the legitimacy of a prize claim. In the *La Nereyda*, on appeal to the U.S. Supreme Court (1823),[71] regarding the conduct of a U.S. privateer (Danels), the Court was required to assess whether his fitting out a cruiser and serving under Letters of Marque from both the Buenos Ayres (against Spain) and Banda Oriental (against Portugal) insurgent governments breached the U.S. Neutrality Act. A core issue, as noted, was that if his conduct had indeed been in breach of that statute, then the prize he claimed in respect of

67. Kent, Kent's Commentary on International Law, 275, 283–85.

68. *See, e.g.*, Fred Hopkins, *For Freedom and Profit: Baltimore Privateers in the Wars of South American Independence*, 18 Northern Mariner 93 (2008); Joel Samuels, *The Full Story of* United States v. Smith, *America's Most Important Piracy Case*, 1 Penn. St. J. L. Int'l Aff. 320 (2012); Patrick Browning, *The Gran Para: The Delicate Dance of South American Privateering from Baltimore*, Legal History Publications 56, https://digitalcommons.law.umaryland.edu/mlh_pubs/56.

69. United States v Smith, 18 U.S. 153 (1820).

70. *See, e.g.*, Samuels, *The Full Story of* United States v. Smith, *America's Most Important Piracy Case, 355–60*; Hopkins, *For Freedom and Profit: Baltimore Privateers in the Wars of South American Independence*, 103.

71. La Nereyda, 21 U.S. 108 (1823).

La Nereyda (under Spanish flag, and actually awarded in the prize court of the allied insurgent government of Venezuela) was invalid under U.S. law and restitution to Spain was thus due. However, another key issue considered by the Court was the effect of a statement by President Monroe on the seeming existence of a "civil war" in parts of the Spanish colonial empire. Mr. Hoffman for the Spanish Consul (who was seeking restitution on behalf of Spain) did not disagree that this status could indeed alter the complexion of the case. He argued, rather, that in this specific case, the acknowledgment of civil war did not extend to the Artegan Banda Oriental insurgency, and thus invalidated the privateering commission *ab initio*. As summarized by Justice Story,

> the principles established by cases recently decided in this Court, do not impugn the doctrine contended for, as they occurred in the case of commissions granted by such of the South American provinces as our government, in the opinion of the Court, had recognised to be engaged in a civil war with Spain. That our government, and this Court, having, in no instance whatever, recognised Artegas as engaged in a war with Spain, he is as incompetent to grant commissions of prize, as any other individual in the Spanish provinces.[72]

In his judgment, Justice Story—in the absence of a clear executive statement as to whether a civil war was in train between the Banda Oriental and Spain—looked to the veracity of the prize court as an indicator of validity, finding that the inability of the party claiming ownership rights based on the prize court award, to produce a copy of the order, was fatal to his cause:

> The general usage of maritime nations to proceed in prize causes to adjudication in this manner either by a formal libel or by some equivalent proceeding is so notorious that the omission of it is not to be presumed on the part of any civilized government, which professes to proceed upon the principles of international law.[73]

That is, the effect of formal recognition of belligerency by the executive did alter the legal context. In this case, its very absence, and the absence of a prime indicator (a recognizable prize court order) reduced the original seizure to illegality at both international and U.S. law, and thus allowed the U.S. courts to intervene to return the vessel. However, as Justice Story was quick to note, had the prize court been valid, then the U.S. courts would have had no place in entertaining the suit, except in a very narrow set of circumstances centring around determining initial justiciability:

> where, as in the present case, the capture is made by captors acting under the commission of a foreign country, such capture gives them a right which no

72. *Id.* at 111–12.

73. *Id.* at 161.

> other nation neutral to them has authority to impugn unless for the purpose of vindicating its own violated neutrality. The courts of another nation, whether an ally or a co-belligerent only, can acquire no general right to entertain cognizance of the cause unless by the assent or upon the voluntary submission of the captors. In such a case it is peculiarly proper to show the jurisdiction of the court by an exemplification of the proceedings anterior to the sentence of condemnation. And in all cases it is the habit of courts of justice to require the production of the libel or other equivalent document to verify the nature of the case and ascertain the foundation of the claim of forfeiture as prize.[74]

Where, however, the executive had made a clear statement, the court in general applied this in its assessment of consequences. For example, President Cleveland's several proclamations in relation to the Cuban insurgency of 1895–1898[75] recognized Cuban insurgency but specifically refused to recognize belligerency. Yet he also proclaimed that U.S. citizens should nevertheless "abstain . . . from doing any of the acts prohibited by the neutrality laws."[76] This direction was closely followed by the U.S. Supreme Court—not least in *The Three Friends* (1897), where the court, dealing with such a situation, clearly indicated,

> We are thus judicially informed of the existence of an actual conflict of arms in resistance of the authority of a Government with which the United States are on terms of peace and amity, although acknowledgement of the insurgents as belligerents by the political department has not taken place; and it cannot be doubted that, this being so, the act in question [the *Neutrality Act*] is applicable.[77]

The first iterations of the British Foreign Enlistment Act were primarily focused upon Jacobean and French threats, and were inconsistently employed in relation to the colonial wars of independence against Spain in South America in the first quarter of the nineteenth century. Indeed, a string of opinions by Foreign Office legal advisers over the period 1813–1824 (Britain commencing recognition of the full independence of many of the former colonies from 1825[78]) tend to emphasise, time and again, that the original Acts were difficult to apply and did little to restrain British citizens from commercial dealings with, and support of, insurgent governments, including recruiting and even fighting for them.[79] During

74. *Id.* at 169.

75. John Bassett Moore, 1 A Digest of International Law § 74 (1906).

76. *Id.*

77. The Three Friends, 166 U.S. 1, 65–66 (1897).

78. Britain and the independence of Latin America, 1812–1830 12–17 (Charles Webster ed., 1938); William Kaufmann, British Policy and the Independence of Latin America 1804–1828, 128–81 (1951).

79. *E.g.*, Advice by Christopher Robinson (Jan. 27, 1817), *in* 79 Law Officers' Opinions to The Foreign Office 1793–1860 11 (Clive Parry ed., 1971) (discussing one "Mr Brown," who

the American Civil War, the relevance of the Foreign Enlistment Act was on several occasions noted in legal advice touching upon colonial British jurisdiction over Confederate sailors and privateers of British nationality ("the defence that they were in the service of then Confederate States involves (at the very least) an admission that they violated the *Foreign Enlistment Act*"[80]), who for whatever reason found themselves within British jurisdiction, or were present on-board Confederate vessels currently in British ports.[81]

The British Foreign Enlistment Act was judicially tested in *The Alexandra* (1864), and found wanting.[82] This case concerned a vessel suspected of being fitted out in Liverpool for the Confederate States, which was then seized under the Foreign Enlistment Act. The alleged equipping of the vessel by British nationals was thus for a recognized belligerent party (Britain having recognized the Confederate belligerency via a declaration of neutrality on 13 May 1861).[83] The prosecution failed, partly because the Act was considered to be arbitrary and incomplete in scope. As the court at first instance asked, why the special attention on ships? Why did the Act permit sale of munitions to the rebel party, but not the sale of a vessel that might later be fitted out as a warship?[84] The key difficulty however appears to have been that there were practical and political divergences between the use of certain terms in national laws, and use of the same legal terms of art in international discourse. Thus while the operation of neutrality at international law could only arise, de jure, upon the recognition of belligerency, the British Foreign Enlistment Act and U.S. Neutrality Acts were generally designed for domestic use in an attempt to prevent citizens from enlisting with, or supplying war material to, insurgents as equally as recognized belligerents.[85] Indeed, the same divergences

had been fighting with the Buenos Ayres insurgent maritime force against Spain, and who had been captured by Spain); *see also* Advice of Robinson, Shepherd, and Gifford (Aug. 25, 1817), *in* 79 LAW OFFICERS' OPINIONS, 80 (concluding that the Foreign Enlistment Act did not readily apply to British subjects serving in the military forces of an insurgent power as it was directed at those serving in the military forces of foreign princes, states, or potentates).

80. Legal Advice of Roundell Palmer, Robert Collier, and Robert Phillimore to Earl Russell (Jan. 27, 1861), *in* UK Archives File: FO 881/2068, item 12, enclosure 2.

81. E.g., Letter from Edward Cardwell to Sir C. Darling (Apr. 26, 1863), *in* UK Archives File: FO 881/2068, item 17.

82. Attorney-General v. Sillem and Others (1863), 176 Eng. Rep. 295. This case later followed, as Lord Bingham noted, a "tortuous" path on appeal, which ultimately left the decision in place. *See* TOM BINGHAM, LIVES OF THE LAW: SELECTED ESSAYS AND SPEECHES: 2000–2010 23–24 (2011).

83. *See, e.g.*, Admiralty War Staff (Trade Division): The American Civil War 1861–1862—Orders Issued to the United States Navy and Other Subjects Relating to the Blockade of the Southern Ports, *in* UK Archives File: FO 800/924; Harcourt, 330–31.

84. Attorney-General v. Sillem and Others, 311.

85. It is interesting to note that the Foreign Enlistment Act was, much later, pressed into service by the Admiralty in an attempt to dissuade serving and retired Royal Navy personnel who

in use of terms of art also bedeviled judicial dealings with "piracy" as a marine insurance issue in rebellion-insurgency-belligerency contexts.

There were, consequently, positive effects for the conflict state of the imposition of neutrality upon third states, particularly in terms of limiting the ability of those states to support the NSAG. Yet as has been noted in the case examples, there was also a concurrent negative perspective on the consequences (from the conflict state point of view) of granting recognition of belligerency to an adversary rebel group. This concern centered upon whether such recognition could likewise legitimize interference by other states unconcerned at entering into an adversarial Law of War relationship with the conflict state. This perspective is well expressed in a note sent by the British Foreign Secretary, Viscount Halifax, to the British representative in Barcelona, recording the outcomes of a discussion with the (Republican) Spanish Ambassador in London on 14 December 1938:

> Before he left, the Ambassador again emphasised the extreme anxiety of his Government in regard to any possible proposal to grant General Franco belligerent rights. To do this, quite apart from its immediate consequences, would destroy any chance there might be of making progress with any such reasonable solution as he had sketched. We should, in fact, be granting belligerent rights to the Italians and Germans and there would, of course, be no inducement left on the side of moderation.[86]

The political point is clear: belligerency would offer a sheen of legitimacy to existing Italian and German support to the Nationalists.[87] The legal point, however,

were sympathetic to the Republican cause from joining the Republican navy during the Spanish Civil War. *See, e.g.*, Minute M05722/36 (Dec. 23, 1936), *in* UK.Archives File A.D.M. 116/6315 (indicating "[t]hat Foreign Office and Home Office should be asked to consider the possibility of instituting proceedings under the Foreign Enlistment Act against the Holborn communist organisation, and any other similar organisations or ratings intending to proceed to Spain which may be unearthed by M.I.5.").

86. W. 16591/83/41 (No.446) Confidential Note from Viscount Halifax to Mr. Stevenson (Dec. 14, 1938), ¶ 7, *in* UK Archives File: A.D.M. 116/6315.

87. One interesting aspect of the diplomatic wrangles concerning the Non-Intervention Agreement, and the legal nature of support to Franco (from, in this case, Italy) is manifested in correspondence between the British and Republican Spanish governments in relation to Italian warships operating with Nationalist forces. In a note dated January 12, 1939, the Spanish Ambassador "denounced the naval assistance which the Italian Government are affording the Spanish rebels, making it possible, by means of sales or transfers, for units of the Italian fleet to collaborate with the rebel naval forces. As usual these denunciations have been totally ignored and have not had the least result or consequence." Note Received in Foreign Office Signed by P. (Pablo) Azcarate (Jan. 12, 1939), *in* UK Archive File: A.D.M. 116/6315. The note then cited the examples of four destroyers and two submarines, described in the December 1938 edition of *Janes Fighting Ships List* (a UK publication) as, variously, "purchased from Italy by Spanish Nationalist Government' or "sold to Spanish Nationalist Government [by Italy]." *Id.* The note concludes: "These sales constitute further examples of the many open and declared violations, on the part of the Italian Government, of the Non-Intervention Agreement. It is impossible to

is that the standard consequence of recognition of belligerency for third states—neutrality—was the expectation, and German and Italian non-neutrality in support of Franco would thus formalize, to the detriment of the Republican government, the international nature of that civil war.

D. THE NSAG PERSPECTIVE

From the perspective of the conflict state, and depending upon the purposes sought, there were clear advantages to recognizing the belligerency of an adversary NSAG. Of course, the quid pro quo was that the legal benefits of such recognition would equally flow to the NSAG. However, not all of these benefits necessarily paralleled those accruing to the conflict state. In order to assess the scope and utility of the doctrine on recognition of belligerency from the perspective of the adversary NSAG, I will examine seven particularized sets of legal consequences: the functionally limited (but significant) international legal recognition that followed from the status; the application of Law of War rules to both NSAG and conflict state conduct; the consequences for captured NSAG fighter status and treatment, that is, the application of the PW regime de jure; the associated according of combatant status; the consequences of recognition of belligerency for NSAG prize courts and other fiscal matters; the requirements for NSAG compliance with treaties; and the effects of belligerent status upon the application of NSAG laws.

(i) Functionally limited recognition

For the NSAG, recognition of belligerency brought with it a limited international status—both temporally and in terms of scope—and afforded access to similarly circumscribed international legal rights. Lorimer called the recognition of belligerency "the recognition of the inchoate State as a jural claimant for separate recognition—that is to say, the acknowledgement of its right to contend for recognition."[88] But this recognition was not, he went on to clarify, in any way a judgment "either on the merits of the claim or the probability of its ultimate vindication."[89] Similarly, Harcourt argued that recognition of belligerency was "not a liberty during the pendency of an actual struggle to speculate on the result, or to assume the probability of the ultimate failure of the ancient Sovereign,"[90] but rather was a limited first step short of, and different to, recognition of independence. As he stated, "First of all, there is the recognition of the belligerency; and secondly, if their independence should be established, there will be recognition of

believe that at least the British Government, whose naval intelligence service has the reputation of being one of the most reliable and effective in the world, did not have knowledge of them." *Id.*

88. Lorimer, The Institutes of the Law of Nations, 141.

89. *Id.* at 142.

90. Harcourt, Letters by Historicus on Some Questions of International Law, 8.

independence. But those are two different things, and stand on a wholly different footing."[91] Any recognition of "the inchoate independence of the insurgents" while "the contest is not absolutely or permanently decided," Harcourt concluded, "is a hostile act towards the sovereign State which the latter is entitled to resent as a breach of neutrality and friendship."[92] Stowell similarly described recognition of belligerency as juridically distinct from recognition of independence, but often understood as a step along that path. However, the fact that the two forms appeared in some analyses as points along the same status spectrum meant that it was vital that they be understood distinctly and separately. As Stowell continued,

> Recognition [of belligerency], when justified by the pressing need of the state to deal with the de facto authorities is not interference. It is merely the exercise of an undoubted right. But any state that goes beyond the limits of what is required to secure the adequate protection of its immediate interest is guilty of a violation of the sovereignty of a sister state.[93]

Similarly, as Judge Daly observed in the context of the American Civil War, recognition of belligerency and recognition of independence were quite distinct, and "one may exist without the other, and by exchanging prisoners, therefore, we concede nothing and admit nothing, except what everybody knows, that actual war exists, and that as a Christian people we mean to carry it on according to the usages of civilised nations."[94] British legal advice to colonial governors as to the marks of respect to be paid to Confederate warships provides a technical, but most telling, illustration of the scope of rights conferred by recognition of belligerency as compared to full recognition:

> Her Majesty's Government have had occasion to consider whether salutes can properly be exchanged between forts in Her Majesty's Colonies and vessels of war of the Confederate States.
>
> I have to instruct you that, in case the Commander of any such vessel should offer you a salute, it will be your duty to decline it, and that if the salute should be fired without having been previously offered, it should not be returned.
>
> In each case the Commander of the vessel should be informed that the reason for declining to receive or return such salutes is that the Confederate States have not been acknowledged by this country otherwise than as belligerents.[95]

Almost a century later, British advice in relation to the Nationalist-Communist Chinese conflict as at 1956 was similarly clear and succinct: "If we recognised a

91. Harcourt, *The Rights and Duties of Neutrals in Time of War: Part I*, 319.

92. Harcourt, 9.

93. Stowell, Intervention in International Law, 348.

94. The Daly Letter (1861).

95. Letter of Downing Street (Jan. 11, 1864), *in* UK Archives File: FO 881/2068, item 11.

state of belligerency we should merely be saying that the hostilities waged were of such a character and scope as to entitle the parties to be treated as belligerents engaged in a war in a sense ordinarily attached to the term in international law. Our action would not involve recognising the nationalists as a Government."[96]

Thus the status and rights afforded to a recognized belligerent were expressly limited to the purposes of the conflict only. However, this category of rights and status was wider than simply the right to have its conduct assessed and characterized in accordance with the international Law of War. For Lawrence, the grant encompassed "all the rights and all the obligations of an independent state so far as the war is concerned, but no further."[97] Edward Hertslet, Foreign Office librarian and adviser on treaty affairs, in a memorandum for the Foreign Office dated 3 May 1875, quoted the apparently orthodox view as follows:

> Professor Bernard describes the 'recognition of belligerency'[98] as entitling the contending parties, in respect of the neutrals, to all those exceptional rights and powers with which Sovereign States at war with each other are clothed by International law; adding, that since those rights can only be regularly exercised by means of a certain known machinery, the recognition of them draws after it a recognition of the machinery.[99]

In terms of time, the grant was for the duration of the civil war only. If the NSAG lost, the grant ended (as was the effect of the Confederate surrender upon the *Shenandoah*'s commission, as noted in Chapter 2); if it won, then it most likely became the state.[100] Thus the recognized belligerent could not send or receive ambassadors to third states,[101] and such communications as were necessary were to be "strictly confined to matters affecting the private and business interests of the nationals of both parties."[102] Likewise, the status of its communications with the parent (conflict) state—even to discuss the terms of surrender—remained informal and unofficial.[103] Nor could the NSAG negotiate

96. Belligerency in the Formosa Strait: Memorandum by the Foreign Office (Feb. 1956), ¶ 3, *in* UK Archives File: FO 371/120939.

97. T.J. Lawrence, The Principles of International Law 78 (1910).

98. Bernard, A Historical Account of the Neutrality of Great Britain during the American Civil War, 114–17.

99. Edward Hertslet, Memorandum on the Recognition of Belligerent rights between Contending Parties, Foreign Office, (May 3, 1875), *in* UK Archives File: FO 881/2897 (parts of this summary by Hertslet are direct quotes form Bernard).

100. Great Britain and the Law of Nations, 262, 325.

101. Lorimer, The Institutes of the Law of Nations, 143.

102. Hershey, The Essentials of International Public Law and Organization, 204.

103. U.S. Secretary of State Seward (Mar. 13, 1865), *in* Wharton, A Digest of the International Law of the United States, 514.

treaties,[104] although there is some recognition of a right to enter into limited commercial arrangements with third states.[105] The Dutch, for example—albeit much to Britain's fury—provided loans to the American party during the War of Independence, covered by what was described as a "treaty."[106] Similarly, it was accepted that the Confederacy, during the American Civil War, "could float loans, purchase war materials, and contract the building of ships not fitted for war."[107] Even in the event of the belligerent NSAG's ultimate failure, contracts raised in its currency were nevertheless to be respected after the conflict for, at the time such contracts were made, "[t]o the extent, then, of actual supremacy, however unlawfully gained, in all matters of government within its military lines, the power of the insurgent government cannot be questioned."[108] The NSAG could also—as an incident of its prosecution of the war—engage in some wider economic activities, such as floating bonds.[109] Indeed, there was some pressure upon the British government, from both Polish Nationalists and British businessmen, to conclusively indicate whether it would recognize Polish insurgent belligerency in 1863, for this was a prerequisite for the loans being sought by the Polish Nationalist "government."[110] As Henryk Wereszycki explained,

> Prince Czartoryski, the national government's authorized agent, demanded belligerent rights for the insurgents. Poles needed money to buy arms. They wanted to put bonds on foreign markets, especially in London; this could only be done after the insurgents had been recognized as a belligerent party, since otherwise the bonds would be considered invalid.[111]

Additionally, it was clearly understood that a recognized belligerent NSAG could establish and maintain Prize Courts as an incident of their right to

104. Lawrence, The Principles of International Law, 78.

105. Harcourt, Letters by Historicus on Some Questions of International Law, 35.

106. Memorandum of Instances in which Belligerents Have Enforced the Right of Searching Neutral Vessels on the High Seas for the Persons or Property of their Enemies, 1780–1855, *in* UK Archives File: FO 881/1014, item 1.

107. Howard Jones, Blue and Gray Diplomacy: A History of Union and Confederate Foreign Relations 47 (2011).

108. Thorington v. Smith, 75 U.S. 1, 11 (1868) ("It seems to follow as a necessary consequence from this actual supremacy of the insurgent government as a belligerent within the territory where it circulated, and from the necessity of civil obedience on the part of all who remained in it, that this currency must be considered in courts of law in the same light as if it had been issued by a foreign government, temporarily occupying a part of the territory of the United States.").

109. Hershey, The Essentials of International Public Law and Organization, 204.

110. John F. Kutolowski, *Mid-Victorian Public Opinion, Polish Propaganda, and the Uprising of 1863*, 8 J. Brit. Stud. 86, 95 (2014).

111. Henryk Wereszycki, *Great Britain and the Polish Question in 1863*, 50 Eng. Hist. Rev. 78, 100 (1935).

implement blockade and exercise visit and search.[112] Therefore, as Bernard records,

> The sentences . . . of [recognised belligerent NSAG] Prize Courts sitting within the territory occupied by a population in revolt and under the authority of a Government established there—commissions issued by that Government—the flag which it has chosen—are accepted and recognised within the jurisdiction of the neutral, as emanations and symbols not, indeed, of the sovereignty to which the Government lays claim, but of that substantial though temporary and precarious power which it possess in fact.[113]

A most eloquent summative description of the scope of the grant, informed by U.S. Supreme Court cases such as *United States v Palmer*,[114] is furnished by Puente thus:

> Persons or vessels employed in the service of a self-declared government, thus acknowledged by the United States to be maintaining its separate existence by war, must be permitted to prove the fact of their being actually employed in such service, by the same testimony which would be sufficient to prove that such persons or vessels were employed in the service of an acknowledged State. But the seal of such unacknowledged government cannot be permitted to prove itself . . . and the fact that such persons or vessels are so employed may be proved without proving the seal.[115]

Yet even though the potential grant of legal personality was quite limited in nature, it was nevertheless highly prized. The legal, financial, and political benefits sought by the Poles in 1863 have been noted previously. Another, more recent case in point is the importance placed upon recognition of Spanish Nationalist belligerency by Franco during the Spanish Civil War. Indeed, this option was floated as one component of a draft general plan "providing for the withdrawal of foreign volunteers from Spain, for the grant in certain circumstances of belligerent rights to the two parties in Spain, and for the observation of the Spanish frontiers by land and sea."[116] The then-recognized (Republican) Spanish government responded sharply against this proposal:

> [The Republican Spanish government] must not, however, allow this opportunity to pass without reiterating its ruling criterion, which is entirely opposed

112. *See, e.g.*, Foreign Office Law Officers' Opinion on "Consequences of the recognition of belligerency" (Feb. 1956), ¶ 2(d), *in* UK Archives File: FO 371/120939.

113. Bernard, A Historical Account of the Neutrality of Great Britain during the American Civil War, 115.

114. United States v. Palmer, 16 U.S. 610 (1818).

115. Julius I. Puente, International law as Applied to Foreign States, 37 (1928).

116. Confidential Note (W 10089/83/41) from the Spanish Ambassador in London (Azcarate) to Viscount Halifax in the Foreign Office (July 26, 1938), ¶ 1, *in* UK Archives File: A.D.M. 116/6315.

> to any recognition of belligerency, whether limited with a greater or a lesser degree, in favour of the Spanish rebels. First, because there can be no possible doubt that foreign assistance, and foreign assistance exclusively, has made it possible for the rebels to prolong the rebellion. And secondly, because the condition for any recognition of belligerency, which it has always been necessary to fulfil, is the strictest abstention from the deliberate employment of war methods contrary to the principles of humanity.[117]

For Franco, however, recognition of Nationalist belligerency was "both essential and fundamental" to any implementation of an offer he had made to "withdraw immediately 10,000 foreign volunteers."[118] Franco informed Francis Hemming (who was compiling a report for the governments of Britain, France, Germany, Italy, and Portugal) that "should it prove impossible for the [Non-Intervention] Committee to give General Franco satisfaction on the question of belligerent rights, little advantage would be served by an examination of the administrative and technical aspects of the other portions of the Committee's plan."[119] Franco's desire for the Nationalist rebels to gain the "juridical personality" afforded by recognition of their belligerency clearly permeates the Hemming Report.[120] Hemming's conclusions were, inter alia,

> (1) General Franco considers that the conditions under which his Administration is conducted—an Administration which covers the greater part of the territory of Spain—gives him an unquestionable right under international law to be accorded belligerent rights. . . .
> (2) The opinions summarised in Conclusion (1) above are so strongly held by General Franco that from his point of view no compromise is possible, the question of belligerent rights being regarded by him as a question of fundamental importance involving Spanish national dignity and Spanish national honour.[121]

(ii) Application of the Law of War

As noted previously, the primary specific benefit for the NSAG—whether actual or hortatory—was the required de jure application of the Law of War as

117. *Id.*, ¶ 16.

118. Report by Mr. Francis Hemming on his Mission to National Spain (Nov. 17, 1938), ¶¶ 71–72, *in* UK Archives File: A.D.M. 116/6315.

119. *Id.*, ¶ 73.

120. *E.g.*, *id.*, ¶¶ 74–81, 165–70, 222.

121. *Id.*, ¶ 222(1)–(2).

between the conflict parties in the hope of reducing the levels of barbarity employed in prosecuting the conflict. One of the most significant and important consequences for the NSAG was thus the treatment of its captured fighters. No longer mere municipal criminals, they would now be the beneficiaries of "combatant immunity" for battlefield conduct according with the Law of War.[122] This very important concession raises the direct question as to whether the doctrine actually incorporated a specific change of status for the NSAG (from criminal, to combatant), or for its acts (from criminal, to legitimate under the Law of War). In the *Lieber Code*, for example, the precise legal status of partisan forces associated with the military of a state, as differentiated from those who were equivalently organized, but who had no link to a legitimating sovereignty, was critical to considerations linked to combatant immunity and PW status.[123] This is of particular importance when assessing the criminality of a use of force by NSAG fighters, the benefit for the insurgents being that once they were recognized as belligerents they escaped the legal vacuum into which rebels against the sovereign were traditionally cast in terms of the severe battlefield methods, and subsequent reprisals (often veiled under the guise of martial law, as noted in Chapter 2), which the sovereign could employ against them. This change in legal status followed from the doctrine's alteration of the status of the rebels (the NSAG), and as a consequence of that change in status, its creation of an obligation upon the conflict state to now fight those rebels according to the "standard" rules of the Law of War as applicable on an interstate basis. Dana, in the 1866 Wheaton, argued that recognition of belligerency certainly wrought a change in legal status for members of the recognized NSAG insofar as neutral third states were concerned:

> If it is a war, the insurgent cruisers are to be treated by foreign citizens and officials, at sea and in port, as lawful belligerents; if it is not a war, those cruisers are pirates and may be treated as such. . . . Within foreign jurisdiction, if it is a war, acts of the insurgents in the way of preparation and equipments for hostility may be breaches of neutrality laws, while if it is not war, they do not come into that category, but under the category of piracy or of crimes by municipal law.[124]

122. *See, e.g.*, Jordan Paust, et al, International Criminal Law: Cases and Materials 678, 685, 698 (4th ed. 2013); U.S. Army, F.M. 27–10, The Law of Land Warfare 9, ¶ 11(a) (1956); Stephen Neff, War and the Law of Nations: A General History ch. 7 (2005).

123. Instructions for the Government of Armies of the United States in the Field (Lieber Code), http://www.icrc.org/ihl.nsf/FULL/110?OpenDocument (The Union treated Confederate soldiers (and ultimately mariners) as PW.); *see also* Quinta Jurecic, *The Lieber Code*, Lawfare (July 23, 2015), https://www.lawfareblog.com/throwback-thursday-lieber-code.

124. Wheaton, Elements of International Law, §23 n. 15, 29–32.

This passage, as Wharton notes, was cited with approval by Sir Alexander Cockburn in his Alabama Claims Arbitration opinion, as having "been nowhere more fully and ably, or more fairly, stated."[125]

The accepted position in international law thus unambiguously held that the armed forces of NSAGs with recognized belligerent status could access the rights of, as well as require others to obey the obligations of, the Law of War. Importantly, these invocations bound not only the adversary parties, but neutral third states as well in their dealings with the parties to the conflict. In an advice relating to the Cretan insurrection of 1867, for example, John Karslake, Charles Selwyn, and Robert Phillimore were explicit that if rebels were recognized as belligerents, it was permissible for those rebels to commission privateers, for they could, "according to the general principles of International Law resort to this means of self-defence and of aggression against their enemy." If, however, they were not entitled to "the status of belligerents" then such privateers "would be liable to be treated generally as pirate vessels, and especially to be treated as such, if they should attempt to interfere in any way with the vessels of any foreign State."[126] Lawrence neatly summarized the legal consequence for the NSAG: "Its armies are lawful belligerents, not banditti; its ships of war are lawful cruisers, not pirates; the supplies it takes from invaded territory are requisitions, not robbery; and at sea its captures made in accordance with maritime law are good prize, and its blockades must be respected by neutrals."[127] As late as 1956, in her advice on recognition of belligerency as an option in relation to the conflict between Nationalist Chinese and Communist Chinese forces, Gutteridge noted that the obligation on the third state was "to detain, and if necessary, to intern members of the armed forces of the contesting parties who come within their territory"[128]—a clear invocation of the duties of a neutral state under the Law of War.

125. Wharton, A Digest of the International Law of the United States, 519. For an excellent summary and analysis of the Alabama Claims Arbitration, *see* Bingham, 22. The ACA was referred to by many at the time as "the Geneva Tribunal."

126. Advice of John Karslake, Charles Selwyn, and Robert Phillimore to Lord Stanley (FO 83/2396) (Aug. 14, 1867), *in* Great Britain and the Law of Nations, 262–65.

127. Lawrence, The Principles of International Law, 78; *see also* International Law Institute, *Rights and Duties of Foreign Powers as Regards the Established and Recognised Governments in Case of Insurrection*, art. 6 (1900) ("A government which has recognized its revolting nationals as belligerents cannot consider it a cause of complaint against a third Power that it receives those armed insurgents who take refuge on its territory kindly, disarming them and interning them until the end of hostilities. Consequently, it is powerless to object if its own soldiers, refugees in the same territory, are disarmed and interned. It is, moreover, liable for indemnity only for the support of its own troops.").

128. Gutteridge, Consequences of the Recognition of Belligerency, ¶ 3(f).

(iii) Prisoner of War status

Did international law require neutral third states to treat the forces of both parties who happened into that third state's control in the same manner as it would require the third state to treat the forces of two contending states? This was a question that would be informed by the law of neutrality as well as the Law of War. In other words, were neutral third states required to treat captured NSAG fighters as PWs under the Law of War? Certainly, Hershey expressly stated that NSAG combatants were to be treated as "prisoners of war instead of as traitors and pirates."[129] Zorgbibe similarly felt secure in writing, in 1971, that

> Most authors, however, have laid stress on the sacrifices imposed upon itself by the established government. In particular, they have contrasted the recognition of belligerency and the application of penal law. When ties of allegiance have been shed, the captured insurgent is no longer subject to trial but is a prisoner of war.[130]

The weight of logic and practice also indicates that this was the case. First, the humanitarian imperative—that both sides would apply the Law of War so as to reduce barbarity—was clearly understood to be reciprocal. As Daly observed in his letter of 1861 on Confederate privateers, and Lauterpacht reiterated in 1947, "If the lawful government were to claim belligerent rights whilst denying them to the insurgents, such illogical and one-sided conduct would invalidate its continued recognition as a belligerent."[131] One of the most evident signs of a reduction in barbarity was considered to be the treatment of rebels as legitimate combatants, thus removing from the conflict state's arsenal the occasionally employed punishment of summary execution, but also the more frequently employed sanction of execution of captured "rebels" or "pirates" after truncated summary proceedings.[132]

Second, state practice in those situations where recognition of belligerency was granted by the conflict state to the adversary NSAG was clear that legitimate NSAG forces were treated as PWs, as was the case, noted previously, in

129. Hershey, The Essentials of International Public Law and Organization, 202.

130. Charles Zorgbibe, *Sources of the Recognition of Belligerent Status*, 17 Int'l Rev. Red Cross 111, 116 (1977); *see also* Daoud Khairallah, Insurrection Under International Law, with Emphasis on the Rights and Duties of Insurgents 196 (1973) ("When rebel forces are recognized as belligerent by the lawful government, they gain, until the end of the hostilities, the status of prisoners of war in international conflicts with all its privileges. They are also under an obligation to give the same treatment to captured government forces."); *id.* at 197–210 (case studies of treatment of captured NSAG fighters in Algeria, Congo, Yemen, and Vietnam); G.I.A.D. Draper, *Humanitarian Law and Internal Armed Conflicts*, 13 Ga. J. Int'l & Comp. L. 253, 258 (1983).

131. Lauterpacht, Recognition in International Law, 200.

132. On piracy, for example, *see* The Piracy Act 1698 (11 Will 3 c 7) ("An Act for the more effectual suppression of Piracy"); The Offences at Sea Act, 1806 (46 Geo. 3, c. 54.) (Imperial) ("An Act for the more speedy Trial of Offences committed in distant Parts upon the Sea.").

the American Civil War.[133] Indeed, after the surrender of Lee's and Johnston's Confederate armies in April 1865, U.S. General Grant determined that if the force commanded by General Smith—the single remaining sizable Confederate force in the field—should continue to fight, its members would not be afforded PW status ("he and his men are not entitled to the consideration due an acknowledged belligerent"[134]). They were no longer to be considered as recognized belligerents because their "ostensible Government" had ceased to exist. "Theirs is the condition," Grant instructed, "of outlaws, making war against the only Government having an existence over the territory where war is now being waged."[135]

Third, there are some statements of law and policy on the obligation of the conflict state government to treat as PWs any U.S. or British nationals captured while fighting with a belligerent NSAG. The U.S. view—although it is unclear as to whether the legal basis for the statement was full formal independence, or ongoing recognition of belligerency—is encapsulated in an 1842 memorandum from U.S. Secretary of State Webster to the U.S. Minister in Mexico (Thompson) regarding the Texan war of independence from Mexico. Having noted that Texas had apparently maintained an independent government for several years (the United States having effectively recognized Texan belligerency in 1832 via adoption of neutrality as between the parties[136]), Webster then went on to assert that

> If, under these circumstances, any citizen of the United States in whose behalf this Government has a right on any account or to any extent to interfere, should, on a charge of having been found with an armed Texan force acting in hostility to Mexico, be brought to trial and punished as for a violation of the municipal laws of Mexico, or as being her subject engaged in rebellion, after his release has been demanded by this government, consequences of the most serious character would certainly ensue.[137]

There are official British documents that make this point even more unambiguously. One example is the advice of Christopher Robinson to Lord Canning on 1 April 1823. This advice concerned representations by a British woman regarding her son, who had apparently been serving in a rebel vessel (*Heroine*) in the service

133. *See, e.g.*, Cushman K. Davis, A Treatise on International Law Including American Diplomacy 108 (2018) ("it was never heard during the war between the United States and the Confederate States that any Englishman or other foreigner landing in either the north or the south for the purpose of taking service in the army of either came under any code of murder or assassination.").

134. Lester Nurick and Roger W. Barrett, *Legality of Guerrilla Forces under the Laws of War*, 40 Am. J. Int'l L. 563, 573 (1946).

135. *Id.*

136. U.S. Secretary of State Forsyth to Mexican Minister Gorostiza (Sept. 20, 1836), *in* Moore, 1 A Digest of International Law, 176–77.

137. U.S. Secretary of State Webster to the U.S. Minister to Mexico (Thompson) (Apr. 15, 1842), *in* Moore, 1 A Digest of International Law, 178.

of a rebellious South American colony. He had been captured by a Portuguese warship and taken to Lisbon for detention. Robinson's opinion was that the British government could make representations on behalf of British subjects. However, he cautioned, "But if the lad has been serving on board a vessel bearing a commission against Portugal or exercising present hostilities against Portuguese ships, he will be subject to be detained as a prisoner of war."[138]

A second example relates to the rebellion by Malagasy forces (which counted among its fighters both local Hovas and British subjects) against French forces asserting a French protectorate over Madagascar. Reports of a French policy of executing any British subjects who were captured serving in the Malagasy forces had agitated concern in London, and on 16 April 1895, Robert Reid and Frank Lockwood (as Foreign Office legal advisers) were asked for an opinion by the War Office. The first two of the three questions were directly on point:

> 1. Whether the French authorities are entitled to discriminate between British subjects serving in the armed forces of the Malagasy Government and Hovas in the like service, to the prejudice of the former.
> 2. Whether the French authorities are entitled to shoot British subjects serving in the Hova forces whom they may take prisoners in open fight during the pendency of the present hostilities in Madagascar.[139]

The legal advice was unequivocal. First, because the fighting between the Malagasy and French forces was more than "merely a civil brawl, or a local popular tumult," the French were no longer able to "legitimately treat persons who take part in it as rioters and murderers." Second, although Britain had yet to make a formal announcement of recognition of belligerency on the part of the Malagasy, this was because no British interest had yet been engaged by the revolt (a precondition to making such a declaration). This did not, however, alter the requirement for France, and the Malagasy forces, to comply with the Law of War as the conflict was clearly a civil war of belligerency status:

> the duties imposed upon belligerents by international law are in no sense dependent upon, and have no relation to the action of, neutral Powers which is dictated by their own policy and interests. If a state of war exists as distinguished from a civil brawl, the authorized soldiers of one belligerent when captured by the other belligerent must be treated as prisoners of war to whatever nationality they belong, subject always to the risk of such reprisals as are recognized by international law, in case the Government they serve has violated the law.[140]

138. Christopher Robinson to Lord Canning (FO 83/2286) (Apr. 1, 1823), *in* 55 Law Officers' Opinions to The Foreign Office 1793–1860 200 (Clive Parry ed., 1971).

139. Percy Anderson to Robert Reid and Frank Lockwood (Apr. 16, 1895), *in* 3 International Law Opinions 370 (Lord McNair ed., 1956).

140. Report of Robert Reid and Frank Lockwood (Apr. 26, 1895), *in* 3 International Law Opinions, 371, ¶ 4a.

As a consequence, they asserted, the French most certainly were not entitled to simply execute British subjects "regularly incorporated in the regular forces of the Hovas" if taken prisoner "in open fight" during the hostilities.[141]

A third example is the British War Cabinet's August 1944 decision on recognition of Polish partisan belligerent status, which was expressly for the purpose of ensuring that Germany clearly understood "that we recognize the Polish Underground Army as a fully combatant force entitled to normal treatment under the laws and customs of war." A British War Cabinet memorandum of 23 August 1944, entitled "Belligerent Status for Polish Underground Army" (which was also known as the Polish Home Army, as well as the Armia Krajowa ("AK")), proposed a declaration for British and U.S. government approval, which asserted that "[t]he Polish Home Army, which is now mobilised, constitutes a combatant force operating under the orders and directions of the Polish High Command, and forms an integral part of the Polish Armed Forces."[142] "The Polish Government," the memo continued, "have pressed us strongly to issue a declaration recognising the belligerent status of the Polish Underground forces and calling upon the German armed forces to respect that status. They have quoted General Eisenhower's similar declaration in regard of the French forces of the Interior."[143] The express purposes of this declaration were to offer, "in the absence of more effective support" a morale boost for Polish forces, as well as to put Germany on notice that the Allies were aware that captured Polish fighters "are being treated by the German military authorities in a manner contrary to the laws and customs of war." There was an identified "technical legal difficulty" related to the fact that many of the Polish Underground fighters did not wear uniform or distinguishing marks and "probably do not fulfil the strict requirements of international law which are necessary to qualify them as lawful combatants." However, it was anticipated that careful drafting of "any statement invoking for them the protection of international law" would see the problem addressed.[144] The contents of the declaration focused particularly on elements two and three of the recognition of belligerency (likely because element one, given the scale of the conflict in Poland, could be taken for granted, and element four was obviously already satisfied as Britain had decided to recognize belligerency): a clear statement that the Polish Home Army "constitutes a combatant force operating under the orders and directions of the Polish High Command"; that they "operate under responsible commanders," "bear their arms openly against the enemy," and "are provided with a distinctive emblem or with Polish uniforms"; and that members of the Polish Home Army

141. *Id.*, ¶ 2.

142. "Belligerent Status for Polish Underground Army," Memorandum for the War Cabinet by the Secretary of State for Foreign Affairs (Aug. 23, 1944), *in* UK Archives File: CAB/66/54/12.

143. Cable No.2476, Foreign Office to Moscow (Aug. 11, 1944), ¶ 1, *in* UK Archives File: FO 954/20B.

144. Note (Aug. 14, 1944), *in* UK Archives File: FO 954/20B.

"are instructed to conduct their military operations in accordance with the rules of war."[145] The consequence, the declaration concluded, was that

> in these circumstances reprisals against members of the Polish Home Army violate the rules of war by which Germany is bound. His Majesty's Government, together with their Polish Allies, are determined to track down and punish all those responsible for such crimes. Steps to this end are already being taken.[146]

Britain and the United States then made a unilateral declaration to this effect on 29 August 1944, recognizing the AK as part of the Polish Armed Forces.[147] The negotiation of this recognition through the British Cabinet is, however, once again indicative of the ways in which the political context overtly and legitimately informed the assessment and application of the recognition of belligerency test. Prior to the recognition decision, for example, it was essential, in the British view, that Soviet consent, or even better a Soviet statement recognizing Polish Underground belligerency to which Britain could acquiesce, was an important preliminary step, given that the Polish Underground was active in "the area of Russian operational responsibility."[148]

Nevertheless, it is worth noting that some disagreement on this core issue remained as late as 1937, when Philip Jessup, in the American Society of International Law discussion on belligerency and insurgency, took issue with Padelford on just this point.

> Jessup: I should be much obliged if [Professor Padelford] would elaborate his point that international law prevents a State from treating as traitors or persons guilty of treason those in insurrection against it after their belligerency has been recognized. I was not aware that international law so restrained the State in the treatment of its nationals, particularly on land, in the course of a civil war or rebellion. . . .
>
> Padelford: With regard to the matter of refraining from treating insurgents as traitors after the recognition of belligerency, that principle has been stated unanimously by writers on the subject, that once belligerency has been recognized the parent government is expected to treat captured rebels as prisoners of war and to apply the rules for the conduct of international warfare to the contest.[149]

145. War Cabinet W.P. (44) 462, Belligerent Status for Polish Underground Army—Draft Declaration (Aug. 23, 1944), ¶¶ 1–2, *in* UK Archives File: C.A.B. 66/54/12.

146. *Id.*, ¶ 3.

147. David Williamson, The Polish Underground, 1939–1947 155 (2012).

148. Cable No.2476, Foreign Office to Moscow (Aug. 11, 1944), ¶ 5, *in* UK Archives File: FO 954/20B; Note (Aug. 14, 1944), *in* UK Archives File: FO 954/20B; Office of the War Cabinet Letter (Aug. 17, 1944), *in* UK Archives File: FO 954/20B.

149. "Discussion," 31 Am. Soc. Int'l L Proc 153, 161 (1937).

After a balanced, more recent assessment, Lootsteen is ultimately, and justifiably, convinced that the weight of academic analysis on this issue since 1937 also evidences a robust understanding of the implication that where belligerency status was accorded, "[c]aptured members of the rebel armed forces, as well as soldiers of the incumbent government, were entitled to prisoner of war status."[150] The only issue upon which any uncertainty remained was whether a third state's recognition of belligerency could bind the conflict state to treat not only the third state's nationals serving with the NSAG as PWs, but also the conflict state's own nationals serving with the NSAG. There is, I suspect, no easy answer to this question.

(iv) Combatant status

A second and intimately linked consequence of the application of the Law of War was the accompanying authority to commission warships and crews (and, if not bound by the *Paris Declaration* of 1856, privateers), which could then legitimately enforce blockades, carry out naval operations against the adversary conflict state, and conduct visit and search in relation to neutral third state vessels.[151] Edward Hertslet, in a memorandum compiled for the Foreign Office, dated 3 May 1875, listed a series of historical incidents of belligerency and concluded, "Blockade is, in fact, a belligerent right, and the refusal of belligerent rights implies that no war exists."[152] An example of the capacity to commission warships and crews was recounted by T.S. Woolsey in 1896:

> Thus, early in our Civil War, the *Sumter* put in at Curacao, Holland having recognized the belligerency of the Confederacy. The commission of the *Sumter's* captain was accepted as granted by a lawful belligerent and the ship admitted on the same footing with ships of the North, though Mr. Seward [U.S. Secretary of State] tried to fasten a piratical character upon her.[153]

Of equal importance for a NSAG afforded belligerent status by a third state, however, was the requirement that those neutral third states refrain from assisting the conflict state in enforcing its own blockade against the NSAG, at the risk of imperiling their neutral status. During the Spanish blockade of rebel ports in northern Spain in 1834–1835, the Foreign Office legal adviser (Jenner) was very clear that "His Majesty's ships of war are not authorised to warn neutral vessels from entering blockaded ports, and certainly that they have no right to turn

150. Yair M. Lootsteen, *The Concept of Belligerency in International Law*, 166 Mil. L. Rev. 109, 110 (2000).

151. Gutteridge, Consequences of the Recognition of Belligerency, 17, ¶ 2(a)–(c).

152. Hertslet, Memorandum on the Recognition of Belligerent rights between Contending Parties, Foreign Office, 2.

153. Woolsey, *The Consequences of Cuban Belligerency*, 183.

such vessels from their course, or to detain those which, after notice, may persist in attempting to pursue their course in violation of the blockade." As a consequence of the implicit recognition of belligerency afforded to the rebels through the Spanish declaration of a blockade, the Royal Navy could not "afford any assistance to the Spanish Government with a view to causing the blockade to be respected."[154] Given the British government's assumption that the blockade was effective, Hertslet's memorandum cites this advice as indicative of the "de facto and de jure" result that "the Carlists would henceforth become belligerents, and Her Majesty's Government would be obliged to issue a Proclamation of Neutrality."[155] Similarly, as T.S. Woolsey, analyzing the issue in the context of the Cuban "insurgency" of 1895–1898, noted,

> If a 'recognized' insurgent blockades a port after due notification, the neutral submits to such blockade. It admits his right to search for and seize contraband articles belonging to its subjects and destined for his enemy's use, on the high seas. The insurgent thus gains considerably from recognition of his belligerency. He gains in caste; he gains in rights; he gains in the facilities for carrying on war.[156]

Gutteridge, in her advice regarding China and Formosa in 1956, similarly indicated that it was settled law that recognition of belligerency created, in third states so recognizing that belligerency, "the duty to acquiesce in the exercise of belligerent rights by the contesting parties."[157]

(v) Prize and fiscal relations

A further important consequence of recognized belligerent status for NSAGs was that third states accepted the NSAG's authority to tax activities within the territory they controlled,[158] and apply prize law using their own prize courts.[159]

154. Letter from Herbert Jenner to Viscount Palmerston (FO 83/2368) (Sept. 30, 1834), *in* 82 Law Officers' Opinions to The Foreign Office 1793–1860, 41 (Clive Parry ed., 1971).

155. Hertslet, Memorandum on the Recognition of Belligerent rights between Contending Parties, Foreign Office 2.

156. Woolsey, 183–84; *see generally* George Grafton Wilson, *Insurgency and International Maritime Law*, 1 Am. J. Int'l L. 46, 55–59 (1907); Raoul Ghent, *The Charge of Piracy in the Spanish Civil War*, 32 Am. J. Int'l L. 253, 260 (1938); Padelford, 272.

157. Gutteridge, ¶ 3(b).

158. Hall, at 35 (describing this as "a reasonable measure of self-protection" by a third state). It is not uncommon for NSAGs to tax activities in areas they control, and to establish courts that police criminal and fiscal matters as one measure of the control they assert over the civilian population, and the service provision obligations this control correspondingly engages. *See also* Darragh Murray, Human Rights Obligations of Non-State Armed Groups 3–6 (2016).

159. Gutteridge, ¶ 2(d).

The decisions of these courts were to be accepted as legitimate by all states who recognized the belligerency, so long as the prize courts themselves met minimum requirements. As vested in belligerent status NSAGs, the right to take in prize any neutral vessels captured in accordance with the Law of War applicable in naval warfare was one of the earliest components of the evolving doctrine on recognition of belligerency. As early as 1818, the then-Foreign Office legal adviser (Robinson) was firm in his advice that the situation of a Spanish vessel (*Santa Theresa del Jesus*) captured by Buenos Aires-based insurgents rebelling against the Spanish authorities, was "to be assimilated to the case of a Prize of War between the two Belligerents," with which Royal Navy warships ought not interfere.[160] In May 1829, Sir Herbert Jenner advised that a Provisional Government of Greece prize court established at Egina was invalid, because the make-up of the court made "it highly improbable that justice will be impartially administered."[161] Upon rectifications, including an appropriate avenue of judicial review, wrought by a provisional government decree, the prize court was then held to be unobjectionable in advice dated 30 June 1829.[162] Robinson further advised the British government, on 3 April 1830, that the condemnation as prize of part of the cargo of a British vessel (*Laurel*) was legitimate and lawful. This had followed the initial capture of the vessel by a Greek privateer, its liberation by a British warship, the detention of the Greek captain and that part of the *Laurel*'s cargo he had seized as contraband, the intervention of the Austrian representative in Venice, and the ultimate subjection of the seized cargo to the Greek provisional government prize court.[163]

This recognition of the validity of the prize courts of a recognized NSAG belligerent was paralleled for neutral third states by a valid claim in international law against any attempt by the conflict state to levy taxes against activities and transactions under the control of the NSAG, or to seek compensation for vessels or cargoes condemned in belligerent NSAG prize courts.[164] Indeed, according to William Atherton, Roundell Palmer, and Robert Phillimore in advice to Earl Russell concerning the activities of the Confederate warship *Alabama*, it was the very fact that the belligerent had established legitimate prize courts that actually transformed the conduct of the warship from piracy into lawful conduct in accordance with the Law of War. As they stated in their advice,

160. Advice of Sir C. Robinson (FO 83/2365) (Aug, 11, 1818), *in* 79 Law Officers' Opinions to The Foreign Office 1793–1860, 206 (Clive Parry ed., 1971).

161. Sir Herbert Jenner to the Earl of Aberdeen (FO 83/2286) (May 19, 1829), *in* 38 Law Officers' Opinions to The Foreign Office 17931860, 164–65 (Clive Parry ed., 1971).

162. Sir Herbert Jenner to the Earl of Aberdeen (FO 83/2286) (June 30, 1829), *in* 38 Law Officers' Opinions to The Foreign Office 1793–1860, 169–70 (Clive Parry ed., 1971).

163. Sir Herbert Jenner to the Earl of Aberdeen (FO 83/2286) (Apr. 3, 1830), *in* Law Officers' Opinions to The Foreign Office 1793–1860, 171–78 (Clive Parry ed., 1971).

164. Lawrence, The Principles of International Law 158.

> [t]he Government of the neutral submits to the exercise of this authority [the contraband regime and associated visit and search], the creature of war, on the faith that the conduct and property of its subjects will be submitted to the impartial jurisdiction of a legal tribunal, bound to regulate its procedure and its decisions according to recognised principles, not of municipal, but of international law.
>
> Every belligerent is obliged to have such tribunals so constituted and conducted.
>
> A belligerent which carried on war without them would be rightly considered and treated by States not otherwise concerned in the war, as piratical.
>
> It is not the act of the captor, but the decree of the Prize Court, that permanently changes the property of the vessel or goods seized, and gives to a new owner a new judicial title, a title universally respected by all States because it is judicial.[165]

Similarly, it was also accepted that recognized belligerent authorities were entitled to decree, and enforce in relation to neutral third states, measures relating to currency.[166] As Foreign Office legal adviser Hardinge advised Lord Malmesbury in 1858, in relation to the revolution in San Domingo,

> [e]ach 'de facto' Government engaged in a Civil War is 'prima facie' a regular Government in relation to those Foreign Nations, who remain Neutral, and is entitled, as such, to exercise complete Sovereign authority within the Territory actually in its power. The regulation of the currency, and the forbidding the uttering or circulation of certain kinds of paper Money under certain penalties (especially as to the paper Money of hostile Powers during a civil war), appears to me to be within the Sovereign authority ordinarily exercised by, and as it were incidental to regular Governments.[167]

Should the rebellious NSAG be unrecognized, then none of these rights accrued to it. However, by the same token, the conflict state could not employ the fact of an insurgency as a basis for levying tariffs or other dues as if materials imported from a part of its territory subject to insurgent control had been imported from a foreign entity. In *Lincoln v United States* (1905), the U.S. Supreme Court reversed a series of rulings that had recognized some Philippines insurgents as belligerents.[168] This decision meant that tariffs collected on goods shipped from Manila to New York

165. William Atherton, Roundell Palmer, and Robert Phillimore to Earl Russell (FO 83/2215) (Nov. 12, 1862), *in* 3 International Law Opinions 360 (Lord McNair ed., 1956).

166. For a slightly different view, *see* Planters' Bank v. Union Bank, 83 U.S. 483 (1872).

167. Advice of John Harding to Lord Malmesbury (FO 83/2262) (Apr. 14, 1858), 27 Law Officers' Opinions to the Foreign Office 1793–1860, 208–13 (Clive Parry ed., 1971).

168. Lincoln v. United States, 202 U.S. 484 (1905). For the reversed rulings, *see*, for example, Warner Barnes & Co. v. United States, 40 Ct. Cl. 1, 29 (1904).

as imposed via a Presidential Order of 1898 (mandated prior to the treaty with Spain in relation to the Philippines but not withdrawn after U.S. annexation of the Philippines), had to be repaid to the importers. The reason, as Justice Holmes explained, was that

> we are of opinion that the cases before us are governed by the decision, in *Fourteen Diamond Rings v. United States* (*The Diamond Rings*). In that case it was decided that after the title [to The Philippines] passed to the United States there was nothing in the Philippine insurrection of sufficient gravity to give to the islands the character of foreign countries within the meaning of a tariff act.[169]

Consequently, he continued,

> Manila was not like Nashville during the Civil War, a part of a state recognized as belligerent and as having impressed a hostile status upon its entire territory. . . . The fact that there was an insurrection of natives not recognized as belligerents in another part of the island, or even just outside its walls, did not give the President power to impose duties on imports from a country no longer foreign.[170]

(vi) NSAG Treaty obligations

While the recognition of belligerency afforded the NSAG certain fiscal and taxation rights, the broader issue of belligerent NSAG succession to, and binding by, treaties, was considerably more restricted. This was particularly the case where the belligerent NSAG was ultimately defeated and the writ of the parent government once again imposed over the rebelling entity. The nuance inherent within these considerations is perhaps best illustrated by reference to the American Civil War,[171] where these issues were most clearly ventilated, and through the elucidation of two imperfect, but roughly summative, rules that appear to emerge from this context. However, there are other relevant contexts as well, one of which I shall briefly note.

The first rule concerns the parent state's pre-conflict treaties. Once the conflict began, the parent state considered the belligerent status entity to remain bound by such treaties entered into by the unified state prior to the rebellion. Furthermore, the parent state believed that it was not the place of third states to intervene in

169. *Id.* at 428.

170. *Id.* at 428–29.

171. *See generally* Roscoe Ralph Oglesby, Internal war and the Search for Normative Order 84–99 (1971).

related arguments insofar as they might be litigated in the parent state's courts.[172] However, under the rule just referenced, some allowances could be made by third states, in the name of neutrality, such that during the period of the conflict the belligerent status NSAG was not automatically bound by certain treaty obligations adopted by the unified state prior to the civil war. The most illustrative example of this rule is in relation to British declarations regarding the *Webster-Ashburton Treaty* (1845), which dealt with cooperative action in respect to suppression of the slave trade.[173] British legal advice was sought as to two questions, recorded by Oglesby as,

> (1) whether British cruisers are to treat vessels flying the flag of Southern seceding states as vessels belonging to established governments with which Britain has no treaty for the suppression of the slave trade and therefore subject to molestation;
> (2) whether the treaty made with the parent government (the United States) is binding on the seceding states (and hence their vessels are not subject to capture and confiscation according to the terms of the treaty).[174]

British legal advice was to the effect that while rebelling entities did take with them preexisting treaty obligations, once recognition of belligerency had been granted in May 1861, it was not appropriate to characterize Confederate vessels as U.S. vessels for the purposes of the treaty. Thus, Confederate vessels would not be subject to the terms of that treaty. Additionally, it would not be appropriate for Britain to report to the United States on the slave trading activities of Confederate flagged vessels, as part of the broader treaty cooperation obligation, as this would "constitute a violation of neutrality."[175]

172. *See* Advice of Robert Phillimore to Lord Stanley (Feb. 13, 1867), *in* Great Britain and the Law of Nations 412–16 (H. A. Smith ed., 1932); Advice by Collier, Coleridge, and Twiss (Feb. 23, 1869), *in* 2 International Law Opinions 365 (Lord McNair ed., 1956).

173. *The Webster-Ashburton Treaty. Treaty to Settle and Define the Boundaries between the Territories of the United States and the Possessions of Her Britannic Majesty in North America, for the Final Suppression of the African Slave Trade, and for the Giving Up of Criminals Fugitive from Justice, in Certain Cases*, U.S.-UK, Aug. 9, 1842, arts. VIII, IX, http://avalon.law.yale.edu/19th_century/br-1842.asp.

174. Oglesby, Internal war and the Search for Normative Order, 91.

175. *Id.* at 92. This aspect of the Webster-Ashburton Treaty, 173, was ultimately superseded by another treaty signed in 1862. *Treaty between United States and Great Britain for the Suppression of the Slave Trade*, U.S.-UK, Apr. 7, 1862, http://avalon.law.yale.edu/19th_century/br1862.asp. Article 1 of the Treaty provided that "The two high contracting parties mutually consent that those ships of their respective navies which shall be provided with special instructions for that purpose, as hereinafter mentioned, may visit such merchant vessels of the two nations as may, upon reasonable grounds, be suspected of being engaged in the African slave trade, or of having been fitted out for that purpose; or of having, during the voyage on which they are met by the said cruisers, been engaged in the African slave trade, contrary to the provisions of this treaty;

This rule is also evident in the negative in the situation of requisitions from Rio Tinto mines in Nationalist controlled territory during the Spanish Civil War. On 1 March 1937, the Foreign Secretary brought to the Cabinet's attention "the serious position which has arisen from the action of the insurgent authorities in requisitioning the products of the mines of Rio Tinto Company (Limited), the Tharsis Copper and Sulphur Company and certain other concerns." The problem, in essence, was that copper and pyrites were being requisitioned by the nationalists for both their own use, but also "for export to Germany and Italy."[176] This problem had catalyzed around correspondence between Sir Auckland Geddes (then Chairman of Rio Tinto) and Sir Robert Vansittart (then Permanent Under-Secretary of State for Foreign Affairs), culminating in a letter from Geddes to Vansittart dated 24 February 1937. The concern underpinning this correspondence was that quite apart from the commercial and legal concerns inherent in Nationalist requisitions, the diversion of the materials from Rio Tinto mines under insurgent control in Spain to Germany, and away from Britain, served to greatly benefit the former and harm the latter. As Geddes wrote,

> [s]ince the occupation of the pyrites mining district by the Insurgents at the end of August, the sequence of events and all our researches in Spain and Germany give credibility to the reports that a bargain was struck between the Insurgents and the aggressive elements directing German foreign policy from the Foreign Office of the NSDAP, together with those directing the Göring Four-Year Plan of economic self-sufficiency.[177]

Sir Geddes continued, "Under pressure from Germany and Italy, the Insurgents have refused to give permits to export copper to the United Kingdom, and have diverted it to Germany and Italy. This is plain robbery."[178] Additionally, the requisitions meant that Rio Tinto refineries now had no raw material to process, workers were being laid off, and the company was suffering from the effects of forced currency conversions between the insurgent currency and pounds sterling.[179] The problem, he concluded, was that, "unsupported," the company could not "oppose the will of a military commander in de facto possession of its mines." Unless and until the British government was "prepared to enforce the rights of

and that such cruisers may detain, and send or carry away, such vessels, in order that they may be brought to trial in the manner hereinafter agreed upon." *Id.*, art. 1.

176. Position of Certain of the British Mining Companies in Spanish Insurgent Territory (Mar. 1, 1937), ¶¶ 1–2, *in* UK Archives File: CAB/24/268. The memorandum also notes that there was "reason to believe that General Franco has guaranteed to Germany the export of the greater part of the products of the iron ore mines of Spain as, and when, these fall into his hands." *Id.*, ¶ 7.

177. Letter from Sir Auckland Geddes to Sir Robert Vansittart (Feb. 24, 1937), at 4, *in* UK Archives File: CAB/24/268.

178. *Id.* at 5.

179. *Id.* at 6–7.

this British Company not spasmodically but unremittingly," the only option the company had was to "walk warily, to comply with every insurgent demand, no matter how extravagant or costly it may be."[180]

In a most apt summation of the facts on the ground, Sir Geddes signed off by observing, "My intention in writing has been to make it clear that as a result of forces beyond our control, Germany, acting through the Spanish Insurgent Headquarters, is practically master in our house."[181] However, the basic legal position, as the Foreign Secretary advised, was relatively clear: the provisions of a 1922 treaty with Spain that exempted British subjects from "any military exaction or requisition" continued to apply. As the Foreign Secretary set forth, "The Treaty of 1922 is, of course, applicable to the whole of Spain and is valid in respect of the territory administered by the insurgents."[182] This was entirely in keeping with the implications of the three-level scheme and the doctrine on recognition of belligerency. Because the nationalists remained characterized by Britain as insurgents, not belligerents, such preexisting treaties continued to apply in full. The situation may have been different—as it had been in relation to the Confederacy as noted earlier—if Franco's nationalists had been accorded recognition of belligerency. The question, consequently, was not whether Franco was in breach of international law—he clearly was. Rather, in light of the deteriorating security situation, the question posed by the Foreign Secretary was whether the Royal Navy ought to be employed to "intercept any ship which leaves Huelva carrying such products to Germany or Italy [in order] . . . to end this state of affairs."[183]

The second discernible rule on NSAG treaty obligations was that the conflict state could not bind the belligerent NSAG, nor the territory and people under its control, to treaty obligations entered into subsequent to the commencement of the conflict. An illustrative example of this rule was the early 1861 U.S. attempt to accede to the prohibition against privateering contained within the Paris Declaration of 1856. Strategically, the Union could see that the Confederacy would be particularly reliant upon privateers for its naval forces. The Union hoped that its accession to the prohibition would be considered binding across the entire territory and citizenry of the United States, including the rebelling states, and thus would deny the Confederacy access to this means of warfare.[184] The United States also believed that this act would create an obligation among neutral third states to treat Confederate privateers as pirates, given that many of these states were signatories to the Paris Declaration and were thus obliged to apprehend and treat

180. *Id.* at 7.

181. *Id.* at 8.

182. Position of Certain of the British Mining Companies in Spanish Insurgent Territory, 176, ¶ 10.

183. *Id.*, ¶ 13.

184. *See generally* Oglesby, Internal war and the Search for Normative Order, 93–94.

privateers as criminals.[185] However, while opening negotiations with the United States on the matter, Britain and France indicated that any such U.S. accession to the prohibition would not prospectively affect the lawfulness of Confederate privateering during the American Civil War. That is, the United States could not bind the recognized Confederate belligerent party through the act of accession.[186]

(vii) The validity of NSAG legislative acts

That the legislative acts of a defeated belligerent status NSAG are voided by their defeat is a well-accepted component of the doctrine on recognition of belligerency. Thus compliance with such legislation could not be relied upon as a defense against subsequent enforcement proceedings in relation to, for example, contract or debt liabilities that existed and were not satisfied before initiation of the conflict. This situation generally arose where such preexisting debts were subsequently voided or acquitted by belligerent-entity legislation, but in relation to which delayed resolution was now sought after the conclusion of the conflict.

This rule is best illustrated by the U.S. Supreme Court case of *Williams v Bruffy* (1877).[187] The facts of this case concerned the payment to Confederate authorities, by the administrator of Bruffy's estate, of a prewar debt owed to Williams. This payment was in compliance with Confederate legislation, passed in August 1861, which required the payment to the Confederate treasury of all such debts owed to "enemy aliens." This was said to be a full discharge of the debt. Subsequent to the surrender of the Confederacy and the reunification of the United States, Williams sought payment of the debt, which was opposed by Bruffy's estate on the grounds that it had already been paid in accordance with laws applicable in the Confederacy at the relevant time. Bruffy's estate administrator argued that this should act as a defense against any order to repay the debt a second time, albeit to the original creditor. Two issues of law were significant. The first, which shall not be further explored here, related to a U.S. constitutional prohibition regarding "discriminating legislation by one state against the citizens of another state and to secure to them the equal protecting of its laws," itself an assertion that the U.S. Constitution continued to apply across the entirety of the United States during the Civil War.[188] The second issue concerned the lingering effect or status to be afforded to the legislation of a defeated recognized belligerent entity. On this

185. *See, e.g.*, Letter from the Duke of Newcastle to Governor Hincks (Windward Islands) and Relayed to Other Colonial Governors (Nov. 30, 1861), it. 5, encl. 1, *in* UK Archives File: FO 881/2068 (in response to a request for instructions regarding "the course which should be taken by the British authorities in regard to privateers carrying the flag of the so-styled Confederate States."); Legal Advice of Harding, Atherton, and Palmer to Earl Russell (Oct. 5, 1861), *in* 2 INTERNATIONAL LAW OPINIONS 369–60 (Lord McNair ed., 1956).

186. For a full account of this negotiation, *see* BERNARD, A HISTORICAL ACCOUNT OF THE NEUTRALITY OF GREAT BRITAIN DURING THE AMERICAN CIVIL WAR, 173–86.

187. Williams v Bruffy, 96 U.S. 176 (1877).

188. *See, e.g.*, *id.* at 183–84.

issue, the Court was very clear: "The validity of its acts, both against the parent state and its citizens or subjects, depends entirely upon its ultimate success. If it fail to establish itself permanently, all such acts perish with it."[189] Furthermore,

> [t]he concession made to the confederate government in its military character was shown in the treatment of captives as prisoners of war, the exchange of prisoners, the recognition of flags of truce, the release of officers on parole, and other arrangements having a tendency to mitigate the evils of the contest. The concession placed its soldiers and military officers in its service on the footing of those engaged in lawful war, and exempted them from liability for acts of legitimate warfare. But it conferred no further immunity or any other rights. It in no respect condoned acts against the government not committed by armed force in the military service of the rebellious organisation; it sanctioned no hostile legislation; it gave validity to no contracts for military stores; and it impaired in no respects the rights of loyal citizens as they had existed at the commencement of hostilities.[190]

Thus because recognition of belligerency "yielded nothing to [Confederate] pretensions of legality," and the United States had "never for one moment renounced their claim to supreme jurisdiction over the whole country and to the allegiance of every citizen of the republic,"[191] then "when its military forces were overthrown, [the Confederacy] utterly perished, and with it all its enactments."[192] The Court agreed that a party could be released from liability "had such property [been] taken from them by force." However, in this case "debts not being tangible things subject to physical seizure and removal, the debtors cannot claim release from liability to their creditors by reason of the coerced payment of equivalent sums to an unlawful combination."[193] Although interpreted by some as inconsistent with the rule as expounded in later cases, and as explained by McNair on the basis of British Legal Adviser opinions,[194] the decision in *Williams v Bruffy* appears to support rather than undermine the general rule that a "voluntary"—including a legislatively coerced, but not physically forced—payment or handing over of property to a belligerent entity in accordance with belligerent legislation will not bring relief from liability, while a physically enforced seizure of money or physical property may.[195]

189. *Id.* at 186.

190. *Id.* at 187.

191. *Id.* at 188.

192. *Id.* at 191–92.

193. *Id.* at 187.

194. Oglesby, for example, appears uncertain as to the full adherence of *Williams v Bruffy* with later cases. Oglesby, Internal war and the Search for Normative Order, 88–90.

195. Note, however, that the general position relating to the subsequent liability of the successful state to honor loans made to an unsuccessful insurgent during a civil war was that the

This said, however, the doctrine on recognition of belligerency clearly incorporated an express provision for the continuing post-conflict validity of compliant Law of War-governed acts of the defeated belligerent NSAG. This preservation existed regardless of any parallel and subsequently invalidated NSAG legislation to the same effect, and such acts were not impugnable before the unified state courts subsequent to the conclusion of the conflict. As with *Williams v Bruffy*, the U.S. Supreme Court case of *Ford v Surget* (1878)[196] dealt with the issue of subsequent liability for debts resulting from belligerent entity action, after that entity had failed and the writ of the state had been reaffirmed across the entire territory and citizenry of the state. In this case, however, the liability at issue was the value of a cotton crop (two hundred bales) that had been burned by Confederate authorities in May 1862. The basis for the action was twofold. First, a Confederate law required that military commanders destroy cotton "should the same be about to fall into the hands of the United States." Second, orders by the Confederate military commander, General Beauregard, required the burning of "all cotton along the banks of the Mississippi River likely to fall into the hands of the forces of the United States."[197] Affirming the rule in *Williams v Bruffy*, the Court clearly agreed that the Confederate legislation was irrelevant to the case as it had failed with the Confederacy, and could not form the basis of any claim against liability.[198] However, the Court concluded that the second authority—the orders of the military commander—could provide a relief from liability if those orders and their implementation complied with the Law of War. Noting that cotton was a key source of finance for the war effort,[199] Justice Harlan, for example, observed that where the burning of cotton to prevent it falling into the hands of the enemy forces "was an act of war upon the part of the military forces of the rebellion, for which the person executing such orders was relieved from civil responsibility at the suit of the owner voluntarily residing at the time within the lines" of the Confederacy, then so long as this act was carried out by those Confederate forces "consistently with the laws and usages of war," then it was a lawful act and not subject to subsequent liability.[200] However, the more fully elaborated judgment was that of Justice Clifford, who clearly based his reasoning around the observation that "it is as clear as anything in a legal decision can be that the Confederate States were belligerents in the sense attached to that word by the law of nations."[201]

state was not bound by those contracts. *See* Haig Silvanie, Responsibility of States for Acts of Unsuccessful Insurgent Governments 19 (1939).

196. Ford v. Surget, 97 U.S. 594 (1878).

197. *Id.* at 604–608.

198. *Id.* at 604.

199. *Id.* at 605; *id.* at 614–15 (Clifford, J., concurring).

200. *Id.* at 605–606.

201. *Id.* at 612 (Clifford, J., concurring).

Consequently, because the Law of War, which was applicable de jure as between the parties, clearly recognized the right "to seize and confiscate all contraband goods,"[202] whether enemy or neutral, it was permissible under the Law of War to destroy the cotton. This action could not, therefore, be complained of, and no redress was due for its value.

E. THE PERSPECTIVE OF NEUTRAL THIRD STATES

For third states, the essence of recognition of belligerency lay in placing a legal framework around their dealings with both parties to the conflict. Once belligerent status was afforded, the rebel NSAG could be dealt with as a separate legal authority for the purposes of the third state's relations with that party, rather than as a legal nonperson, which could only be dealt with via the conflict state's own authorities. As Hyde records of recognition of belligerency, "By such action, the foreign State undertakes to treat both parties to the conflict as belligerents, and also to assume itself in relation to them the position of a neutral with the burdens and rights incidental to such status."[203] President McKinley, facing a difficult political decision as to whether to recognize the belligerency of Cuban insurgents, stated in his 6 December 1897 message that "In the code of nations there is no such thing as a naked recognition of belligerency unaccompanied by the assumption of international neutrality."[204] In order to illustrate the consequences of a recognition of belligerency for an affected third state, I will outline three benefits accruing from the perspective of such states: the capacity to engage in certain forms of relationship with the NSAG; the higher degree of legal certainty afforded to interactions with the NSAG in relation to taxation and tariffs; and the opportunity the doctrine offered in terms of navigating a "middle way" between the conflict state and the NSAG.

(i) Relations with the NSAG

As previously discussed, by recognizing the belligerency of a NSAG, a neutral third state gained the benefit of clarity as to the legal status of its own nationals who fought alongside the armed forces of the conflict state or NSAG. It also derived benefit from the recourse to settled relationships with neutral shipping that

202. *Id.* at 611 (Clifford, J., concurring).

203. Charles Chaney Hyde, 1 International Law Chiefly as Interpreted and Applied by The United States § 47(1) (1922); *see also* Great Britain and the Law of Nations 261 (H. A. Smith ed., 1932); Henry Wager Halleck, International Law, or Rules Regulating the Intercourse of States in Peace and War 74 (1861) ("a foreign state should remain a passive spectator, or, if its own relations require diplomatic intercourse with the revolted society, it should treat such revolted society as a de facto government only."). On the specifically maritime dimensions of neutrality, *see*, inter alia, Tucker, 196–262.

204. William McKinley, Annual Message (Dec. 6, 1897), *in* Moore, 1 A Digest of International Law, 199.

accompanied the subjection of the conflict to the Law of War rules of blockade, contraband, and visit and search.[205] A further significant benefit accruing to neutral third states from recognizing the belligerency of the NSAG was that such recognition permitted the third state to accept the realities on the ground in rebel held territory. This allowed the third state to instruct its citizens that it was lawful to deal with the de facto authority on day-to-day issues such as commercial transactions, claims for damages, payment of customs levies in ports, and other administrative activities necessary for normal private intercourse and transactions (noting, however, the risks for conflict state citizens that attended the nullity of all NSAG legislation in the event of failure, in the U.S. interpretation). Smith described the impetus for this consequence as being that

> the prolonged exercise of actual authority over substantial territories by an insurgent government may compel neutrals to carry on such intercourse with that government as is required for the protection of their own subjects. Here again the according of belligerent recognition is really a consequence of the inability of the legitimate government to assert its authority over certain territories. The right and duty of the British crown to protect its subjects everywhere cannot be diminished by the default of the legitimate government, and the crown is thus compelled to conduct intercourse, although in a provisional and informal manner, with such authorities as in fact exist.[206]

Stowell went so far as to argue that this pressing need of the state to deal with the de facto authorities is not interference because, "When, after a protracted struggle, neither side is able to vanquish the other, or to preserve the tranquillity of the territory over which it claims jurisdiction, there arises a just ground for impeachment of sovereignty." This was particularly so given that the conflict "is almost certain seriously to injure the commerce of all other states, and to impose upon the nearer ones great burdens of police in the fulfilment of their obligations."[207] In relation to a post-American Civil War seizure by U.S. authorities of cotton purchased by British subjects during that war, via an agent based in (Confederate) Charleston, Foreign Office legal advisers Roundell Palmer, Robert Collier, and Robert Phillimore were of no doubt as to the state of the law:

> To treat the dealings of foreigners with persons in the Confederate States as bound by the Acts of Congress of the United States during the time while the de facto Government of the Confederate States continued, would be a most questionable course of proceeding; but to hold bona fide transactions of this kind, which took place in 1862 and 1863, defeated ex

205. Gutteridge, Consequences of the Recognition of Belligerency, 17, ¶ 3.

206. Great Britain and the Law of Nations 262 (H. A. Smith ed., 1932).

207. Stowell, Intervention in International Law, 348–55.

> post facto by an Act of Congress passed in 1864, would be nothing less than monstrous.[208]

Similarly, Wharton cites the pre-American Civil War U.S. view as follows:

> A revolutionary party, like a foreign belligerent power, is supreme over the country it conquers as far and as long as its arms can carry and maintain it. Foreign vessels obtaining and using licences and clearance from such a party, are not liable to punishment by the other party afterwards for so doing.[209]

The logic and efficacy of this consequence of recognition of belligerency was often attributed to simply accepting the situation as it actually was, and thus allowing neutral third states to engage with an effective partner—the de facto authority—in relation to issues involving that third state's nationals, and their interests, in the rebel held area.[210] However, as Mr. Hoffman, arguing before the U.S. Supreme Court in *The Gran Para* (1822) made clear, even if (in that particular case) the Banda Oriental was viewed by the United States as engaged in a civil war with Spain, to which the Law of War applied, this did not furnish in its wake any power for that insurgent entity to engage in war with other nations.[211] That is, the grant of belligerent rights to the NSAG was to be construed narrowly and did not extend to the exercise of belligerent rights against third states, except insofar as was provided for under the laws of war and neutrality.

(ii) Taxation and tariffs

A second major benefit for neutral third states was that they could avoid double payment of customs and taxes. Once the third state had recognized the NSAG as a belligerent, it was considered to be a good defense to subsequent claims for taxes and customs made by the conflict state authorities in relation to rebel held territory. Thus, third state and third state nationals' transactions with rebel authorities within or in relation to rebel held territory were to be considered as having already been legitimately levied by, and paid to, the relevant

208. Advice of Roundell Palmer, Robert Collier, and Robert Phillimore (FO 97/47) (Feb. 3, 1866), *in* LAUTERPACHT, 223–24.

209. WHARTON, 520.

210. *See, e.g.*, HANNIS TAYLOR, A TREATISE ON INTERNATIONAL PUBLIC LAW 457 (1904) ("If the disturbance is in the interior and of local importance, it should not be officially noticed except for the purpose of holding the general government liable for all damages to foreigners and their interests. If the revolt reaches the border, especially a seaport, the case is altered. Foreign interests, particularly of the neighbouring state, are apt to be so involved as to force the sending of warships by different states for the protection of their citizens. In that event, if the insurrection is formidable and so organized and continued as to effect such interests, a recognition of belligerency should follow.").

211. The Gran Para, 20 U.S. 471 (1822).

authorities.[212] This point on the validity of levies imposed by a belligerent status NSAG underpinned British advice on a Peruvian rebel decree, issued from Lima (which the rebels had captured) purporting to require anyone who paid customs duties at Callao (where the fleeing government had re-established itself) to pay them again to the de facto Lima government. In the opinion of Herbert Jenner, as advised to Viscount Palmerston, this decree was invalid as to goods staying in areas under the control of the de jure government. However, should those goods subsequently be transported to areas under the control of the de facto government, then "the party in possession" of the area "is not bound to admit them duty free, upon the ground that the proprietors have already been compelled to pay the duty at Callao."[213] By 1865, this position had hardened, and Robert Phillimore advised

> [t]hat according to the universal usage of nations dues paid by foreigners, who take no part whatever in a civil war which breaks out in the country where they are peaceably resident and carrying on trade under the faith of treaties and general international law, to a de facto Government which demands and has the power of compelling this payment, must be considered to be paid to the government of the country.[214]

This position was not without nuance, however. As McNair reports, in situations where the payment was not compelled (and thus could be assimilated to voluntary support of the rebels, a point also made by the U.S. Supreme Court in *Bruffy* and other cases), or where the rebels had not in fact established a de facto government of sufficient effectiveness, Foreign Office legal advice was that the de jure government may be in a position to levy such duties a second time.[215]

(iii) The political utility of a middle way between non-interference and armed intervention in support of independence-seeking peoples

That the recognition of belligerency served important diplomatic and domestic political purposes for neutral third states should of course come as no surprise. As noted earlier, diplomatic recognition of belligerency could provide a form of legal abeyance from observing certain treaty obligations concluded with the parent state, where these conflicted with the dictates of neutrality. However, the domestic

212. 2 International Law Opinions 395 (Lord McNair ed., 1956).

213. Herbert Jenner to Viscount Palmerston (FO 83/2317) (July 29, 1834), 52 Law Officers' Opinions to the Foreign Office 1793–1860, 91–95 (Clive Parry ed., 1971).

214. Advice of Robert Phillimore (FO 83/2379) (May 11, 1865), *in* 2 International Law Opinions 398 (Lord McNair ed., 1956).

215. *Id.* at 398–99 (citing advice in relation to the Carlist rebellion in Spain (1874), and rebellions in Mexico (1875), Peru and Columbia (1885), and Chile (1891)).

political purposes served by recognition of belligerency for the neutral third state must also be appreciated, and in this context a primary purpose of recognition of belligerency appears to have been the assuaging of domestic public opinion. To this end, it is instructive to briefly describe two situations that evidence this particular strength of the doctrine.

The first, arising at the very cusp of the doctrine's emergence in the first quarter of the nineteenth century, involves the wars of independence in South America against Spain and, to a lesser extent, Portugal.[216] As Tyson Reeder has described, the difficulty presented for "aligning geography and law,"[217] as well as public opinion, in dealing with the wars of independence in South America, was particularly acute for the young, democratic, liberal U.S. Republic, which had within living memory fought its own war for independence. There was, understandably, strong public sympathy for the independence-seeking entities, and there is a solid literature dealing with the ways in which this sympathy was acknowledged by the U.S. government. One significant consequence of this sympathy was initially weak enforcement of the U.S. Neutrality Act in respect of the estimated fifteen to twenty thousand U.S. mariners at that time engaged as privateers by these entities in struggles with their colonial powers.[218] According to a contemporary Portuguese assessment, the privateers' actions resulted in almost two million dollars-worth of losses of ships and cargoes, "not including damage and interest."[219] Indeed, the early U.S. declaration to the effect that it would maintain strict neutrality between all parties to this interlinked civil war—particularly that by President Monroe in his "Instructions to the Treasury," echoed by Secretary of State Adams to the Spanish Minister—specifically permitted use of U.S. ports and harbors on equal footing by both Spanish and Portuguese vessels and those of the rebelling entities (excepting pirates), so long as they paid the necessary tariffs and dues and

216. Enoch Resnick, *Spain's Reaction to Portugal's Invasion of the Banda Oriental in 1816*, 73(74) J. Am. Hist. 131 (1972).

217. Tyson Reeder, *"Sovereign Lords" and "Dependent Administrators": Artigan Privateers, Atlantic Borderwaters, and State Building in the early Nineteenth Century*, 103 J. Am. Hist. 323, 324 (2016).

218. Hopkins, *For Freedom and Profit: Baltimore Privateers in the Wars of South American Independence*, 99–103; Kevin Arlyck, *Plaintiffs v. Privateers: Litigation and Foreign Affairs in the Federal Courts, 1816–1822*, 30 L. Hist. Rev. 245, 257 (2012). It is difficult to verify this figure. Gillespie notes a range of other estimates of privateering in relation to the American War of Independence and South American rebellions in the first half of the nineteenth century, which, while still substantial, would tend to suggest lower estimates. Alexander Gillespie, 1 A History of the Laws of War 52 (2011).

219. Letter from the Portuguese Consul in the United States, Mr. de Figaniere, to U.S. Secretary of State Daniel Webster, *extracted in* W. Vernon Harcourt, *The Rights and Duties of Neutrals in Time of War: Part II (June 30, 1865)*, *in* 9 J. Royal U. Serv. Inst. 329, 342 (1865). It is estimated that "well over 5000 British volunteers" also joined rebel South American forces in their rebellions against Spain. *See* Nir Arielli, Gabriela A. Frei, and Inge Van Hulle, *The Foreign Enlistment Act, International Law, and British Politics, 1819–2014*, 38 Int'l Hist. Rev. 636, 637 (2016).

obeyed port state law as required.[220] President Monroe's First Annual Message (2 December 1817) was most explicit:

> It was anticipated at an early stage that the contest between Spain and the colonies would become highly interesting to the United States. It was natural that our citizens should sympathize in events which affected their neighbors. It seemed probable also that the prosecution of the conflict along our coast and in contiguous countries would occasionally interrupt our commerce and otherwise affect the persons and property of our citizens. These anticipations have been realized. Such injuries have been received from persons acting under authority of both the parties, and for which redress has in most instances been withheld.
>
> Through every stage of the conflict the United States have maintained an impartial neutrality, giving aid to neither of the parties in men, money, ships, or munitions of war. They have regarded the contest not in the light of an ordinary insurrection or rebellion, but as a civil war between parties nearly equal, having as to neutral powers equal rights. Our ports have been open to both, and every article the fruit of our soil or of the industry of our citizens which either was permitted to take has been equally free to the other.[221]

Similarly, attempts pressed upon the U.S. government by Spain and Portugal to tighten and enforce U.S. law as a means of attaining commercial sanctions against the privateers,[222] if not a political concession deleterious to the entities whose Letters of Marque they bore, caused significant debate.[223] As Kevin Arlyck observes of the cases from this period,

> At the nexus of war, revolution, and commerce, the primary goal in litigation was not to create good law, it was to use law to recover the goods . . .
>
> The court's role in United States foreign relations was shaped by large-scale transatlantic dynamics funnelled into quotidian litigation, in which private parties went to court to realize the best possible outcomes in the collision of maritime commerce and inter-imperial war.[224]

220. *See* Harcourt, The Rights and Duties of Neutrals in Time of War: Part I, 317–18; *see also* Moore, 1 A Digest of International Law, 170.

221. James Monroe, First Annual Message (Dec. 2, 1817), http://millercenter.org/president/monroe/speeches/speech-3594.

222. *See* Harcourt, *The Rights and Duties of Neutrals in Time of War: Part II (June 30, 1865)*, 242–43; Arlyck, *Plaintiffs v. Privateers: Litigation and Foreign Affairs in the Federal Courts, 1816-1822*, 218.

223. Browning, 8–9; Ayrlick, *Plaintiffs v. Privateers: Litigation and Foreign Affairs in the Federal Courts, 1816-1822, 246–47.*

224. Arlyck, *Plaintiffs v. Privateers: Litigation and Foreign Affairs in the Federal Courts, 1816-1822*, 248, 250.

This path was often selected in preference to other avenues of redress because even though the courts were cognizant and cautious of the "delicate" political and public issues enmeshed with the issue of civil war and belligerent recognition at international law, they were quite at home with a long-accepted domestic law doctrine to the effect that a prize taken by a U.S. national, even if apparently authorized under a Letter of Marque from a foreign power or belligerent status entity, where that mariner was nevertheless in breach of U.S. neutrality law, could indeed be a matter for the U.S. courts.[225] In this way, U.S. judges did not interfere with the law of nations as it applied in terms of granting the power to validate prizes to belligerent courts, because the issue they entertained was not the validity in international law of the prize taken by the U.S. privateer. Rather, the issue upon which they were adjudicating was that U.S. domestic law had made accepting such privateer commissions unlawful for U.S. nationals within the United States, and thus any prize disposed of within U.S. jurisdiction was amenable to U.S. law for the purposes of restitution to the deprived original owner.[226] As Chief Justice Marshall noted in *The Gran Para*, "The principle is now firmly settled that prizes made by vessels which have violated the acts of Congress that have been enacted for the preservation of the neutrality of the United States, if brought within their territory, shall be restored."[227] Similarly, the sentence of execution passed on U.S. mariners convicted in relation to a particularly notorious incident of piracy unmitigated by a valid Letter of Marque, albeit in the Banda Oriental and Buenos Ayres belligerency context,[228] was remitted primarily because of government fears as to the "odium" that would accrue if the sentences were carried out. This was in no small part due to the general support of the population for the revolutionary entities.[229] To this end, recognition of belligerency, and the consequent neutrality it invoked, could be utilized as an intermediate step that assuaged popular support for the revolutionary entities seeking independence[230] through not being legally characterizable as support for the colonial states against the rebels. Furthermore, recognition of belligerency also maintained a superficial gloss of non-intervention, and genuflection to the state system, by not supporting (at least officially) the rebels against their European colonial masters. Ostensibly employing U.S. precedent in relation to South America in the first quarter of the nineteenth century to illustrate U.S. inconsistency in relation to British recognition of Confederate

225. *See also* discussion in Chapter 3 on the intersection between insurgency, belligerency, and commercial litigation.

226. Arlyck, *Plaintiffs v. Privateers: Litigation and Foreign Affairs in the Federal Courts, 1816-1822*, 253, 364.

227. *The Gran Para*, 20 U.S. at 486.

228. *Smith*, 18 U.S at 169.

229. Samuels, *The Full Story of* United States v. Smith, *America's Most Important Piracy Case*, 356–59.

230. David B. Roe and Russell K. Osgood, *United States Supreme Court February Term 1824*, 84 Yale L. J. 770, 784 (1975).

belligerency in 1861, Vernon Harcourt cited U.S. correspondence recognizing belligerency in 1815, and then argued that

> [t]he recognition of the independence of the South American colonies did not take place till 1822—that is, seven years afterwards. Therefore, this is the principle laid down in the clearest form by the American Government themselves, of what is the course which ought to be taken by a neutral Government towards parties engaged in war, where, on one side, there is an old established Government, and on the other side an insurrection in arms against it; because at that period there was nothing like consolidation or stability in the South American Republics that would have entitled them to recognition, as independent States, and, as I have said, recognition did not take place until seven years later.[231]

The second example is the British response to the Polish uprising against Russian overlordship in the early 1860s.[232] In this case, the British government clearly acknowledged within its policy-making processes strong British public opinion in favor of the Polish insurgents, and expressed routine disquiet with the atrocities perpetrated by Russian forces combating the insurgency.[233] As one commentator argued,

> The guerrilla war which she [Poland] has now for nearly six months carried on with such bravery and success may yet last a few years, but it must in the end die out before disciplined armies and resources almost unlimited. The results of such a struggle are terrible to anticipate. Poland would be a desert, and the best and bravest of her sons lie under her soil, or die a living death in the mines of the Oural, or the mysterious oubliettes of the Siberian fortresses. Her towns would be in ruins, her villages in ashes, her women and children dying of famine and the plague. Such are a few of the horrors which can alone be prevented by a strong power coming forward to aid the Poles in the contest which they are evidently determined to fight out to the last.[234]

231. Harcourt, The Rights and Duties of Neutrals in Time of War: Part I, 318.

232. For an account of the United States' response, within the context of the ongoing American Civil War, *see* Joseph Wieczerzak, *American Reactions to the Polish Insurrection of 1863*, 22 Pol. Am. Stud. 90 (1965); Laurence J. Orzell, *A "Favourable Interval": The Polish Insurrection in Civil War Diplomacy*, 1863, 24 Civil War Hist. 332 (1978).

233. *See, e.g.*, Events in Poland, Fremden Blatt (Mar. 19, 1863), *in* UK Archives File: FO 417/311 (encl. to item 248); Letter from Mr. Mounsey to Lord Bloomfield (Apr. 7, 1863), *in* UK Archives File: FO 417/311 (cncl. to item 373).

234. *See, e.g.*, *Art IX—Poland*, 24 Westminster Rev. 171, 189 (1863); *see generally* Wereszycki, *Great Britain and the Polish Question in 1863*, 78, 80–81, 85–88; Kutolowski, *Mid-Victorian Public Opinion, Polish Propaganda, and the Uprising of 1863*, 89, 91; Orzell, *A "Favourable Interval": The Polish Insurrection in Civil War Diplomacy*, 1863, 332.

Recognition of Polish rebel belligerency was explicitly canvased and considered in public meetings, the press, by commentators,[235] and by the British government. In one contemporary opinion piece, for example, the author argued that the Polish insurgent "national government repudiates all foreign intervention; it asks only for a recognition by Europe of the same belligerent rights as those she has hitherto extended to every insurgent nation; to the Greeks in 1826, to the Belgians in 1830, and to the Confederate States of America since the beginning of the present civil war."[236]

Britain ultimately decided to withhold the grant of belligerent status.[237] As previously discussed in relation to this conflict context, several factors militated against progressing recognition from insurgency to belligerency, including the balance considered necessary as between of the humanitarian impulse and the legal availability of a recognition option on one hand, and the clear British policy goals of avoiding military entanglement on the other; preserving the balance of power created by the Congress of Europe in 1815; and concerns about French territorial ambitions, along with fears of a Russian-U.S. Union alliance should the Polish rebels be accorded full belligerent status.[238] As Edward Stanley observed in the House of Lords in February 1863, the risk with a half-measure of recognition in a situation where sympathies with the rebels were strong was that it implied, ultimately, a readiness to intervene with arms:

> Another set of circumstances under which recognition is legitimate is where other nations, having in the interests of humanity determined that a desolating warfare shall no longer be continued, in order to put an end to it agree to recognise the revolting party. But in that case recognition is always followed by something further, for it means nothing unless the Powers who join in it are ready to support by force of arms the claims of the State which they recognise.[239]

Nevertheless, the idea that recognition of belligerency offered an intermediate step between consigning the Polish rebels to Tsarist internal and extrajudicial

235. *See, e.g.*, Remigiusz Bierzanek, *Humanitarian Law in Armed Conflicts: The Doctrine and Practice of Polish Insurgents in the 19th Century*, 17 Int'l Rev. Red Cross 128 (2010); Stowell, Intervention in International Law, 91, 102 ("Evidently this sentiment in favor of the insurrectionists was too widespread and too profound to be ignored by governments dependent upon popular support.").

236. *E.g.*, *Art V—The Treaty of Vienna: Poland*, 24 Westminster Rev. 412, 429–33 (1863).

237. *See generally* Wereszycki, *Great Britain and the Polish Question in 1863*, 101; Kutolowski, *Mid-Victorian Public Opinion, Polish Propaganda, and the Uprising of 1863*, 102, 105–106.

238. *See, e.g.*, Orzell, *A "Favourable Interval": The Polish Insurrection in Civil War Diplomacy*, 1863, 335, 338; Wereszycki, *Great Britain and the Polish Question in 1863*, 94; Kutolowski, *Mid-Victorian Public Opinion, Polish Propaganda, and the Uprising of 1863*, 103.

239. Earl of Derby (Edward Stanley), Address to Her Majesty on the Lords Commissioners (Feb. 5, 1863), http://hansard.millbanksystems.com/lords/1863/feb/05/address-to-her-majesty-on-the-lords#S3V0169P0_18630205_HOL_23.

discipline, and full recognition of a resurrected Polish state, was a clear driver of debate and policy formulation. As John Kutolowski has observed, Polish propagandists at work in England at the time recognized that "however strong middle- and upper-class sentiment for Poland was, influential Englishmen disliked war,"[240] and thus agitation for recognition of Polish rebel belligerency was the aim of the Polish Nationalists and their sympathizers. This would have created an obligation of neutrality, placing Russia and the insurgents on an equal legal footing for the purposes of the civil war, but would not have required of Britain an unwilling and politically destabilizing intervention. That is, it offered something in between "diplomatic humiliation" from the Russian rejection of the British-French-Austrian remonstrance, and "unwanted war."[241] Similarly, as Vernon Harcourt wrote, in relation to the contemporaneous issue of recognition of Confederate belligerency in the American Civil War, this mechanism offered a useful middle ground, employing the guise of neutrality, for "those who wish to recognise the South, and yet not to intervene in the American quarrel."[242]

F. CONCLUSION

In this chapter, I have examined some of the purposes served by the doctrine on recognition of belligerency. While these purposes range from the evidently humanitarian to the explicitly political, they were nevertheless primarily expressed via the language and application of law. The means by which humanity was to be encouraged, for example, was to invoke de jure application of the Law of War as to means and methods, treatment of PWs, and conduct vis-à-vis neutral third states. The means by which political ends were served included the application of the law of neutrality to characterize maritime interactions between third states on the one hand, and the conflict state and belligerent NSAG on the other, and employing recognition of belligerency as a middle path between assuaging public agitation in support of insurgents and the countervailing diplomatic imperative to maintain the veneer of non-intervention against fellow states. However, the doctrine also evinced a level of legal novelty and progressive development in response to perceived needs, such as the limited status and attributes afforded a recognized belligerent NSAG in terms of raising funds, taxing activity, and taking responsibility for treatment of and consequences for third state nationals. All of these doctrinal attributes and consequences speak clearly to the doctrine's fitness for purpose, and its coherence within the wider corpus of international law. In the next chapter, I will therefore turn to an examination of some of the legal and situational challenges faced in applying this apparently well-tailored and eminently flexible doctrine.

240. Kutolowski, *Mid-Victorian Public Opinion, Polish Propaganda, and the Uprising of 1863*, 93.

241. *Id.* at 98. Although, as a number of historians argue, it was probable that the Polish aim was for a recognition of belligerency to soften barriers to, and thus pave the way for, British military intervention in support of the Polish insurgents.

242. Harcourt, Letters by Historicus on Some Questions of International Law, 7.

5

Some Challenging Issues and Case Studies in Recognition of Belligerency

> Once the norm of belligerent recognition had been firmly established as operational in the international community it immediately went into decline. What are the reasons for the disuse of belligerent recognition within the past hundred years? Almost surely one cause was the resentment on the part of the United States of Britain's action vis-à-vis the Confederacy.[1]
>
> —Roscoe Oglesby (1971)

A. INTRODUCTION

Although it formed a recognizably coherent legal scheme from the early 1820s, a relatively settled appreciation of the scope, content, and stability of the doctrine on recognition of belligerency remains evident still today. This is testament to both the doctrine's longevity and its utility. Amos Hershey's 1939 revised edition of *The Essentials of International Public Law and Organization*, for example, noted that "the recognition of insurgent political communities which have revolted from the parent country" had "given rise to more definite rules and a more regular and consistent practice" than even international law on the recognition of new states.[2] The doctrine was consciously employed during World War II (for example, the recognition of Polish Underground Army belligerency by the Allies), and has continued to feature subsequently (as the discussions surrounding the progressive development of the law, and the short case studies examined in the final section of this chapter, attest). But this is not to say that the doctrine has remained unchallenged by conflict contexts, evolving law, and political realities. Indeed, the

1. Roscoe R. Oglesby, Internal War and the Search for Normative Order 103 (1971).

2. Amos S. Hershey, The Essentials of International Public Law and Organisation 201 (1939).

very fact that it is an almost forgotten component of the Law of War/LOAC today indicates that the doctrine must have evinced a degree of fragility because it is now subject to some level of existential doubt.

In this chapter, I will deal with four of the challenges faced by the doctrine on recognition of belligerency. The first challenge is one of universality: Was recognition of belligerency ever a widely recognized legal doctrine, or was it a uniquely British and U.S. legal construct that, while useful, was of relevance only in British and U.S. legal discourse? The second challenge is factual: How did the doctrine fare when applied to especially complicated (legally and politically) situations, such as the Boer Wars and the Spanish Civil War? The third challenge is one of legal exegesis: Has the evolution of the Law of War/LOAC since 1949 extinguished any legal space in which the doctrine might practically operate? The final challenge is one of relevance: Has the doctrine on recognition of belligerency fallen into desuetude, or is there evidence of its persistence as an analytical construct applied in the assessment of recent, doctrinally conducive, conflict situations?

B. THE CHALLENGE OF UNIVERSALITY: WAS RECOGNITION OF BELLIGERENCY SOLELY U.S. AND BRITISH PRACTICE?

(i) Crystallization in British and U.S. legal advice and practice

As has been described elsewhere in this book, the formal, crystallized, doctrine on recognition of belligerency initially emerged primarily as a response to early nineteenth-century colonial rebellions and the disruption they caused to maritime communications.[3] Certainly, by the time of the American Civil War—considered by many scholars to have been the doctrine's apogee—it was undoubtedly a fully elucidated and coherently integrated legal scheme. As a consequence, its development and deployment was undeniably tethered to the needs and concerns of the two major maritime powers of the day—Britain and the United States—and thus found its widest expression in maritime terms, and in civil war contexts that included a maritime dimension.[4] This maritime dimension

3. *See* Sir Hersch Lauterpacht, Recognition in International Law 176–82 (1947) (citing for example, the list of UK and U.S. nineteenth-century recognitions of belligerency—primarily by declaration of blockades by conflict states, and compliance with those blockades by third states).

4. This is readily evident in the focus of an early "founding document" in the evolution of the doctrine of recognition of belligerency. Christopher Robinson provided legal advice to Viscount Castlereagh, dated 6 February 1817, in regard to the capture of a British vessel, *Perthshire*, in the Caribbean during hostilities between Spain and her rebellious South American colonies, stating, "It must be allowable for any Nation I conceive to maintain public relations with Countries in the situation of Insurgent Provinces, after a certain time." 79 Law Officers' Opinions to the Foreign Office 1793–1860, 24–28 (Clive Parry ed., 1970).

was central to formal British recognition of Greek belligerency during the Greek Rebellion of 1821–1825, to recognition of blockades in Haiti, San Domingo, and several other South American contexts in the second half of the nineteenth century, and for structuring relations with the two contesting parties during the American Civil War. Similarly, the maritime dimension—including the preponderance of U.S. nationals among the ranks of rebel privateers—was critical to U.S. recognition of belligerency in the South American wars of independence up to 1826, as was the experience of recognition of Confederate belligerency during the American Civil War. Yet, the doctrine was also fundamental as a political, diplomatic, and legal frame of reference for other conflict contexts—such as the Polish Rebellion in 1863—even though, ultimately, recognition of belligerency was not conferred.

The doctrine was, however, not purely a creature of Foreign Office and State Department legal advice. The British and U.S. courts also employed the doctrine in nineteenth- and twentieth-century decisions. As previously outlined, U.S. courts appear to have paid greater attention to the executive on this issue, whereas in Britain, the most directly relevant case law often hinged around the interpretation and application of the *Foreign Enlistment Act*.[5] Thus, in some respects, there was little distinction between insurgency and recognized belligerency because that Act's restrictions on service in, or supply of war materiel to, foreign forces applied in both contexts. Similarly, in both jurisdictions, case law concerning insurance provisions related to piracy or war risk was far more slave to the technicalities of commercial and marine insurance litigation than to the parallel legal framework of insurgency-belligerency. Nevertheless, the legal differences between these two terms of art in international law, and as contextually distinct conflict characterizations, were clearly in the mind of the courts.

Thus, in the previously noted case of *The Chesapeake* (1864), decided in the Vice-Admiralty Court of New Brunswick, the right of mariners of a recognized belligerent (in this case Confederate sailors and privateers) to act "free from the imputation of piracy" was compared with the liability of neutral nationals serving the belligerent NSAG as privateers, but without a commission, to be treated as pirates.[6] In *The Salvado*r (1870), the Privy Council, hearing an appeal from the Vice-Admiralty Court of the Bahamas, found that a ship employed in the service of Cuban insurgents, who had not been granted belligerency status, could indeed be seized in accordance with the UK *Foreign Enlistment Act*.[7] Similarly, in *The*

5. *See* James Kent, Kent's Commentary on International Law 268–97 (2d ed., 1878) (showing a contemporaneous comparison of the U.S. and British Foreign Enlistment Acts).

6. *See* Norman MacKenzie and Lionel Laing, Canada and the Law of Nations 528–29 (1938) (including extracts of the 1864 Chesapeake case).

7. The Queen v. James Carlin (ship "Salvador") [1870] 3 LRPC 218 (appeal taken from Bah.), http://www.bailii.org/uk/cases/UKPC/1870/1870_25.html.

Three Friends (1897),[8] the U.S. Supreme Court—citing much precedent as well as the influential Wheaton's *Elements of International Law*—determined that:

> And as, agreeably to the principles of international law and the reason of the thing, the recognition of belligerency, while not conferring all the rights of an independent state, concedes to the government recognized the rights, and imposes upon it the obligations, of an independent state in matters relating to the war being waged, no adequate ground is perceived for holding that acts in aid of such a government are not in aid of a state, in the sense of the statute [the U.S. *Neutrality Act* - Rev. Stat. sec. 5283].[9]

Finally, it is clear that the 1939 Draft Convention on Rights and Duties of Neutral States in Naval and Aerial War, fundamentally the product of U.S. and British academic analysis, was perhaps the most comprehensive (but by war, interrupted) statement as to the doctrinal status of recognition of belligerency. As Article 1(b) of that draft expressly noted, "A 'belligerent' is a State or a politically organised group at war with a State or with a politically organised group," adding (at Article 1(f)) that "The 'territory' of a State or of a belligerent comprises its land and territorial waters and the airspace above them."[10] The commentary to this provision then begins with the assertion that:

8. The Three Friends, 166 U.S. 1 (1897). This case concerned the November 7, 1896, seizure in Florida, by the Collector of Customs, of a steamer, *The Three Friends*, which was being fitted out as an armed vessel intended to be operated in support of Cuban insurgents rebelling against Spain. The United States had not formally recognized the Cuban insurgents as belligerents, and the case turned—controversially—on the extent to which the alleged offense in U.S. statute (Rev. Stat. §5283—) could be excluded from operation in respect of some situations of insurgency, as well as the more generally accepted situations of recognized belligerency.

9. Section 5283 of the Revised Statutes states:

> Every person who, within the limits of the United States, fits out and arms, or attempts to fit out and arm, or procures to be fitted out and armed, or knowingly is concerned in the furnishing, fitting out or arming, of any vessel with intent that such vessel shall be employed in the service of any foreign prince or state, or of any colony, district or people, to cruise or commit hostilities against the subjects, citizens or property of any foreign prince or state, or of any colony, district or people, with whom the United States are at peace, or who issues or delivers a commission within the territory or jurisdiction of the United States for any vessel, to the intent that she may be so employed, shall be deemed guilty of a high misdemeanor, and shall be fined not more than ten thousand dollars, and imprisoned not more than three years. And every such vessel, her tackle, apparel and furniture, together with all materials, arms, ammunition and stores, which may have been procured for the building and equipment thereof, shall be forfeited; one-half to the use of the informer and the other half to the use of the United States.

The Three Friends, 53 (citing Section 5283 of the Revised Statutes).

10. Draft Convention on Rights and Duties of Neutral States in Naval and Aerial War art. 1(b), 33 Am. J. Int'l L. Supp. 175 (1939).

> This explanation is included to bring out the fact that a belligerent may be a party to an international or to a civil war provided, in the latter case, that belligerency has been recognised . . . It seems clear that if the government of State A recognises the belligerency of Group B either directly or indirectly by establishing a blockade or by exercising other belligerent rights, State A cannot object if State C also recognises the belligerency of Group B and proclaims the neutrality of C . . . there is [also] much authority for the proposition that State C is free to grant or to withhold recognition in its own discretion, provided that it does not extend premature recognition and thus be charged with illegal intervention in the domestic affairs of another State.[11]

Yet, despite the fact that recognition of belligerency was to some extent built around what often appeared to be at core British and U.S. concerns, other states also employed the doctrine as a means of discriminating between rebellion contexts. Wharton stated that France, Holland, and Denmark all recognized U.S. belligerency during the American War of Independence,[12] and although retrospectively correct, as a historical claim, this assertion should be treated with caution given that the formal doctrine on recognition of belligerency did not really evolve in its modern form until the early 1800s. The French and Dutch did, however, clearly recognize Confederate belligerency during the American Civil War,[13] as did Britain and Brazil.[14] This then leads us to the critical challenge of universality—was the doctrine employed or referred to by other states as a legal frame of reference in relation to civil wars?

(ii) Indicators of broad acceptance of the doctrine

As will be evident from the incidents and case studies examined thus far, and from those examined later in this chapter, it is fair to say that while the doctrine on recognition of belligerency appears to have been substantially driven by British and U.S. interests, concerns, advisers, and publicists, it was clearly accepted as an operative legal framework on a much broader basis. As has been noted thus far, Portugal and Spain certainly considered the doctrine operative in the nineteenth

11. *Id.* at 209–13.

12. Francis Wharton, A Digest of the International Law of the United States, Taken From Documents Issued By Presidents and Secretaries of State, and From Decisions of Federal Courts and Opinions of Attorneys-general 570 note 9 (1886).

13. *See* James Lorimer, The Institutes of the Law of Nations: A Treatise of the Jural Relations of Separate Political Communities 42 (1884) (on France); *see also* Joseph H. Beale Jr., *The Recognition of Cuban Belligerency*, 9 Harv. L. Rev. 406 (1896) (on France); *See* 1 Henry Wheaton, Elements of International Law 34–36 (on Holland in §23); *see also* Pieter J. Kuyper, *Recognition: Netherlands Theory and State Practice*, 1 Int'l L. Neth. 371, 384 (1978); *see generally* Quincy Wright, *International Law and the American Civil War*, 61 Am. Soc'y Int'l L. Proc. 50, 50–58 (1967).

14. John Bassett Moore, 1 A Digest of International Law 185 (1906).

century. Justice Brown, in *The Ambrose Light* (1885), assessed from the documentary record that,

> France, as early as 1776, expressly recognized our belligerent rights, and set at liberty a corsair arrested by procurement of the British vice-admiral . . . while Portugal alone, by decree of June 4, 1776, refused us recognition, shut her ports to our merchantmen, and denounced confiscation of all our vessels found with contraband goods on board.[15]

France also specifically recognized Confederate belligerency during the American Civil War, and considered, but did not ultimately afford, recognition of Polish rebel belligerency in 1863—in part because the rebels did not meet the necessary tests insofar as exhibiting "sufficient cohesion to establish governmental agencies of some stability."[16] Similarly, Austria refused to grant recognition of belligerency to Greek rebels against Ottoman rule in the 1820s, and during the Polish rebellion, Austria was most concerned about avoiding any diplomatic action that could be interpreted as recognition of belligerency. The Polish rebels of 1863 worked tirelessly, but unsuccessfully, to secure recognition of belligerency—particularly from Britain and France—and Harcourt (as Historicus) argued that the 1830 Belgian rebellion against, and separation from Holland, was also an early form of recognized belligerency.[17] An 1863 assessment in the *Westminster Review* asserted that upon the Dutch King's refusal of a proposed armistice that had been accepted by the Belgian rebels, "The belligerent rights of the Belgians were then recognized" by many European powers, resulting in negotiations and the ultimate independence of Belgium.[18] In 1913, Mexican Constitutionalists expressly sought recognition of belligerency from the United States in their insurrection against the Huerta dictatorship.[19] The Mexican Constitutionalists pleaded that the United States should enforce its declared neutrality in accordance with domestic U.S. law (the *Neutrality Act*) to halt the supply of arms to Huerta's forces across the Texas-Mexico border.[20]

15. *The Ambrose Light*, 25 F. 408, 414 (S.D.N.Y. 1885).

16. Lauterpacht, Recognition in International Law, 177 note 1, 183; Remigiusz Bierzanek, *Humanitarian Law in Armed Conflicts: The Doctrine and Practice of Polish Insurgents in the 19th Century*, 17 Int'l Rev. Red Cross 128, 131 note 2 (1947).

17. William Vernon Harcourt, Letters by Historicus on Some Questions of International Law 36–37 (1863).

18. *Art. V—The Treaty of Vienna: Poland*, 80 Westminster Rev. 412, 429 (1863).

19. Telegram from L.L. Fierros, representing certain Constitutionalists, to the President, (Apr. 14, 1913), *in* Papers Relating to the Foreign Relations of the United States, With the Address of the President to Congress December 2, 1913, 878, https://history.state.gov/historicaldocuments/frus1913, File No: 812.113/2100.

20. *See, e.g.*, Letter from the Secretary of State to the Governor of Texas, (May 13, 1913) *in* Papers Relating to the Foreign Relations of the United States, With the Address

Brazil recognized Confederate belligerency in the American Civil War, and the Brazilian naval rebels of 1894 specifically sought this status. During the "Paulista War" (also referred to as the Brazilian Civil War or Constitutionalist Revolution of 1932), the Governor of Sao Paulo specifically requested "the recognition of belligerency between the State of Sao Paulo and the Dictatorship."[21] Similarly, Brazil engaged in an insurgency-belligerency status assessment when dealing with the seizure of the *Santa Maria* in 1961. Peru recognized Cuban rebels as belligerents in 1869, and Bolivia recognized the belligerency of Chilean rebels in 1891.[22]

Denmark was also an early advocate for, and subject of something like the doctrine on recognition of belligerency. "In 1779," records O'Rourke, "John Paul Jones, having made prizes of several English merchant vessels, sent them into Norwegian ports. Shortly thereafter the Danish Government delivered them up to the British on the grounds that Jones' commission, issued by a government not yet recognised by the world was not valid in the eyes of Danish law."[23] The United States demanded compensation, and later Danish partial acceptance of the U.S. claim to respect for its War of Independence commissions, gave rise to lengthy diplomatic debate as to the compensation demand. Justice Brown, in the 1885 U.S. case of *The Ambrose Light*, made specific and detailed documentary reference to this ultimate Danish acceptance of the application of neutrality law and prize law during the American War of Independence: "The reclamations made by this country upon Denmark for the prizes of Paul Jones restored by her to England in 1779, furnish no exception to the rule here laid down." Citing a range of congressional sources as well as commentary by Barnard and documents in Wheaton's *Elements of International Law*, Justice Brown concluded that

> from these documents it appears that Denmark had previously professed to act as neutral, and had thus, either expressly or by implication, already recognized

OF THE PRESIDENT TO CONGRESS DECEMBER 2, 1913, 879, File No: 812.00/7443; Letter from Governor of Texas to the Secretary of State, (May 19, 1913), *in* PAPERS RELATING TO THE FOREIGN RELATIONS OF THE UNITED STATES, WITH THE ADDRESS OF THE PRESIDENT TO CONGRESS DECEMBER 2, 1913, 880 File No: 812.00/7578; The Constitutionalists indeed cited U.S. Statutes and Congressional statements back at the Secretary of State to underscore the domestic legal obligations the United States had assumed toward both parties in the Mexican Civil War, in line with the U.S. Neutrality Act. *See* Letter from The Confidential Agent of the Constitutionalist Government of Mexico to the Secretary of State, (Jun. 26, 1913), *in* PAPERS RELATING TO THE FOREIGN RELATIONS OF THE UNITED STATES, WITH THE ADDRESS OF THE PRESIDENT TO CONGRESS DECEMBER 2, 1913, 881, File No: 812.00/7897.

21. Telegram from U.S. Consul General at Sao Paulo (Cameron) to the Secretary of State, (Aug. 1 1932), *in* FOREIGN RELATIONS OF THE UNITED STATES DIPLOMATIC PAPERS, 1932, THE AMERICAN REPUBLICS, VOLUME V, U.S. Department of State, Washington, D.C., document 434, File No: 832.00 revolutions/286, https://history.state.gov/historicaldocuments/frus1932v05/d434,.

22. LAUTERPACHT, RECOGNITION IN INTERNATIONAL LAW, 177 note 1, 183.

23. Vernon O'Rourke, *Recognition of Belligerency and the Spanish War*, 31 AM. J. INT'L L. 398, 405 (1937).

> our belligerency . . . To deliver up our prizes as captured piratically, after professions of neutrality or implied recognition of our belligerency, without notice prohibiting our entry to her ports, was so inconsistent with her previous attitude as to afford just ground for reclamations.[24]

The diplomatic record thus appears to evidence Danish acceptance of a precursor form of recognition of belligerency as early as the late eighteenth century. Ultimately, however, Chen is undoubtedly correct that

> There was no formal recognition of belligerency during the American War of Independence. The attitude of the European Powers varied from the prompt acknowledgement of independence (such as that by France and Spain) to the release of American prizes by Denmark. In no case, however, was there any evidence that the governments concerned had acted in accordance with the doctrine that the revolting colonies had no rights until recognised.[25]

So far as Prussia was concerned, an early instance of a clear appreciation and application of the doctrine arose out of the "Sonderbund War" within the Swiss Confederacy in 1847. During this conflict, a group of seven predominantly Catholic cantons, which had declared a "separate alliance," were swiftly defeated by the remaining forces of the Federal Diet.[26] Although the conflict was a rebellion (and was called at the time a "civil war"), the Commander of the Federal Swiss Forces required that the Law of War be followed, and—on the whole—it was.[27] Stowell, assessing the conflict from the perspective of the norm against intervention, described the situation thus:

> During the Sonderbund conflict in Switzerland . . . which arose in part over the question of the expulsion of the Jesuits, France and the reactionary powers espoused the cause of the revolting cantons and threatened to impose upon Switzerland the arbitration of the Pope. This support of the revolt was so patently an unjustifiable interference in the internal affairs of Switzerland that Lord Palmerston was able to thwart it by diplomacy alone until Switzerland had overthrown the Sonderbund. This is a striking example of the respect paid

24. *The Ambrose Light*, 25 F. 408, 437–39 (S.D.N.Y. 1885).

25. Ti-Chiang Chen, The International Law of Recognition 337 (Stevens and Sons, London, 1951).

26. *See generally* Thomas Maissen, *The 1848 Conflicts and their Significance in Swiss Historiography*, *in* The Making of Modern Switzerland, 1848–1998, 3, 3–34 (Michael Butler et al. eds., 2000).

27. François Bugnion, *Jus ad Bellum, Jus in Bello and Non-International Armed Conflicts*, 6 Y.B. Int'l Humanitarian L. 167, 179 (2003).

> to international law in a case where the States interfering in violation of law were much more powerful than its defenders.[28]

In a direct reference to the applicability of the Law of War and the law of neutrality in civil wars, Frederick William IV of Prussia, as Prince of the Canton of Neuchatel, declared that "on the solid basis of the letter and spirit of the Federal Pact, of the public law of Europe, and the principles of general European policy . . . the Canton of Neuchatel had a perfect right to declare itself neutral during the present civil war."[29] Similarly, the Cape Town-based German Consul-General's 1899 statement regarding the neutrality to be observed by German nationals with respect to both the British and Boer parties was clearly informed by an awareness of the doctrine on recognition of belligerency, as well as the potential consequences for third states of the lesser status of insurgency.[30]

An interesting vignette of the international appreciation of the doctrine is offered by a 1959 treatise by Djojohadikusumo Sumitro, a French and Dutch educated economist and former Indonesian Finance Minister. At this time, Sumitro was living abroad as a member of the rebel Permesta (PRRI) movement, and in this role, he passed to his U.S. interlocutors a substantial document outlining the background and aims of the PRRI struggle. This is of direct relevance to the issue of the scope of acceptance of recognition of belligerency as a legal and political analytical framework for two reasons. First, as the accompanying file notes attest, Sumitro's aim was "to request the US government to slow down, or rather discontinue, delivery of military goods to the Djakarta government, and to adopt a neutral position with regard to Indonesia's striving parties."[31] Second, this particular document indicates that the doctrine was understood much more broadly than as merely a British-U.S. legal innovation because it refers directly to recognition of belligerency and to one particular nuance of its interpretation. First, Sumitro assessed that "the PRRI as an unrecognized government had yet to prove to the outside world that it was able to meet the requirements for international recognition, even if only for a status as a belligerent power."[32] Second, Sumitro's analysis paid specific homage to the tendency for adoption by a NSAG of guerilla tactics to be assessed as a negative factor in affording recognition of belligerency: "It is true that guerilla war could ultimately not be avoided in view of the enemy's numerical strength, but the fact that guerilla tactics were adopted prematurely

28. Ellery C. Stowell, Intervention in International Law 347 note 73 (1921).

29. Letter from Chevalier Bunsen (Prussian Legation) to Viscount Palmerston, Nov. 28, 1847 (1847), *in* UK National Archives File: FO 881/43, 323.

30. *See, e.g.*, Robert G. Campbell, *Neutral Rights and Obligations in the Anglo-Boer War*, *in* 26 Johns Hopkins University Studies in Historical and Political Science, 47–48 (1908), https://archive.org/details/neutralrightsan00campgoog/page/n6.

31. Memorandum, May 9, 1959, in UK Archives File: FO 371/144071.

32. The Sumitro Document, 3, Part VI, *in* UK National Archives File: FO 371/144071.

did have an adverse effect on the general position of the [PRRI] Revolutionary Government."[33]

Further evidence of the broad acceptance and use of the doctrine on recognition of belligerency is also found in other twentieth-century civil war and legal negotiation contexts. More than twenty states were participants in the non-intervention arrangements for the Spanish Civil War, a key component of which was (as shall be discussed in the next section of this chapter) an agreement to collectively withhold and consider recognition of belligerency. Declarations, legislation, and other instruments by a collective of concerned European states such as Albania, Lithuania, and Sweden all contemplated the doctrine.[34] Further, as shall also be noted later, a wide range of states continued to refer to the doctrine during negotiations for the Geneva Conventions of 1949 and the Additional Protocols of 1977.

C. FACTUAL CHALLENGES: TWO CASE STUDIES OF CONTENTIOUS APPLICATION OF THE DOCTRINE ON RECOGNITION OF BELLIGERENCY

As the nineteenth century waned, the doctrine on recognition of belligerency had retained—indeed, arguably increased—its relevance and authority in terms of political, legal, and academic analysis in relation to late nineteenth-century rebellions. The language and implications of the scheme routinely appeared in U.S. presidential announcements,[35] and British and U.S. administrative correspondence—such as in relation to the Brazilian Naval Revolt of 1893–1834,[36] and the Cuban Revolution of 1895–1898.[37] It also featured a number of influential

33. *Id.*

34. *See, e.g.*, NORMAN J. PADELFORD, INTERNATIONAL LAW AND DIPLOMACY IN THE SPANISH CIVIL STRIFE App. I, III, V, and VII (1939) (displaying a substantial collection of annexed documents).

35. For example, the messages—exactly 28 years apart, but both on Cuban rebellions—of Presidents Grant (December 6, 1869) and McKinley (December 6, 1897) encompassing a long-standing refusal by the U.S. executive to grant the Cuban "insurgents" the status of formal belligerents (albeit in the face of some contrary views—such as Congressional resolutions/votes in 1896, and the near contemporary academic opinions of Cushman Davis and others). *See* CUSHMAN DAVIS, A TREATISE ON INTERNATIONAL LAW 106 (1901) *See, e.g.*, MOORE, 1 A DIGEST OF INTERNATIONAL LAW, 194 (citing President Grant's 1869 message, "The contest [in Cuba] has at no time assumed the conditions which amount to a war in the sense of international law, or which would show the existence of a de facto political organisation of the insurgents sufficiently to justify a recognition of belligerency."). *Id.* at 198–200 (citing President McKinley's 1897 message: "For these reasons I regard the recognition of the belligerency of the Cuban insurgents as now unwise and therefore inadmissible. Should that step hereafter be deemed wise as a measure of right and duty the Executive will take it.").

36. Joseph Smith, *Britain and the Brazilian Naval Revolt of 1893–1894*, 2 J. LATIN AM. STUD. 175 (1970).

37. T. S. Woolsey, *The Consequences of Cuban Belligerency*, 5 YALE L.J. 182 (1896); Beale, 406; George Grafton Wilson, *Insurgency and International Maritime Law*, 1 AM. J. INT'L. L. 46 (1907).

attempts to consolidate and crystallize the state of international law around the *fin de siècle*—including the Institute for International Law's resolutions in 1900, on (inter alia) the "relations of foreign governments to insurrections"[38] and "responsibility of states for injuries to aliens."[39] In the next section of this chapter, I shall examine two conflict situations from the first half of the twentieth century. These two contexts each provided particularized legal and political challenges to the application of the doctrine on recognition of belligerency. The outcomes from each illustrate the ongoing adaptability and evolution of the doctrine, but also the limitations on application that can accompany civil war contexts that are tethered to intensely complicated international political currents.

(i) The South African Wars: Civil war or international war?

After annexation of the infant republic of Natal by the British, and grudging recognition of the Afrikaner states—The Orange Free State, and the South African Republic (Transvaal)[40]—in May 1875, Britain proposed discussion of a South African Federation.[41] Transvaal was considered unlikely to acquiesce to existence

38. *Rights and Duties of Foreign Powers as Regards the Established and Recognised Governments in Case of Insurrection, in* RESOLUTIONS OF THE INSTITUTE OF INTERNATIONAL LAW: DEALING WITH THE LAW OF NATIONS 157, 157–59 (James Brown Scott ed., 1916).

39. *Regulations Respecting the responsibility of States by reason of Damages suffered by Aliens in case of Riot, Insurrection or Civil War, in* RESOLUTIONS OF THE INSTITUTE OF INTERNATIONAL LAW: DEALING WITH THE LAW OF NATIONS 159–61 (James Brown Scott ed., 1916).

40. The Sand River Convention (1852) with respect to Transvaal states:

> The Assistant Commissioners guarantee in the fullest manner, on the part of the British Government, to the emigrant farmers beyond the Vaal River the right to maintain their own affairs, and to govern themselves according to their own laws without any interference on the part of the British Government, and that no encroachment shall be made by the said Government on the territory beyond to the north of the Vaal River, with the further assurance that the warmest wish of the British Government is to promote peace, free trade, and friendly intercourse with the emigrant farmers now inhabiting or who hereafter may inhabit that country, it being understood that this system of non-interference is binding upon both parties.

G.W. EYBERS, SELECT CONSTITUTIONAL DOCUMENTS ILLUSTRATING SOUTH AFRICAN HISTORY 1795–1910, 357, 357–59 (1918). The Orange River (or Bloemfontein) Convention of 1854 with respect to Orange Free State states, "Article I. Her Majesty's Special Commissioner, in entering into a Convention for finally transferring the Government of the Orange River Territory to the representatives delegated by the inhabitants to receive it, guarantees, on the part of Her Majesty's Government, the future independence of that country and its Government." *Id.* at 281–85.

41. Lynn Berat, *Constitutionalism and Mineral Law in the Struggle for a New South Africa: The South African War Revisited*, 15 SUFFOLK TRANSNAT'L L.J. 61, 71–72 (1992).

as a British entity, and thus was annexed by Britain,[42] the Proclamation being read on 12 April 1877:[43]

> The reading of the Proclamation took place on the 12th April, 1877, at about ten or twelve in the morning, in the presence of a few townspeople, when Mr. Burgers [President of Transvaal from 1872 until annexation in 1877], without consulting his Volksraad (which, by the way, he was strongly warned by Sir T. Shepstone [former Secretary of Native Affairs in Natal, the UK Special Commissioner] not to assemble), and, in defiance of their resolution, handed over the Government offices to the High Commissioner. Having issued the Protest, as well as a Proclamation calling on the inhabitants to maintain order, and await in peace the result of the Protest, the President of the Republic sold off the whole of his effects and left the Transvaal.[44]

The annexation was vehemently renounced and resisted by many.[45] As *The Spectator* reported on 12 May 1887,

> The annexation of the Transvaal Republic is, however, a very different affair from the admission of Fiji to the privileges of a British colony. The Transvaal is colonised by a population of European descent, with a Government of their own, with traditions, placing them in an attitude of fierce hostility to the British Government, and with an obstinacy of nature characteristic of their

42. The reasons behind the annexation are myriad. Strategically, Britain was concerned at the increasing German presence in Africa, and German links with the Transvaal government; politically, the idea of a South African Union under the British flag was considered the best way to preserve and ensure British interests; on a nationalist level, the discriminatory treatment of Uitlanders (non-Afrikaaners) in Transvaal law and commerce; and economically, there were clear interests on the part of major British business interests in accessing the mineral wealth being discovered in Transvaal. All of these concerns, and others, played a role. *See* Edward J. Gibbs, England and South Africa 24–46 (1889); Karl Blind, *The Transvaal War and European Opinion*, 169 N. Am. Rev. 760 (1899); Alfred Thayer Mahan, *The Merits of the Transvaal Dispute*, 170 N. Am. Rev 312 (1900); Shula Marks and Stanley Trapido, *Lord Milner and the South African State*, 8 Hist. Workshop 50 (1979); Casper Sylvest, *Our Passion for Legality: International Law and Imperialism in Late Nineteenth Century Britain*, 34 Rev. Int'l Stud. 403, 415–21 (2008); J.L. Hilton, *Theodor Mommsen and the Liberal Opposition to British Imperialism at the Time of the Second South African War of Independence (1899–1902)*, 6 Classical Receptions J. 48, 48–50 (2014). Grievances continued well after the establishment of the Union. *See, e.g.*, T.R.H. Davenport, *The South African Rebellion of 1914*, 78 Eng. Hist. Rev. 73 (1963).

43. Eybers, Select Constitutional Documents Illustrating South African History 1795–1910, 448–53.

44. George P. Moodie, *Annexation of the Transvaal: A Reply to Sir Bartle Frere's Letter to "The Times," 25 Feb. 1881 and a Letter on the Subject of Alleged Slavery in the Transvaal (reprinted from "The Daily News" 23 Feb. 1881)*, 8–9 (1881).

45. *See* John Laband, *Burying The Union Jack: British Loyalists In The Transvaal During The First Anglo-Boer War, 1880–1881*, 4 Hist. of Intell. Culture 1 (2004) (showing the internal tensions and debate between pro- and anti-annexation British and Boer Transvaalers).

> Dutch origin . . . the Dutch of the 'South-African Republic' had not only not invited us to rule them, but had vehemently rejected our proffered sovereignty and protection.[46]

Transvaaler discontent simmered until a two-month armed "rebellion" (from 16 December 1880, with the first major clash at Bronkhorstspruit on 20 December 1880,[47] until the British defeat at the Battle of Majuba on 27 February 1881[48]) forced Britain to negotiations.[49]

> Following three humiliating border defeats, ending with Majuba, all that remained was armistice and a peace agreement, the 1881 Pretoria Convention. A muddy kind of settlement, conceding the substance of Transvaal independence while clinging to a residual Crown 'suzerainty', its legacy was, as . . . Laband emphasizes, 'trouble stored up for the future'.[50]

The complicated nature of the legal relationship between Transvaal and Britain thus posed problems for the characterization of the Transvaal parties to the conflict. It was a "rebellion" within the Empire, but the British government took a conscious decision to "treat the Boers in all respects according to the rules of civilized warfare."[51] The instructions continued:

> Lord Kimberley would therefore suggest that Mr Secretary Childers should inform Sir George Colley [the General Officer Commanding Natal] by telegraph that although the occasion has not arisen for determining any question of belligerent rights, he is instructed to treat the Boers according to the recognized rules of civilized warfare, including exchange of prisoners.[52]

46. *The Annexation of the Transvaal*, THE SPECTATOR (UK), May 12, 1877, at 8–9, http://archive.spectator.co.uk/article/12th-may-1877/8/the-annexation-of-the-transvaal.

47. Laband, *Burying The Union Jack: British Loyalists In The Transvaal During The First Anglo-Boer War, 1880–1881*, 8.

48. *See* Bill Nasson, *The Jameson Raid of its Day*, 47 J. AFR. HIST. 335. In February 1881, a British force of around 600 men was engaged by a Boer force on Majuba Mountain. The Boers lost one man and the British "lost over half their complement, dead, wounded or captured" including the commander, Major-General Colley. *Id.*

49. See Laband, *Burying The Union Jack: British Loyalists In The Transvaal During The First Anglo-Boer War, 1880–1881*, 1; Hilton, *Theodor Mommsen and the Liberal Opposition to British Imperialism at the Time of the Second South African War of Independence (1899–1902)*, 49–50; *see also* Stanley Palmer, *Review: The Transvaal Rebellion: The First Boer War, 1880–1881*, 48 VICTORIAN STUD. 571 (2006).

50. Nasson, *The Jameson Raid of its Day*, 336.

51. Letter from Earl of Kimberly (John Wodehouse), Secretary of State for Colonies, to The Under Secretary of State, War Office, January 28, 1881, in UK National Archives File WO 32/7799.

52. *Id.*

General Colley replied on 29 January that he had "avoided proclamation or raising question of belligerent right," but as the Boers had released British prisoners, he proposed "to do the same with any we take," noting that the Boers had "acted with courtesy and humanity in the matter of our wounded."[53] The Secretary of State for War, Mr. Childers, approved "Colley's telegram about belligerency,"[54] and confirmatory instructions were duly sent: "Your action as to belligerent rights approved."[55]

At the conclusion of this short conflict, Transvaaler and British officials negotiated a new arrangement, the Pretoria Convention (1881),[56] which recognized "complete self-government, subject to the suzerainty of Her Majesty,"[57] and subject to reservations and limitations relating to (inter alia) the presence of a British Resident, the right to move troops through the territory of Transvaal "in time of war, or in the case of apprehension of immediate war," and "the control of the external relations" of Transvaal.[58] Further negotiations resulted in the London Convention (1884),[59] from which reference to British "suzerainty" was absent, and separate articles in that treaty confusingly referred to the continuing duties of the Resident, as well as a position of "Consular Officer" entitled to "the protection and assistance of the Republic [Transvaal]," and a relaxation of treaty-making authority to the extent that "The South African Republic will conclude no treaty or engagement with any State or nation other than the Orange Free State, nor with any native tribe to the eastward or westward of the Republic until the same has been approved by Her Majesty the Queen."[60] This state of ambiguous independence was that which pertained at the outbreak of the Second Boer War in 1899. Indeed, as late as 1897, the British and German governments were in dispute "over the precise legal standing of the London Convention of 1884," with Germany arguing that it granted Britain "no special control over the Transvaal," while the British government (albeit after a period of official ambiguity on this

53. Telegram from General Colley, January 29, 1881, in UK National Archives File WO 32/7799.

54. Note, Secretary Childers, January 29, 1881, in UK National Archives File WO 32/7799.

55. Telegram from Secretary of State, War Office to General Officer Commanding Natal, January 29, 1881, *in* UK National Archives File WO 32/7799.

56. Eybers, SELECT CONSTITUTIONAL DOCUMENTS ILLUSTRATING SOUTH AFRICAN HISTORY 1795–1910, 455–63.

57. Convention of Pretoria, UK-S. Afr. R., pmbl. Aug. 3, 1881, https://www.sahistory.org.za/archive/convention-pretoria-convention-settlement-transvaal-territory-3-august-1881.

58. *Id.* at art. II.

59. Eybers, SELECT CONSTITUTIONAL DOCUMENTS ILLUSTRATING SOUTH AFRICAN HISTORY 1795–1910, 471–74.

60. *Id.* at art. 3, 4, 10; *see* the debate on these interpretive issues among, *e.g.*, Blind, *The Transvaal War and European Opinion*, 762–64; Mahan, *The Merits of the Transvaal Dispute*, 314–17.

issue[61]) asserted that it was "an agreement between a sovereign and a dependant state."[62]

This argument as to the nature of the Britain-Transvaal relationship in 1899 colored perceptions of both the justice of the Second Boer War (1899–1902), as well as the nature of the conflict—a war between states, or a rebellion within the British Empire. Alfred Thayer Mahan, on one side, was adamant that British suzerainty continued to exist after the signing of the London Convention, asserting that the UK "Has, in dealing with the Transvaal . . . a particular right and duty—as distinguished from those general rights which all nations possess as members of the international community. This particular right is called suzerainty, a term admittedly vague at the present day."[63] Karl Blind, on the other hand, argued that "While the Queen's suzerainty undoubtedly existed between 1881 and 1884," it was "arrant hypocrisy" to assert that the suzerainty had not been abolished by the London Convention in 1884, and that, consequently, Britain from that time forward held "no right to interfere in the internal affairs of the South African Republic."[64] In his critique, he addressed the issue of insurgency-belligerency consequences:

> Imagine the consequence this [declaring the conflict to be 'a revolt of the vassal', and refusing to recognise the Boer republics as belligerent powers] would have for the English soldiers now in Boer captivity, if the Governments at Pretoria and Bloemfontein had taken reprisals for such treatment as mere 'rebels'! Happily, those Governments were more humane, and acted as belligerent foreign Powers toward their prisoners.[65]

61. *See, e.g.*, Sylvest, *Our Passion for Legality: International Law and Imperialism in Late Nineteenth Century Britain*, 417–19.

62. Hilton, *Theodor Mommsen and the Liberal Opposition to British Imperialism at the Time of the Second South African War of Independence (1899–1902)*, 50. Hilton notes that Germany ultimately recognized British interests in Transvaal in 1898 as part of a policy focused on gaining territory from Portugal in South East Africa.

63. Mahan, *The Merits of the Transvaal Dispute*, 314. Interestingly, John Westlake also asserted that despite uncertainty over the term "suzerainty," it was clear that Transvaal was a "self-governing state within the British Empire"; however, he also argued the justification for Britain going to war on other grounds, focusing upon the justice of propagating the liberal British form of governance over the "Transvaal idea," racially based on Dutch custom and culture and illiberal treatment of the natives. *See* Sylvest, *Our Passion for Legality: International Law and Imperialism in Late Nineteenth Century Britain*, 419–20. Theodore Mommsen also noted that the Second Boer war, in many ways, "a conflict between the sixteenth century and the twentieth century." *See* Hilton, *Theodor Mommsen and the Liberal Opposition to British Imperialism at the Time of the Second South African War of Independence (1899–1902)*, 57.

64. Blind, *The Transvaal War and European Opinion*, 763–64.

65. *Id.* at 768–69.

The previously noted Cape Town-based German Consul-General's 1899 statement regarding the neutrality to be observed by German nationals was clearly informed by an awareness of the doctrine on recognition of belligerency, as well as the potential consequences for third states of the lesser status of insurgency.[66] But it is also representative of the pervasive legal uncertainties that attended the characterization of the Boer parties—independent powers, recognized belligerents, or rebels? James Bryce—a noted legal academic and Member of Parliament—declared during debate in 1902 that the 1 June 1900 proclamation by Lord Roberts (who served as the military commander in South Africa), to the effect that captured members of Boer Commandos would be treated as rebels subsequent to the May 1900 annexations, had been a "monstrous proclamation, a proclamation opposed to the first principles of international law . . . which purported to treat the inhabitants of the two republics as rebels."[67] Previously, Bryce had welcomed its withdrawal, but noted the reputational damage it had wrought:

> That proclamation was taken by everybody who read it as a refusal of belligerent rights to the Boers in the field. The impression naturally produced by the text was that His Majesty's Government considered the time had come when the Boers should be treated no longer as belligerents but as rebels. That construction has been completely abandoned by the Colonial Secretary, and I think that is a real gain. This proclamation has been regarded in foreign countries as a declaration that the Boers were not to be treated as belligerents. For that reason I look upon its terms as having been most unfortunate, and I hope the disclaimer of the Colonial Secretary will obtain the same publicity as the unhappy proclamation itself.[68]

Ultimately, captured Boer fighters were treated as PW, as were captured British nationals who served with Boer Commandos. Indeed, a Cabinet Memorandum dated 8 December 1902 dealt with the legally complex issue of whether, and how, to prosecute for treason British subjects who had been captured serving with Boer forces and had been held as PW (in this case, the individuals at the center of the issue were Mr. Enright and Mr. Hodgson). The legal advice provided was that

> We think that there are grave objections to a prolonged detention of such persons . . . before bringing them to trial. A prisoner of war might be brought to trial for treason after any lapse of time upon the discovery of the fact that he is a British subject. But if it is from the first known that he is a British subject, and with that knowledge the Crown detains him a prisoner of war, we think that this must in fairness be taken to be an election not to treat such person as a traitor . . . We think that when the fact that the person is a British subject comes

66. *See, e.g.*, Campbell, *Neutral Rights and Obligations in the Anglo-Boer War*, 54–55.

67. 20 Jan. 1902, 101 Parl Deb HC (4th ser.) (1902) col. 324–436, 423.

68. 15 Aug. 1901, 99 Parl Deb HC (4th ser.) (1901) col. 978–1051, 1021–22.

> to the knowledge of the authorities they ought to decide whether they will treat him as a prisoner of war or as a rebel, and act accordingly. To detain him as a prisoner of war while the war lasts, and then bring him to trial for high treason, would be to punish the man twice for the same offence.[69]

The recommendation was that the cases not be proceeded with,[70] and this cohered with the general approach to a "light touch" with respect to prosecutions for treason within the Cape Colony itself[71]—informed to a large extent by deep concerns over the execution of martial law.[72] What is clear, however, is that captured Boer fighters were treated as recognized belligerents—given the formal British position on persisting "suzerainty" over the Boer Republics—and that this status could also be applied to British subjects who were captured while fighting in Boer Commandos. The *Vereeniging Peace Treaty* (1902) with the Orange Free State[73] specifically referred to the conflict in rebellion terms, requiring that the "Burgher Forces in the field will . . . desist from any further resistance to the authority of His Majesty . . . whom they recognise as their lawful sovereign,"[74] and providing that

> No proceedings, civil or criminal, will be taken against any of the burghers so surrendering or so returning for any acts in connection with the prosecution of the war. The benefit of this clause will not extend to certain acts contrary to the usage of war which have been notified by the Commander-in-Chief to the Boer Generals, and which shall be tried by Court-Martial immediately after the close of hostilities.[75]

69. Cabinet Memorandum, Proposed Prosecution of Enright and Hodgson, British Subjects, for Rebellion during the Boer War, Dec. 8, 1902, ¶ 2, *in* UK National Archives File CAB 37/63 No.164.

70. *Id.* at ¶ 8.

71. *See* Keith Surridge, *Rebellion, Martial Law and British Civil-Military Relations: The War in Cape Colony 1899–1902*, 8 Small Wars & Insurgencies 35 (1997) (regarding treason trials and martial law in the Cape Colony, 1899–1902).

72. *See, e.g.*, South African Vigilance Committee, Memorandum Regarding the Administration of Martial Law in the Cape Colony, forwarded to the British High Commissioner, Alfred Milner, August 21, 1901, *in* UK National Archives File WO 32/8122); Confidential Memorandum from Lord Milner to Mr. Chamberlain, September 2, 1901, *in* UK National Archives File WO 32/8122; Confidential Memorandum, Governor Sir Hely-Hutchinson to Mr. Chamberlain, September 2, 1901, *in* UK National Archives File WO 32/8122.

73. Vereeniging Peace Treaty, May 31, 1902, *reprinted in* Eybers, Select Constitutional Documents Illustrating South African History 1795–1910, 345–47.

74. *Id.* at art. 1.

75. *Id.* at art. 4.

If Britain had not specifically recognized Boer belligerency with a formal declaration, it had clearly done so by conduct.

(ii) The Spanish Civil War: Non-intervention and non-recognition of belligerency?

The most iconic twentieth-century situation for consideration of recognition of belligerency, and for many scholars the primary talisman of the desuetude of the doctrine, was the Spanish Civil War. Indeed, much academic discussion of this conflict—in terms of the challenges it presented to international law—tended to focus upon the applicability or otherwise of recognition of belligerency, and the consequences flowing therefrom.[76] Many contemporary analyses of the conflict concluded that—to cite but one writer, Vernon O'Rourke—"the scope of the Spanish war today legally justifies recognition of belligerency by foreign States."[77] Padelford likewise lamented that European states employed a policy of non-intervention with "inadequate legal protection" such that it effectively "amounted in reality to a form of intervention in the civil strife in Spain and operated against the established government."[78] Oglesby asserted that the Spanish Civil War "clearly and unequivocally met all the standard criteria justifying belligerent recognition." The primary reason the status was not afforded, he (and others) argued, was—paradoxically, considering the "non-intervention" agreement—"the presence of widespread intervention by outside powers."[79] Van Wynen Thomas and Thomas Jr. agreed that

> When the Spanish conflict reached the magnitude of war, which probably occurred within a very few months of the rebellion's outbreak, belligerency should have been recognised and neutrality observed. In failing to recognise belligerency and to grant full belligerent rights when all necessary conditions were present, the several European powers appear to have violated international law and to have intervened in Spanish affairs.[80]

76. Arnold McNair, *The Law Relating to the Civil War in Spain*, 53 L.Q. Rev. 71 (1937); Robert R. Wilson, *Recognition of Insurgency and Belligerency*, 31 Am. Soc'y Int'l L. Proc. 136 (1937); Fred K. Nielsen, *Insurgency and Maritime Law*, 31 Am. Soc'y Int'l L. Proc. 144, 153 (1937); O'Rourke, 405; Norman J. Padelford, *Foreign Shipping During the Spanish Civil War*, 32 Am J. Int'l L. 264 (1938); Raoul Genet, *The Charge of Piracy in the Spanish Civil War*, 32 Am J. Int'l L. 253 (1938); *see also* Kuyper, *Recognition: Netherlands Theory and State Practice*, 385–86 (discussing the contemporaneous debate in Dutch circles—including the scholars H.A. Helb and J.W.H. Verzijl—as to whether recognition of belligerency, or of insurgency, should be considered).

77. O'Rourke, *Recognition of Belligerency and the Spanish War*, 404.

78. Padelford, International Law and Diplomacy in the Spanish Civil Strife, 201.

79. Oglesby, Internal War and the Search for Normative Order, 104–105.

80. Ann Van Wynen Thomas and A.J. Thomas Jr., *International Legal Aspects of the Civil War in Spain, 1936–39*, *in* International Law of Civil War 111, 176 (Richard A. Falk ed., 1972).

Edwin Firmage, in his "Summary and Interpretation" concluding chapter in Richard Falk's important 1971 volume on *The International Law of Civil War*, was convinced that, in retrospect,

> the scope and territorial nature of the nationalist revolt resulted in a status of de facto belligerency which would be hard to distinguish from the status of de jure belligerency enjoyed by the Confederacy in the American Civil War. The rules of war would seem to have been as binding upon the conduct of the Spanish Civil War as upon the American.[81]

Equally, however, the contemporaneous political discourse in Britain was ultimately characterized by a tortuous application of non-interference policy thinly veiled with—among other things—a counterintuitive claim to "non-intervention." This was accompanied by a clear bastardization of the law of piracy, so as to deny (for political reasons) the application of the doctrine.[82] This is plainly evident in the fact that British political and legal appreciations of the Spanish Civil War were informed, from the very outset, by the contextually inescapable doctrine on recognition of belligerency.

A British Foreign Office memorandum on "Italian Foreign Policy in the Spanish Civil War," dated 31 August 1936 and circulated to the Cabinet, addressed the need to ensure that Italy fully understood the sensitivity of His Majesty's Government "in case Italy should by some means or another upset the existing balance in the Western Mediterranean."[83] The memorandum warned that if Italy did not sign up to the "agreement for non-intervention which we are trying to achieve," then Britain

> could not remain indifferent to any alteration in the balance of sea and air power in the western Mediterranean, which was due not to the action of Spain within her own jurisdiction (a matter which it is not open to us to question),

81. Edwin Brown Firmage, *Summary and Interpretation, in* International Law of Civil War 405, 415 (Richard A. Falk ed., 1972); *see also* Van Wynen Thomas and Thomas Jr., *International Legal Aspects of the Civil War in Spain, 1936–39*, 123, 128, 141–46 (discussing respectively the humanitarian protections; the interplay between the legal schemes for belligerency, insurgency; and non-intervention in relation to third states).

82. Genet, *The Charge of Piracy in the Spanish Civil War*, 53. The animating political imperative for a number of concerned third States was to deny both sides the formal status of belligerency; the consequence was the tortured characterization of the large-scale and significant maritime (including submarine) operations carried out by both sides against third State shipping as "piracy", best represented in the Nyon Agreement of September 14, 1937, which never entered into force. *See* Nyon Agreement, Sep. 14, 1937, 181 L.N.T.S 137, https://www.icrc.org/applic/ihl/ihl.nsf/Treaty.xsp?documentId=8CFA247BE2EE0CA2C12563CD002D6A76&action=openDocument.

83. Italian Foreign Policy in the Spanish Civil War, Foreign Office memorandum for Cabinet CP.233 (36), dated 31 August 1936, *in* UK National Archives File: CAB/24/264.

> but to the action of some other Power which had taken advantage of civil war in Spain to enter into some kind of special relationship with either side.[84]

The concern was, it seems clear, that Italy might recognize the belligerency of the parties in the Spanish Civil War, and then use that status as a pretext to support the Fascist belligerent, thereby enlivening its Law of War powers in support of a party to the conflict and to the detriment of British interests in the area. Alternatively, the concern was that allowing the belligerent parties to employ the Law of War in respect to neutrals—including blockades and visit and search—would also be to the grave detriment of British interests in the area and was therefore equally unacceptable. Even if Britain itself did not follow suit with recognition of belligerency, and a formal declaration of consequential neutrality, the fact that a major third state—Italy—had done so would thus have greatly complicated the situation for Britain.[85]

The question of belligerent rights in the Spanish Civil War continued to bedevil the British government throughout the period 1936–1939. Notes from the British Cabinet meeting of 22 November 1936 are indicative of the range of concerns that the question of recognition of belligerent rights provoked at this early stage of the conflict. The notes disclose that the Board of Trade was "urging that belligerent rights at sea should be publicly recognised as soon as possible."[86] The letter from the President of the Board of Trade (Walter Runciman) to the Prime Minister (Stanley Baldwin) is dated 21 November 1936 and is very instructive as to the interaction of the legal doctrine with commercial concerns. The Board of Trade argued that the grant of belligerent rights was "desirable . . . as soon as possible if we are not prepared in effect to protect British merchant ships against any interference on the high seas."[87] This reasoning was based upon the interrelated concerns that while British merchant shipping interests were "under the impression that they can count on protection from British warships against any interference on the high seas," unless belligerent rights were granted, the Board of Trade understood that the Royal Navy (RN) had determined not to interfere with the Francoist blockade. That is, despite there being no recognition of belligerent rights at sea, "protection will not be afforded to British ships beyond that which would be given if belligerent rights were recognised."[88] This position, the Board of Trade correctly believed was "full of anomalies" and as such the Board was "strongly of the opinion that in the interests of traders generally and of shipping certainty is desirable."[89] The Minister for Co-ordination of Defence and the Admiralty both

84. *Id.*

85. *See* Lauterpacht, Recognition in International Law, 250–53.

86. Notes of Cabinet Meeting, Nov. 22, 1936, at 1, *in* UK National Archives File: CAB/24/265.

87. *Id.* at 1 (app. III, Board of Trade letter from Runciman to Baldwin dated Nov. 21, 1936).

88. *Id.*

89. *Id.* at 2.

observed that recognition of belligerency might also soon become necessary at any rate, "owing to the development of trade negotiations" with Franco's regime.[90] Indeed, by November 1937, these relations had subsequently deepened to the extent that the cross-appointment of "agents" between the Nationalists and the British government was deemed appropriate—although, in keeping with a strict three-level scheme legal analysis, it was noted that because the Nationalist NSAG remained categorized as "insurgent," the nature of these agencies was "nominally at all events—purely a commercial one."[91]

The Admiralty also argued in favor of recognizing belligerency from two additional perspectives. First, they argued that to do so would be "merely adopting our traditional attitude in recognising belligerent rights," and thus Britain could safely take this act without being accused of "following their [German and Italian] lead" in recognizing the Nationalists as a government in Spain.[92] Second, the Admiralty advised that recognition of belligerency should be granted because non-recognition created "uncertainties" for the RN.[93] This was particularly so with respect to the RN's protective responsibilities in relation to British vessels they knew to be involved in arms smuggling into Barcelona, and the risk of escalation if these vessels were intercepted by German or Italian warships on behalf of the Francoist forces, possibly requiring the RN to intervene. That is, if belligerent rights were granted, the RN could properly allow such inspections as a part of a legitimate blockade. However, if belligerent rights were not granted, the RN would be expected to defend British shipping from the unlawful exercise of blockade rights by Nationalist forces, thus raising the probability of interactions with any German or Italian units that intercepted those British vessels in support of Franco's purported blockade.

In order to provide some clarity, the Admiralty had issued an evolving set of instructions over the period 20–22 November 1936. The first iteration, dated 20 November, had instructed that upon receipt of a request from a British vessel for assistance in the face of interdiction by a Spanish warship, the normal response of assistance or protection was not to be offered if the vessel in question was "carrying war material destined for Spain." In this situation, the instructions added, "you should inform the master that HM Government are not prepared to accord him protection."[94] These instructions were then amended on 22 November to provide that while Britain did not recognize either party's right to conduct visit and search outside of Spanish territorial waters, if a British vessel was halted for this purpose, and then asked a British warship in the vicinity for assistance, "the master is to be advised to submit to visit and search but a British naval officer is to

90. *Id.* at 6–7.

91. Note, Foreign Office to Sir Alexander Hardinge, Nov. 29, 1937, *in* UK National Archives File: FO/954/27A.

92. *Id.* at 2–3.

93. *Id.* at 2.

94. *Id.* at 1.

take part in the search."[95] If the vessel was found to be carrying war material destined for either party in Spain, then the vessel would forfeit British protection.[96] If not, then the interdicting Spanish vessel would be informed that the British vessel "cannot be controlled unless visit and search has proved that war material destined for Spain is being carried."[97]

Conversely, the Foreign Secretary was of the view that "it would be preferable not to recognise belligerent rights to General Franco's forces at present." This was because any such grant—coming hard on the heels of Franco's declaration of a blockade of Barcelona—would "be held to be taking a preliminary step indispensable to his acting, and thus helping his cause."[98] Indeed, recognizing Franco as a belligerent would legitimize the blockade and would thus act to "curtail supplies of food to Madrid, and we ought not to facilitate this."[99] The Home Secretary also pointed out that if belligerency were recognized, then the British government would be signaling an expectation (and acceptance) of Nationalist prize courts and contraband lists.[100] He also discussed the consequences of not recognizing belligerency, including that Franco's actions in enforcing his blockade against British vessels might be "piracy,"[101] as well as the implications of "an extension of the Foreign Enlistment Act so as to prevent British ships from carrying war material from foreign ports to Spain."[102] The Minister for Co-ordination of Defence (while reminding Cabinet of the de jure government of Spain's right to exercise authority within "the three mile limit"[103]) suggested that "if we were not prepared to grant belligerent rights," then the minimum required was some specific legislation "to make the carriage of war material from a foreign port by a British ship a penal offence."[104] The Foreign Secretary added that this policy would have to be applied to both

95. *Id.* at 4.

96. *Id.*

97. *Id.* at ¶ (f).

98. *Id.* at 1. A three-page Foreign Office note on "The Question of Belligerent Rights" was tabled at the Cabinet meeting and is attached to the notes as App. I, dated Nov. 21, 1936. This note is interesting for the amalgam of political, diplomatic, and legal reasoning presented, including the observation that recognizing belligerent rights at that stage might "place us in a humiliating position in that we could be accused of having done so only on account of General Franco's threat and our consequent fear of an incident in the Mediterranean with a Spanish ship." *Id.* at 2.

99. *Id.* at 2.

100. *Id.* at 3.

101. *Id.* at 13.

102. *Id.* at 5. The Home Secretary elsewhere noted that the "it was already illegal to export arms from this country to Spain" under the *Foreign Enlistment Act*, and that the proposed legislative action "would merely make it illegal to carry them to Spain from anywhere." *Id.* at 10.

103. *Id.* at 5.

104. *Id.*

parties.[105] The Prime Minister—demonstrating either a nuanced grasp of, or an excellent brief on, the intricacies of blockade law (i.e., that it must be effective, not merely declared)—also observed that "even if we granted Belligerent rights, we should be a long way off recognising a blockade."[106]

The Cabinet then assessed the Admiralty's 22 November 1936 instructions to the Mediterranean and Home Fleets,[107] alongside draft statements on the British government's attitude to the contending parties as prepared by the Home Office,[108] and the Exchequer.[109] It was determined that the existing policy of "non-intervention" would remain in place, and Admiralty instructions would revert to the 20 November 1936 version.[110] It was also decided that a note would be dispatched to Franco indicating that while Britain would "continue to not accord belligerent rights at sea to either side in the Spanish struggle," and that British policy was "to take no part in the conflict on either side," the government would act to ensure "that British shipping should not carry war material to any port in Spain."[111] As noted previously, this contorted policy of acting neutrally, but denying belligerency, remained in place even until the Hemming Report,[112] which placed Franco's continuing demands for recognized belligerent status, and the Republicans' equally trenchant continuing demand that this status be denied to the Nationalists,[113] at the core of any potential agreement on mitigating the international consequences of the conflict.

In 1951, the British government responded to assertions in a Spanish Note Verbale (No.190 of 1950) concerning claims for compensation by British subjects arising from the Spanish Civil War. The Note Verbale included diplomatic and legal claims as to partisan British conduct during the Spanish Civil War, including that the non-intervention arrangements were a cover for British support to the Republican side. Reviewing the context and history of the issue, Mr. Aiken-Sneath advised that the British government had at the time determined that recognition of belligerency of both sides was legally justified, but had proposed that it only be accorded "by all the members of the Non-Intervention Committee . . . contingent on the withdrawal of foreign nationals from Spain," and only to "become effective when the Non-Intervention Committee place on record their opinion

105. *Id.* at 7.

106. *Id.*

107. *Id.* at 3–6.

108. *Id.* at 8–9.

109. *Id.* at 8.

110. *Id.* at 16.

111. *Id.* at app. IV.

112. Report by Mr Francis Hemming on his Mission to National Spain, dated Nov. 17, 1938, ¶¶ 71–81, 167, 170–71, 222, *in* UK Archives File: ADM 116/6315.

113. Communication from Mr. Azcarate to Viscount Halifax, Jul. 27, 1938, ¶ 16, *in* UK Archives File: ADM 116/6315; Note from Viscount Halifax to Mr. Stevenson (Barcelona), Dec. 14, 1938, ¶ 7, in UK Archives File: ADM 116/6315.

that the arrangements for the withdrawal of foreign nationals are working satisfactorily."[114] That the British had trod an uncomfortable legal path in the name of an elusive and ultimately unachieved political aim was certainly recognized by, among others, Legal Adviser Sir Eric Beckett:

> The Spanish Government have, I think, really a moral though not a legal case against us here. There is no doubt, I think, that international law indicated as proper though not, I think, obligatory a recognition of belligerency from the beginning of the Spanish civil war and much difficulty and many insoluble problems would have been avoided if only HMG and other Governments had, at the beginning of the Spanish civil war, taken the course which international law indicated as appropriate in these circumstances. Instead of this they tried to deal with the matter through the non-intervention committee and denying belligerent rights at sea . . .
>
> The Spanish civil war has always seemed to me to be one of those cases which illustrate the series of tangles which one gets into if one is confronted with a situation where international law provides the obvious course of action and where, for reasons which are supposedly good at the time, another course is taken.[115]

The point—very, very clearly—is that it was the political determination to *avoid* recognizing the belligerency of the parties that led to this particular legally obtuse characterization outcome; that is, the recognition of belligerency was clearly understood to be the core characterization issue, and strenuous efforts were made in order to deny its applicability. Again, this is not indicative of a dead or dying doctrine.

At this point, a brief interrogation of two specific legal vignettes arising from this context will serve to further indicate how clearly the recognition of belligerency was consciously accepted as the background to Spanish Civil War legal debates. This assessment will also serve to illustrate some of the diverse effects that the conscious decision to avoid this outcome ultimately entailed. The first vignette is a British Admiralty jurisdiction case; the second is the non-intervention system.

(A) Government of Republic of Spain v. SS Arantzazu Mendi (1939)

It is instructive to briefly describe the *Arantzazu Mendi* case as an instance of (at that time) contemporary judicial expression of the "confusing, nebulous, and

114. Memorandum, F. Aiken-Sneath, 1952, ¶ 13, *in* UK Archives File: FO 371—WS 1483/1.

115. Memorandum by Sir Eric Beckett, Legal Adviser, Jun. 18, 1951, ¶ 7, *in* UK Archives File: FO 371—WS 1483/6. Ultimately, Sir Beckett advised, "As to the question of HMG's attitude toward the insurgents during the Civil War, and the propriety of withholding belligerent status from them, I should be disposed to avoid being drawn into a paper controversy on this subject." in Note from RSB Best to Sir Eric Beckett, Jun. 14, 1951, ¶ 3(b), *in* UK Archives File: FO 371—WS 1483/6.

unsettled"[116] legal consequences of insurgency and belligerency. Although it is a case, as Herbert Briggs points out, more about the distinction between de facto and de jure recognition,[117] *Arantzazu Mendi* is nevertheless indicative of the state of the law in relation to insurgency and belligerency in the fulcrum of the Spanish Civil War. The *Arantzazu Mendi* was a privately owned vessel registered in Bilbao. She was requisitioned by the Spanish (Republican) government on 28 June 1937. At the time, however, Bilbao was in the hands of the Nationalist rebels, and the vessel itself was at sea. Upon arrival in London on 11 August 1937, the owner commenced proceedings to recover possession (formally, for it appears that the vessel was not actually following Spanish government orders) from the Republican government. On 5 April 1938, the Nationalist government (still considered an insurgent force, and not recognized as a belligerent by Britain) also requisitioned the vessel, and her owners opted to recognize the Nationalist order. On 13 April 1938, the Republican government applied to have possession of the vessel assigned to its own agents. "The Franco insurgents—called 'the nationalist Government of Spain' by the court—entered a conditional appearance to set the [Republican] writ aside on the ground that it impeded a foreign sovereign state which was unwilling to submit to the jurisdiction of the court."[118]

Counsel for the Republican government explicitly referred to the legal consequences of recognition of insurgency as opposed to recognition of belligerency:

> In the present case there has been merely a recognition of insurgency [of the Nationalists]; and it is contrary to the principles of international law to concede full sovereign status to a body which confessedly has not attained its full aim . . . A recognition of insurgency does not carry with it all the attributes of true sovereignty, even provisionally.[119]

However, counsel for the Nationalists did not address the insurgency-belligerency issue, but argued the case rather from the perspective of previous British recognition—as a matter of political expediency—of de facto governments insofar as their conduct affected British interests: "On the main question as to the position of the respondents [Nationalists] in international law, a de facto Government having the occupied territory completely under its control has necessarily full responsibility, and its acts have the status of acts of a Government which will be recognised."[120]

116. Van Wynen Thomas and Thomas Jr., *International Legal Aspects of the Civil War in Spain, 1936–39*, 158–59; *see also* CHEN, THE INTERNATIONAL LAW OF RECOGNITION, 320–23.

117. Herbert W. Briggs, *De Facto and De Jure Recognition: The Arantzazu Mendi*, 33 AM. J. INT'L L. 689 (1939).

118. *Id.* at 693; *Government of Republic of Spain v. S.S. Arantzazu Mendi And Others*, 33 AM. J. INT'L L. 583 (1939); LAUTERPACHT, RECOGNITION IN INTERNATIONAL LAW, 279–82, 288–91.

119. Government of Republic of Spain v. S.S. Arantzazu Mendi, [1939] AC 256 (H.L) (appeal taken from Rep. Gov't).

120. *Id.* at 261.

The issue of recognition for the purposes of assessing the Nationalist government's claim was ultimately resolved through acceptance by the Court of the Foreign Secretary's response to a question on the recognition afforded by the British government to both parties. In essence, the British government de facto recognized the Nationalist government as responsible for the administration of the area including Bilbao, and that "the nationalist Government is not a Government subordinate to any other Government in Spain." This decision has been criticized for its failure to engage with the parallel doctrine on recognition of belligerency and insurgency,[121] and it is fair to say that the House of Lords did abdicate the field in terms of rationalizing the intersections apparent in this case between recognitions of state, government, belligerency, and insurgency. Briggs, rhetorically inquiring how the Court decided "this question of law," concluded that:

> They said in effect: A government which is recognised as having as much power as the Foreign Office letter attributes to the nationalist Government *must* be a state; therefore we must grant this recognised de facto government the same immunities we should grant a recognised de jure government; and besides, it can grant us reciprocal immunity; and if we take jurisdiction over Franco's property he may have a 'feeling of injured pride' and may attack us.[122]

Indeed, it is interesting to ask whether the Foreign Secretary's letter was in part based upon the understanding that recognition of belligerency for the Nationalists was both overdue and imminent, as would appear to have been the case by reference to the Hemming Report.

(B) Incoherence within the Non-Intervention System

Italian and German support for the Nationalists was an early fact on the ground in the Spanish Civil War.[123] European security fragility, and concerns as to the potential knock-on effects of the conflict if intervention became the norm, led to the development of the non-intervention accord—actually a series of substantially similar declarations agreed between twenty-seven governments that signed up to the policy, coupled with relevant domestic legislative acts that purported to ensure the governments and nationals of each non-intervention state maintained strict impartiality and non-intervention.[124] The policy, as analyzed by Padelford, hinged around nine pillars, the first three being of most relevance to discussions of non-intervention and non-recognition of belligerency:

121. *See, e.g.*, Oglesby, Internal War and the Search for Normative Order, 77–78.

122. Briggs, *De Facto and De Jure Recognition: The Arantzazu Mendi*, 698.

123. *See generally* Van Wynen Thomas and Thomas Jr., *International Legal Aspects of the Civil War in Spain, 1936–39*, 111–15.

124. *See generally* Padelford, International Law and Diplomacy in the Spanish Civil Strife, 56–69; Van Wynen Thomas and Thomas Jr., *International Legal Aspects of the Civil War in Spain, 1936–39*, 115–20.

> (1) a collective admission of insurgency and acknowledgement of the fact that hostilities were in progress; (2) collective determination of the question of granting belligerent rights; (3) a collective embargo upon the exportation of war materials and a collective ban on the departure of volunteers and troops for both sides in Spain. [125]

But the non-intervention policy was, to say the least, riddled with legal, political, and factual incoherencies from the very outset. Non-intervention states often allowed, or were ineffective in halting, the influx of their nationals into the conflict as fighters and their goods as war material, and despite significant institutionalization and continuous revision,[126] the non-intervention policy did not ultimately prevent interventions.

As Padelford noted in 1939, "The Non-Intervention system gradually atrophied as the Spanish strife took its wearisome course towards its ultimate denouemont." The Non-Intervention Committee did not meet after July 1938, the foreign fighter withdrawal plan was not implemented, and states began to withdraw from the system in November 1938.[127] Lauterpacht's cutting, concise, and contemptuous observation in the 1948 edition of Oppenheim's *International Law* is exactly on point: "These agreements consisted in an undertaking on the part of certain powers to refrain from committing an international illegality in consideration of the promise of other powers to refrain from action in a manner in which they were entitled—and according to some—legally bound to act."[128]

Of particular note within this system was the approach taken by the non-intervention states to acts of maritime warfare carried out on the high seas by and on behalf of the conflict parties—that is, outside and apart from the generally recognized right of either or both of the parties to control navigation within the Spanish territorial sea (at that time agreed to be out to three miles). In essence, the refusal to recognize belligerency, when coupled with a policy of non-intervention, necessitated the legal characterization of conduct at sea by the NSAG as piracy, for the Law of War applicable at sea did not de jure apply as between the parties, nor as between the NSAG and third states. However, in this case, the policy of non-intervention—read here as impartiality—required that conduct by Republican forces also be labeled piratical, despite the fact that the Republican party to the

125. Padelford, International Law and Diplomacy in the Spanish Civil Strife, 118–19. The other six pillars were: (4) an international organization to coordinate and monitor non-intervention; (5) an observation and control scheme; (6) collective appeals to both parties to respect foreign life and property; (7) collective protests against inhumane conduct of the war; (8) withdrawal of foreign troops and volunteers; and (9) collective proposals for mediation and termination of the conflict.

126. *See, e.g.*, Padelford, International Law and Diplomacy in the Spanish Civil Strife, 72–12.

127. *Id.* at 117; Lauterpacht, Recognition in International Law, 250–52.

128. 1 Lassa Oppenheim, International Law: A Treatise 273 (H. Lauterpacht ed., 7th ed., 1948).

conflict was the generally recognized government and thus its forces could not legally commit piracy. If belligerency had been recognized, then both parties would have been entitled to conduct operations on the high seas in accordance with the Law of War, and third states would have interacted with these operations from a legally unimpeachable position of neutrality. This absurdity found its fullest expression in the *Nyon Arrangement* of 1937,[129] which was described by Green as a legal instrument

> directed against *unknown* submarines which were attacking merchant vessels legitimately trading with the Spanish government. In this case the law was enforced not against the parties to the conflict, but the *officially* unidentified powers whose vessels were indulging in these unlawful attacks against *neutral* shipping.[130]

This attempt to redraw the lines between piracy, insurgency, belligerency, and neutrality at sea[131]—while tortuously and inconsistently applied during the Spanish Civil War—ultimately failed to gain traction. As Alfred Rubin observed in 1976, discussing draft articles and negotiations for what would become the 1982 Law of the Sea Convention, adopting a Nyon sense of "illegality" (and its implications for the concept of "private ends") would do great harm to the orthodox view as to the line between piracy and insurgency at sea:

> The violence of those allied with a rebellion can, of course, be considered as acts for 'private ends'; it has always been the obvious tactic of a government seeking to suppress rebellion to label the rebels 'bandits' and members of a self-seeking clique. That tactic has customarily been ignored by second states, which normally have no interest in the enforcement of the criminal laws of a state suffering outbreaks of robbery, mutiny, or treason . . . While the law relating to piracy has in some cases been applied to rebels, it has never been applied to favour them, and the overwhelming practice of states has been to refuse to mingle in foreign rebellions by stigmatizing one foreign political group or another as 'piratical'.[132]

129. The text of the arrangement and its supplementary agreement are annexed in PADELFORD, INTERNATIONAL LAW AND DIPLOMACY IN THE SPANISH CIVIL STRIFE, 603–609.

130. Leslie C. Green, *Strengthening Legal Protection in Internal Conflicts: Low-Intensity Conflict and the Law*, 3 ILSA J. INT'L & COMP. L. 493, 497–98 (1997).

131. Of some interest to this issue is the associated debate that ensued between Hersch Lauterpacht and Carl Schmitt in relation to the assimilation of submarine warfare with piracy evident in the *Nyon Arrangement*, along with the related dispute regarding the concept of an "enemy of mankind" and the criminalization of "public enemies." *See* Walter Rech, *Rightless Enemies: Schmitt and Lauterpacht on Political Piracy*, 32 OXF. J. LEG. STUD. 235 (2012).

132. Alfred P. Rubin, *Is Piracy Illegal?*, 70 AM. J. INT'L L. 92, 93–94 (1976). Rubin, incidentally, is of no doubt that as of 1976, the consequences of insurgency, and the doctrine on recognition of belligerency, remained very much operative in international law.

In summary, perhaps the most damning assessment of the legal incoherence and inconsistency of the non-intervention system in its many facets is that offered by O'Rourke. Noting the "new practice in international law—non-intervention" adopted in relation to the Spanish Civil War, he asked whether this "supplanting" of neutrality as the applicable "policy" actually achieved the effect desired. That is, because "declarations of neutrality on the part of foreign Powers amount to recognition of belligerency," did it follow, that assiduous avoidance of that term was sufficient to also avoid the legal consequence?[133]

O'Rourke did not think so. First, if a situation was not one of recognized belligerency, then it remained an insurgency. For example, in insurgencies, the conflict state was entitled to a continued supply of munitions from third states, while the insurgent force was not entitled to any support from third states: "Until an insurrection has achieved the status of belligerency . . . the established government may expect partial treatment from third powers."[134] Second, the requirements of the agreed non-intervention stance included control of private transactions and dealings by third state nationals to a much more restrictive degree than did the adoption of neutrality.[135] Third, on the basis of his survey of the evidence, he assessed that "the policy and practice of non-intervention in many ways is even more deep-reaching than the observance of simple neutrality."[136] "If the latter entails recognition of belligerency," he then asked, "why not the former?"[137] Ultimately, he therefore concluded: "Non-intervention, which treats both combatants impartially, amounts to neutrality."[138]

133. O'Rourke, *Recognition of Belligerency and the Spanish War*, 409.

134. *Id.* at 410.

135. *Id.* at 409.

136. *Id.* at 411.

137. *Id.*

138. *Id.* at 410. Wyndham L. Walker, *Recognition of Belligerency and Grant of Belligerent Rights*, 23 Transactions Grotius Soc'y 177, 206–207 (1937). Walker similarly pointed out the legal incoherence of the non-intervention substitute for having to recognize belligerency:

> the first principle we adopt is that of non-intervention . . . designed to prevent or minimise the effects of outside interference in Spain. But at the same time we refuse to admit the legality of visit and search or the exercise of any belligerent rights on the high seas to either side in the contest, or to recognise the validity of the establishment of blockades. But the facts force us into certain dealings with the insurgents, who are in de facto control of two-thirds of Spain.

He continued, "However much I may dislike dictatorships, whether black or red, I cannot find our present practice to be strictly in accordance with the practice or opinion of the past. The law is not always such an ass as the legislator may be tempted to suppose." *Id.* at 210; *see also* Van Wynen Thomas and Thomas Jr., *International Legal Aspects of the Civil War in Spain, 1936–39*, 145–46; Chen, The International Law of Recognition, 248 (who similarly make this point).

D. THE CHALLENGE OF LEGAL EXEGESIS: RECOGNITION OF BELLIGERENCY AND SOME POST-1945 LEGAL DEVELOPMENTS

Perhaps the most important and iconic representation of the enduring status and relevance of the recognition of belligerency by the mid-twentieth century is Lauterpacht's seminal 1947 monograph *Recognition in International Law*, in which he devoted entirely one-quarter of the book to recognition of belligerency and insurgency. He certainly treated the doctrine as one of significant nuance, settled content, and enduring effect: "There is general agreement as to the nature of the conditions which impose the duty of recognition of belligerency—or which, according to others, justify recognition of belligerency."[139] There can be no doubt that his analysis was underpinned by a clear assumption that the doctrine was most certainly not defunct. Similarly, the U.S. Military Tribunal in Nuremberg, in *The Hostages Trial (List and Others)* in 1948, dealt specifically with the issue of partisans and the conditions of their access to PW treatment rights.[140] But this does not mean that the doctrine's continuance has remained unproblematic in terms of post-1945 developments in international law. In this section, I will briefly address three legal interpretive challenges that arise in relation to a continuing role for recognition of belligerency in the post-1945 international legal scheme—The UN Charter and "intervention"; the 1949 Geneva Conventions; and the 1977 Additional Protocols—in order to come to a conclusion about the continued existence or otherwise of a legal "space" in which recognition of belligerency might still persist and operate. As will be seen, this persistence in LOAC is arguably evident on two levels: as a customary Law of War doctrine that was not extinguished in toto by the 1949 reconfiguration of much of the Law of War into LOAC; and as a conflict typology that remains independent of and distinct from the orthodox NIAC thresholds.

139. Lauterpacht, Recognition in International Law, 175–76.

140. The U.S. Military Tribunal in Nuremberg addressed the issue of partisans and the conditions of their access to PW treatment rights.

> We agree, therefore, with the contention of the defendant List that the guerrilla fighters with which he contended were not lawful belligerents entitling them to prisoner of war status upon capture. We are obliged to hold that such guerrillas were *francs tireurs* who, upon capture, could be subjected to the death penalty. Consequently, no criminal responsibility attaches to the defendant List because of the execution of captured partisans in Yugoslavia and Greece during the time he was Armed Forces Commander Southeast.

The Hostages Trial: Trial of Wilhelm List and Others (Case No. 47), 8 L. Rpts. of Trials of War Criminals 34, 75 (UN War Crimes Comm. 1948) (quoting U.S. Military Trib., Nuremberg 8th July, 1947, to 19th February, 1948).

(i) The UN Charter 1945

There can also be no doubt that recognition of belligerency creates challenges in terms of interpretation and application within the context of the UN Charter.[141] This challenge is most particularly acute in relation to the purposes enshrined in Article 2 (especially non-intervention in the domestic affairs of states, and the prohibition of threats and uses of force against the territorial integrity and political independence of states), and the Chapter VII jurisdiction of the United Nations Security Council (UNSC) in relation to international peace and security. As Charles King has observed, "One of the characteristics of modern revolutionary war is the apparent need of all guerrilla movements for at least some foreign assistance to provide them with the necessary armaments to effect the transition from guerrilla to conventional warfare."[142] Stowell considered recognition of belligerency to be a legitimate international law rule set, but argued from the position that the doctrine was properly cognizable as an (often illegitimately claimed) exception to the general rule on non-intervention.[143] Wyndham Walker, discussing the Spanish Civil War, recognized the challenge of integrating non-intervention and recognition of belligerency, but never assessed that the former had displaced or extinguished the latter:

> If non-intervention is in any sense a principle of law, not merely a principle of State policy, the State that recognises belligerency prematurely will find itself legally culpable as an intervener, and the state which long withholds recognition of undoubted belligerents may find itself in a situation in which the efficient protection of its own subjects' interests appears to call for measures quite inconsistent with non-interference in the military struggle in progress—it may have to choose between recognition and acts of military or naval interference in the operations carried on by one side against its enemy.[144]

John Norton Moore also analyzed the Soviet intervention in Afghanistan and U.S. intervention in El Salvador in terms of a Charter-based rule set centered around the difficult triptych of a norm of non-intervention leavened by permissible situations of intervention and counter-intervention.[145] The ICJ, in the *Nicaragua Case (Merits)*, has similarly made clear that "provision of weapons or logistical or other support"—while not an armed attack for the purposes of

141. William P. Bobulsky, *Beyond Vietnam to Indo-China—The Legal Implications of the United States' Incursions into Cambodia and Laos*, 3 Case W. Res. J. Int'l L. 163, 174 (1971).

142. Charles R. King, *Revolutionary War, Guerrilla Warfare, and International Law*, 4 Case W. Res. J. Int'l L. 91, 101 (1972).

143. Ellery C. Stowell, Intervention in International Law 345–55 (1921).

144. Walker, *Recognition of Belligerency and Grant of Belligerent Rights*, 199.

145. John N. Moore, *Legal Standards for Intervention in Internal Conflicts*, 13 Ga. J. Int'l & Comp. L. 191 (1983).

the UN Charter—could nevertheless constitute intervention in the domestic affairs of a state,[146] thus indicating that support to a recognized belligerent NSAG would continue to sit uncomfortably alongside the norm on non-interference. In this sense, the relationship between recognition of belligerency and the parallel legal doctrine of non-intervention has always been both messy and uneasy. Counterintuitively, however, deconfliction of the doctrine on recognition of belligerency with this current Charter norm has been very little analyzed, although—as will be noted—Jessup did provide a brief commentary as to how these two norm sets might readily be integrated.

There are three ways to look at this norm deconfliction (or integration) challenge, and although this book is focused upon the interaction of recognition of belligerency with the Law of War / LOAC, as opposed to its interaction with the broader corpus of international law, it is appropriate to briefly address this issue before moving on to assess the doctrine's continued existence within the Law of War / LOAC. The first approach is to simply argue that non-intervention has a long history as a norm in international law—a history that well predates the UN Charter. Consequently, these two rule sets had coexisted well enough before 1945. Lauterpacht, for example, argued in 1928 that "there is nothing, so far as conventional international law is concerned, to warrant the assertion that states have assumed the obligation to protect their neighbours from every conceivable kind of revolutionary design directed against them."[147] Thus the adoption by a third state of a position of neutrality as between a conflict state and a recognized belligerent NSAG, while it could be construed by the conflict state as an unfriendly act, did not involve an interventionary act: "So far as hostile propaganda and revolutionary activities falling short of preparations for a hostile expedition are concerned," Lauterpacht continued, "a state is not bound to accede to requests the fulfilment of which is incompatible with its laws and constitution."[148] Thus apart from prohibitions on a third state from sponsoring or permitting its territory to be used as a base from which hostile expeditions are mounted, or as a venue for political assassinations of conflict state or NSAG personnel, "States are not bound to prohibit, on their territory, the commission of acts injurious to other states."[149] That is, he concluded, the third state's obligation, including in situations of civil war, was "a negative one . . . it is not a duty of active protection" of the interests of that conflict state.[150]

If, however, the conduct amounted to "foreign military intervention on the insurgent's side," then the orthodox interpretation—as consistently argued by the

146. Military and Paramilitary Activities in and Against Nicaragua (Nicar. v. U.S.), Judgment, 1986 I.C.J. 14, ¶195 (June 27).

147. Lauterpacht, *Revolutionary Activities by Private Persons Against Foreign States*, 22 Am. J. Int'l L. 105, 121 (1928).

148. *Id.* at 123.

149. *Id.* at 126.

150. *Id.* at 129.

International Committee of the Red Cross (ICRC)—is that "there would seem to be no doubt that the laws and customs [of war] . . . should be applied as a whole to the conflict, which thus becomes of an international nature."[151] Thus, if states and publicists prior to 1945 on the whole accepted that recognition of belligerency was a valid exception to, or was already interstitially factored into, the norm on non-intervention, then it is fair to ask whether the fact of subsequent transcription and elucidation of the norm within (inter alia) Article 2(4) of the UN Charter has necessarily negated this long-held interpretation. Fifty years after Lauterpacht's signal assessment, the Committee of Privy Counsellors appointed to inquire into the recruitment of mercenaries, and to advise on the need or otherwise for updating the British *Foreign Enlistment Act* (the 1976 "Diplock Report"), took a similar view: Yes, "the principal public interest . . . harmed by the presence of United Kingdom citizens serving as mercenaries abroad is the maintenance of good international relations between the United Kingdom and other states"; but equally, the Privy Counsellors observed, "There is an important juristic distinction, as well as a practical one, between a law which seeks to control what is done by people when they are within the United Kingdom and what is done by them when they are not."[152]

The second approach is to maintain—as is the case still today[153]—that the outcomes achieved from an orthodox application of a Law of War- or LOAC-based assessment are not invalidated merely by the fact that the outcome conflicts with another rule set. That is, the *jus ad bellum* (the legal question as to the lawfulness of the intervention) does not and should not color the *jus in bello* (legal assessments relating to the conduct of the operation).[154] This would also appear to be the view adopted by the UN General Assembly in its dealings with, for example, apartheid in South Africa, calling for "freedom fighters" to be treated as PWs in accordance with international law, particularly [Geneva Convention III].[155] That is, the illegality of the *jus ad bellum* basis for the conflict did not negate the applicability of *jus in bello* within the conflict.

The third approach is to ask if, and how, post-1945 commentary has assessed and resolved (if at all) this specific problem of norm deconfliction. One approach—intimated by Louis Sohn in 1963—is that the two issues are premised

151. 21st International Conference of the Red Cross, *Reaffirmation and Development of the Laws and Customs of War Applicable in Armed Conflicts*, 100 (Sept. 1969).

152. Report of the Committee of Privy Counselors Appointed to Inquire into the Recruitment of Mercenaries ¶¶ 12, 9 (1976) [hereinafter the Diplock Report].

153. *See, e.g.*, Bugnion, *Jus ad Bellum, Jus in Bello and Non-International Armed Conflicts*, 170–76.

154. Rob McLaughlin, *Common Article 2 as a Paradigmatically Challenging Threshold for the Application of IHL*, Int'l L. Ass'n Rep. (Austl. Branch) Nov. 11, 2016, http://ilareporter.org.au/2016/11/common-article-2-as-a-paradigmatically-challenging-threshold-for-the-application-of-ihl-rob-mclaughlin/.

155. G.A. Res. 2396 (XXIII), ¶ 8(c) (Dec. 2, 1968).

upon different thresholds. Where recognition of belligerency was based in a well-calibrated and politically nuanced test applied by states,

> [T]he question of the power of the United Nations to intervene in a civil war depends on the factual situation: Does a particular civil war in fact create a threat to international peace? Such threat might arise, if other countries assist either the government in power or the insurgents, or if two groups of countries give assistance to both sides in the civil war.[156]

Another approach is that of Roscoe Oglesby, who argued in 1971 that the collective security norm, and in particular UN Charter Article 39, had effectively extinguished the possibility of neutrality: "the decline of neutrality as a norm of international law suggests that the reasons why modern nations in a system oriented toward collective security are reluctant to grant belligerent rights since for third states this requires a proclamation of neutrality *jure gentium*."[157] Evan Luard similarly concluded that the "imprecise" distinctions that governed the three-level scheme had since 1945 been overtaken by a more general conception of "civil strife" that required the application of "more objective criteria for determining recognition" in relation to rebellions against "any government officially accepted as a member of the UN."[158] I—with great respect—disagree, and will address this point about the "desuetude" of neutrality in the final section of this chapter; suffice it to say that the law of neutrality remains alive and well, and thus this parallel desuetude argument in relation to recognition of belligerency tends to fail at this point.

Other perspectives on this interrelationship between the collective security mandate of the UNSC, neutrality, and recognition of belligerency also exist. At the Geneva Conference of 1949, for example, the Representative of Greece, Mr. Pesmazoglu, asked:

156. Louis B. Sohn, *The Role of the United Nations in Civil Wars*, 57 AM. SOC'Y INT'L L. PROC. 208, 211 (1963); Sohn also further argued this point:

> There is clearly a conflict here between the interest of the United Nations in the maintenance of international peace and the right of a people to self-determination and enjoyment of fundamental freedoms. In the interest of peace, the United Nations should either support the legitimate government or the stronger party in order to bring the conflict quickly to an end, before other nations become involved. The right of self-determination seems to imply that the matter should be left to the people itself, even if a prolonged conflict would result therefrom. But the right of self-determination could also form the basis of United Nations intervention on the side which is more likely to grant a greater measure of freedom to the people . . .

Id. at 214.

157. OGLESBY, INTERNAL WAR AND THE SEARCH FOR NORMATIVE ORDER, 107.

158. EVAN LUARD, CONCLUSIONS, *in* THE INTERNATIONAL REGULATION OF CIVIL WARS 215, 226–27 (Evan Luard ed., 1972).

> The recognition of belligerency entailed certain rights; but who would be competent to recognize belligerency in the case of civil war? The Greek Delegation had proposed one form of wording, and others might be forthcoming. It might for example be decided that a majority of members of the Security Council of the United Nations should be competent for the purpose.[159]

The USSR representative, General Slavin, was not fond of this idea;[160] others, such as Mr. de la Pradelle of Monaco found it unnecessary.[161] Nevertheless, the idea retained attraction for some well beyond 1949: Jessup, for example, noted that civil wars could readily be subject to UNSC action as threats to international peace and security, but also that "if the Security Council took no action, no obligation under the Charter would be violated if a member state proclaimed its neutrality, thus recognising the belligerency of the contending factions."[162] Yet, he continued, there is no doubt that "three centuries of experience" has proved that neutrality and (latterly) recognition of belligerency can create international frictions. The solution, he proposed, was that "recognition of insurgency or belligerency should therefore be an act of the [UN] Organisation."[163] Further, in the absence of UNSC action, Jessup saw no reason why the General Assembly itself could not "adopt a resolution recording its view that the contending factions were or were not entitled to recognition as belligerents."[164] Judge Ammoun certainly believed that such action was open to the UN:

> The recognition by the United Nations of the legitimacy of the Namibian people's struggle against the South African aggression is nothing less than a recognition of belligerency. For the recognizing States, namely the States Members of the United Nations, it transforms the hostilities between a State and another subject of law, which the Namibian people is, into an international war.[165]

159. II FINAL RECORD OF THE DIPLOMATIC CONFERENCE OF GENEVA OF 1949 § B, at 10–11 (1949) [hereinafter FINAL RECORD] (statement by the representative of Greece, Mr. Pesmazoglu). Mr. Pesmazoglu clarified his proposal subsequently stating that "He did not wish it to be understood that recognition as belligerents should be given to rebels by the Security Council but given individually by the majority of the countries represented in the Council." *Id.* at 16.

160. *Id.* at 13–14 (statement by the representative of the USSR, General Slavin).

161. *Id.* at 14 (statement by the representative of Monaco, Mr. de la Pradelle).

162. Philip C. Jessup, A Modern Law of Nations 54–55 (1948).

163. *Id.*

164. *Id.*

165. Legal Consequences for States of the Continued Presence of South Africa in Namibia (South West Africa) Notwithstanding Security Council Resolution 276 (1970), Advisory Opinion, 1971 I.C.J. Rep. 16, ¶ 13 (June 21) (separate Opinion of Vice-President Ammoun). As Mastorodimos points out, however, this did not mean that there was room for neutrality.

Lauterpacht, however, again advised caution—the "collectivisation of the process of recognition of belligerency," while an admirable goal ("a rational and desirable consummation"), had not been spectacularly successful in its guise as the non-intervention system during the Spanish Civil War. He did agree, however, that the UN Charter encapsulated promising institutional, moral, and legal possibilities for achieving this consummation.[166]

As will be well evident from even this briefest of outlines, the challenges posed by the interaction of the doctrine on recognition of belligerency as a normative scheme, with the parallel but differently focused normative scheme around non-intervention, are not new. Nor, however, could this challenge be said to have been so total and debilitating for the doctrine on recognition of belligerency that it mandated the doctrine's extinction, either before or since 1945, and the coming into effect of the UN Charter. This is a subject worthy of a book in itself, and it is my sincere hope that some scholar, somewhere, might take it up as a topic for deeper, sustained analysis. However, for the purposes of this book, my aim has simply been to ensure that the challenge is identified. I will now unashamedly sidestep it (with a slight revisitation in the conclusion), as my focus now returns to the task of assessing the existence or otherwise of a legal space for any continuity of the doctrine on recognition of belligerency within the post-1949 LOAC scheme.

(ii) Common Articles 2 and 3 of the Geneva Conventions of 1949

At the Diplomatic Conference of Geneva of 1949, from whence the four 1949 Geneva Conventions ultimately emerged, those delegations, which publicly turned their mind to the issue, appeared to understand that nothing in Common Articles 2 and 3 (CA2, CA3) necessarily abjured the older customary doctrine on recognition of belligerency. Gerald Draper noted that "reversion to the classical criteria of recognition of belligerency as the necessary precondition for the application of the full Geneva Convention to the parties engaged in an internal armed conflict . . . failed to be adopted." This indicated that the doctrine and CA3 were not coterminous, and Draper lamented that the certainty—and the restraint—inherent to the doctrine on recognition of belligerency was thus lost to any literal interpretation of CA3.[167] Draper's conclusion was that

> It is possible to advance the contention that the rebel faction enjoys a degree of persona adequate to bear the obligations imposed by article 3. This appears

See Konstantinos Mastorodimos, *Belligerency Recognition: Past, Present and Future*, 29 Conn. J. Int'l L. 301, 320–21 (2014).

166. Lauterpacht, Recognition in International Law, 253–55.

167. G.I.A.D. Draper, *Humanitarian Law and Internal Armed Conflicts*, 13 Ga. J. Int'l & Comp. L. 253, 264 (1983).

> to have been the basis upon which recognised insurgent belligerents were considered to be bound by the customary law of war.[168]

Lauterpacht, in the sixth edition of Oppenheim's *International Law*, argued that CA2 and CA3 in effect entailed no change to the doctrine on recognition of belligerency, except to note that where NSAG belligerency is recognized by the conflict state, "the rules of the Geneva Conventions apply *in toto* if the legitimate Government is a party to them and if the recognised insurgents formally accept and apply the provisions of these Conventions." "Failing this," he continued, "the accepted customary rules of war apply in this as in other spheres."[169] Van Wynen Thomas and Thomas Jr. (discussing the Spanish Civil War) note as an aside that the Geneva Convention 1949 rules on PW treatment clearly apply in a civil war where it is "a war of an international character [because] belligerency has been recognised."[170] Even Jean Pictet observed at the time that

> It was . . . highly desirable that the Geneva Conventions should be applicable also in case of civil war. Many difficulties have arisen in this connection, owing to the fact that the conventions are signed by states as such, and are only binding between signatories, whereas in the event of civil war, one of the parties concerned is usually not a recognized belligerent.[171]

That is, there was no doubt in his mind that the Law of War as refined and encapsulated in the new Geneva Conventions of 1949 of course continued to apply with no legal difficulty in situations where the NSAG was a recognized belligerent.

Richard Baxter, on the other hand, was concerned that the Geneva Conventions had in fact confused the once-clear delineations between different categories of NSAGs:

> The Geneva Conventions of 1949 . . . instead of clarifying the status of these individuals, destroyed what little certainty existed in the law. It is probably safe to say that the Conventions are at their weakest in delineating the various categories of persons who benefit from the protection of each.[172]

168. *Id.* at 268.

169. 2 Lassa Oppenheim, International Law: A Treatise 211–12 (H. Lauterpacht ed., 6th ed., 1944).

170. Van Wynen Thomas and Thomas Jr., *International Legal Aspects of the Civil War in Spain, 1936–39*, 123.

171. Jean S. Pictet, *The New Geneva Conventions for the Protection of War Victims*, 45 Am. J. l Int'l L. 462, 468–69 (1951).

172. Richard R. Baxter, *So-Called "Unprivileged Belligerency": Spies, Guerrillas, and Saboteurs*, 28 Brit. Y.B. Int'l 323, 327 (1951).

Alfred Rubin was similarly concerned as to the correlation, if any, between the customary concepts of belligerency and recognition of NSAGs, and the new Geneva Convention CA2 term (or status) of a "Power in the conflict."[173] Georg Schwarzenberger, however, assessed that CA3 "extended . . . to any guerrilleros, irrespective of whether or not their internal enemies recognize them as insurgents or belligerents."[174] Indeed, to have perpetrated any other outcome would have been, as Akande and Hill-Cawthorne note, "regressive" rather than progressive.[175] At the Diplomatic Conference, the representative of Norway, Mr. Castberg, was clear that

> As for belligerency, when belligerency was recognized in an internal conflict, serious legal consequences were entailed; but it was to be hoped that the Conference would agree that purely humanitarian rules should be applied in armed conflicts independently of any recognition of belligerency.[176]

Similarly, the U.S. Representative, Mr. Harrison, elaborated upon the relationship of CA2 with the older customary scheme:

> Every government had a right to put down rebellion within its borders and to punish the insurgents in accordance with its penal laws. Conversely, premature recognition of the belligerency of insurgents was a tortious act against the lawful government and a breach of international law. The United States of America therefore considered that the Convention should be applicable only where the parent government had extended recognition to the rebels or where those conditions obtained which would warrant other States in recognizing the belligerency of the rebels whether or not such recognition was accorded by the Power on which they depend in this latter eventuality. The application of this Convention could not be regarded as recognition of belligerency by any party thereto.[177]

In discussion over Common Article 2/2A, the Danish delegate, Mr. Cohn, was also very explicit:

173. Alfred P. Rubin, *The Status of Rebels under the Geneva Conventions of 1949*, 21 Int'l & Comp. L.Q. 472 (1972).

174. Georg Schwarzenberger, *Human Rights and Guerrilla Warfare*, 1 Is. Y.B. Hum. Rts. 246, 254 (1971).

175. Dapo Akande and Lawrence Hill-Cawthorne, *The Lieber Code and the Regulation of Civil War in International Law*, 53 Colum. J. Transnat'l L. 638, 643 (2015).

176. FINAL RECORD, 11 (statement by the representative of Norway, Mr. Castberg).

177. FINAL RECORD, 12 (statement by the Representative of the United States of America, Mr. Harrison). The Representative of Monaco, Mr. de Geouffre de la Pradelle, also referred to recognition of belligerency in terms of interaction with, not displacement by, the 1949 Geneva Convention. *See* FINAL RECORD, 14.

> The real truth is that we are in certain cases obliged in international law, to recognize as belligerents, Parties which are not States, and the question cannot be solved unless rules and conditions of this kind are embodied in the Convention. The only way out is to take a decision as to whether a Party to the conflict, which is not a State, is entitled to claim the benefit of the rules laid down in the four Conventions.
>
> This is why the Danish Delegation has prepared a draft resolution intended to decide whether the question of the recognition of a Party to the conflict by a Party outside the conflict shall be determined, not by a Convention, but in accordance with the general rules of international law, in all special cases.[178]

Similarly, Colonel Du Pasquier of Switzerland, although disagreeing with Mr. Cohn about the existence of "regulations in international law which do or do not obligate the States to recognize belligerency in case of civil war," recognized that the interaction of recognition of belligerency with what would ultimately be settled as CA2, was indeed a complex issue.[179] This discussion was clearly informed by an appreciation (and in some quarters a very deep appreciation) of the tripartite customary scheme, with delegates clearly distinguishing between rebellion, insurgency, and belligerency—evident, for example, when Mr. Bolla of Switzerland reminded the Conference that

> [e]ven among other provisions [of GC IV] which can be conceived as being applicable, either directly or by analogy, to civil war, there were a considerable number, which, if they were applied, would put obstacles in the way of the legitimate government whose duty it is, in a non-international war, to compel rebels and insurgents to respect the national law of the country.[180]

"The question of belligerency," he continued, "is completely outside this scope of the provisions and of the solutions proposed in the four Conventions."[181]

During the preparatory stages of the Conference, it had indeed been proposed that recognition of belligerency be explicitly incorporated into the provisions anticipated to be applicable in Non-International Armed Conflict (NIAC); however, this option was ultimately rejected:

> A further possible solution was to make the criterion the recognition of the rebels as belligerents by the State in conflict with them or by other States. But in view of the enormous practical difficulties to which these differentiations would have given rise, and the very thorny problems presented by the application to civil war of Conventions drawn up for international war, an attempt

178. FINAL RECORD, 322 (statement by the representative of Denmark, Mr. Cohn).

179. FINAL RECORD, 332 (statement by the Rapporteur, Colonel Pasquier).

180. FINAL RECORD, 334 (statement by the representative of Switzerland, Mr. Bolla).

181. *Id.* at 336.

> was made to find another principle which might provide a solution, and it was proposed to restrict the obligations of the legitimate government and the rebel authority to the most obvious and imperious rules of the Conventions, that is, to humanitarian duties as a whole.[182]

The British delegation was concerned at the outset that any regulation of internal conflict included in the Geneva Conventions be structured such that it did not imply recognition of belligerency:

> In the United Kingdom Delegation's view, paragraph 4 of Article 2 was a source of serious difficulties, not only because the Conventions would be applicable to situations which were not war, but because the application of the Conventions would appear to give the status of belligerents to insurgents, whose right to wage war could not be recognized.[183]

This sentiment was widely echoed—General Oung of Burma, for example, expressed his concern that "The proposed Convention should not give legal status to insurgents who sought by undemocratic methods, to overthrow a legally constituted government by force of arms."[184] In discussions around the substitution of "parties to the conflict" for the term "belligerents," the British delegation legal adviser, Miss Gutteridge (the drafter of legal advice to the British Cabinet on recognition of belligerency in relation to the Formosa Strait in 1956), also spoke of recognition of belligerency as having a continuing existence quite apart from CA2 (and the debated idea of an additional Common Article 2A):

> The word 'belligerent', I need hardly remind the Conference, has a well understood meaning in international law and is used in particular in relation to questions of neutrality. Certain rights are accorded in international law to belligerents, and the wholesale replacement of the word 'belligerent' in these Conventions by the expression 'Parties to the conflict', the wholesale replacement of one expression in an international treaty by another expression can lead to legal consequences which I am certain are not intended by the framers of these humanitarian Conventions.[185]

Colonel Hodgson of Australia, and other experts, similarly assessed that references to "parties" must not be interpreted as an automatic conferral of belligerency status.[186] Thus at the time of drafting and debating the 1949 Geneva Conventions, the doctrine on recognition of belligerency was undoubtedly considered extant,

182. FINAL RECORD, 129 (art. 2A/2A/2A/2A).

183. FINAL RECORD, 10 (statement by the Representative of the UK, Sir Robert Craigie).

184. FINAL RECORD, 15 (statement by the Representative of Burma, General Oung).

185. FINAL RECORD, 333 (statement by the representative of the UK, Miss Gutteridge).

186. FINAL RECORD, 53 (statement by the representative of Australia, Colonel Hodgson).

for much effort was expended in assessing the possible consequences of using a customary term of art—belligerent—in a context that might incorrigibly broaden the material scope of CA2. Of clear concern was the potential for use of the term "belligerent" to allow some states to spuriously claim or create CA2 coverage, inappropriately internationalizing an otherwise internal armed conflict through the political act of recognizing NSAG belligerent status. The term "parties to the conflict" (indeed, ultimately, in CA2, "High Contracting Parties") was thus considered to be much more objective and indicative of only de jure states and governments. Ultimately, Resolution 10 made the continuing existence of the doctrine on recognition of belligerency quite clear: "The Conference considers that the conditions under which a Party to a conflict can be recognized as a belligerent by Powers not taking part in this conflict, are governed by the general rules of international law on the subject and are in no way modified by the Geneva Conventions."[187] It was subsequently clear to Erik Castren and others that neither CA2 nor CA3 had removed the possibility, in relevant cases, for recognition of belligerency.[188]

It is clear on its face that the drafters of the Geneva Conventions—quite expressly—did not intend for the Conventions to extinguish the customary doctrine on recognition of belligerency. Additionally, states have, since 1949, continued (even if only occasionally) to refer to the recognition of belligerency as a relevant consideration when assessing their responses to international crises, albeit in almost every case to ultimately exclude its application. As noted previously, Britain and the United States discussed the Indonesian insurrection in 1958 in terms of possible recognition of belligerency: indeed, as the memorandum of a conversation between the Secretary of State and the British Ambassador in Washington, dated 13 April 1958 discloses, recognition of rebel belligerency (dependent upon "the government's failing for the time being in driving the opposition into the mountains") was one of "three possibilities presented . . . for study"—the other two being recognition of Sumatran secession, and the unilateral deployment of U.S. forces into Indonesia to protect U.S. property. The British, the note continued, were "very doubtful that the plan for recognition of belligerent rights would work," but accepted that this would "logically follow" if either of the other two possibilities came to be.[189] This appreciation of the ongoing validity, vitality, and utility of recognition of belligerency has also continued to inform doctrine. The U.S. Army's 1956 Field Manual (FM 27-10) on *The Law of Land Warfare*, for example, succinctly stated that, "The customary law of war becomes applicable to civil war upon recognition of the rebels as belligerents."[190] Australian

187. Resolutions of The Diplomatic Conference, Aug. 12, 1949, 75 U.N.T.S. 21.

188. Erik J. Castren, Civil War 85–86 (1966).

189. Document 57, Memorandum of Conversation (13 Apr. 1958), *in* Foreign Relations of the United States, 1958–1960, Indonesia, Vol. XVII, (1958), https://history.state.gov/historicaldocuments/frus1958-60v17/d57.

190. U.S Dep't of Army, Field Manual 27–10, The Law of Land Warfare ¶ 11a (18 July 1956). Indeed, the new U.S. Dep't of Def., Law of War Manual (June 2015) also refers to

military doctrine as recently as 2006 also preserved recognition of belligerency as a matter of LOAC concern:

> International law has historically regulated relations between states. A state's internal affairs, including responsibility for the maintenance of law and order and the defence of territorial integrity against domestic insurgents, were largely regarded as within the exclusive jurisdiction of the state concerned. The notion of international law regulating a conflict occurring within a state was generally regarded as being at variance with this approach. However, it is possible for insurgents in an internal armed conflict to be recognised as belligerents and for the LOAC to apply.[191]

Similarly, that recognition of belligerency continued to coexist with, and complement, the newer 1949 Geneva Conventions scheme was quite evident in many scholars' writings.[192] The scheme was also still considered to be an operative component of LOAC so far as the UN was concerned: As the Secretary-General's 1970 Report on *Respect for Human Rights in Armed Conflicts* noted, in relation to those types of conflict that would ultimately become the subject of 1977 Additional Protocol I Article 1(4):

> The conflict may gradually come to be regarded as an international one when the liberation movement is formally recognized as belligerent by States. As a rule, such recognition would be granted only if the liberation movement shows that it exercises effective authority over a certain part of the territory involved in the conflict. Some experts have pointed out that, in modern struggles for self-determination and liberation from colonial and foreign rule, characterized by guerrilla warfare, this condition is not easily fulfilled. They have suggested rather a criterion of effective control and allegiance of populations. Even if this more flexible criterion were accepted, its application would probably give rise to much controversy. It may be added that deducing the international character of a conflict primarily from recognition of the liberation movement as a belligerent has the disadvantage of relying decisively upon the discretion of third parties.[193]

recognition of belligerency in terms indicating its continuing legal viability and availability—for example, at ¶¶ 3.3.3, 4.3.2, 17.2.3, at http://www.dod.mil/dodgc/images/law_war_manual15.pdf.

191. Austl. Dep't of Def, Australian Defence Doctrine Publication (ADDP) 06.4, Law of Armed Conflict, ¶1.35 (May 2006).

192. For example, James E. Bond, *Internal Conflict and Article Three of the Geneva Conventions*, 48 Denv. L.J. 263, 270 (1971); Schwarzenberger, *Human Rights and Guerrilla Warfare*, 253–54.

193. U.N. Secretary-General, *Report on Respect For Human Rights In Armed Conflicts*¶209, U.N. Doc. A/8052 (Sep. 18, 1970), http://www.un.org/en/ga/search/view_doc.asp?symbol=A/8052.

The concept of belligerency is also referenced in at least one directly relevant post-1949 regional treaty, the 1957 Protocol to the Convention on Duties and Rights of States in the Event of Civil Strife (1928 Havana Convention),[194] which provides (inter alia):

> Article 1. Each Contracting State shall, in areas subject to its jurisdiction:
> a) Keep under surveillance the traffic in arms and war material that it has reason to believe is intended for starting, promoting, or supporting civil strife in another American State;
> b) Suspend the exportation or importation of any shipment of arms and war material during the period of its investigation of the circumstances relating to the shipment, when it has reason to believe that such arms and war material may be intended for starting, promoting, or supporting civil strife in another American State; and
> c) Prohibit the exportation or importation of any shipment of arms and war material intended for starting, promoting, or supporting civil strife in another American State.
>
> Article 2. The provisions of Article 1 shall cease to be applicable for a Contracting State only when it has recognized the belligerency of the rebels, in which event the rules of neutrality shall be applied.

Indeed, the Havana Convention and the Inter-American Treaty of Reciprocal Assistance 1947 (Rio Treaty) were relevant to advice on recognition of belligerency given to U.S. President Kennedy in 1961, in relation to the insurrection in Cuba (and the Cuban missile crisis). This advice certainly indicated an appreciation of the doctrine as being of continuing validity as a legal frame of reference. Arthur Schlesinger, summarizing the Legal Adviser, informed the President—in terms clearly reflecting the legal nuance of the doctrine on recognition of belligerency—that

> [i]f the insurgents gain control over a particular area and if they organize a framework of government within that area, a case can be made for US recognition of a state of belligerency in Cuba.
>
> If the US recognized a state of belligerency, we would have the position, under international law, of a neutral. Both parties to the war would have the rights of belligerents. While the US Government would be required to practice impartiality in its relations with the two belligerents, private persons and companies in the US could make loans, sell arms, etc., to the insurgents. The Castro regime, on the other hand, would have the right under international

194. Protocol to The Convention on Duties and Rights of States in the Event of Civil Strife (Inter-American), *opened for signature* 1 May 1957, 284 U.N.T.S. 201, *entered into force* 9 Dec. 1957.

> law to blockade ports held by the insurgents and to stop and search American vessels on the high seas and seize vessels carrying contraband of war.[195]

Schlesinger also noted that recognition of Cuban insurgent belligerency carried with it the risk/possibility of characterization as a "fact or situation that might endanger the peace of America" (Article 6 of the *Rio Treaty*[196]). This could open the situation to Organization of American States (OAS) cognizance, creating a "basis for multilateral OAS action calling for an end to hostilities and supervised elections; or, failing this, for OAS quarantine of Cuba or general OAS recognition of belligerency in Cuba."[197] U.S. recognition of belligerency was still being considered in terms of an appropriate and possible legal response to the situation in Cuba in 1963—the fourth draft of a Department of State and Department of Defense "Paper on US assistance to Revolt in Cuba," dated 8 June 1963 proposed the following timeline:

> After the insurgents had issued a public call for help and the US decided that armed assistance constituted the appropriate response or the Soviets had taken forcible action against our aircraft or the insurgents, the US would:
>
> 1) Issue a call for the convocation of the OAS as Organ of Consultation . . . and recommend (i) the immediate establishment of a full quarantine, (ii) the furnishing of all necessary help to the insurgents, possibly under an 'OAS Assistance Command' and (iii) formal recognition of the insurgents including their belligerent status under the 1928 Habana Convention.[198]

Such advance planning for the employment of a legal scheme—in this case, the doctrine on recognition of belligerency—hardly indicates that it is defunct.

Similarly, the doctrine was not necessarily felt to have fallen into desuetude by courts faced with explicit questions as to its application. The Prize Court sitting in Alexandria, Egypt, in the November 1950 case of *The Fjeld*, determined that "creating a Prize court governed by the principles of international law" (among

195. Document 114, Memorandum from the President's Special Assistant (Schlesinger) to President Kennedy (17 Apr. 1961), *in* Foreign Relations of the United States, 1961–1963, Volume X, Cuba, January 1961–September 1962, (1961) (referencing a memorandum forwarded to Schlesinger on 17 April 1961 under a covering memorandum from Executive Secretary Lucius D Batt entitled 'Various Considerations if an Insurrectionary Movement Gains Control of a Specific Area in Cuba', dated 7 April 1961, at https://history.state.gov/historicaldocuments/frus1961-63v10/d114).

196. Inter-American Treaty of Reciprocal Assistance, Sept. 2, 1947, 62 Stat. 1681, 1700, 21 U.N.T.S. 77, 95, https://www.loc.gov/law/help/us-treaties/bevans/m-ust000004-0559.pdf [hereinafter Rio Treaty].

197. Document 114, Memorandum.

198. Memorandum from James K. Patchell to Mr. Joseph A.Califano, subject: Comments on Fourth Draft of State—Defense Paper on U.S. Assistance to Revolt in Cuba 15 (8 June 1963), https://catalog.archives.gov/id/304979.

other indicia) provided belligerent recognition of the Jewish armed party to the conflict in Palestine.[199] In the *Societe Purafina Francaise* case before the French Court of Cassation in 1962, the validity of a "war" damage claim relating to sabotage by Algerian FLN rebels against a Purafina installation in metropolitan France in part hinged around the characterization of the situation in Algeria as either civil war or mere insurgency.[200] As noted previously, ICJ Vice-President Ammoun, in his separate opinion in the *South West Africa Advisory Opinion* (1971) (the *Namibia Case*), also referred to recognition of belligerency as a live, and applicable, legal framework:

> The recognition by the United Nations of the legitimacy of the Namibian people's struggle against the South African aggression is nothing less than a recognition of belligerency . . . Consequently, when there is aggression by a State against a people for the purpose of subjugating it by force, then whatever its manifestations, it cannot be denied that it has the character of a war, or at least of a state of belligerency, with all the legal effects attaching thereto, including in particular the status of neutrality imposed on third-party States.[201]

Finally, on the very cusp of the finalization of the 1977 Additional Protocols, the 1976 Diplock Report presented to the British Parliament, clearly took as its stepping off point that the concept of recognition of belligerency remained extant. The Privy Counsellors indeed argued—employing a doctrinal test drawn from the recognition of belligerency scheme—that

> the description of the offences [in the *Foreign Enlistment Act*] requires that the persons on whose behalf the force is raised should also constitute an entity possessed of characteristics which in international law entitle it to recognition as being "at war" with another state so as to enable it to exercise belligerent rights vis-à-vis neutral states.[202]

Consequently, the fact that the Act, as a penal statute, was to be strictly interpreted, in effect, required a recognition of belligerency of the NSAG by the British government prior to it becoming applicable. This, they concluded was a significant shortfall in utility of the Foreign Enlistment Act for dealing with the concern standing

199. The Fjeld, Prize Court of Alexandria 17 ILR 345, 349 (1950).

200. Societe Purafina Francaise v. Cie. D'Assurances la Nationale, 44 ILR 439 (1962); *see also* Leslie C. Green, International Law Through the Cases 733–34 (4th ed. 1978).

201. Legal Consequences for States of the Continued Presence of South Africa in Namibia (South West Africa) Notwithstanding Security Council Resolution 276 (1970), Advisory Opinion, 1971 I.C.J. Rep. 16, ¶ 13 (June 21) (Separate Opinion of Vice-President Ammoun), https://www.icj-cij.org/files/case-related/53/053-19710621-ADV-01-02-EN.pdf

202. Diplock Report.

behind the original referral to the commission—the recruitment of around 160 British nationals to serve with rebel groups in Angola.[203]

(iii) Expressions as to continuity of the doctrine as a matter of law since the Additional Protocols of 1977

As states gathered to negotiate the Additional Protocols, the customary doctrine on recognition of belligerency was again referenced—even if only rarely—in terms of its continuation as an operative component of the legal framework regulating armed conflict. During negotiations for AP II, a number of states expressed views—in line with those expressed thirty years earlier—that provisions dealing with internal armed conflict should be carefully crafted so as not to automatize recognition of belligerency.[204] Certainly, the ICRC *Commentary on the Additional Protocols of 8 June 1977*, published in 1987, makes only limited reference to the customary doctrine on recognition of belligerency. On one hand, the *Commentary* notes that recognition of belligerency forms part of "the legal situation before 1949." On the other, however, the *Commentary* clearly employs headings that refer to recognition of belligerency by both the "legitimate government of the state" and by "third states."[205] Additionally, the *Commentary* expressly reflects upon three highly relevant points. The first is the formal legal distinction between insurgents and belligerents[206] (as already noted), indicating that use of these legal terms of art within the *Commentary* is neither careless nor accidental. Second, the *Commentary* specifically cautions against the temptation to "incorrectly" assume recognition of belligerency is "a consequence of the application of common article 3 and of Additional Protocol II."[207] This indicates a clear appreciation of the doctrine as extant, rather than defunct. Finally, in analyzing Article 1 of AP II, the *Commentary* indicates that, "Insurgents (usually part of the population), fight against the government in power acting in the exercise of the public authority vested in it. This distinction sets the upper threshold for the applicability of the Protocol."[208] Some scholars, such as Andrew Sanger, have argued that AP I Article 1(4) effectively "replaced" recognition of belligerency, the implication being that the doctrine was irrelevant to both AP I and AP II: "The law today—arguably

203. *Id.*

204. 9 OFFICIAL RECORDS OF THE DIPLOMATIC CONFERENCE ON THE REAFFIRMATION AND DEVELOPMENT OF INTERNATIONAL HUMANITARIAN LAW APPLICABLE IN ARMED CONFLICTS, GENEVA (1974–1977), at 314 (1978) (Mr. Torres Avalos for Argentina), https://www.loc.gov/rr/frd/Military_Law/pdf/RC-records_Vol-9.pdf. *Id.* at 315 (Mr. Ortega Jugo for Venezuela).

205. INT'L COMM. OF THE RED CROSS, COMMENTARY ON THE ADDITIONAL PROTOCOLS OF 8 JUNE 1977 TO THE GENEVA CONVENTIONS OF 12 AUGUST 1949, at ¶¶ 4342–49 (Yves Sandoz et al. eds., 1987) [hereinafter 1977 ADDITIONAL PROTOCOLS COMMENTARY].

206. *See, e.g., Id.* at ¶ 4343.

207. Indeed, the authors quantify this tendency as "often."

208. 1977 ADDITIONAL PROTOCOLS COMMENTARY, ¶4458.

reflecting an international climate that is not as sympathetic to wars of national liberation as it once was—appears unable to respond as it once did: we no longer have the recognition of belligerency doctrine and its replacement—Article 1(4)—has never been applied."[209] Other scholars, such as Gerald Draper, have argued the opposite—that AP I Article 1(4) does not replace recognition of belligerency but rather "render[s] more numerous and complex the types of internal conflicts now known to the law."[210] For Draper, this burgeoning lexicon of "types"—CA3 NIACs, AP II NIACs, AP I Article 1(4) conflicts, civil wars, recognized belligerencies, insurgencies—continues to coexist in the law:

> We now consider 'national liberation' struggles, as defined in protocol I, article 1(4), as international armed conflicts insofar as the humanitarian law of war is concerned. Then we have the classical forms of civil war in which recognition of belligerency has been accorded to the rebel elements by the government of the state concerned or by third states. This category will bring down upon it the customary law of war, which includes the Hague Convention No. IV of 1907, and may possibly now include the Geneva Conventions of 1949.[211]

Michael Bothe, discussing the application of LOAC in the Biafran conflict, has argued that there are several parallel and equally valid paths by which this outcome may have been achieved. "An application of the rules of international warfare, in whole or in part, is possible" he asserted, in the following circumstances: "if the parties conclude an agreement to this effect under paragraph 3 of article 3"; "if there is a declaration of belligerency"; "or if customary international law is applied to Biafra as a local de facto regime." He also noted that AP II would have applied if it had existed at that time.[212] There is no hint in the writings of these eminent scholars that they view the doctrine on recognition of belligerency as having been extinguished by either the Geneva Conventions or the Additional Protocols.

Given the technical care taken in the *Commentary* to distinguish the terms "insurgency" and "belligerency"—a clear genuflection to the customary scheme—and the indication that AP II applies up to (but not beyond) the threshold between insurgency and belligerency, it thus seems clear that the recognition of belligerency was still considered by the three distinguished editors to be relevant to the interpretation and application of LOAC in 1977 when the Additional Protocols were settled, and perhaps as late as 1987 when the *Commentary* was published. Indeed, a British Foreign Office policy document of 1984, dealing with the question of "Is Intervention ever Justified?," observed that the predominant

209. Andrew Sanger, *The Contemporary Law of Blockade and the Gaza Freedom Flotilla*, 13 Y.B Int'l Humanitarian L. 397, 434 (2010).

210. Draper, *Humanitarian Law and Internal Armed Conflicts*, 274–75.

211. *Id.* at 275.

212. Michael Bothe, *Article 3 and Protocol II: Case Studies of Nigeria and El Salvador*, 31 Am. U. L. Rev. 899, 901 (1982).

"western" view was that assistance to national liberation movements asserting a right of self-determination (with the exception of humanitarian and economic measures) "infringes the sovereignty of the state, at least until the rebels establish belligerent rights by controlling part of the territory."[213] This continued role for recognition of belligerency was also indicated by reference to the obligation of third state neutrality within the context of the discussion on "restrictions on the lawfulness of states providing outside assistance to other states":

> One [restriction] is that any form of interference or assistance is prohibited (except possibly of a humanitarian kind) when a civil war is taking place and control of the state's territory is divided between warring parties. But it is widely accepted that outside interference in favour of one party to the struggle permits counter-intervention on behalf of the other, as happened in the Spanish Civil War and, more recently, in Angola.[214]

Running in parallel with this development was a select, but nevertheless consistent, academic discourse during the 1970s and 1980s, which dealt with the doctrine as one of continuing relevance, albeit challenged by a parallel discourse that accepted the doctrine as historically significant, and not necessarily extinguished, but which simultaneously questioned its contemporary practical validity.[215]

213. British Foreign Office, Foreign Policy Document No. 148, 57 BRIT. Y.B. INT'L L. 614, 619 (Section II.23).

214. *Id.* at 616 (Section II.7). The UN General Assembly, in reference to rebellions against Portugal (primarily Mozambique and Angola), had in 1968 demanded that native guerrillas be treated as PW in accordance with GCIII: G.A. Res. 2395 (XXIII), Question of Territories under Portuguese Administration, ¶ 12 (Nov. 29, 1968).

215. For example, John N. Moore, *The Control of Foreign Intervention in Internal Conflict*, 9 VA. J. INT'L L. 5, 20 (1969); Richard A. Falk, *Introduction*, *in* THE INTERNATIONAL LAW OF CIVIL WAR 11–13 (Richard A. Falk ed., 1971) Kuyper, 382–87; Michel Krauss, *Internal Conflicts and Foreign States: In Search of the State of Law*, 5 YALE J. INT'L L. 173 (1980); Draper, *Humanitarian Law and Internal Armed Conflicts*, 253; Robert W. Gomulkiewicz, *International Law Governing Aid to Armed Opposition Groups in Civil War: Resurrecting the Standards of Belligerency*, 63 WASH. L. REV. 43 (1988); Lindsay Moir, *The Historical Development of the Application of Humanitarian Law in Non-International Armed Conflicts to 1949*, 47 INT'L & COMP. L. Q. 337 (1998); Yair M. Lootsteen, *The Concept of Belligerency in International Law*, 166 MIL. L. REV. 109, 109 (2000). Recent commentary (scarce as it is) appears split on whether the doctrine remains extant; the views of the "nay" faction are well represented by, for example: Rosalyn Higgins, *International Law and Civil Conflict*, *in* THE INTERNATIONAL REGULATION OF CIVIL WARS 169, 171 (Evan Luard ed., 1972) ("But it must be said that, because the four criteria [for recognition of belligerency] seem not to cover contemporary situations, and because governments do not wish to harness themselves to the legal consequences of a recognition of insurgency or belligerency, recognition of this status has lost all practical significance."); HEATHER A. WILSON, INTERNATIONAL LAW AND THE USE OF FORCE BY NATIONAL LIBERATION MOVEMENTS 33 (1990) ("In the case of belligerency third States should remain neutral, although this is no longer common practice"); and Anthony Cullen, *Key Developments Affecting the Scope of Internal Armed Conflict in International Humanitarian Law*, 183 MIL. L. REV. 66, 68 (2005) (*see* note

Nevertheless, authors from as wide a variety of political and legal contexts as Lebanon,[216] India,[217] and the Philippines,[218] for example, have continued to refer to the doctrine as an extant component of the applicable law. Similarly, Natalino Ronzitti proposed in 1974 that "the classical theory of the recognition of the 'status of belligerency'" might be employed—with a UN recognition element—to bring "liberation movements" more clearly within post-1949 LOAC.[219] Donald deKieffer and David Hartquist, analyzing the status in international law of Transkei in 1978, referred to recognition of belligerency as a potential, but in this case situationally irrelevant, consideration.[220] In the 1995 decision on the defense motion for interlocutory appeal on jurisdiction in *Prosecutor v. Tadic*, the ICTY spent some time analyzing the customary law of belligerency, noting "the trend initiated with the Spanish Civil War . . . whereby the central authorities of a State where civil strife has broken out prefer to withhold recognition of belligerency but, at the same time, extend to the conflict the bulk of the body of legal rules concerning conflicts between States."[221] The Institut de Droit International, in a 1999 Resolution concerning the application of LOAC in situations where NSAGs are parties, certainly referred to the doctrine in terms that at the very least recognize a continued potential existence:

> II. All parties to armed conflicts in which non-State entities are parties, irrespective of their legal status, as well as the United Nations, and competent regional and other international organizations have the obligation to respect international humanitarian law as well as fundamental human rights. The application of such principles and rules does not affect the legal status of the

9 where he argues that "the doctrine of belligerency, used in traditional international law for the recognition of internal armed conflict, has fallen into disuse and is now considered obsolete."); James Crawford, The Creation Of States In International Law 419 (2d ed., 2006) ("There was no clear twentieth century case of recognition of belligerency: the result, it has been persuasively argued, has been the desuetude of recognition of belligerency.") Douglas Guilfoyle, *The Mavi Marmara Incident and Blockade in Armed Conflict*, 81 Brit. Y.B. Int'l L. 171, 191–94 (2011) (for example, "However, it is unclear, even doubtful, that the doctrine survived the nineteenth century."); *see generally* Sandesh Sivakumaran, The Law Of Non-International Armed Conflict 156–62 (2014).

216. *See, e.g.*, Daoud L. Khairallah, Insurrection under International Law with Emphasis on the Rights and Duties of Insurgents 27–62 (1973).

217. Vidya D. Mahajan, Public International Law 210–12 (5th ed., 1974).

218. Jorge R. Coquia and Miriam Defensor -Santiago, Public International Law 82–87 (1984).

219. H.N. Boon, *Natalino Rontitte—Le Guerre di Liberazione Nationale e il Dritto Internazionale, Pacini Editore, Pisa 1974*, 26 Neth. Int'l L. Rev. 204, 205 (1979) (book review).

220. Donald deKieffer and David Hartquist, *Transkei: A Legitimate Birth (1977–1978)*, 13 New Eng. L. Rev. 428, 437.

221. Prosecutor v. Tadic, Case No. IT-94-1-I, Defense Motion for Interlocutory Appeal on Jurisdiction, ¶ 96–106 (Int'l Crim. Trib. for the Former Yugoslavia Oct. 2, 1995).

parties to the conflict and is not dependent on their recognition as belligerents or insurgents.[222]

Insurgent groups in the Philippines have in the recent past reportedly made recognition of their belligerent status a precondition for peace negotiations,[223] and the Moro Islamic Liberation Front has periodically claimed that Philippines and other international declarations have effectively recognized its belligerent status.[224] More recently, the Venezuelan Assembly recognized the belligerency of the Fuerzas Armadas Revolucionarias de Colombia—Ejército del Pueblo (FARC-EP) and Ejército de Liberación Nacional (ELN) NSAGs in Columbia, and advocated that others do likewise, squarely locating the action within the context of a "live" legal regime on recognition of belligerency:

> Chavez argues recognition of the guerrillas as a 'belligerent force' would open the path to peace and require the guerrillas to abide by the Geneva Protocols by desisting from using such methods as hostage taking and terrorist acts against civilians . . .
>
> While belligerent status would make the guerrillas accountable to international human rights provisions in the Geneva Protocols, it also has political implications that the Colombian government does not want to cede such as recognition of FARC and ELN control over huge swathes of Colombian territory.[225]

222. Institut de Droit International Res., *The Application of International Humanitarian Law and Fundamental Human Rights, in Armed Conflicts in which Non-State Entities are Parties* (Aug. 25, 1999), http://www.idi-iil.org/idiE/resolutionsE/1999_ber_03_en.PDF.

223. Soliman M. Santos Jr., *Evolution of the Armed Conflict on the Communist Front*, 14 (Human Development Network Foundation, Inc. for the Philippine Human Development Report 2005, Background Paper), http://hdn.org.ph/wp-content/uploads/2005_PHDR/2005%20Evolution_Communist_Conflict.pdf.

224. Mary Ann O. Arguillas, *The Non-Traditional Moro Elites and the Organization of Islamic Conference (OIC)*, 22 Phil. Pol. Sci. J. 97, 110 (2001). Also of much more attenuated relevance was the situation in July 27, 2003 when Philippines' President Gloria Macapagal-Arroyo declared a short-lasting (and constitutionally doubtful) state of "rebellion" in relation to the Magdalo group (the "Oakwood mutineers," a dissident group within the Philippines Armed Forces); *see* Soliman M Santos Jr., *Correspondent's Reports: The Philippines*, 6 Y.B. Int'l Humanitarian L. 561, 561–64 (2003).

225. Kiraz Janicke, *Venezuelan Legislature Supports Belligerent Status for Colombian Rebels*, VENEZ. ANALYSIS, Jan. 19, 2008, http://venezuelanalysis.com/news/3080; Dmitry Sudakov, *Bolivar's Sword: Venezuela's Recognition of the Colombian Insurgency*, PRAVDA, Jan. 25, 2008, http://english.pravda.ru/world/americas/25-01-2008/103640-venezuela_colombia-0/; *see also* Chris Krual, *Chavez keeps up campaign to get rebels off terrorist list*, L.A. Times, Jan. 20, 2008, http://articles.latimes.com/2008/jan/20/world/fg-farc20 ('It might sound like mere semantics. But when Venezuelan President Hugo Chavez proposed this month that Colombia's largest rebel group be recognized as "belligerents," not terrorists, the reverberations reached to Washington and Europe, and relations between the two Latin American nations plunged to what one observer called perhaps the lowest point in their history.

Chavez has appealed to European and South American nations to strike [FARC and ELN] . . . from their lists of terrorist groups.

Similarly, a Georgian "blockade" instituted against the "breakaway territory" of Abkhazia as early as 2004, but more consistently since 2008 (focused particularly on the Abkhaz held port of Sukhumi), was exercised by Georgian warships in 2009 against at least twenty-three Abkhaz and third state vessels (including a Cambodian flagged vessel in August 2009 and a Turkish flagged vessel in September 2009).[226] However, as with the Sri Lanka blockade, the precise legal basis of the measure—a Law of War blockade, or a municipal act in relation to the territorial sea (or contiguous zone)—is difficult to ascertain. For example, one Georgian statement on the blockade was as follows: "Citing the [Law of the Sea] convention, the Georgian Foreign Ministry said Tbilisi was authorized to exercise its rights in contiguous zone 'to prevent and punish infringement by Russia of its customs, fiscal, immigration or sanitary laws and regulations within its territorial sea.' "[227] Russian assistance to Abkhazia in terms of escorting vessels so as to avoid the Georgian blockade was also characterized as a "territorial sea" measure: "An agreement between the Russian Federation and Abkhazia on joint protection of the state border envisages joint measures to provide security in the Republic's territorial waters," Interfax news agency reported, quoting the Chief of Abkhaz Border Guard Service.[228] A recent analysis of the Libyan conflict also specifically highlighted the coming into effect for rebels of the formal status of recognized belligerents as a legal milestone in the rebellion;[229] another recent analysis of the

The rebels should be viewed as "belligerents," Chavez said, a change that could open the way for diplomatic recognition of the groups—at least by Venezuela.' For more detailed context, *see generally* Felicity Szesnat and Annie Bird, *Columbia, in* International Law and the Classification of Conflicts 217, 221, (Elizabeth Wilmshurst ed., 2012); *The FARC Files*, The Economist, May 22, 2008, http://www.economist.com/node/11412645; the Venezuelan government complied and released a "factsheet" subsequent to U.S. House Resolution 1049 ("H. Res. 1049 (110th): Calling for the Bolivarian Republic of Venezuela to be designated a state sponsor of terrorism, 13 March 2008, at https://www.govtrack.us/congress/bills/110/hres1049/text), which referenced information regarding alleged Venezuelan links to, and support of, FARC, which was gleaned during the intelligence exploitation of killed FARC leader Raul Reyes' captured computer and its files: At "Resolution and Reality: H.Res 1049," Venezuelan Embassy, Washington, D.C., 2008, at http://www.embavenez-us.org/factsheet/HRes1049.pdf.

226. *Georgia: Abkhazia Protests Blockade*, N.Y. Times, Aug. 21, 2009, http://www.nytimes.com/2009/08/21/world/europe/21briefs-Georgiabrf.html?mcubz=0; Deborah Sanders, Maritime Power in the Black Sea 137 (2016).

227. *Russian Warns Georgia Against Ship Seizures*, Civil Georgia, Sept. 3, 2009; *see generally* Daniel McLaughlin, *Georgia to Meet Russians over Abkhazia Sea Blockade*, Irish Times, Sept. 8, 2009, http://www.irishtimes.com/news/georgia-to-meet-russians-over-abkhazia-sea-blockade-1.733622.

228. *Russia to Protect Ships Bound to Abkhazia*, Civil Georgia, Aug. 29, 2009, http://www.civil.ge/eng/article.php?id=21405.

229. Institute for National Security and Counterterrorism (INSCT), *Libya in Conflict: Mapping The Libyan Armed Conflict*, 7–10, 28 (2012); *see also* Sam Foster Halabi, *Traditions of Belligerent Recognition: The Libyan Intervention in Historical and Theoretical Context*, 27 Am. Univ. Int'l L. Rev. 321 (2012).

Afghanistan conflict asserts that the Taliban is a recognized belligerent in accordance with "customary laws of war."[230]

These instances, along with several other post-1949 case studies to be explored in the final section of this chapter, point to a trickling but clearly discernible set of diverse national and contextual references to recognition of belligerency as a relevant legal analytical framework for assessing modern "civil war" situations. This is hardly indicative of a dead doctrine, and squarely raises the following query: If the doctrine persists, is there actually any legal space remaining in which it could irreproachably be said to operate? As a matter of legal analytical practice, it is relatively clear that recognition of belligerency remains a valid and viable framework for analyzing certain NIAC situations, at least in the minds of some scholars and some state legal advisers, and at least as a general conceptual scheme. The next question, therefore, is whether there remain any substantive and legally circumscribed conflict contexts within which the scheme could still be employed.

(iv) Is there a legal space within LOAC in which the doctrine could still operate?

It must be accepted that contemporary discussions referencing the recognition of belligerency are relatively sparse in comparison with the burgeoning and essential discourse focused upon the interpretation and application of the substantially codified post-1949 corpus of LOAC. However, the fundamental question remains: Has the doctrine, and thus its attendant status of recognized belligerent, survived codification and the post-1949 progressive development of LOAC? Certainly, as is hopefully evident from the analysis thus far, some state practice (including that to be addressed in more detail to come), some treaties, some commentary, and some academic discussion would tend to indicate that it has. This then brings us to a fundamental question in terms of the possible continuing validity of the doctrine: If recognition of belligerency remains legally relevant and available as a framework for legal analysis of conflict and the allocation of LOAC-governed status, rights, and obligations, what is the minimum scope of application over which it might still apply? It is important to engage with this issue because the effective residual scope available for material application of the doctrine is a different question to its subsistence in law as a generally available tool for legal comment and analysis. It is my view, as shall likely be evident, that recognition of belligerency remains broadly afoot as a legal doctrine; however, the interests of concision are better served by proving a discrete instance of continuity as an indicator of both a minimum persisting scope as well as potentially broader application. To this end, I shall thus focus upon one indicator: the difference between the test for recognition of belligerency and the scope of AP I Article 1(4).

On a cautious reading, treating codified rules as having effectively extinguished any parallel components incorporated within the doctrine, it is still possible to

230. Jordan J. Paust, *NIAC Nonsense, the Afghan War, and Combatant Immunity*, 44 GA. J. INT'L & COMP. L. 555, 563 (2016).

identify situational lacunae governed—or at least governable—by the doctrine on recognition of belligerency. This may be briefly illustrated by reference to the example of AP I Article 1(4), which does not extinguish the recognition of belligerency's "third on-ramp" into International Armed Conflict (IAC) LOAC, persisting as it still does in tandem with (but separate and not entirely parallel to) the well-recognized CA2 and AP I Article 1(4) "on-ramps."[231] Further, there is no doubt that the AP I Article 1(4) mechanism was at the time of negotiation, and remains, intensely controversial and has yet to be formally and definitively applied or acknowledged in any particularized context, thus leaving even greater scope for an argument that recognition of belligerency subsists in the background regardless of AP I Article 1(4). Again, however, the interests of concision and brevity are perhaps best served by a focused assessment of one clear instance that proves the general proposition without necessarily establishing its full schematic scope.[232]

The first element of substantive difference is evident in the manner by which the trigger for application is defined. The trigger in AP I is clear in law, if difficult in practice:

> Article 1
>
> 3. This Protocol, which supplements the Geneva Conventions of 12 August 1949 for the protection of war victims, shall apply in the situations referred to in Article 2 common to those Conventions.
> 4. The situations referred to in the preceding paragraph include armed conflicts in which peoples are fighting against colonial domination and alien occupation and against racist regimes in the exercise of their right of self-determination, as enshrined in the Charter of the United Nations and the Declaration on Principles of International Law concerning Friendly Relations and Co-operation among States in accordance with the Charter of the United Nations.[233]

Article 1(4) thus provides for the removal of the category of conflict it describes from the realm of NIAC, and its legal re-definition as an IAC. The consequence

231. That is, recognition of belligerency, if it remains extant, offers a legally distinct alternative path into the de jure application of IAC LOAC—one that is separate to both the existing Tadic threshold, and Additional Protocol I article 1(4) threshold, even though it shares some of the elements and sub-tests apparent in each of these thresholds. I am indebted to Douglas Guilfoyle for this most eloquent analogy.

232. *See, e.g.*, Lootsteen, *The Concept of Belligerency in International Law*, 109. However, Lootsteen's view is that the doctrine has fallen into desuetude, with the last occasion on which it was seriously considered being the Spanish Civil War; *see also* Dapo Akande, *Classification of Armed Conflicts: Relevant Legal Concepts*, *in* INTERNATIONAL LAW AND THE CLASSIFICATION OF CONFLICTS 32, 49 (Elizabeth Wilmshurst ed., 2012).

233. Protocol I Additional to the Geneva Conventions of 12 August 1949, and Relating to the Protection of Victims of International Armed Conflicts art. 1, June 8, 1977, 1125 U.N.T.S. 3. [hereinafter Additional Protocol I].

is that the panoply of IAC LOAC then applies as a matter of course, by treaty and through customary rules. Certainly, recognition of the context as one fitting within the Article 1(4) scope clearly requires some states to say something about the nature of the conflict. But this serves as evidence of the threshold rather than a core requirement of the application of the test, for the test is fundamentally beholden to the extent to which the facts on the ground meet the required definition in the specified instruments. One such inherent requirement asserted by Leslie Green, for example, was that qualification as a "national liberation movement"—a precondition for the operation of AP I Article 1(4)—was in part dependent upon whether "the entity making the claim . . . [was] recognized as such by the regional organization in the area in which it is operating."[234] In relation to recognition of belligerency, however, the state prerogative—either of the imperiled conflict state, or of third states—was a fundamental, overtly political, interest-based element of the test to be met in order to legitimately generate recognition of belligerency.

A second element of difference between the test for recognition of belligerency and the AP I Article 1(4) threshold goes to the scope of application of each characterization scheme. In this sense, the question is this: Are there any conflict contexts where the application of the customary doctrine on recognition of belligerency would bring IAC LOAC rules into play, but which are not covered by the material scope of application carved out by AP I Article 1(4)? Draper, among others, certainly felt this to be the case.[235] It is arguably this "gap" that presents the most difficult transference problem between the pre-1949 internal conflict and civil war scheme, and the post-1949 NIAC LOAC context. Clearly, many decolonization belligerency situations would fall within the AP I Article 1(4) scope of "wars of liberation against colonial domination and racist regimes," which are equated to IACs for the purposes of LOAC application. However, recognition of belligerency was not specifically limited to anti-colonial conflicts, although many of the situations where recognition of belligerency status was discussed by third states as a possible response, were in fact tied to rebellions against colonial powers. But there remain pre-1949 internal conflict contexts where belligerency was either recognized (American Civil War) or was seriously considered, although not granted (such as with respect to the Spanish Civil War), which do not neatly fit within the post-1949 AP I Article 1(4) conception of a rebel group fighting a war of national liberation against colonial domination or a racist regime.

In the American Civil War, for example, it was arguably the rebelling entity that could have been described as the more racist regime. During the Brazilian Naval Revolt of 1893–1894, the conflict was between a post-1889 revolutionary government, and Brazilian naval mutineers,[236] who were generally perceived to be pro-monarchy. The result, consequently, is that there were pre-1949 belligerency

234. Green, *Strengthening Legal Protection in Internal Conflicts: Low-Intensity Conflict and the Law*,, 503.

235. Draper, *Humanitarian Law and Internal Armed Conflicts*, 275.

236. *See* Moore, 1 A Digest of International Law, §70.

contexts that do not fall within the scope of AP I Article 1(4), and within which the pre-1949 scheme asserted (or at the very least considered) the applicability of the Law of War (modern IAC LOAC). Or put another way, there are clear instances of pre-1949 internal conflict contexts afforded belligerency status, and within which the Law of War applied, which still fall outside the modern AP I Article 1(4) group of internal conflict contexts in which IAC LOAC must be applied.

E. THE RELEVANCE CHALLENGE: THE APPLICATION OF RECOGNITION OF BELLIGERENCY TO SELECTED ISSUES AND SITUATIONS SINCE 1949

The ultimate question we arrive at, as presaged by the analysis thus far, is whether the recognition of belligerency has been treated by states as of continuing relevance—either as a justification or explanatory framework or, more particularly, as a characterization to be avoided—precisely because it is still believed to bring into play a set of clear and well-defined legal consequences that concerned states may wish to avoid. Some of these situations and analyses have already been canvassed—the Communist-Nationalist China conflict, and Biafra, for example. In this concluding section of the chapter, I will deal with two legal questions and three conflict situations of more recent provenance, and which have hitherto been only briefly noted in this book. The two legal questions are as to desuetude and the continuing utility of the doctrine in maritime contexts; the three situations are Algeria, the *Mavi Marmara*, and Yemen.

(i) The issue of desuetude

Might it be said that the doctrine on recognition of belligerency has fallen into irreversible desuetude? A number of notable scholars certainly believe so.[237] Richard Falk argued in 1964 that the trend in rebellions to manifest as focused putsches targeted at elites and control of government apparatus, rather than (in the first instance) as extended physical presence across territory and a population, meant that the recognition of belligerency criteria were by then "inadequate for modern needs."[238] Thomas Franck and Nigel Rodley similarly argued in 1970 that the doctrine had at the very least fallen into disuse.[239] David Elder, in 1979, was

> of the opinion that both the doctrines of belligerency and insurgency, despite recent scholarly criticisms of why and how they were not applied in a

237. Thomas M. Franck and Nigel Rodley, *Legitimacy and Legal Rights of Revolutionary Movements with Special Reference to the Peoples' Revolutionary Government of South Viet. Nam*, 45 N.Y.U. L. Rev. 679, 683–84 (1970).

238. Richard A. Falk, The International Law of Internal War 218–20 (Richard A. Falk ed., 1971).

239. Franck and Rodley, *Legitimacy and Legal Rights of Revolutionary Movements with Special Reference to the Peoples' Revolutionary Government of South Viet. Nam*, 683.

> particular conflict, are, for the most part, useless. These doctrines derail intelligent commentators and statesmen from the more productive pursuit of a genuine consensus on minimal humanitarian principles applicable in such domestic settings.[240]

The Columbian government, in a statement on the status of FARC dated 16 June 1999, referred to the fact that the "political status conferred on FARC" for the purposes of seeking a peaceful settlement of the conflict, was not to be read as recognition of a "state of belligerence," adding that "The institution of belligerence, which is part of the international customary law, is in practice obviously in disuse."[241]

However, it is Oglesby—arguing in 1971—who has made the strongest direct claim as to the desuetude of the doctrine. He begins his assessment by asserting that the turning point in the doctrine's influence was also its apogee—the American Civil War. The inconsistent and itinerant application of the doctrine after 1865, and the—in his view—"negligible" commentary on the doctrine (with the exception of the Spanish Civil War, where the status was not ultimately granted) were indicative of desuetude, he asserted. Further, the advent of UN Charter Article 39 (with its attendant "impossibility" of an attitude of neutrality once an internal conflict is subject to UNSC attention[242]) was also a development, Oglesby argued, that proved the doctrine's extinction. In order to affirm his opinion, Oglesby explored the concept of desuetude in relation to recognition of belligerency, and arrived at the following criteria:

> On the basis of the experience derived from systems of law using the principle of desuetude, it is possible to set up at least four valid tests for determining when nonuse has been translated into desuetude.
>
> (1) That the disuse be of such duration that the disuse itself has become established as a custom.
> (2) That another customary law has been substituted for it.
> (3) That the contrary practice approaches the universal in its acceptance.
> (4) That the opportunities must have presented themselves for the law to have been applied.[243]

Oglesby's conclusion is that each of the four tests is met in relation to recognition of belligerency —to wit: (1) The doctrine evolved over fifty years, but then

240. David A. Elder, *The Historical Background of Common Article 3 of the Geneva Convention of 1949*, 11 Case W. Res. J. Int'l L. 37, 40 (1979).

241. *Statement of Government of Columbia Regarding the Status of FARC, 16 June 1999*, 2 Y.B. Int'l Humanitarian L. 440, 441(1999).

242. Oglesby, Internal War and the Search for Normative Order, 101–108.

243. *Id.* at 112.

was relatively unused for the next one hundred years; (2) Insurgency has replaced belligerency as the relevant doctrine since the American Civil War; (3) The collective approach to international security evident in the UN Charter "suggests that such a concept [recognition of belligerency], founded on pre-World War I rules of neutrality, is inappropriate and ineffective for present conditions"; and (4) the application of the doctrine in the Spanish Civil War was "studiously avoided."[244]

These conclusions are, however, arguable on both the basis of the tests used and the facts. First, as to the test, Jan Wouters and Sten Verhoeven note in their entry on "desuetudo" in the *Max Planck Encyclopedia of Public International Law*, that the "rejection of a rule [or inference that the obligation has ceased to exist] through subsequent non-enforcement or non-compliance" is more readily demonstrated when dealing with custom than with treaties; indeed, they assert, it is "the legal ground par excellence for terminating rules of customary international law." However, as they note, "A mere inconsistent practice will not be sufficient. Opinio iuris should be deduced from the conflicting practice in respect of the extinction or modification of the previous norm."[245] The recent ICRC 2016 *Commentary on Geneva Convention I*, addressing certain provisions within GC I which have been the subject of little or no recent practice (such as articles 8 and 10 on Protecting Powers), cites Wouters and Verhoeven with approval, observing that

> [t]he absence of practice in the application of a provision does not, in and of itself, lead to the falling into desuetude of such a provision. Desuetude means that a treaty rule is no longer applicable or has been modified, a conclusion that should not be reached lightly. It is subject to stringent conditions and requires the agreement, at least tacit, of the Parties or the emergence of an inconsistent rule of customary international law.[246]

Admittedly, the concern here is with desuetude of treaty rules; but the test—as formulated by Woutens and Verhoeven—with respect to a customary doctrine remains similar: mere inconsistent, sparse, or even negligible practice is not sufficient; conflicting practice is necessary. In the case of recognition of belligerency, this would effectively nullify Oglesby's first test—that of time. This is perhaps reinforced when the issue of piracy is considered: the fact that there were no

244. *Id.* at 112–14.

245. Jan Wouters and Sten Verhoeven, *Desuetudo*, *in* 3 Max Planck Encyclopedia of Public International Law 70 (Rudiger Wolfrum ed., 2013), http://opil.ouplaw.com/view/10.1093/law:epil/9780199231690/law-9780199231690-e1027?prd=EPIL.

246. International Committee of the Red Cross, Commentary on the First Geneva Convention: Convention (I) for the Amelioration of the Condition of the Wounded and Sick in Armed Forces in the Field, ¶¶ 51–52 (2016); *see also* International Committee of the Red Cross, Commentary on the Second Geneva Convention: Convention (II) for the Amelioration of the Condition of Wounded, Sick and Shipwrecked Members of Armed Forces at Sea, ¶¶ 65–66 (2017), https://ihl-databases.icrc.org/applic/ihl/ihl.nsf/Comment.xsp?action=openDocument&documentId=514012CC1D2DA6C8C1258115004AE0CC#_Toc478490304.

customarily defined piracy prosecutions for almost a century, until the rise of Somali piracy off the Horn of Africa in the late 2000s, was never understood to have meant that the customary international law norms in relation to piracy had fallen into desuetude.[247]

Second, as has been discussed in this chapter, the post-1949 evolution of modern LOAC has in no way extinguished the pre-1949 Law of War; indeed, the pre-1949 Law of War remains an integral part of post-1949 LOAC, and in some areas, remains the most recently settled applicable law. The example par excellence is the Law of War applicable at sea, where the majority of directly applicable, maritime-focused treaty law is still drawn from Hague 1907 Conventions VI–IX, XI, and XIII.[248] As Natalino Ronzitti observed in the introduction to his compendium on *The Law of Naval Warfare* in 1988:

> The corpus of Declarations and Conventions which concur in forming what is known as the law of warfare at sea was almost entirely established at the time of the Hague codifications of 1899 and 1907. Some of these rules were drafted even earlier, such as those embodied in the 1856 Paris Declaration, which is still of great importance for the law of blockade and the discipline of economic warfare . . . the law of naval warfare is a subject which has been neglected by the contemporary literature, with the exception of seminal works devoted to the topic by the late D.P. O'Connell.[249]

Oglesby's conclusions as to the third test—contrary practice—appears to be based on two factors. The first is an assessment of the parallel desuetude of the law of neutrality, itself based in an assumption that all conflicts will be subject to UNSC mandatory measures under Chapter VII of the Charter, thus diminishing the possible assertion of neutrality by a third state obliged to assist in the implementation of those measures. Other scholars have similarly argued that the law of neutrality is at the very least in "partial retreat."[250] This symbiotic link between the persistence of recognition of belligerency on the one hand, and neutrality on the other,

247. *See* James Gathii, *Kenya's Piracy Prosecutions*, 104 Am. J. Int'l L. 416 (2010); Douglas Guilfoyle, *Prosecuting Somali Pirates: A Critical Evaluation of the Options*, 10 J. Int'l Crim. Just. 767 (2012); Eugene Kontorovich, *International Legal Responses to Piracy off the Coast of Somalia*, 13 Am. Soc'y Int'l L Insights, Feb. 6, 2009, https://www.asil.org/insights/volume/13/issue/2/international-legal-responses-piracy-coast-somalia; Lawrence Azubuike, *International Law Regime Against Piracy*, 15 Ann. Surv. Int'l & Comp. L. 43, 44–46 (2009).

248. *See* Louise Doswald-Beck, *San Remo Manual on International Law Applicable to Armed Conflict at Sea*, 35 Int'l Rev. Red Cross 5, 67–69 (1995).

International Institute of Humanitarian Law, San Remo Manual on International Law Applicable to Armed Conflicts at Sea 5, 67–69 (Louise Doswald-Beck ed., 1995); UK Ministry of Defence, The Manual of the Law of Armed Conflict, ¶¶13.1–13.4 (2004).

249. The Law of Naval Warfare: A Collection of Agreements and Documents with Commentaries 1 (Natalino Ronzitti ed., 1988).

250. Mastorodimos, *Belligerency Recognition: Past, Present and Future*, 319.

is unsurprising. Lauterpacht in his 1928 assessment of the extent of the non-interference obligation for a third state in its dealings with a conflict state, and with revolutionaries who are located within third state jurisdiction, observed that the Anglo-American tradition of interpretation of this norm was built around and structured to implement the obligations of neutrality. He differentiated this approach from the German-Austrian-Russian approach, which was reflective of a "system of mutual insurance," and from the "Latin" approach, which referred back to international law in order to determine the specific criminality or otherwise of individual acts.[251]

It is very clear, however, that the formalization of international security management norms has not in fact extinguished the need for the law of neutrality. Indeed, there have been, and remain, many conflict contexts that were not, or are not, subject to UNSC Chapter VII mandatory measures, and in which the law of neutrality still clearly applied de jure: The Israel-Arab Wars; India-Pakistan;[252] Georgia-Russia;[253] and China-Vietnam[254] being but a few examples. Additionally, as George Politakis and others have amply illustrated, the law of maritime neutrality remains very much a live consideration in assessing maritime incidents within armed conflict contexts, and has certainly not been extinguished by the advent of formal mechanisms for collective security.[255] There is similarly no doubt that the drafters of the *Tallinn Manual 2.0* took as fundamental the continued existence and application of neutrality as a legal concept.[256] The second factor is Oglesby's argument that recognition of insurgency replaced recognition of belligerency as the relevant doctrine. However, the vast bulk of commentary and practice traversed in the course of this book is clearly to the effect that insurgency and belligerency are successive and distinct options within the three-level scheme, with differing legal and political consequences; they are not interchangeable.

Finally, Oglesby's conclusion that the Spanish Civil War offered an opportunity for application of the doctrine on recognition of belligerency, which was then studiously avoided, perhaps approaches the interpretation of the role played by recognition of belligerency in this situation from the wrong end of the desuetude spectrum. Oglesby's view is that precisely because the doctrine was consciously

251. Lauterpacht, *Revolutionary Activities by Private Persons Against Foreign States*, 113–19.

252. *See, e.g.*, Elihu Lauterpacht, *The Legal Irrelevance of the "State of War,"* 62 Am. Soc'y Int'l L. Proc. 58, 60 (1968).

253. *See, e.g.*, *Russia Reaffirms Neutrality*, Civil Georgia, Mar. 16, 2004, http://www.civil.ge/eng/article.php?id=6451&search=Russia.

254. *See, e.g.*, Daniel Tretiak, *China's Vietnam War and its Consequences*, 80 China Q. 740,748 (1979).

255. George Politakis, Modern Aspects of the Laws of Naval Warfare and Maritime Neutrality 7–9, 381–407 (1988).

256. Tallinn Manual 2.0 on the International Law Applicable to Cyber Operations 245, 555–62 (Michael N. Schmitt ed., 2d ed., 2017) (discussing cyber operations in the territorial sea during armed conflict in Rule 49 and neutrality in Rules 150–54).

and overtly central to the characterization debates surrounding the Spanish Civil War, the fact that the status was not formally accorded to the Nationalist party—in spite of a clear factual permission to do so—equates to a finding that the doctrine was no longer effective. However, the opposite view is equally tenable—the very fact that the doctrine was at the core of legal debates about the Spanish Civil War is clear evidence that states (including the imperiled state itself, as is clear from the lengths the Republican government went to in order to ensure the Nationalists were not recognized as belligerents), and publicists, considered it to be the operative analytical framework. Similarly, the fact that the status of belligerent was not ultimately accorded to the Nationalists could as equally speak to the robust health of the critical fourth element of the recognition of belligerency test—that third states would ultimately make their decision based on their own political and diplomatic interests—rather than indicate the irrelevance of the test. Konstantinos Mastorodimos, after a review of various incidents and authorities, concluded that

> If anything comes out of . . . [this] inquiry, it is that recognition of belligerency still exists in customary international law, to the extent that significant authorities certify it, albeit verbally. State practice, on the other hand, tends to ignore it, with the possible exception of states that are either in the American continent or are deeply influenced by US legal tradition.[257]

I would, respectfully, rate the record on state practice much higher—the fact that states have continued to employ the doctrine on recognition of belligerency as a contextual analytical tool fundamentally speaks against desuetude. The fact that there was no conviction for piracy in the international law sense for close to a century, prior to the Somali piracy phenomenon,[258] was never sensibly leveraged to argue that piracy as a legal concept had fallen into desuetude. Instead, it would seem clear that there are ongoing—albeit rare—references in judicial and quasi-judicial contexts, treaties, and negotiations. When coupled with the myriad post-1949 instances where states have specifically addressed recognition of belligerency as an animating factor within their analytical and decision-making processes, and the absence of any clear statements by states to the effect that the doctrine is dead, the record tends to militate against a finding of desuetude.

(ii) The enduring predominance of maritime concerns and contexts

On a maritime-focused reading, it is certainly possible to argue that the doctrine on recognition of belligerency remains afoot in its entirety. The ICJ has

257. Mastorodimos, *Belligerency Recognition: Past, Present and Future*, 318.

258. Tamsin Paige, *Piracy and Universal Jurisdiction*, 12 Macquarie L.J. 131 (2013).

determined in the *Nicaragua Case*[259]—a case within an arguably NIAC context, including maritime LOAC applications[260]—that customary rules can coexist with treaty crystallization, and that both parallel sets of rules may exhibit differences in nuance. Indeed, in the absence of any post-1949 instruments conclusively extinguishing the doctrine and given that some post-1949 maritime NIAC state practice appears to hearken back to this scheme, it is difficult to see why the pre-1949 scheme, as applied at sea, should be considered entirely defunct. Certainly, we must accept that the scheme has been amended by post-1949 developments in means and methods LOAC, conflict characterization LOAC, and contextual overlays such as the Law of the Sea Convention. But this does not extinguish it entirely, nor alter it beyond all recognition such that reference back to the customary doctrine is rendered, ab initio, nugatory or deceptive. Even if we decide that post-1949 treaty crystallization has extinguished all of those elements of the pre-1949 conflict categorization scheme that have any correspondence to the post-1949 scheme's scope, concepts, or context, we are still left with the legal possibility that a subset of (at the very least) maritime belligerency situations in which the Law of War was historically applied nevertheless persists outside the scope of post-1949 codifications of IAC and NIAC LOAC.

As a matter of state practice, the most obvious post-1949 NIAC contexts in which the recognition of belligerency has been clearly available for consideration, if not application, have been maritime. This is unsurprising given the substantially maritime origins of the doctrine and the maritime concerns it was originally designed to address. In many of these post-1949 maritime contexts, recognition of belligerency was not afforded, and the conflict state (and where necessary, third states) tended to characterize NSAG maritime elements as criminals and terrorists domestically, and as terrorists or pirates internationally. The most obvious example is the Liberation Tigers of Tamil Eelam (LTTE) "Sea Tigers," who were always dealt with by Sri Lankan forces as criminal insurgents, and whose conduct in international waters was generally characterized (but not prosecuted) as criminal—even piratical—rather than being characterized as legitimate activity by a belligerent force in accordance with the applicable maritime LOAC.[261] The Sri Lankan "blockade," as Wolff Heintschel von Heinegg and others have correctly pointed out, was actually a domestic law enforcement measure limited to the Sri Lankan territorial sea (and by extension into the contiguous zone), as opposed to a LOAC-based means or meathod of warfare—even if the Sri Lankan Navy on at least one occasion carried out an interdiction outside of the territorial sea and contiguous zone. The key issue is that Sri Lanka did not claim a Law of War

259. Military and Paramilitary Activities in and Against Nicaragua (Nicar. v. U.S.), Judgment, 1986 I.C.J. 14, ¶ 177 (June 27).

260. Rob McLaughlin and Dale Stephens, *International Humanitarian Law in the Maritime Context: Characterization in Judicial and Quasi-Judicial Contexts*, *in* Applying International Humanitarian Law in Judicial and Quasi-Judicial Bodies 103 (Derek Jinks, Jackson Maogoto, and Solon Solomon eds., 2014).

261. *See, e.g.*, Guilfoyle, *The Mavi Marmara Incident and Blockade in Armed Conflict*, 193.

blockade; they claimed a "maritime surveillance zone." This is a historically well-attested and well-calibrated legal option for states seeking to achieve maritime security objectives against an insurgent without resort to the Law of War techniques of blockade or visit and search, and the recognition of belligerency that implicitly accompanied such actions.[262]

Similarly, Mastorodimos's analysis of the Papua New Guinean "blockade" in relation to the rebellious Bougainville province is that it was an embargo only extending out to twelve nautical miles (the territorial sea), and thus was clearly within the realm of a law enforcement prerogative of the state as opposed to a LOAC-based act.[263] He is undoubtedly correct. However, there are two clear situations where the legal consequences of recognition of belligerency in the maritime context appear to have been consciously considered, and tacitly invoked, and one further situation where recognition of belligerency appears to be relevant, but unappreciated.

(iii) Algeria, 1954–1962

The relevant maritime operations arising out of the Algerian Revolution center around interdiction of third state shipping on the high seas by French forces in connection with prosecution of the armed conflict ashore. For some analysts there is little doubt that the French had, in practice, imposed and enforced a LOAC blockade.[264] Under the customary law on recognition of belligerency, the

262. Wolff Heintschel von Heinegg, *Methods and Means of Naval Warfare in Non-International Armed Conflicts*, 88 Int'l L. Stud. 211, 215–16 (2012); Guilfoyle, *The Mavi Marmara Incident and Blockade in Armed Conflict*, 193. Some dispute this characterization, pointing to other reports that one particular interdiction—of the *Captain Ali*, in June 2009—took place not at 18 nautical miles off the Sri Lankan coast, but rather further off the coast (the reporting is unclear); *see* Eugene Kontorovich, *Iran's Relief Ship and the Blockade of Yemen*, Opinio Juris (May 11, 2015), http://opiniojuris.org/2015/05/11/guest-post-irans-relief-ship-and-the-blockade-of-yemen/. One Sri Lankan news report purports to quote a Sri Lankan Navy source thus: "Naval Media Spokesman & Special Boat Squadron Director Capt. D.K.P. Dassanayake said, 'the vessel was seized about 100 nautical miles off the Western coast at about 4.00 am. Thursday, June 4 2009.'": Walter Jayawardhana, "Captain Ali, a Ship Carrying Alleged LTTE Cargo Seized by Sri Lanka Navy during the Wee Hours of Thursday," LANKA WEB, 4 June 2009, at http://www.lankaweb.com/news/items/2009/06/04/captain-ali-a-ship-carrying-alleged-ltte-cargo-seized-by-sri-lanka-navy-during-the-wee-hours-of-thursday/.

263. Mastorodimos, *Belligerency Recognition: Past, Present and Future*, 314–15.

264. For example, Charles Zorgbibe, *Sources of the Recognition of Belligerent Status*, 17 Int'l Rev. Red Cross 111, 115 (1977); James Kraska, *Rule Selection in the case of Israel's Naval Blockade of Gaza: Law of Naval Warfare or Law of the Sea?*, 13 Y.B. Int'l Hum. L. 367, 388 (2010); Rob McLaughlin, *The Law Applicable to Naval Mine Warfare in a Non-International Armed Conflict*, 90 Int'l L. Stud. 475, 477 (2014); Russell Buchan's article is very clear on this point and states, "Moreover, in the late 1950s France imposed a naval blockade against Algeria, which was a colony of France at the time, in order to prevent war material from reaching the Algerian insurgents that were seeking liberation from French colonisation. Significantly, however . . . the Algerian insurgents were recognised as belligerents." *The International Law of Naval Blockade and Israel's Interception of the Mavi Marmara*, 58 Neth. Int'l L. Rev. 209, 218 (2011);

consequence, of course, was that this amounted to a clear invocation of the Law of War and thus comprised tacit—but nevertheless effective—recognition of Algerian NSAG belligerency. One indicative example of French "blockade"-based conduct related to the *Athos/Saint Briavels*, a British registered, but at the time unflagged, vessel interdicted in the Mediterranean in October 1956 on suspicion of carrying "contraband" to Algerian rebels. The vessel was diverted to the French port of Nemours and investigations disclosed a significant cargo of arms and ammunition, and a number of individuals said to have been trained in Egypt for roles within Algerian rebel forces.[265] One might put this specific act down to the "unflagged" appearance of the vessel and a robust reading of the right of visit, but other vessels—of Czechoslovak, Yugoslav, and West German registration—were also interdicted, including in the English Channel.[266] Another indicative incident was the *West Breeze*, a British flagged vessel interdicted in international waters, in February 1961. Britain had not recognized FLN belligerency, and thus responded to a French request to recall the vessel to a British port for inspection (on suspicion of carrying contraband for the FLN) by indicating that it had no routine peacetime power to do so. The French then diverted *West Breeze* to Mers el Kebir, and upon finding no contraband, allowed the vessel to proceed.[267] The issue was debated in the House of Commons on 27 February 1961 in terms that clearly evidenced an ongoing appreciation of recognition of belligerency as a legal option:

> Mr. Healey (by Private Notice): asked the Lord Privy Seal what protest Her Majesty's Government have made to the French Government concerning the interception of the British ship 'West Breeze' in international waters off the Algerian coast.
>
> The Joint Under-Secretary of State for Foreign Affairs (Mr. J. B. Godber): Representations were made to the French Government both in London and Paris on 24th February. They were asked for a full explanation of the circumstances surrounding this incident. We are now considering what further action we should take.

see also Rear Admiral Bernard Estival, *The French Navy and the Algerian War*, 25 J. Strategic Stud. 79, 81–82 (2002) (referring to a "coastal blockade" and a "maritime surveillance" operation). If LOAC blockade was not the actual legal basis, then some of the interdictions carried out were, it seems fair to say, without appropriate legal foundation.

265. Letter from the Representative of France Addressed to the Secretary-General, October 25, 1956 (S/3689), http://www.un.org/en/ga/search/view_doc.asp?symbol=S/3689.

266. Arnold Fraleigh, *The Algerian Revolution as a Case Study in International Law*, *in* The International Law of Civil Wars, 179, 203–204 (Richard Falk ed., 1971); Eldon Van Cleef Greenberg, *Law and the Conduct of the Algerian Revolution*, 11 Harv. Int'l L.J. 37, 40–44 (1970); Katherine Draper, *Why a War Without a Name May Need One: Policy-Based Application of International Humanitarian Law in the Algerian War*, 48 Tex. Int'l L. J. 575, 592–601 (2013).

267. Anna Van Zwanenberg, *Interference with Ships on the High Seas*, 10 Int'l & Comp. L. Q. 785, 791–92 (1961).

> Mr. Healey: Can the Under-Secretary tell us whether he has had a reply from the French Government in the light of which he could give further consideration to this matter? Is it not the case that the French Government are not at war in Algeria, the only situation in which such interception would be legally permissible, and that the interception therefore represents an illegal interference with the freedom of the seas? . . .
>
> Mr. Godber: . . . This is a matter on which we obviously need further information before making further representations. We shall, naturally, want to see the master's report. We do not accept that the action of the French Government in this case was in any way correct and we shall wish to take further action, but we wish to have our facts first.
>
> Mr. Paget: Do we also take it that the action of the French Government in arresting this ship amounted to a recognition of the belligerent rights of the F.L.N., and that from now onwards all nations are entitled to treat F.L.N. as a lawful belligerent?
>
> Mr. Godber: That is an interesting question, but I do not feel disposed at the moment to say what interpretation should be placed on the actions of the French. This is not the first occasion on which the French have intercepted a vessel, although it is the first on which a British ship has been involved.[268]

Arnold Fraleigh, in his analysis of the Algerian Revolution, clearly notes the delicacy of the French legal position, characterized as it was by a lack of clarity as to whether they were applying maritime Law of War measures or not, combined with a general non-responsiveness to queries. Clearly, if France was not applying Law of War measures, their interference with third state shipping on the high seas was clearly unlawful. This opacity appears to have been informed by a political decision to avoid doing anything that looked like recognizing Algerian rebel belligerency. The FLN, Fraleigh continued, "cited [the interdictions] as evidence that the French actually recognized the FLN as a belligerent," and the French, for their part, "could not set up a prize court to handle complaints by shipowners without acknowledging the belligerent status of the rebels."[269] Certainly, the Algerian Revolution was widely discussed in terms of a possible and probable instance of recognition of belligerency. Equally clearly, France employed maritime Law of War regimes such as visit and search (traditionally a tacit recognition of belligerency), but veiled this conduct with a conscious effort to avoid any formal indications to that effect. Further, a range of formal French instruments (indicative in the array of examples and references marshaled by, inter alia, Mohammed Bedjaoui, and Eldon Van Cleef Greenburg) tend to illustrate the extent to which recognition of belligerency, and the wish to avoid this characterization, was a clear animating concern. Similarly, French determination to treat Algerian rebels as PW—following a conscious decision not to prosecute them as criminals—was characterized by the ICRC as paralleling the IAC PW provisions; the rebels had

268. 635 Parl Deb HC (5th ser.) (1961) col. 1196–97.

269. Fraleigh, *The Algerian Revolution as a Case Study in International Law*, 206.

also undertaken early in the conflict to treat captured French soldiers as PW.[270] When added to the previously noted *Societe Purafina Francaise* case (where a French court faced with legally characterizing the situation determined that it was indeed a "civil war," albeit not one that enlivened the relevant "war" insurance provisions) it is possible to conclude that both parties, and many third states, clearly viewed the conflict context through the lens of the doctrine on recognition of belligerency. Some of these actors did so using the doctrine as an analytical tool for ascribing possible legal rights and obligations; others assiduously and delicately structured public statements to avoid having to address the issue and raise the prospect at all. This is not indicative of a doctrine in desuetude.

(iv) The Gaza Blockade, 2010

A second example that indicates the continued application of the doctrine on recognition of belligerency is the 2010 boarding of *Mavi Marmara*. More than any other recent event, this incident squarely raised the issue of application of maritime Law of War rules in a an ostensibly NIAC context. Consequently, some of the more nuanced reporting and analysis has not shied away from the question as to how it might be that the Law of War regime of blockade might have operated de jure in relation to the Gaza Strip in 2010. The Turkel Commission, and the UN-appointed Palmer-Uribe Inquiry, both concluded that the Israeli blockade was lawful, albeit in the context of an IAC characterization.[271] However, other analyses—including by the ICC Office of the Prosecutor, and in the Palmer-Uribe report—have also concluded that while it is probable that the conflict context was one of IAC, deriving from the effects of an ongoing (legally contentious) "occupation,"[272] the situation in fact may have been a NIAC. This is significant because

270. *See* James E. Bond, *Application of the Law of War to Internal Conflicts*, 3 GA. J. INT'L & COMP. L. 345, 368–69 (1973).

271. *See, e.g.*, The Public Commission to Examine the Maritime Incident of 31 May 2010—The Turkel Commission Report (Part 1) (2011), ¶¶56–60, http://www.turkel-committee.gov.il/files/wordocs//8707200211english.pdf [hereinafter The Turkel Report]. The Turkel Report states,

> Historically, in order for the rules of international humanitarian law that govern international armed conflicts to apply to non-international ones, recognition of a 'belligerency' was required of other States. Such recognition was limited to circumstances in which the level of the conflict has reached 'a certain threshold of intensity manifesting a situation similar to that of a war between states.' However, it should be noted that this has become less important and today is almost irrelevant.

Id. at ¶39; *see also* Geoffrey Palmer, Alvaro Uribe, Joseph Itzhar and Suleyman Sanberk, UN Secretary-General, *Report of the Secretary-General's Panel of Inquiry on the 31 May 2010 Flotilla Incident*, ¶¶ 20–24, 73–81 (September 2011) [hereinafter the Palmer-Uribe Report].

272. *See, e.g.*, Office of the Prosecutor of the International Criminal Court, Situation on Registered Vessels of Comoros, Greece and Cambodia: Article 53(1) Report ¶¶ 29, and 42 (Nov. 6, 2014) [hereinafter ICC OTP Mavi Marmara Report]; *see generally* Guilfoyle, *The Mavi Marmara Incident and Blockade in Armed Conflict*, 171.

the OTP, for one, has concluded—albeit with thin explanation—that even if this was the case, the law of blockade could still be applicable. The OTP's reasoning is as follows:

> The Office's assessment below of alleged acts constituting war crimes focuses on the relevant provisions under articles 8(2)(a) and 8(2)(b) of the Statute as a result of the conclusion reached above concerning the existence of a military occupation. The analysis conducted would also be generally relevant and applicable if it was concluded, alternatively, that the law applicable in the present context and in light of the Israel-Hamas conflict, is the law of non-international armed conflict. Given the crimes of possible relevance to the present situation, which are substantially similar in the context both of international and non-international armed conflicts, it is not necessary at this stage to reach a conclusive view on the classification of the conflict.[273]

The authority for, or mechanism by which, the Law of War regime of blockade applies within the NIAC context is left unstated. However, given that the customary Law of War admitted of only one circumstance where blockade could be invoked against a NSAG—that is, upon overt or tacit recognition of that NSAG's belligerency—the implication is clear. Marko Milanovic and Vidan Hadzi-Vidanovic's treatment of the process of "internationalization through redefinition" justifies an argument that recognition of belligerency—if still relevant—probably offers a cleaner pathway into IAC LOAC in this case, than either AP I Article 1(4) or any contentious, emerging norm on internationalization as a result of the engagement of an international organization.[274] The Palmer-Uribe Report also specifically raises this possibility: "The *Prize Cases* decision therefore suggests that in addition to an international armed conflict, the law of blockade would also be applicable in non-international armed conflicts 'in' which the parties and/or neutral countries recognize each other as belligerents."[275] A number of scholars have also assessed the de jure application of maritime Law of War rules relating to blockade as evidence of a tacit Israeli recognition of the belligerency of Hamas in the Gaza Strip.[276] Indeed, it seems relatively clear that (1) Blockade is a Law of War / LOAC scheme that can only apply in relation to NSAGs where the situation

273. ICC OTP Mavi Marmara Report, ¶35; additionally, *see also* the manner in which the OTP dealt with contextual issues of fact and law—such as the obligation to make a blockade effective, which must be taken into account when assessing the lawfulness of the boarding operation: at, for example, ¶¶32, 91–92.

274. Marko Milanovic and Vidan Hadzi-Vidanovic, *A Taxonomy of Armed Conflict*, *in* Research Handbook on International Conflict and Security Law 256, 298–300 (Nigel White and Christian Henderson, eds., 2013).

275. Palmer-Uribe Report, ¶23.

276. *See, e.g.*, Kevin Heller, *The Civil War and the Blockade of Gaza (a Response to Posner)*, Opinio Juris, (June 4, 2010), http://opiniojuris.org/2010/06/04/eric-posners-incomplete-editorial-on-the-blockade-of-gaza/:

is one in which the Law of War / IAC LOAC applies de jure; (2) a declaration of blockade is considered to be the example par excellence of tacit recognition of belligerency; and (3) the implication that there was a recognition of belligerency in this situation is very strong indeed.

(v) Yemen, 2015–2017

A difficult, and still slippery, example of current potential application of the doctrine on recognition of belligerency stems from the reported imposition of what may be a Law of War visit and search regime, or even a blockade, by Saudi forces supporting the Yemeni government in its NIAC with Houthi rebels.[277] One report, for example, indicated that

> Iran's foreign ministry insisted it would not allow Saudi-led naval forces to inspect an aid ship bound for [the rebel held port of] Hudaydah under military escort. The US has urged Iran to redirect the ship—said to be carrying 2,500 tonnes of food, medicine, tents and blankets—to Djibouti, where the UN has set up a hub. Saudi Arabia has accused Iran of providing military assistance to the Houthis, a charge it denies.[278]

> In short, the evidence does not support Posner's claim that the Civil War indicates there is "a certain latitude for countries to use blockades against internal as well as external enemies." On the contrary, the reaction of both Europe and the Supreme Court to the blockade indicates a very different customary rule: namely, that the institution of a blockade is itself evidence that a conflict with a non-state actor is sufficiently serious that the blockading party must treat the non-state actor as a belligerent, not as an insurgent.
>
> The importance of this rule for Israel's blockade of Gaza is clear. It does not indicate that Israel does not have the right to blockade Gaza. What it indicates is that, for the blockade to be legal, Israel must recognize that a state of belligerency exists between it and Hamas. Which means, in turn, that Hamas soldiers, as the armed forces of the non-state actor that is Gaza, are entitled to engage in hostilities with Israel's armed forces, cannot be prosecuted for acts of violence against those armed forces that comply with the laws of war, and must be treated as POWs upon capture.

Id. See also Kontorovich, *Iran's Relief Ship and the Blockade of Yemen*, Opinio Juris (May 11, 2015) and the associated comments by Guilfoyle, Paust, and Heller.

277. *See generally The War the World Ignores*, The Economist 11 (Dec. 2, 2017); *From Bad to Worse*, The Economist, 19–22 (Dec. 2, 2017); European Council on Foreign Relations, *Mapping the Yemen Conflict*, http://www.ecfr.eu/mena/yemen (last visited Nov. 29, 2018); *In Yemen, Anti-Houthi Operations Confront Forceful Opposition*, Stratfor Worldview 3, 23, 37 (August 21, 2015), https://worldview.stratfor.com/article/yemen-anti-houthi-operations-confront-forceful-opposition#/entry/jsconnect?client_id=644347316&target=%2Fdiscussion%2Fembed%3Fp%3D%252Fdiscussion%252Fembed%252F%26vanilla_identifier%3D268937%26vanilla_url%3Dhttps%253A%252F%252Fworldview.stratfor.com%252Farticle%252Fyemen-anti-houthi-operations-confront-forceful-opposition%26vanilla_category_id%3D1%26title%3DIn%2BYemen%252C%2BAnti-Houthi%2BOperations%2BConfront%2BForceful%2BOpposition.

278. *Yemen conflict: Aid effort begins as truce takes hold*, BBC (May 13, 2015), http://www.bbc.com/news/world-middle-east-32719194.

The Saudi-led force supporting the Yemeni government in its NIAC against the Houthi force has apparently stated that it "will destroy any naval ships trying to enter Yemeni ports."[279] Although public details on this quarantine/temporary closure of the territorial sea/blockade/visit and search regime are exceedingly difficult to come by, it is entirely possible that the regime imposed is nothing more than a measure of municipal waters policing, limited to the territorial sea.[280] This regime is then overlaid by a partial UNSC sanctions regime,[281] as well as by UNSC concerns as to the effects of the closure of ports on the flow of humanitarian aid into Yemen, and the need to ensure "navigational rights and freedoms in and around Bab al-Mandeb strait."[282]

However, this "blockade" could also be an invocation of maritime Law of War rules,[283] a source of authority for such actions being their right to attack warships performing unneutral service for the adversary; and to capture, and in some cases attack, neutral merchant vessels that engage in unneutral service through breach of a blockade or by "intentionally and clearly" resisting visit and search.[284] Similarly,

279. Greg Botelho and Saeed Ahmed, '*Saudi-led coalition strikes rebels in Yemen, inflaming tensions in region*, CNN (Mar. 27, 2015), http://edition.cnn.com/2015/03/26/middleeast/yemen-saudi-arabia-airstrikes/.

280. *See, e.g.*, Identical letters dated 26 March 2015 from the Permanent Representative of Qatar to the United Nations addressed to the Secretary-General and the President of the Security Council (S/2015/217), Mar. 27, 2015, which do not elaborate upon the blockade.

281. S.C. Res. 2342 (Feb. 23, 2017), renewing the iteratively amplified sanctions regime implemented in S.C. Res. 2140, (Feb. 26, 2014).

282. Statement by the President of the Security Council, S/PRST/2017/7, 15 June 2017:

> The Security Council further calls on the parties to allow the safe, rapid and unhindered access for humanitarian supplies and personnel to the populations of all affected governorates, and to facilitate access for essential imports of food, fuel, and medical supplies into the country and their distribution throughout. In this regard, the Security Council stresses the importance of keeping all Yemen's ports functioning, including Hodeida port, as a critical lifeline for humanitarian support and other essential supplies, in line with the Special Envoy's latest proposals for Hodeida port and city . . .
>
> The Security Council takes threats to shipping around Bab al-Mandeb, a strategically important shipping passage, extremely seriously and stresses that the continued exercise of navigational rights and freedoms in and around Bab al-Mandeb strait in accordance with relevant international law must be upheld.

Id. See also Tom Ruys and Luca Ferro, *Weathering the Storm: Legality and Legal Implications of the Saudi-Led Military Intervention in Yemen*, 65 INT'L & COMP. L. Q. 61, 75 (2016) (discussing one particular interception of a vessel (23 January 2013) alleged to have been carrying Iranian arms to the Houthi forces).

283. *See, e.g.*, Philippe Sands, Andrew Clapham and Blinne Ni Ghralaign, Legal opinion on The Lawfulness of the Authorisation by The United Kingdom of Weapons and Related Items for Export to Saudi Arabia in the Context of Saudi Arabia's Military Intervention in Yemen, ¶ 2.25 (Dec. 11, 2015) (discussing the application of *San Remo Manual* Rule 102).

284. Doswald-Beck, *San Remo Manual on International Law Applicable to Armed Conflict at Sea*, 98.

the Pakistan Parliament voted on 10 April 2015 to maintain "neutrality" in the conflict: Parliament, it was reported, "desires that Pakistan should maintain neutrality in the Yemen conflict so as to be able to play a proactive diplomatic role to end the crisis."[285] Alternatively, this move may have been prompted by the fact that "Pakistan's growing relation[s] with Iran might have to a considerable extent compelled Pakistan to maintain neutrality on the issue."[286] Whatever the political imperative, however, neutrality is only an option for third states in an IAC, or—as the doctrine on recognition of belligerency expressly incorporates—in customary Law of War terms, a civil war where the NSAG has been recognized as having belligerent status, and thus that the Law of War rules, including neutrality, come into effect. The armed conflict in Yemen is clearly a NIAC; the Pakistan statement is clearly a declaration of neutrality; and under the customary doctrine on recognition of belligerency, a statement of neutrality by a third state is clear recognition of the belligerency of the relevant NSAG by that third state. This is not the first occasion on which Saudi Arabia, in support of Yemeni authorities engaged in their NIAC against Houthi NSAGs, has declared a blockade over some Yemeni ports. The fact that the declared blockade of 2009 was at least in part motivated by direct concerns that the NIAC was spilling across the border into southern Saudi Arabia,[287] does not alter the nature of the conflict (a NIAC) nor the possibility that the declaration provides tacit recognition of the Houthis as belligerents, and of Saudi Arabia as a party to the conflict as opposed to a neutral.

Ultimately, the precise legal nature of the Yemen "blockade" will likely remain ambiguous. As the North of England P&I Association factsheet on Yemen reported in April 2015:

> Members and P&I correspondents have reported instances where their entry into Yemen's ports has been blocked by coalition vessels and ships are routinely boarded outside Yemen's territorial waters. On 12 April [2015] Yemen's Ministry of Foreign Affairs formally confirmed that

285. Mohammad Mukashaf, *Pakistan declines Saudi call for armed support in Yemen fight*, Reuters (Apr. 10, 2015), http://www.reuters.com/article/2015/04/10/us-yemen-security-idUSKBN0N10LO20150410.

286. Angana Kotokey, *Pakistan's Neutrality on Yemen Crisis: A Domestic Compulsion*, Centre for Studies in International Relations and Development (Aug. 22, 2015), http://csird.org.in/wp-content/uploads/2017/02/Pakistan.pdf.

287. Salah Nasrawi, *Saudi Arabia imposes naval blockade on coast of northern Yemen*, Wash. Post (Nov. 11, 2009), http://www.washingtonpost.com/wp-dyn/content/article/2009/11/10/AR2009111018351.html; Bethan McKernan, *Saudi Arabia lifts blockade on Yemen air and seaports to allow in vital aid*, The Independent (Nov. 22, 2017), http://www.independent.co.uk/news/world/middle-east/yemen-saudi-arabia-blockade-sanaa-hodeida-airport-seaport-lifted-humanitarian-crisis-a8069916.html.

navigation in Yemen's territorial waters is no longer permitted, unless first inspected and approved by Saudi-led coalition forces.[288]

Such action, straddling as it does the line between an act of municipal policing and passage suspension within territorial waters jurisdiction,[289] and the employment of what effectively amounts to a precondition of visit and search on the high seas (that is, outside the Yemen territorial sea) prior to authorization to enter the Yemen territorial sea, is difficult to legally characterize definitively.

F. CONCLUSION

Although intensely flexible and well suited to its purposes, the doctrine on recognition of belligerency has faced significant challenges over the course of its customary existence. These challenges have included questions as to its universality; its applicability in certain intensely complicated political and military situations; its survival in relation to the post-1949 reconfiguration of the Law of War and the creation of LOAC; and the lack of recent definitive state practice in terms of clear, express, and overt genuflection to and application of the doctrine. Yet indications of its utility and vitality persist, albeit often as a sub-narrative to the more mainstream NIAC-IAC analysis of conflict characterizations and contexts. If the doctrine does indeed persist, customarily independent of the NIAC-IAC plurality that defines modern LOAC, then it remains appropriate to ask how it might assist in overcoming some of the challenges faced by the application of LOAC in NIAC contexts today. It is to this question that I now turn in the final chapter of this book.

288. North of England P&I Association, Loss Prevention: Yemen Information Sheet (Apr. 2015), http://www.nepia.com/media/249646/Yemen-Information-Sheet-April-2015.PDF.

289. A coastal state may temporarily suspend innocent passage within its territorial sea "if such suspension is essential for the protection of its security." United Nations Convention on the Law of the Sea Art. 25(3), Dec. 10, 1982, 1833 U.N.T.S. 397.

6

What if Recognition of Belligerency Remains Legally Available?

Here again the according of belligerent recognition is really a consequence of the inability of the legitimate government to assert authority over certain territories.[1]

—H.A. Smith (1932)

This Protocol . . . shall apply to all armed conflicts which are not covered by Article 1 of the Protocol Additional to the Geneva Conventions of 12 August 1949, and relating to the Protection of Victims of International Armed Conflicts (Protocol I) and which take place in the territory of a High Contracting Party between its armed forces and dissident armed forces or other organized armed groups which, under responsible command, exercise such control over a part of its territory as to enable them to carry out sustained and concerted military operations and to implement this Protocol.[2]

—1977 Additional Protocol II, Article 1(1)

Most armed conflicts that occur globally now and in recent decades, regardless of their legal characterization as international or internal, involve non-state armed groups as parties. Those armed groups frequently exercise effective control over a territory and its inhabitants. Yet, the law governing armed conflict does not properly and adequately address the issue in a concrete and comprehensive manner.[3]

—Tom Gal (2017)

1. Great Britain and the Law of Nations 261 (Herbert A. Smith ed., 1932).

2. Protocol Additional to the Geneva Conventions of 12 August 1949, and Relating to the Protection of Victims of Non-International Armed Conflicts (Protocol II) art. 1(1), June 8, 1977, 1125 U.N.T.S. 609 [hereinafter APII].

3. Tom Gal, *Territorial Control by Armed Groups and the Regulation of Access to Humanitarian Assistance*, 50 Isr. L. Rev., Mar. 2017, at 25.

A. INTRODUCTION

Why revisit the doctrine on recognition of belligerency? What problems might it solve? If recognition of belligerency does indeed remain extant and available for states to employ in defining the legal rules governing their relationship with and/or between the conflict state and NSAG, what might be the consequences? The answer, it is hopefully evident, is that the doctrine on recognition of belligerency offers a specially and specifically designed (albeit relatively forgotten) legal analytical framework through which to approach some of the challenges and nuances that make NIAC LOAC a fundamentally more amorphous and difficult study than IAC LOAC. In this concluding chapter, I will offer some thoughts on the utility of the doctrine—if it persists—for addressing some of these challenges. I shall approach this task under three general thematic headings: status and treatment, means and methods, and interacting with NSAGs as entities.

B. STATUS AND TREATMENT

The "sovereignty concerns"[4] that coalesce around the interrelated concepts of "status," "combatant immunity," and targetability provide an unparalleled set of talismanic issues upon which to base an assessment of the ongoing utility of the doctrine on recognition of belligerency as regards LOAC within a modern NIAC context. To this end I shall briefly engage with two issues of status and treatment: combatant immunity and Prisoner of War (PW) treatment, and the default characterization of NSAG conduct as criminal. In each case I shall first briefly describe the challenge, and then outline how application of the doctrine on recognition of belligerency might serve to overcome that challenge.

(i) Combatant immunity

The primary issue confronting assessments of the legal status of incidents of use of force by state military forces engaged in a NIAC is whether the definition of "combatant" applies in NIAC LOAC. This question heralds a series of significant legal implications, for combatant status carries with it—in general LOAC—not only obligations but also certain rights and protections.[5] The most critical of these—in terms of assigning legal character to each incident of use of force—is combatant immunity from prosecution for acts that result in death, injury,

4. Dapo Akande and Lawrence Hill-Cawthorne, *The Lieber Code and the Regulation of Civil War in International Law*, 53 COLUM. J. TRANSNAT'L L. 638, 645 (2015).

5. *See, e.g.*, Jens Ohlin, *The Combatant's Privilege in Asymmetric and Covert Conflicts*, 40 YALE J. INT'L L. 337 (2015).

destruction, or damage, which would otherwise be transgressions of the applicable criminal law. This question can be complicated by the variety of contextual permutations available: state forces fighting a NIAC against rebels within the territory of the state, with no interventions by third parties on either side (Sri Lanka and the LTTE, after the withdrawal of Indian peacekeeping forces); state forces of a third party supporting the state forces of the state within whose territory the NIAC is being fought, in their operations against the rebels (e.g., International Security Assistance Force (ISAF) in Afghanistan); state forces of a third party supporting the rebels against the state forces of the state within whose territory the NIAC is being fought (e.g., Rwandan Defence Force support to M23 rebels in the Democratic Republic of Congo[6]); and state forces of a third party who intervene in a NIAC but are formally aligned with neither the state forces nor the rebel forces (e.g., formally, North Atlantic Treaty Organization (NATO) operations in Libya in 2011). Yet while this variety of contextual nuances should not be discounted, they do not fundamentally alter the core legal attribute of any state force engaged in any of these contexts—their sovereign character.[7]

This is the key theoretical device that stands behind the distinction between a pirate and a privateer, and between a criminal and a battlefield captive entitled to PW status or treatment. Consequently, when thinking about the status of use of force by state military forces engaged in a NIAC, contextual nuance (while important in many other respects) is arguably not a differentiating attribute that governs the applicable law.[8] The primary attribute is sovereign status or association. There is one exception to this rule—the *levee en masse*—but it is an IAC focused and heavily caveated option only available in the immediate stages of response to an invasion.[9]

The central question in terms of legally characterizing culpability for use of force in NIAC LOAC governed situations is, consequently, whether "combatant immunity" operates in a NIAC context. The key feature of combatant immunity

6. David Smith, *Rwandan soldiers joined forces with Congo rebels, UN told*, GUARDIAN (Dec. 4, 2012), http://www.guardian.co.uk/world/2012/dec/04/rwandans-congo-rebels-un.

7. This is the essence of the U.S. Supreme Court's decision in The Schooner Exchange v McFaddon, 11 U.S. 116, 144 (1812) (citing the language: "She [a public armed ship] constitutes a part of the military force of her nation; acts under the immediate and direct command of the sovereign; is employed by him in national objects. He has many and powerful motives for preventing those objects from being defeated by the interference of a foreign State. Such interference cannot take place without affecting his power and his dignity."); This notion is also the underpinning precept in the *Corfu Channel Case*. Corfu Channel (U.K., N. Ir. v. Alb.), Judgment, 1949 I.C.J. 4, 30 (Apr. 9).

8. Setting aside the live question as to whether interventions in circumstances akin to the NATO operation in Libya are actually situations of a concurrent NIAC (Libyan state forces against rebels) and IAC (NATO state forces against, inter alia, Libyan state forces).

9. Geneva Convention for the Amelioration of the Condition of the Wounded and Sick in Armed Forces in the Field, art. 13(6), Aug. 12, 1949, 75 U.N.T.S. 31 [hereinafter Convention I].

in IAC LOAC is that a member of a state military force who uses force that kills, injures, destroys, or damages will be immune from prosecution/criminal sanction under any applicable national legal regime. This includes immunities in relation to own state law, host state law, adversary "law" if such exists (the LTTE, for example, claimed a relatively stable legal system and scheme of laws for around three decades), third state law, or international legal regimes (e.g., the *Rome Statute of the International Criminal Court (ICC)*), so long as the conduct and the consequence was permissible under LOAC.[10] This is clearly reflected in the rule that a legitimate (or privileged) combatant who falls into the hands of his or her opponent must not be prosecuted for conduct that was within the bounds of LOAC.[11]

Ken Watkin argues that "it is logical to conclude that the concept of combatant immunity would apply to the armed forces of the state tasked with using force in a non-international armed conflict."[12] As Ian Henderson notes, given the silence of the treaties on this point, the argument for a corresponding combatant immunity for state military forces in NIAC contexts is primarily one of logic rather than textual analysis.[13] But the strength of this conclusion is well-buttressed by state practice, which is clearly that state military forces engaged in a NIAC are legally characterized as, and hold the status of, "combatants" along the same lines as in IAC. In some cases this recognition may be readily implied or inferred from its negative—in Australia's war crimes legislation (Division 268 of the *Commonwealth Criminal Code*), there is, for example, an offense of murder in a NIAC that is structured to exclude culpability where the killed person was DPH, a member of an organized armed group, or the death was a consequence of a legally permissible incidental injury.[14] The effect is to recognize a facsimile of, if not the actual grant of, combatant immunity.

10. *See* Geneva Convention Relative to the Protection of Civilian Persons in Time of War, art. 1, Aug. 12, 1949, 75 U.N.T.S. 287 [hereinafter Convention IV]; *see also* Hague Convention Respecting the Laws and Customs of War on Land and Its Annex: Regulations Concerning the Laws and Customs of War on Land, art. 1, Oct. 18, 1907 [hereinafter Hague Convention IV]; *see also* Protocol Additional to the Geneva Conventions of 12 August 1949, and Relating to the Protection of Victims of International Armed Conflicts, art. 43(2), Jun. 8, 1977, 1125 U.N.T.S. 3 [hereinafter API].

11. Of note, this is where the status of members of a *levee en masse* as legitimate combatants under LOAC is probably most complicated—determining whether an otherwise lawful act under LOAC, when perpetrated by a member of a *levee en masse* (e.g., killing an enemy combatant), retains its immunity from criminal sanction.

12. Kenneth Watkin, *Warriors Without Rights? Combatants, Unprivileged Belligerents, and the Struggle over Legitimacy*, Program on Humanitarian Pol'y & Conflict Res., Winter 2005, no. 2; *see also* Kenneth Watkin, Fighting at the Legal Boundaries: Controlling Use of Force in Contemporary Conflict 43–46, 92–97 (2016).

13. Ian Henderson, *Civilian Intelligence Agencies and the Use of Armed Drones*, 13 Y.B. Int'l Humanitarian L. 133, 150–52 (2010).

14. *See Criminal Code Act 1995* (Cth), s F (Austl), *available at* https://www.legislation.gov.au/Details/C2005C00524 (stating that "[w]ar crimes that are serious violations of article 3 common

This outcome is entirely coherent with placing the sovereign nature, disciplining, and legal character of state military and associated forces at the very center of the issue of combatant status. LOAC is most particular as to who may access this status, going so far as to the establish both the conditions under which, and the formal process by which, state nonmilitary forces (such as formed police units) are to be assimilated to state military forces in order to gain combatant status.[15] This means that status and task are in constant and conscious focus as the implications of nuance are particularly acute in the use of force sphere—a lawful killing under LOAC will not necessarily meet the paradigmatically distinct preconditions for a lawfully excused killing under general criminal law.

For state military forces, the domestic "rebel" adversary retains his/her character as a criminal, regardless of the fact that (provided the context is a NIAC) they may be pursued using lethal LOAC-based authorizations as equally as with routine law enforcement powers.[16] The reach of combatant immunity—in terms

to the Geneva Conventions and are committed in the course of an armed conflict that is not an international armed conflict"). Section 268.70 states:

> War crime-murder
> (1) A person (the perpetrator) commits an offence if:
> (a) the perpetrator causes the death of one or more persons; and
> (b) the person or persons are neither taking an active part in the hostilities nor are members of an organised armed group; and
> (c) the perpetrator knows of, or is reckless as to, the factual circumstances establishing that the person or persons are neither taking an active part in the hostilities nor are members of an organised armed group; and
> (d) the perpetrator's conduct takes place in the context of, and is associated with, an armed conflict that is not an international armed conflict.
> Penalty: Imprisonment for life.
> (1A) Subsection (1) does not apply if:
> (a) the death of the person or persons occurs in the course of, or as a result of, an attack on a military objective; and
> (b) at the time the attack was launched:
> (i) the perpetrator did not expect that the attack would result in the incidental death of, or injury to, civilians that would have been excessive in relation to the concrete and direct military advantage anticipated; and
> (ii) it was reasonable in all the circumstances that the perpetrator did not have such an expectation . . .

Id.

15. *See, e.g.*, Convention I, art. 13(2) and (4); *see also* API, art. 43(3).

16. *See, e.g.*, the Goodman—Schmitt debate: Ryan Goodman, *The Power to Kill or Capture Enemy Combatants*, 24(3) Eur. J. Int'l L. 819 (2013); Michael Schmitt, *Wound, Capture, or Kill: A Reply to Ryan Goodman's "The Power to Kill or Capture Enemy Combatants,"* 24(3) Eur. J. Int'l L. 855 (2013). *See also* Nils Melzer, Interpretive Guidance on the Notion of Direct Participation in Hostilities under International Humanitarian Law 82 (2009); Rob McLaughlin, *Legal-Policy Considerations and Conflict Characterisation at the Threshold Between Law Enforcement and Non-International Armed Conflict*, 13(1) Melb. J. Int'l. L. 94 (2012); On the example of targetable status of drug "barons" in Afghanistan, *see*, inter alia, Dan

of actor, object, and context—thus goes beyond simply assigning the appropriate legal status to an incident of use of force which takes place in a broadly NIAC context; it is also simultaneously determinative of a range of associated issues. One such issue, for example, is whether the use of force is a defense against "attack" under LOAC,[17] or an exercise of the right of self-defense in line with the applicable municipal criminal law concept of individual self-defense or the defense of others.[18]

One recent example indicative of state practice was the prosecution of several Australian Defence Force members in relation to a civilian casualty incident in Afghanistan in February 2009.[19] The incident took place within an expressly NIAC context, and the Chief Judge Advocate's ultimate dismissal of the charges was based fundamentally in a finding that a World War II precedent on immunity of military members from suit for an alleged breach of a duty of care to civilians, when inflicted in the course of operations against the enemy, applied in this context (a NIAC) and was dispositive of the law.[20] Another example is the Columbian record in prosecuting military members for use of force in the context of the NIAC against FARC, involving targeting Rules of Engagement for which the reference point is clearly Additional Protocol I (AP

Karpenchuk, *NATO troops to go after Afghan drug lords*, ABC (Feb. 7, 2009), http://www.abc.net.au/news/stories/2009/02/07/2484955.htm?site=news.

17. API, art. 49(1) (explaining that "attacks" means acts of violence against the adversary, whether in offense or in defense).

18. *See generally* Ian Henderson and Bryan Cavanagh, *Military Members Claiming Self-Defence during Armed Conflict: Often Misguided and Unhelpful*, *in* ACCOUNTABILITY FOR VIOLATIONS IN INTERNATIONAL HUMANITARIAN LAW: ESSAYS IN HONOUR OF TIM MCCORMACK 73–94 (Jadranka Petrovic ed., 2016).

19. *Re Civilian Casualty Court Martial* (2011) 259 FLR 208 (Austl.); *see* Joshua Kelly, *Re Civilian Casualty Court Martial: Prosecuting Breaches of International Humanitarian Law Using the Australian Military Justice System*, 37(2) MELB. U. L. REV. 342 (2013) (providing commentary and analysis); *see also* Emily Crawford, *International Humanitarian Law in the Courts of Australia*, *in* APPLYING INTERNATIONAL HUMANITARIAN LAW IN JUDICIAL AND QUASI-JUDICIAL BODIES: INTERNATIONAL AND DOMESTIC ASPECTS 335 (Derek Jinks, Jackson Maogoto, and Solon Solomon eds., 2014).

20. *See Re Civilian Casualty Court Martial* (2011) 259 FLR 208. at 226 stating

> In summary, having regard to the restrictions on the soldier, sailor or airman's ability to choose to refrain from inherently dangerous conduct, his or her positive obligation to conduct operations against the enemy and the life and death ramifications of hesitation, I can see no basis on which to distinguish the approach taken by the High Court in *Shaw Savill*. For the same reasons that it is opposed alike to reason and policy to concede a tortious liability, it is in my view contrary to reason and policy to impose a criminal duty. If it were to be imposed clear words would be needed by the parliament.

Id. (referencing *Shaw Savill & Albion Company Ltd v. The Commonwealth* (1940) 66 CLR 344 (Austl.)).

I).[21] A further example is the German Prosecutor's assessment of the conduct of German military personnel in the Kunduz tanker incident.[22] Another is the initial conviction of Royal Marine SGT Blackman, where it was clearly, albeit tacitly, accepted that killing NSAG fighters in accordance with IAC LOAC targeting rules, in the context of the Afghanistan NIAC, was not an illegal act[23]—although, of course, killing a person *hors de combat* obviously was, as it also is within IAC LOAC.

In each of these situations, the assumption that the IAC targeting rules in AP I (or parallel custom) also apply in NIAC carries with it an implicit but clearly operative assumption that conduct in accordance with those rules is by definition lawful and free from the application of criminal sanction. Thus, the concept of combatant immunity does have legal resonance in NIAC contexts, even if a modicum of uncertainty as to the precise operation of the concept remains. One such uncertainty, for example, is whether the immunity is based in international law, or rather in a shared tendency to domestic prosecutorial discretion against prosecution. My own view is that state practice indicates that combatant immunity for state military forces engaged in NIACs exists as a matter of customary international law, and is based in an implicit determination that this aspect of LOAC crosses the IAC-NIAC divide. If the rebels were recognized belligerents, however, their could be no debate as to the de jure availability of combatant immunity.

(ii) PW treatment

One intensely significant possible consequence of revisiting the doctrine on recognition of belligerency is that such recognition offers a clear legal pathway to overcoming, when the doctrine applies, the current imbroglio regarding the

21. *See, e.g.*, Juan Carlos Gomez, *Twenty-First Century Challenges: The Use of Military Forces to Combat Criminal Threats*, 88 Int'l L. Stud. 279, 284–86, fn 17 (2011).

22. *See* Wolff Heintschel von Heinegg and Peter Dreist, *The 2009 Kunduz Air Attack: The Decision of the Federal Prosecutor-General on the Dismissal of Criminal Proceedings Against Members of the German Armed Forces,* 53 Ger. Y.B. of Int'l L. 833 (2010); *See also* Timo Noetzel, *The German Politics of War: Kunduz and the War in Afghanistan*, 87(2) Int'l Aff. 397 (2011); *See also* Constantin Schüßler and Yee-Kuang Heng, *The Bundeswehr and the Kunduz Air Strike 4 September 2009: Germany's Post-Heroic Moment?*, 22(3) Eur. Security 355 (2013); *See also* Elisabeth Henn, *The Development of German Jurisprudence on Individual Compensation for Victims of Armed Conflicts: The Kunduz Case*, 12(3) J. Int'l Crim. Just. 615 (2014).

23. Steven Morris, *Judges quash UK marine Alexander Blackman's murder conviction—Briton who killed injured Taliban fighter found guilty of manslaughter on grounds of diminished responsibility instead*, Guardian (Mar. 15, 2017), https://www.theguardian.com/uk-news/2017/mar/15/alexander-blackman-royal-marine-a-judges-quash-murder-conviction; *See* R v. Alexander Wayne Blackman [2017] EWCA (Crim) 190 [paras. 17–19, 23] (Eng.) (*citing* findings in original Court Martial that "[The insurgent] had been seriously wounded having been engaged lawfully by an Apache helicopter and when [the appellant] found him he was no longer a threat.").

existence or otherwise of a power to detain in NIAC LOAC.[24] This question, currently crystallized around the judgments in the UK case of *Serdar Mohammed v Ministry of Defence*,[25] is one of significant legal nuance and serious operational consequence. However, by making the IAC LOAC regime on detention the applicable law, recognition of belligerency mandates de jure recourse to a clearly articulated, and almost universally accepted[26] detention regime. That is, current uncertainty as to the international law power of detention in a NIAC could be neatly and legitimately sidestepped through the application, as a matter of law, of well-established and accepted IAC LOAC on detention, by virtue of the fact that the NSAG had been afforded belligerent status.

This consequence would obviate the *Serdar Mohammed* conundrum of having to identify and justify another appropriate international law power to balance against national law bases for detention of NSAG members.[27] Lawrence neatly summarized the customary legal consequence for the NSAG in particular: "Its armies are lawful belligerents, not banditti; its ships of war are lawful cruisers, not pirates; the supplies it takes from invaded territory are requisitions, not robbery; and at sea its captures made in accordance with maritime law are good prize, and its blockades must be respected by neutrals."[28] Upon recognition of belligerency it is abundantly clear that NSAG members must be treated as PW in accordance

24. Kenneth Watkin, *Opportunity Lost: Organized Armed Groups and the ICRC Direct Participation in Hostilities Interpretive Guidance*, 42(3) N.Y. U. J. Int'l L. & Pol. 641, 652 (2009) (observing characterization of irregulars in the Law of Armed Conflict applicable to International Armed Conflict is much clearer and subject to less debate).

25. *See* Serdar Mohammed v MOD [2014] EWHC (QB) 1369 (Eng.); *See also* Serdar Mohammed v MOD [2015] EWCA (Civ) 843 (Eng.); *See also* Serdar Mohammed v. MOD [2017] UKSC 1 (Eng.); *See also* Serdar Mohammed v MOD [2017] UKSC 2 (Eng.); *See, e.g.*, Rogier Bartles, *IHL Does Not Authorise Detention in NIAC: A Reply to Sean Aughey and Aurel Sari*, EJIL Talk!, Feb. 16, 2015, http://www.ejiltalk.org/ihl-does-not-authorise-detention-in-niac-a-reply-to-sean-aughey-and-aurel-sari/ (an example of the debate surrounding detention in NIAC); *See also* Ryan Goodman, *Authorization versus Regulation of Detention in Non-International Armed Conflicts*, 91 Int'l L. Stud. 155 (2015); *See also* Gabor Rona, *Is There a Way Out of the Non-International Armed Conflict Dilemma?*, 91 Int'l L. Stud. 32 (2015); Sean Aughey and Aurel Sari, *Targeting and Detention in Non-International Armed Conflict: Serdar Mohammed and the Limits of Human Rights Convergence*, 91 Int'l L. Stud. 60 (2015).

26. *See, e.g.*, Hassan v. United Kingdom, 2014-VI Eur. Ct. H.R.; *See* Diane Webber, *Hassan v. United Kingdom: A New Approach to Security Detention in Armed Conflict?*, ASIL Insights (Apr. 2, 2015), http://www.asil.org/insights/volume/19/issue/7/hassan-v-united-kingdom-new-approach-security-detention-armed-conflict#_edn1.

27. *See, e.g.*, Daniel Abebe and Eric Posner, *The Flaws of Foreign Affairs Legalism*, 51 Va. J. Int'l L. 507, 509–511 (2011) (providing an example of how the phenomenon of eroding "executive primacy" carries with it a stronger susceptibility for the consequences of such a recognition decision (but probably not the decision itself) to be subject to judicial review. This could to some extent resurrect the potential for confusion between, or stove-piping of (for example) commercial, contract, and insurance law, with the public law consequences of recognition of belligerency).

28. T. J. Lawrence, The Principles of International Law 78 (2nd ed., 1900).

with the Law of War/IAC LOAC, and that the NSAG must do likewise to those conflict state combatants whom they capture.[29] This would seem to offer a solution (provided revenge or retribution are not the underpinning rationale) to avoid the GTMO consequence: rather than create a bespoke and contested regime to allow prosecution and criminal detention for battlefield conduct,[30] employ instead the full suite of the PW regime and hold captured NSAG belligerents until the close of hostilities. This application of the regime would not shut any doors to prosecution of captured NSAG members for non-LOAC-compliant conduct, thus ensuring prosecution of terrorism could continue unhindered.

Despite this simplicity in application however, the potential "loss" for states that attends any revitalized recognition of belligerency is the very correlate of the benefit for the NSAG—that is, the ability to prosecute belligerent status NSAG members for all battlefield conduct regardless of whether it was compliant with LOAC or not. The clear grant of a form of NSAG combatant immunity—not least through PW status—was a fundamental element of any grant of belligerent status to an NSAG, and this would certainly allow states to detain NSAG members in line with the PW scheme. As noted, by making the IAC LOAC regime on detention the applicable law, recognition of belligerency accesses, de jure, a clearly articulated and almost universally accepted detention regime.

But perhaps this is not necessarily a "loss" per se. The more limited, well-defined, and less controversial option of detention until end of hostilities for LOAC-complying NSAG members,[31] coupled with a continuing power to prosecute those NSAG members who have not complied with LOAC, is something worthy of deeper consideration. Such an approach would preserve the right and opportunity to assert criminal jurisdiction over NSAG members who ought to be held to account for rule-breaking battlefield conduct. As the next section notes, this approach might also reduce the sometimes radicalizing and exacerbating effect of attaching a generic "criminality" or "terrorist" status to all NSAGs and

29. Charles Zorgbibe, *Sources of the Recognition of Belligerent Status*, 17(192) Int'l Rev. Red Cross 111, 116 (1977); *See also* Daoud L. Khairallah, Insurrection under International Law with Emphasis on the Rights and Duties of Insurgents 196, 197–210 (1973) (stating "When rebel forces are recognized as belligerent by the lawful government, they gain, until the end of the hostilities, the status of prisoners of war in international conflicts with all its privileges. They are also under an obligation to give the same treatment to captured government forces.") Further exploring treatment of captured NSAG fighters in Algeria, Congo, Yemen, and Vietnam *see also* G.I.A.D. Draper, *Humanitarian Law and Internal Armed Conflicts*, 13 Ga. J. Int'l & Comp. L. 253, 258 (1983).

30. *See, e.g.*, Curtis Bradley, *The Military Commissions Act, Habeas Corpus, and the Geneva Conventions*, 101 Am. J. Int'l L. 322, 344 (2007) (stating "In the MCA, Congress sought to limit judicial review over the detention and trial of what it defined as enemy combatants, and to preclude courts from applying the Geneva Conventions as a source of rights").

31. Geneva Convention Relative to the Treatment of Prisoners of War art. 118, Aug. 12, 1949, 6 U.S.T. 3316, 75 U.N.T.S. 135 [hereinafter Convention III].

NSAG members, regardless of their otherwise LOAC-compliant acts (insofar as such NSAGs exist).[32]

(iii) Criminality

It is quite clear that criminality is the default status for NSAG member conduct in a NIAC context.[33] "If guerrillas are not lawful belligerents," wrote Lester Nurick and Roger Barrett in 1946, "their normal military acts, such as killing or wounding enemies, possession of arms and other forbidden material, and destruction of enemy property, would be treated as criminal offenses."[34] This is not because, as Oppenheim made clear, the acts themselves "really are violations of recognized rules regarding warfare"—for, indeed, the same act done by a state military force member may well be entirely lawful—"but because the enemy has the right to consider and punish them as acts of illegitimate warfare."[35]

Apart from an ad hoc decision made by the state or the NSAG (if it is the eventual victor) to decline to prosecute, or to retrospectively validate such conduct, there are only two narrow exceptions to this general sheen of criminality. The first is the situation previously noted in relation to AP I Article 1(4) whereby civil wars or rebellions characterized by "peoples . . . fighting against colonial domination and alien occupation and against racist regimes in the exercise of their right of self-determination" are to be considered as IACs, and thus governed by, essentially, the full range of IAC LOAC. The consequence for the NSAG is not only that they must comply with IAC LOAC, but also that they can expect and demand that the adversary state conducts itself in the conflict in accordance with IAC LOAC. These demands may include treating captured NSAG combatants as PW with the consequence that they are not to be prosecuted for acts that are LOAC compliant, regardless of the fact that these acts are simultaneously characterizable as breaches of the conflict state's criminal laws. The second possible exception—superficially similar although, as noted in Chapter 5, fundamentally different—is of course the doctrine on recognition of belligerency.

The intersection, and more importantly the parsing of distinctions, between gangs and armed groups, and between violence for private gain and violence for

32. *See, e.g.*, Madeline Morris, *Terrorism: The Politics of Prosecution*, 5(2) Chi. J. Int'l L. 406 (2005); *See also* Boaz Ganor, *Identifying the Enemy in Counterterrorism Operations—A Comparison of the Bush and Obama Administrations*, 90 Int'l L. Stud. 341 (2014).

33. Commentary, I Geneva Convention for the Amelioration of the Condition of the Wounded and Sick in Armed Forces in the Field 39, 43–44, 60 (Jean S. Pictet ed.,1952); *see also* Michael N. Schmitt, *The Status of Opposition Fighters in a Non-International Armed Conflict*, 88 Int'l L. Stud. 119 (2011).

34. Lester Nurick and Roger Barrett, *Legality of Guerrilla Forces under the Laws of War*, 40(3) Am. J. Int'l L. 563 (1946).

35. Lassa Oppenheim, International Law: A Treatise: Disputes, War and Neutrality §254 (1906).

ideological or political purposes, has long posed problems for LOAC.[36] Indeed, as has been discussed through this book, the intersection of political motivation with the pursuit of power through violence is well recognized in the classic pirate/insurgent dichotomy within the three-level scheme. The current legal status of NSAG fighters however equates them, fundamentally, with criminals and their conduct with criminality (that is, never more than "rebels" under the customary three-level scheme). But this one size fits all classification is ahistorical, superficial, simplistic, and problematic. It also refuses to recognize the lost role (except in relation to mercenaries) that motive once played in assessing status in the Law of War. Soviet lawyer and academic IP Trainin, writing in 1946, argued that a "truly people's war"—that is "one for the basic interests of the people, for its rights, honour, freedom, and independence"—is a "justifiable war."[37] Consequently, it was not—to Trainin—the fact of guerrilla tactics that was the key to rebel criminality and status, but rather the motive of the guerrillas that was critical to their status as either privileged or unprivileged belligerents.[38]

Richard Baxter similarly argued in 1951 that

> As long as partisan warfare is inspired by genuine allegiance rather than a desire for pillage and as long as guerrilla activities are looked upon as licit and laudable by the state on whose behalf they are undertaken and by third parties to the conflict, it is highly unreal to regard them as internationally criminal.[39]

This recognition of the importance of motive or cause in assessing the status and treatment entitlements of rebel NSAGs was also a fundamental and constitutive element of the approach adopted by Imperial Russian Admiralty courts in differentiating privateers from pirates in the eighteenth and nineteenth centuries. Because "the Russian government at the end of the eighteenth century was more concerned with how to differentiate privateers from other naval irregulars and the state navy," writes Julia Leikin,[40] the key distinguishing characteristic thus became "whether privateer activities demonstrated commitment to state service":[41]

36. *See* Pierre Hauck and Sven Peterke, *Organised Crime and Gang Violence in National and International Law*, 92 Int'l Rev. Red Cross 407 (2010) (describing the difficult issue of distinguishing between delinquency, more serious collective and organized criminality, and "insurgency" in conflict contexts); *See also* Jennifer Hazen, *Understanding Gangs as Armed Groups*, 92 Int'l Rev. Red Cross 369 (2010).

37. I.P. Trainin, *Questions of Guerrilla Warfare in the Law of War*, 40 Am. J. Int'l L. 534, 554 (1946).

38. *Id.* at 561–62.

39. Richard R. Baxter, *So-Called "Unprivileged Belligerency": Spies, Guerrillas, and Saboteurs*, 28 Brit. Y.B. Int'l L. 323, 337 (1951).

40. Julia Leikin, *The Prostitution of the Russian Flag: Privateers in Russian Admiralty Courts, 1787–98*, 35(4) L. & Hist. Rev. 1049, 1052 (2017).

41. *Id.* at 1073.

> The commission's reasoning [being the Commission for Archipelago Affairs, the relevant Admiralty court] articulated a conceptual understanding of how privateers differed from naval officers . . . [recognizing] that privateers' activities might coincide with state interests, but that their adherence to and execution of the values that stood behind state interest—the common good—mattered as well.[42]

A reconceptualization of the role of motive in the assessment and assigning of status within LOAC is an important piece of work to be done; but it is beyond the scope of this book. What this very brief digression recalls, however, is that there is a history behind another possible benefit accruing from recourse to the doctrine on recognition of belligerency. That benefit is that states can, and have in the past, found legally nuanced ways to overcome the sometimes politically and legally difficult requirements attaching to characterizing NSAG activities as terrorism in a criminal law sense. States often seek to attach this aggravating/stigmatizing element to NSAG conduct in order to illustrate why that conduct is different from "routine" criminal conduct.[43] Equally, however, states once recognized distinctions between the legal character of and opprobrium attached to the acts of (variously) belligerents, insurgents, rebels, and mere criminal conduct. Is moderation of the "one size fits all" allocation of criminality we currently employ for NSAG therefore actually such a long bow to draw? As Frederic Megret observes,

> At a deeper level, international law has an interest in distinguishing between genuine belligerents and terrorist movements in a context where it is not immediately clear which category an armed group falls in. A conditional [privilege of belligerency, or for these purposes, PW status] would therefore mark the official entry of some violent actors into the fold of international law, and would help keep out those who have no intention of conforming to it.[44]

If the law offers a clear pathway by which NSAG members can be detained under the same regime as PW, with no diminution of the ability to prosecute a recognized belligerent NSAG member for a war crime, a state could still achieve, where necessary, the desired level of aggravating/stigmatizing effect in criminal law (that is, a war crime) without necessarily having to employ the more

42. *Id.* at 1074.

43. *See, e.g.*, Madeline Morris, *Terrorism: The Politics of Prosecution*, 5 Chi. J. Int'l L. 405 (2005); *See generally* Boaz Ganor, *Identifying the Enemy in Counterterrorism Operations—A Comparison of the Bush and Obama Administrations*, 90 Int'l L. Stud. 341 (2014); *See generally* Marco Sassoli, *Query: Is There a Status of "Unlawful Combatant?*, 80 Int'l L. Stud. 57, 60–64 (2006); *See generally* James Renwick and Gregory F. Treverton, *The Challenges of trying Terrorists as Criminals: Proceedings of a RAND/SAIS Colloquium*, RAND Corp., 2008, at 13–17.

44. Claus Kreβ and Frédéric Mégret, *The Regulation of Non-International Armed Conflicts: Can a Privilege of Belligerency Be Envisioned in the Law of Non-International Armed Conflicts?*, 96 Int'l Rev. Red Cross 29, 36 (2015)

contested terrorism label.[45] Simultaneously, however, states would not be required to justify—on criminal law or security-related grounds—the ongoing detention of captured but LOAC-complying NSAG members beyond the initial and periodic review required under the existing IAC LOAC PW and detention regime.

C. MEANS AND METHODS

(i) Targeting

Targeting law, for most states, is codified for IAC primarily in AP I, but otherwise resides in customary international law. It is also clearly arguable that recent state practice tends toward applying the fundamentals of IAC targeting law to NIAC targeting operations. Indeed, targeting operations conducted in NIAC contexts are now very widely considered to be governed by the same rules as for IAC. In Afghanistan—clearly a NIAC for many of the ISAF contributing states—there can be no doubt that the detailed targeting requirements of AP I (relevant to IAC), or their customary equivalent, were applied as the default legal regime governing use of force in targeting operations. The United Nations Assistance Mission in Afghanistan and Afghanistan Independent Human Rights Commission *Annual Report 2010: Protection of Civilians in Armed Conflict*, dated March 2011, is one example of an explicit genuflection within a NIAC context to AP I Articles 48, 51, 52, and 57:

> "Customary rules of international humanitarian law also apply to the warring parties in Afghanistan. International judicial bodies have stated that several rules in the Geneva Conventions and the Additional Protocols are part of customary international law."[46]

For example, in the course of detailed analysis on the law applicable to aerial attacks in the context of the NIAC in Afghanistan, the Report further asserted that:

> In the conduct of military operations, constant care must be taken to spare the civilian population and civilian objects. Armed forces must take all feasible precautions to avoid, and in any event to minimize, incidental loss of civilian life, injury to civilians and damage to civilian objects. They must also take all feasible precautions in the choice of means and methods of warfare with a view

45. *See, e.g.*, Alan Greene, *Defining Terrorism: One Size Fits All?*, 66 Int'l & Comp. L. Q. 411, 412 (2017) (discussing the tensions and incompatibilities between "descriptive definitions of the social sciences and the prescriptive exercise that the law undertakes").

46. See United Nations Assistance Mission in Afghanistan/Afghanistan Independent Human Rights Commission, *Afghanistan Annual Report 2010: Protection of Civilians in Armed Conflict* (Mar. 2011). This analysis is maintained in the UNAMA/OHCHR *Afghanistan Mid-Year Report on Protection of Civilians in Armed Conflict: 2012*, pages ii–iii, *available at* http://www.ohchr.org/Documents/Countries/AF/UNAMAMidYearReport2012.pdf.

> to avoiding, and in any event to minimizing, incidental loss of civilian life, injury to civilians and damage to civilian objects. Under international humanitarian law, parties must do everything feasible to assess whether any attack may be expected to cause incidental loss of civilian life, injury to civilians, damage to civilian objects, or a combination thereof, which would be excessive in relation to the concrete and direct military advantage anticipated. Finally, the warring parties must give effective advance warning of attacks which may affect the civilian population.[47]

It could not be more clear that the point of reference for the applicable targeting law in this NIAC is indeed the IAC focused AP I.

Another indicator of this fusion is the previously noted German Prosecutor's Report into the 4 September 2009 Kunduz tanker incident in Afghanistan, where an airstrike approved by a German commander resulted in (although estimates vary quite widely) up to 142 deaths, with a similarly wide range of estimates of between 60 and 90 of the killed being civilians as opposed to civilian's directly participating in hostilities or members of a NSAG.[48] The Federal Prosecutor ultimately terminated proceedings against Colonel Klein and First Sergeant Wilhelm on the basis that their conduct was in accordance with LOAC.[49] However, as a preliminary to this conclusion, the Prosecutor was first required to characterize the conflict, ultimately determining that German forces in Afghanistan were in fact party to a NIAC. Following this, the Prosecutor then employed AP I-based LOAC rules, whether directly or as indicative of the custom applicable in NIACs, to describe and assess the targeting operation.[50]

47. *Id.* at 22–23.

48. *See* Timo Noetzel, *The German Politics of War: Kunduz and the War in Afghanistan*, 87(2) INT'L AFF. 397 (providing a general summary and analysis of the incident); Thomas Ruttig, *The Incident at Coordinate 42S VF 8934 5219: German Court Rejects Claim from Kunduz Air Strike Victims*, AFG. ANALYSTS NETWORK (Dec. 15, 2013), http://www.afghanistan-analysts.org/the-incident-at-coordinate-42s-vf-8934-5219-german-court-rejects-claim-from-kunduz-air-strike-victims.

49. *See* Constantin von der Groeben, *German Federal Prosecutor Terminates Investigation Against German Soldiers with Respect to NATO Air Strike in Afghanistan*, EJIL TALK!, Apr. 29, 2010, at http://www.ejiltalk.org/german-federal-prosecutor-terminates-investigation-against-german-soldiers-with-respect-to-nato-air-strike-in-afghanistan/.

50. *See generally* Wolff Heintschel von Heinegg and Peter Dreist, *The 2009 Kunduz Air Attack: The Decision of the German Federal Prosecutor-General on the Dismissal of Criminal Proceedings Against Members of the German Armed Forces*, 53 GER. Y.B. INT'L L. 833; Constantin von der Groeben, *Criminal Responsibility of German Soldiers in Afghanistan: The Case of Colonel Klein*, 11 GER. L.J. 469 (2010). Several relatives of people killed in this strike subsequently commenced litigation in Germany to seek damages, but the case was halted when a German court determined that Germany was not liable for such damages. *See Kunduz Bombing: German Court Drops Case Over Civilian Deaths*, SPIEGEL.DE (Dec. 11, 2013), http://www.spiegel.de/international/germany/court-says-germany-not-responsible-for-damages-in-afghanistan-attack-a-938490.html.

A third significant example is the United States Army Judge Advocate General Corps' 2012 *Operational Law Handbook*, which describes the concepts of distinction and proportionality utilizing essentially AP I formulations. The handbook opines that these AP I formulations offer examples of customary LOAC provisions applicable across NIAC and IAC.[51] A combined reading of chapters five (LOAC) and eight (targeting) of the U.S. Navy, U.S. Marine Corps, and U.S. Coast Guard *Commander's Handbook on the Law of Naval Operations* similarly makes it clear that the United States' practice is to apply the same law of targeting in both IAC and NIAC contexts.[52] Any reading of successive Commander ISAF Tactical Memoranda on reducing collateral damage in Afghanistan (which for most of the states contributing forces to ISAF, is a NIAC) also indicates that the reference point is the law of targeting as reflected in AP I and parallel custom.[53]

The validity of such examples is complicated, however, by an underpinning debate as to the status of doctrinal statements as an indicator of customary international law. As the Bellinger and Haynes response to the ICRC *Customary IHL* study importantly points out, such statements in military manuals do not necessarily reflect state practice. The question, therefore, is whether the application of IAC LOAC targeting rules in NIAC contexts is carried out as a matter of policy, or as an incident of law. The United States position is that it applies the same LOAC provisions in both forms of conflict as a matter of policy.[54] The U.S. Department of Defense Directive series 2311.01E (promulgated December 1998, updated May 2006, and reconfirmed February 2011), para. 4.1 requires that "Members of the DoD Components comply with the law of war during all armed conflicts, however such conflicts are characterized, and in all other military operations."[55] This view continues to form part of the U.S. legal analysis of use of force against terrorist targets outside of U.S. territory.[56]

51. *See, e.g.*, INT'L & OPERATIONAL LAW DEP'T, THE JUDGE ADVOCATE GENERAL'S LEGAL CENTER AND SCHOOL, U.S. ARMY, JA 422, OPERATIONAL LAW HANDBOOK 9–14 (2018).

52. U.S. DEP'T OF NAVY, MARINE CORPS, & COAST GOARD, US NAVY, MARINE CORPS, AND COAST GUARD, THE COMMANDER'S HANDBOOK ON THE LAW OF NAVAL OPERATIONS, NWP 1-14M (Aug. 2017) [hereinafter NWP 1-14M].

53. *See* Memorandum, Commander, International Security Assistance Force, subject: Tactical Directive (6 Jul. 2009); *See also* Memorandum, Commander, International Security Assistance Force, subject: Tactical Directive (30 Nov. 2011) (stating "I also insist that all planning and execution of operations account for our obligations to employ force consistent with the principles of military necessity, proportionality, distinction and humanity in accordance with LOAC.").

54. Indeed, the United States applies LOAC provisions outside of armed conflict as well.

55. U.S. DEP'T OF DEFENSE, DIR. 2311.01E, DoD Law of War Program (9 May 2006). The DoD originally promulgated this directive in December 1998, updated it in May 2006, and reconfirmed it in February 2011.

56. PRESIDENTIAL POLICY GUIDANCE: PROCEDURES FOR APPROVING DIRECT ACTION AGAINST TERRORIST TARGETS LOCATED OUTSIDE THE UNITED STATES AND AREAS OF ACTIVE HOSTILITIES (May 22, 2013), https://www.justice.gov/oip/foia-library/procedures_for_approving_direct_action_against_terrorist_targets/download.

However, as with much custom in the LOAC field, at some point in time, in the absence of contrary practice or statements, such "policy" decisions take on the veneer of legal obligation. It is clearly arguable that this is now the case (on this issue at least) for the United States. What would be the consequences for the United States—legal, political, and operational—of now walking back from applying IAC LOAC targeting rules in NIAC contexts? What would this body of rules be replaced with? Where is a (nonexistent, in my view) differentiated body of NIAC LOAC targeting law located or expressed? When such questions are clearly rhetorical, we are surely very close to, if not across, the *opinio juris* threshold.

There are also other indications that harmonization of IAC and NIAC LOAC in relation to targeting law has moved from the realm of discretionary policy choice into legal obligation.[57] In his 2010 address to the American Society of International Law on "The Obama Administration and International Law," U.S. Department of State Legal Adviser Harold Koh asserted that "A state that is engaged in an armed conflict or in legitimate self-defence is not required to provide targets with legal process before the state may use lethal force."[58] Leaving aside the "third paradigm" issue,[59] statements such as Koh's support the view that targeting in NIAC contexts is now considered by states, including the United States, to be governed by an equivalent of IAC targeting law rather than by some other rule set that is much less defined or much more permissive.

The first indication of this view lies in the very need to assert a third paradigm for use of lethal force, rather than simply operationalizing the U.S. Supreme Court's grant to the United States of a global CA3 NIAC against AQ and its affiliates,[60] which was an open door to interpreting a different set of targeting criteria into play. The second is the United States' assurance that such strikes are nevertheless subject to the same rigorous targeting assessment processes as for IAC contexts. There are clear indications that there is no other detailed process that is considered available or acceptable in either IAC or NIAC contexts (or indeed, within Koh's analysis, in the third context of "national self-defence" targeting):

> In particular, this Administration has carefully reviewed the rules governing targeting operations to ensure that these operations are conducted consistently with law of war principles, including:

57. *See* Remarks at National Defence University, 2013 Daily Comp. Pres. Doc. 361 (May 23, 2013).

58. Harold Hongju Koh, Legal Advisor, Dep't of St., Speech to the Annual Meeting of the American Society of International Law: The Obama Administration and International Law (Mar. 25, 2010).

59. Certainly, the fundamental analysis informing this justification for extra-judicial targeted strikes, on a national self-defense basis outside of either a LOAC context or an immediate criminal law "self-defense" context, is highly contested; but this is a separate matter.

60. Hamdan v. Rumsfeld, 548 U.S. 557 (2006).

> First, the principle of *distinction*, which requires that attacks be limited to military objectives and that civilians or civilian objects shall not be the object of the attack; and
>
> Second, the principle of *proportionality*, which prohibits attacks that may be expected to cause incidental loss of civilian life, injury to civilians, damage to civilian objects, or a combination thereof, that would be excessive in relation to the concrete and direct military advantage anticipated.[61]

The reference point is clearly AP I, or perhaps more correctly in the U.S. context, the equivalent rules of IAC LOAC as distilled from custom. This approach is further buttressed by other recent statements. For example, in a 2012 speech at Yale (which is now extracted in the *Digest of United States Practice in International Law*), U.S. Department of Defense General Counsel Jeh Johnson, asserted that:

> In the conflict against an *unconventional* enemy such as al Qaeda, we must consistently apply *conventional* legal principles. We must apply, and we have applied, the law of armed conflict, including applicable provisions of the Geneva Conventions and customary international law, core principles of distinction and proportionality, historic precedent, and traditional principles of statutory construction. Put another way, we must not make it up to suit the moment.[62]

More broadly, during United Nations Security Council sanctioned no-fly zone enforcement and humanitarian protection operations in Libya, it is clear that NATO forces followed, and appeared to consider themselves bound to follow, IAC

61. Harold Hongju Koh, Legal Advisor, Dep't of St., Speech to the Annual Meeting of the American Society of International Law: The Obama Administration and International Law (Mar. 25, 2010). *See also* Geoffrey Corn, *Self-Defense Targeting: Blurring the Line between the Jus ad Bellum and the Jus in Bello*, 88 INT'L L. STUD. 57, 59 (2011).

62. Jeh Johnson, General Counsel, U.S. Dep't of Def., National security law, lawyers and lawyering in the Obama Administration (Feb. 22, 2012) (full speech is available at https://www.americanbar.org/content/dam/aba/administrative/litigation/materials/sac_2012/50-5_nat_sec_ns_law_obama.authcheckdam.pdf). Attorney General Eric Holder also confirmed—by description—that the US applies a fundamentally IAC conception of the LOAC principles to these NIAC targeting operations, stating

> Of course, any such use of lethal force by the United States will comply with the four fundamental law of war principles governing the use of force. The principle of necessity requires that the target have definite military value. The principle of distinction requires that only lawful targets—such as combatants, civilians directly participating in hostilities, and military objectives—may be targeted intentionally. Under the principle of proportionality, the anticipated collateral damage must not be excessive in relation to the anticipated military advantage. Finally, the principle of humanity requires us to use weapons that will not inflict unnecessary suffering.

Eric Holder, U.S. Att'y Gen., Attorney General Erick Holder Speaks at Northwestern University School of Law (Mar. 5, 2012) (full prepared speech available at https://www.justice.gov/opa/speech/attorney-general-eric-holder-speaks-northwestern-university-school-law).

targeting rules.[63] Admittedly, this particular situation is complicated by the possibility that NATO was engaged in a concurrent IAC while a NIAC was afoot between Libyan forces and Libyan rebels. In many ways, however, this supports the view that IAC LOAC on targeting has now become the governing legal regime for targeting operations in all LOAC contexts, for there was no reference to—indeed not even a hint of—any alternative scheme as a context-defined option.

If we accept this proposition,then a clear benefit that might accrue from recognition of belligerency is a legal sidestep of the ongoing debate centering on NSAG membership criteria in relation to targeting,[64] most particularly the continuous combat function issue.[65] If, as is fundamental to recognition of belligerency, the NSAG becomes de jure (for the purposes of LOAC) the equivalent of a combatant force in IAC LOAC, with access to the suite of rights and obligations that accompany this status (including combatant immunity and entitlement to PW status), then the criticality surrounding the ongoing debate about "fighter" role and function dissipates. The need to descend into ever more granular and contentious hair-splitting and parsing of the legal status and liabilities of particular roles falls away, and the talismanic "continuous combat function" debate about whether the NSAG cook is within or outside of the targetable envelope becomes significantly easier. This is because the direct correlation with a military force now becomes mandated by the applicable law, and the answer furnished by IAC LOAC is to the effect that a belligerent status NSAG military force cook is indeed targetable, just as a state military force cook is targetable. This is relatively uncontroversial in recognition of belligerency terms and should thus command some attention.

(ii) Blockade, and Visit and Search: Applying maritime IAC means and methods regimes to certain "NIAC" contexts

As any general survey of "means and methods" provisions in LOAC instruments reveals, it is readily apparent that some means and methods rules apply, by force of the relevant treaty, within NIAC contexts. Thus there is no "opt out" for use

63. *See, e.g.*, Letter from Peter Olson, Legal Advisor, North Atlantic Treaty Org., to Judge P. Kirsch, Int'l Commission of Inquiry on Libya (Feb. 15, 2012), https://www.nato.int/nato_static_fl2014/assets/pdf/pdf_2012_05/20120514_120514-NATO_2nd_ICIL_response.pdf); *See also* Letter from Peter Olson, Legal Advisor, North Atlantic Treaty Org., to Judge P. Kirsch, Int'l Commission of Inquiry on Libya (Jan. 23 2012), https://www.nato.int/nato_static_fl2014/assets/pdf/pdf_2012_05/20120514_120514-NATO_1st_ICIL_response.pdf. This example is complicated, however, by the UN Commission's explicit finding that NATO's participation in the Libyan conflict was as a party to an IAC.

64. Geoffrey Corn and Chris Jenks, *Two Sides of the Combatant Coin: Untangling Direct Participation in Hostilities from Belligerent Status in Non-International Armed Conflicts*, 33(2) U. Pa. J. Int'l L. 313 (2011).

65. Nils Melzer, Interpretive Guidance on the Notion of Direct Participation in Hostilities under International Humanitarian Law 32–36 (2009). *See, e.g.*, Watkin, *Opportunity Lost: Organized Armed Groups and the ICRC Direct Participation in Hostilities Interpretive Guidance*, 652–63.

of certain riot control agents as a means or method of warfare in NIAC because Article 1(5) of the *Chemical Weapons Convention* makes no distinction between IAC and NIAC, declaring only that "Each State Party undertakes not to use riot control agents as a method of warfare."[66] The more vexed question is to determine what LOAC means and methods obligations found within expressly IAC focused treaties, are now considered to apply to NIAC by virtue of broad customary rules that cross both contexts. This leads to the question of whether/how the doctrine on recognition of belligerency might simplify this assessment. The poverty of generalization in the face of a necessarily rule-by-rule assessment required as regards the relationship between IAC and NIAC LOAC has been previously noted; to this end, I will thus briefly examine the law of naval warfare means and methods of blockade, and visit and search, in order to indicate the utility of the doctrine on recognition of belligerency in resolving such questions.

The maritime LOAC means and methods of blockade, and separately visit and search, are long-standing components of both the Law of War and IAC LOAC. Indeed, the authors of and contributors to the *San Remo Manual*[67]—considered by most to be an authoritative record of the Law of Naval Warfare (LoNW) as crystallized by the 1990s—consciously sidestepped the issue of NIAC maritime LOAC in the quest for clarity within the already under-instrumentalized field of IAC maritime LOAC. The *San Remo Manual* blockade rules (93–104) begin from, reflect, and summarize the Law of War context underpinning the 1856 *Paris Declaration*[68] and the relevant *Hague 1907 Conventions*, as well as customary LoNW[69] (as reflected to some extent in the 1909 *London Declaration*, which never formally entered into force,[70] and in the 1913 *Oxford Manual on the Laws of Naval War*[71]). It is clear that blockade, and visit and search, as means or methods of warfare, have not generally crossed the NIAC—IAC membrane. Yet it is equally clear that blockade and visit and search have long been considered a valid means or method of war in conflicts where a NSAG in conflict with its parent state has been afforded formal belligerency status.

66. Convention on the prohibition of the development, production, stockpiling and use of chemical weapons and on their destruction, Jan. 13, 1993, 1975 U.N.T.S. 45.

67. Int'l Inst. Humanitarian L., San Remo Manual on International Law Applicable to Armed Conflicts at Sea 73 (Louise Doswald-Beck ed., 1994) (stating "However, it should be noted that although the provisions of this Manual are primarily meant to apply to international armed conflicts at sea, this has intentionally not been expressly indicated in paragraph 1 in order not to dissuade the implementation of these rules in non-international armed conflicts involving naval operations").

68. Declaration Respecting Maritime Law, Apr. 16, 1856, LXI BSP 155.

69. David Letts and Rob McLaughlin, *Law of Naval Warfare: International Humanitarian Law in the Maritime Domain*, *in* Routledge Handbook of the Law of Armed Conflict 268 (Rain Liivoja and Tim McCormack eds., 2016).

70. Declaration Concerning the Laws of Naval War, Feb. 26, 1909, 208 Consol. T.S. 338.

71. *Manual on the Laws of Naval War*, Aug. 9, 1913, in The Laws of Armed Conflicts 858 (D. Schindler and J. Toman eds., 1988).

However, in civil war/NIAC where there has been no recognition of belligerency, neither the state nor the NSAG was recognized as having the legal authority to impose an IAC maritime LOAC blockade or a visit and search regime (as distinct from admissible control measures within internal waters and, to a lesser extent, the territorial sea, as discussed in relation to Taiwan in the 1950s). Indeed, the Sri Lanka—LTTE conflict provides evidence of this limitation in that neither party was considered to have had the option of blockade or visit and search available to them—elsewise, as a minimum, LTTE "Sea Tiger" actions against both third state vessels at sea, and Sri Lankan vessels, would need to have been characterized as something other than maritime terrorism or piracy.[72] Yet, there have clearly been other post-1949 civil war/NIAC contexts in which blockades and visit and search have been employed such as (in descending order of certainty) Gaza, Algeria, and Yemen. The doctrine on recognition of belligerency would (has?) render(ed) this operational fact legally unobjectionable. It would provide a legal pathway for characterizing the maritime conduct of belligerent status (and indeed insurgent status?) NSAG as other than piracy, given that "piracy" is of contextually narrower definition in the three-level scheme, and within the doctrine on recognition of belligerency (a *lex specialis* regime) than is the case in general international law.

D. DEALING WITH NSAGS AS ENTITIES

(i) Providing support to a recognized belligerent NSAG

Many of the organizational and entity relationship structuring purposes served by the doctrine on recognition of belligerency as applied in civil wars—humanitarian, operational, and fiscal—remain potentially relevant for NIACs. Further, there is a modicum of evidence in state practice and academic discourse that the doctrine on recognition of belligerency is considered by some to remain available as a scheme for describing, analyzing, and regulating legal status, obligations, and relationships in some situations characterized in modern LOAC terms as NIAC contexts. As Jennifer Hazen and others have noted in relation to territories subject to NSAG control,

> Often it is not a question of whether there is governance but of what type of governance is being exercised and by whom. Who fills the gaps matters because they become the centre of power in the community. How these gaps are filled matters because this determines the extent of the challenge to the state.[73]

72. For some details on LTTE Sea Tiger operations, *see generally* PK Ghosh, Maritime Security Challenges in South Asia and the Indian Ocean: Response Strategies (Jan. 18–20, 2004) (paper delivered at the Centre for Strategic and International Studies/America-Pacific Sealanes Security Institute, Conference on Maritime Security in Asia, 18–20 January, 2004); Martin N. Murphy, *Suppression of Piracy and Maritime Terrorism: A Suitable Role for a Navy?*, 60(3) NAVAL WAR C. REV. 23 (2007); Paul A. Povlock, *A Guerrilla War at Sea: The Sri Lankan Civil War*, SMALL WARS JOURNAL, http://smallwarsjournal.com/jrnl/art/a-guerilla-war-at-sea-the-sri-lankan-civil-war (last visited Dec. 19, 2018).

73. Hazen, *Understanding Gangs as Armed Groups*, 380.

If the doctrine on recognition of belligerency remains viable and the purposes it served remain useful, what might states have to lose, or indeed to gain, if recognition of belligerency was revitalized as a means of ensuring some degree of additional humanitarian coverage within what would today be characterized as a NIAC situation? I shall raise a few very brief points on this issue, but only as a hopeful catalyst for further discussion rather than to offer settled or detailed legal argument either way.

One potential "loss" for states is undoubtedly that recognition of belligerency does involve conferral of a form of legitimating status upon the belligerent NSAG. This is clearly a problem and a challenge; but from another perspective, it is also an opportunity.[74] There are situations where engaged states sometimes do want to differentiate between NSAGs, and to give some sort of status to one, but not to another. Were, for example, the armed wings of the moderate Syrian opposition on one hand, and ISIS on the other, factually (and should they be legally) the same in all respects? U.S. support to "vetted Syrian rebels in the war against the regime of Bashar al-Assad" is/was a political and legal fact,[75] as is Turkish support to other Syrian NSAGs.[76]

Might not states and/or the international community sometimes wish to use a mechanism that allows legitimation (and thus support for) one NSAG without legitimizing other NSAGs, using apparent compliance/noncompliance with LOAC (a component of the recognition of belligerency test) as a discriminating factor? Such support could be manifested through the strict application of neutrality obligations in relation to a delinquent conflict state (Ghadafian Libya in 2011, Assadist Syria since 2011–2012), resulting in a legally sanctioned reduction of support options available to the delinquent state via the non-discriminatory conduct required of a neutral. Another option is to send a clear political and operational message via a legitimate statement of partiality—that is, non-neutrality—in support of the NSAG and by definition against the delinquent conflict state (the very result that the tortuous non-intervention arrangements with respect to the Spanish Civil War tried to circumvent in terms of German and Italian policy).

Given that overt third state support of NSAGs is often evident in practice at any rate, perhaps reinvigorating a mechanism that allowed—where appropriate—the

74. Dawn Steinhoff, for example, describes a scenario whereby a state admits to a NIAC, and the NSAG then exploits the admission that there is an armed conflict to add to their legal status by claiming self-determination objectives, thus inviting application of API Article 1(4). Suddenly, the conflict is governed by IAC LOAC. Dawn Steinhoff, *Talking to the Enemy: State Legitimacy Concerns with Engaging Non-State Armed Groups*, 45 Tex. Int'l L. J. 297, 318 (2009).

75. Faysal Itani, *The End of American Support for Syrian Rebels Was Inevitable*, The Atlantic (Jul. 21 2017), https://www.theatlantic.com/international/archive/2017/07/trump-syria-assad-rebels-putin-cia/534540/.

76. *See generally Syria war: A brief guide to who's fighting whom*, BBC News (Apr. 7, 2017), http://www.bbc.com/news/world-middle-east-39528673; *See also* Bethan McKernan, *Turkish troops enter Syria in major operation to support anti-Assad rebels*, The Independent (Oct. 9, 2017), http://www.independent.co.uk/news/world/middle-east/turkey-syria-idlib-troops-assad-rebels-support-a7991691.html.

application of just such a limited legal gloss, in situations that otherwise look like a NIAC, is not such a confronting prospect. Additionally, it should also be remembered that recognition of belligerency only affords status to a NSAG in relation to the application of the relevant LOAC rule set—it does not create a state or an entity with standing outside of this narrow context. Also, if in doubt, the status can at any rate be "unreviewably" denied (by virtue of the subjective political/diplomatic element built into the recognition of belligerency test). This is the ultimate guarantee of state control of the mechanism, and of its subjection to state interests, in that no state is bound by another state's grant of recognition of belligerency; any state can refuse such recognition and act accordingly.

(ii) NSAG LOAC and IHRL obligations

As Daragh Murray has convincingly argued, principled denial of the LOAC and IHRL obligations of NSAGs nevertheless serves to create a substantive vacuum in which "international law fails to respond to the realities of international life." One of those realities is that if the territorial state cannot fulfill its roles in relation to the civilian population in NSAG controlled territory, then "who is responsible for their wellbeing?"[77] As Murray continues, it is not unknown to international law that NSAGs hold some degree of legal personality for various purposes, including in LOAC, and his three criteria for identifying NSAGs that ought to be recognized as direct holders of international obligations are both sensible and historically sound.[78] Tom Gal similarly has argued that the legal framework of obligations and duties in relation to humanitarian assistance and access operations in areas controlled by NSAGs needs to be reconceptualized in such a way that the obligation to permit such access is clearly understood to be a component of NSAG responsibilities.[79]

An integral component of the doctrine on recognition of belligerency is that belligerent status NSAGs become *legally* bound, as organizations, to comply with the Law of War, and (today) through LOAC, with imported IHRL obligations.

77. Daragh Murray, Human Rights Obligations of Non-State Armed Groups 7–15 (2016); *See generally* Liesbeth Zegveld, The Accountability of Armed Opposition Groups in International Law (2002); *See also* Theodore Meron, Human Rights in Internal Strife: Their International Protection (1987). This is a different legal conundrum to that crystalized in Article 10(2) of the *Articles on State Responsibility* regarding responsibility for the acts of a successful insurgent NSAG that ultimately becomes the state; as Patrick Dumberry notes, "the attribution to the new state of the acts of insurgents is indeed quite independent from the other question of whether the rebels were exercising de facto power in part of the territory of the predecessor state, which subsequently became a new state." Patrick Dumberry, *New State Responsibility for Internationally Wrongful Acts by an Insurrectional Movement*, 17(3) Eur. J. Int'l L. 605, 609–10 (2006).

78. Murray, Human Rights Obligations of Non-State Armed Groups, 16 (discussing capacity, direct comprehension by the international legal order, and independent existence).

79. Gal, *Territorial Control by Armed Groups and the Regulation of Access to Humanitarian Assistance*, 39–47.

The customary scheme was very clear that recognition of belligerency bound both parties and neutral third states to follow the Law of War, de jure as opposed to merely de facto or as a matter of policy. This obligation also directly bound individuals with a connection to that organization to follow the applicable Law of War and, therefore, in the modern LOAC scheme, all of the IHRL that has been imported into LOAC. Recognition of belligerency would create a clear and direct, as opposed to subsidiary, path for NSAGs and individual NSAG members to be formally credited with obligations and responsibilities in respect of both LOAC and imported IHRL. This is a radically different proposition from NSAG members only being bound by and through the obligations and laws of the adversary state that the NSAG is fighting against. It is certainly valid to raise the issue of potential for actual enforcement, but even getting to that stage would nevertheless be a welcome step beyond the current interpretive hurdle we tend to encounter when asking if and how LOAC and IHRL obligations apply to NSAGs as a matter of law.

Additionally, the belligerency and insurgency legal-historical record is replete with examples of third state legal systems according standing, rights, and obligations to recognized belligerent (and insurgent) NSAGs. If so, why not for human rights enforcement purposes in the same way that other external non-person legal entities are subject to domestic jurisdiction? Further, given that an identifiable capacity and willingness to comply with the applicable LOAC is an element of the legal test for recognition of belligerency, it is at least theoretically possible that such recognition could have the effect of making NSAGs feel legally bound (as distinct from morally or politically motivated, as underpins such important initiatives as Geneva Call's Deeds of Commitment) to follow LOAC. There is some historical evidence to support the contention that such recognition may, in some cases, have acted to improve battlefield compliance by NSAGs, not least because they would now be treated as PW rather than mere criminals, and would not be prosecuted for LOAC-compliant battlefield conduct. NSAG members thus had less reason to resort to atrocity as a response to, or preventative measure for, inevitable treatment as a criminal (rebel) upon capture. The U.S. Supreme Court in (inter alia) *Ford v Suget*[80] was certainly of the view that the application of the Law of War during the American Civil War "was conceded, in the interest of humanity, and to prevent the cruelties of reprisals and retaliations, such belligerent rights as belonged, under the law of nations, to the armies of independent Governments engaged in war against each other." Hall, writing in 1890, felt secure enough to assert that such dictates of humanity definitely underscored the purpose of recognition of belligerency:

> As soon, it is said, as a considerable population is arrayed in arms with the professed object of attaining political ends . . . it would be inhuman for the enemy to execute his prisoners; it would be still more inhuman for foreign states to capture and hang the crews of war-ships as pirates; humanity requires that the members of such a community shall be treated as belligerents.[81]

80. Ford v. Suget, 97 U.S. 594 (1878).

81. William Edward Hall, A Treatise on International Law 33–34 (1895).

Admittedly, as Lauterpacht identified, this humanitarian impulse may well have been overstated, but he nevertheless agreed that "It is often maintained that recognition of belligerency by outside States is an important factor in securing compliance with rules of warfare and in helping to infuse into an otherwise savage and irregular combat an indispensable measure of restraint and humanity."[82] It is perhaps a very slim possibility, but it is a possibility nonetheless.[83]

Consequently, a significant benefit that might be gained through some revitalization of the doctrine on recognition of belligerency is that a clear body of law—the Law of War and, in current terms, IAC LOAC—is incontrovertibly, and de jure, made applicable. While (as noted previously) many of the means and methods rules in IAC have morphed into customary NIAC LOAC, there remain difficult issues and non-sequiturs, such as blockade, or visit and search that, but for recognition of belligerency, would likely be considered piracy if carried out by an NSAG in a NIAC.[84] Recognition of belligerency removes any doubt whatsoever about the applicable law: The NSAG is legally bound as an organization to comply with the Law of War / IAC LOAC, and this at least directly binds NSAG members (in international law) to follow the Law of War / LOAC, as opposed to those individuals only being bound by the obligations and laws of the state they are fighting against, and, depending upon extraterritorial reach, the laws of their state of nationality, if different.

E. CONCLUSION

Despite a relatively recent general silence as to the continued existence or applicability of the doctrine on recognition of belligerency, there are whispers and indications that it stubbornly but quietly refuses to disappear. Some of those who have specifically addressed the doctrine in recent times have concluded that formal recognition of belligerency, although in "disuse," nevertheless remains "relevant."[85] There seems to be state practice that affirms this view. Others allow that the doctrine may even remain vibrantly extant, and yet others have applied the doctrine to current situations as diverse as Libya, Chechnya,[86] and Columbia.

82. HERSCH LAUTERPACHT, RECOGNITION IN INTERNATIONAL LAW 227 (1947)

83. *See, e.g.*, Kreβ and Megret, *The Regulation of Non-International Armed Conflicts: Can a Privilege of Belligerency Be Envisioned in the Law of Non-International Armed Conflicts?*, 10, 11, 13, 22, and 34.

84. *See, e.g.*, Heintschel von Heinegg, *Methods and Means of naval warfare in Non-International Armed Conflicts*, 88 INT'L L. STUD. 211, 215–16 (2011) (providing commentary upon the characterization of certain actions at sea by the LTTE during the Sri Lankan Civil War); *See also* Douglas Guilfoyle, *The Mavi Marmara Incident and Blockade in Armed Conflict*, BRIT. Y.B. INT'L L. 193 (2011).

85. On the potential application of recognition of belligerency to the Israel-Gaza conflict, *see* James Farrant, *The Gaza Flotilla Incident and the Modern Law of Blockade*, 66(3) NAVAL WAR C. REV. 81 (2013).

86. *See* William Abresch, *A Human Rights Law of Internal Armed Conflict: The European Court of Human Rights in Chechnya*, 16(4) EUR. J. INT'L L. 741 (2005); *See also* Duncan Hollis,

It is not immediately apparent—to me, at any rate—why the humanitarian, operational, and fiscal purposes traditionally served by the customary Law of War doctrine on recognition of belligerency are not as relevant today as they were in the past. Indeed, the express and explicit detail provided by recognition of belligerency, in direct response to the challenges posed by "civil war," provides some insight into the agility, relevance, and adaptability of the doctrine during its heyday. In seeking conceptual stability and contextual clarity in order to better define legal arrangements well-fitted to dealing with the humanitarian, operational, and fiscal challenges attendant upon situations of civil war, it is clear that the doctrine on recognition of belligerency was quite successful.

It is, consequently, possible that the customary Law of War doctrine on recognition of belligerency has indeed survived the post-1949 codification of LOAC. It is even more possible, and indeed probable, that some discrete civil war conflict contexts traditionally covered by the doctrine (such as those in which the Law of War was said to apply, but which do not fall within the scope of modern AP I Article 1(4) conflicts) could also be legitimately characterized by reference to the customary recognition of belligerency scheme. It is therefore perhaps justifiable to speak of any potential modern application of this customary scheme as merely a revitalization rather than a resurrection, for it is clearly arguable that the customary scheme on recognition of belligerency is not dead. It was not, and was not understood to have been, collaterally extinguished during the post-1949 codification and progressive development of LOAC. It is my proposition that the doctrine on recognition of belligerency does indeed still subsist in the customary background to LOAC—albeit with a relatively light touch in current mainstream analysis.

Why, then, have we almost, but not irretrievably, forgotten about it? If the doctrine on recognition of belligerency was able to assist in achieving or crystallizing practical legal responses to important civil war humanitarian, operational, and fiscal concerns in the nineteenth and twentieth centuries, what is it—if indeed this is the case—that now makes this doctrine somehow unsuitable for dealing with what are essentially the very same challenges today? The challenges themselves are not new; it is the details and the particularities in which each manifests that are often new. If this is so, what is it about these modern "details" that makes the recognition of belligerency no longer useful in offering an option for legally assessing and managing situations where it might legitimately apply? I do not believe there is some special, intensely contemporary, legal peculiarity or difficulty that acts to reduce, de facto or de jure, the modern fitness for purpose of the doctrine. I would most tentatively suggest that this forgetfulness is rather a case of understandable, but nevertheless regrettable, a-historicity in the face of frenetically evolving responses to the challenge of applying LOAC within modern insurgency and belligerency contexts.

Accountability in Chechnya—Addressing Internal Matters with Legal and Political International Norms, 36 Bos. C. L. Rev. 793, 814 (1995).

If this is so, then there are clear implications for modern NIAC LOAC. One set of implications relates to characterizing, as a matter of law, the rights and duties of those NSAGs that might, in the customary scheme, achieve the first three elements of the recognition of belligerency test. Another set of implications are the clear legal and operational possibilities that might be generated by renewed access to a neat, tested, customary, but relatively forgotten legal scheme, offering the potential to overcome some of the thornier current questions relating to LOAC detention, NSAG labeling, and targeting regimes for NSAG members in NIACs. Perhaps it is an opportune moment to re-examine a tailor made, but almost forgotten, customary regime that was designed to deal with many of these problems. To conclude as I started, with Megret: "The NIAC regime has by and large been a regime by default, one constructed in the shadow of the regime applicable to international armed conflict."[87] Perhaps a customary regime specifically designed to smooth the way for the application of well-developed Law of War rules within selected civil war / NIAC contexts deserves another look. Return to, and even revision of, such a regime may ultimately be easier than, and preferable to, trying to stitch together a piecemeal and perhaps over-complicated solution to current, but historically known, civil war Law of War / NIAC LOAC challenges.

87. Kreβ and Megret, *The Regulation of Non-International Armed Conflicts: Can a Privilege of Belligerency Be Envisioned in the Law of Non-International Armed Conflicts?*, 17.

Bibliography

Books and articles

Daniel Abebe and Eric Posner, 'The Flaws of Foreign Affairs Legalism' (2011) 51 *Virginia Journal of International Law* 507.

William Abresch, 'A Human Rights Law of Internal Armed Conflict: The European Court of Human Rights in Chechnya' (2005) 16:4 *European Journal of International Law* 741.

Charles Adams (ed), *Memoirs of John Quincy Adams Vol IV*, Lippincott and Co, Philadelphia, 1875.

Dapo Akande, 'Classification of Armed Conflicts: Relevant Legal Concepts', in Elizabeth Wilmshurst, ed, *International Law and the Classification of Conflicts*, Oxford University Press, Oxford, 2012.

Dapo Akande and Lawrence Hill-Cawthorne, 'The Lieber Code and the Regulation of Civil War in International Law' (2015) 53 *Columbia Journal of Transnational Law* 638.

Mary Ann O Arguillas, 'The Non-Traditional Moro Elites and the Organization of Islamic Conference (OIC)' (2001) 22:45 *Philippine Political Science Journal* 97.

Nir Arielli, Gabriela Frei, and Inge Van Hulle, 'The Foreign Enlistment Act, International Law, and British Politics, 1819–2014' (2016) 38:4 *International History Review* 636.

Kevin Arlyck, 'Plaintiffs v. Privateers: Litigation and Foreign Affairs in the Federal Courts, 1816–1822' (2012) 30 *Law and History Review* 245.

'Art IX—Poland' (July 1863) XXIV *Westminster Review* 171.

'Art V—The Treaty of Vienna: Poland' (October 1863) XXIV *Westminster Review* 412.

David Armitage, *Civil Wars: A History in Ideas*, Alfred A Knopf, New York, 2017.

Sean Aughey and Aurel Sari, 'Targeting and Detention in Non-International Armed Conflict: Serdar Mohammed and the Limits of Human Rights Convergence' (2015) 91 *International Law Studies* 60.

Lawrence Azubuike, 'International Law Regime Against Piracy' (2009) 15 *Annual Survey of International and Comparative Law* 43.

Stephanie Bangarth, 'The Politics of African Intervention: Canada and Biafra, 1967–70', in Michael K Carroll and Greg Donaghy, eds, *From Kinshasa to Kandahar: Canada and Fragile States in Historical Perspective*, University of Calgary Press, Calgary, 2016.

Rogier Bartels, 'Timelines, Borderlines and Conflicts: The Historical Evolution of the Legal Divide between International and Non-International Armed Conflicts' (2009) 873 *International Review of the Red Cross* 35.

Gary J Bass, *Freedom's Battle: The Origins of Humanitarian Intervention*, Knopf, New York, 2008.

M Cherif Bassiouni, 'New Wars and the Crisis of Compliance with the Law of Armed Conflict by Non-State Actors' (2008) 98:3 *Journal of Criminal Law and Criminology* 711.

Richard Baxter, 'So-Called "Unprivileged Belligerency": Spies, Guerrillas, and Saboteurs' (1951) 28 *British Yearbook of International Law* 323.

Joseph Beale Jr, 'The Recognition of Cuban Belligerency' (1895–1896) 9 *Harvard Law Review* 406.

John B. Bellinger III and William J. Haynes II, 'A US Government Response to the International Committee of the Red Cross study on *Customary International Humanitarian Law*' (2007) 98:866 *International Review of the Red Cross* 443.

Lynn Berat, 'Constitutionalism and Mineral Law in the Struggle for a New South Africa: The South African War Revisited' (1991–1992) 15 *Suffolk Transnational Law Journal* 61.

Mountague Bernard, *On the Principle of Non-Intervention: A Lecture*, Parker, Oxford, 1860.

Mountague Bernard, *A Historical Account of the Neutrality of Great Britain during the American Civil War*, London, 1870.

Remigiusz Bierzanek, 'Humanitarian Law in Armed Conflicts: The Doctrine and Practice of Polish Insurgents in the 19th Century' (1977) 17:192 *International Review of the Red Cross* 128.

Tom Bingham, 'The *Alabama* Claims Arbitration' (2005) 54:1 *International and Comparative Law Quarterly* 1.

Tom Bingham, *Lives of the Law: Selected Essays and Speeches: 2000–2010*, Oxford University Press, Oxford, 2011.

The Earl of Birkenhead, *International Law* (6th Edition, Ron Moelwyn-Hughes, ed), JM Dent and Sons, London, 1927.

Karl Blind, 'The Transvaal War and European Opinion' (1899) 169:517 *The North American Review* 760.

William Bobulsky, 'Beyond Vietnam to Indo-China—The Legal Implications of the United States' Incursions into Cambodia and Laos' (1971) 3:2 *Case Western Reserve Journal of International Law* 163.

James E Bond, *Rules of Riot: Internal Conflict and the Law of War*, Princeton Legacy Library, Princeton, 1974.

James E Bond, 'Application of the Law of War to Internal Conflicts' (1973) 3:2 *Georgia Journal of International and Comparative Law* 345.

James E Bond, 'Internal Conflict and Article Three of the Geneva Conventions' (1971–1972) 48 *Denver Law Journal* 263.

HN Boon, 'Review: Natalino Rontitte, Le Guerre Di Liberazione Nationale E Il Dritto Internazionale (1974)' (1979) 26:2 *Netherlands International Law Review* 204.

Michael Bothe, 'Article 3 and Protocol II: Case Studies of Nigeria and El Salvador' (1982) 31 *American University Law Review* 899.

Curtis Bradley, 'The Military Commissions Act, Habeas Corpus, and the Geneva Conventions' (2007) 101 *American Journal of International Law* 322.

JL Brierly, *The Law of Nations*, Clarendon Press, Oxford, 1928.

Herbert Briggs, 'De Facto and De Jure Recognition: The Arantzazu Mendi' (1939) 33:4 *American Journal of International Law* 689.

Russell Buchan, 'The International Law of Naval Blockade and Israel's Interception of the Mavi Marmara' (2011) 58:2 *Netherlands International Law Review* 209.

Francois Bugnion, 'Jus ad Bellum, Jus in Bello and Non-International Armed Conflicts' (2003) 6 *Yearbook of International Humanitarian Law* 167.

Antonio Cassese, 'The Status of Rebels under the 1977 Geneva Protocol on Non-International Armed Conflicts' (1981) 30 *International and Comparative Law Quarterly* 416.

Erik Castren, *Civil War*, Suómalainen Tiedeakatemia, Helsinki, 1966.

Gary Catron, 'Hong Kong and Chinese Foreign Policy, 1955–60' (1972) 51 *China Quarterly* 405.

Ti-Chiang Chen, *The International Law of Recognition*, Stevens and Sons, London, 1951.

Carl von Clausewitz, *On War* 1832 (Trans. Michael Howards and Peter Paret), Princeton University Press, Princeton, 1976.

Charles Clode, *The Military Forces of the Crown: Their Administration and Government (Vol II)*, John Murray, London, 1869.

Benjamin Coates, *Legalist Empire: International Law and American Foreign Relations in the Early Twentieth Century*, Oxford University Press, Oxford, 2016.

Jerome Cohen and Hungdah Chiu, *People's China and International Law: A Documentary Study, Volume I*, Princeton University Press, Princeton, 1974.

C John Colombos, *The International Law of The Sea* (6th Edition), Longmans, London, 1967.

PE Corbett, 'The Vietnam Struggle and International Law', in Richard Falk, ed, *The International Law of Civil Wars*, Johns Hopkins Press, Baltimore, 1971.

Michael Corcoran, *The Captivity of General Corcoran: The Only Authentic and Reliable Narrative of the Trials and Sufferings Endured, during His Twelve Month's Imprisonment in Richmond and Other Southern Cities*, Barclay and Co, Philadelphia, 1862.

Geoffrey Corn, 'Self-Defense Targeting: Blurring the Line between the Jus ad Bellum and the Jus in Bello' (2011) 88 *International Law Studies* 57.

Geoffrey Corn and Chris Jenks, 'Two Sides of the Combatant Coin: Untangling Direct Participation in Hostilities from Belligerent Status in Non-International Armed Conflicts' (2011) 33:2 *University of Pennsylvania Journal of International Law* 313.

Jorge Coquia and Miriam Defensor Santiago, *Public International Law*, Philippine Jurisprudence Project, Quezon City, 1984.

Emily Crawford, 'Unequal Before the Law: The Case for the Elimination of the Distinction between International and Non-International Armed Conflict (2007) 20:2 *Leiden Journal of International Law* 441.

Emily Crawford, *The Treatment of Combatants and Insurgents under the Law of Armed Conflict*, Oxford University Press, Oxford, 2010.

Emily Crawford, 'International Humanitarian Law in the Courts of Australia', in Derek Jinks, Jackson Maogoto, and Solon Solomon, eds, *Applying International Humanitarian Law in Judicial and Quasi-Judicial Bodies: International and Domestic Aspects*, TMC Asser Press, The Hague, pp 335–353.

James Crawford, *The Creation of States in International Law* (2nd Edition), Oxford University Press, Oxford, 2006.

Clyde Crockett, 'Toward a Revision of the International Law of Piracy' (1976) 26 *De Paul Law Review* 78.

Brian Crozier, *The Rebels—A Study of Post-War Insurrections*, Beacon Press, Boston, 1960.

Anthony Cullen, 'Key Developments Affecting the Scope of Internal Armed Conflict in International Humanitarian Law' (2005) 183 *Military Law Review* 66.

TRH Davenport, 'The South African Rebellion, 1914' (1963) 78:306 *The English Historical Review* 73.

Cushman Davis, *A Treatise on International Law Including American Diplomacy*, Keefe-Davidson, St Paul, 1901.

Edwin D Dickinson, 'The Closure of Ports in Control of Insurgents' (1930) 24:1 *American Journal of International Law* 69.

Yoram Dinstein, 'Concluding Remarks on Non-International Armed Conflicts' (2011) 88 *International Law Studies* 399.

'Discussion' (1937) 31 *American Society of International Law Proceedings* 153.

Louise Doswald-Beck (ed), *San Remo Manual on International Law Applicable to Armed Conflicts at Sea*, International Institute of Humanitarian Law / Cambridge University Press, San Remo / Cambridge, 1995.

'Draft Convention on Rights and Duties of Neutral States in Naval and Aerial War' (1939) 33 *American Journal of International Law Supplement: Research in International Law* 175.

Katherine Draper, 'Why a War Without a Name May Need One: Policy-Based Application of International Humanitarian Law in the Algerian War' (2013) 48:3 *Texas International Law Journal* 575.

GIAD Draper, 'Humanitarian Law and Internal Armed Conflicts' (1983) 13 *Georgia Journal of International and Comparative Law* 253.

Patrick Dumberry, 'New State Responsibility for Internationally Wrongful Acts by an Insurrectional Movement' (2006) 17:3 *European Journal of International Law* 605.

David Elder, 'The Historical Background of Common Article 3 of the Geneva Convention of 1949' (1979) 11 *Case Western Reserve Journal of International Law* 37.

Rear Admiral Bernard Estival, 'The French Navy and the Algerian War' (2002) 25:2 *Journal of Strategic Studies* 79.

GW Eybers, *Select Constitutional Documents Illustrating South African History 1795–1910*, Routledge & Sons, London, 1918.

Richard Falk, 'The International Law of Internal War', in James Rosenau, ed, *International Aspects of Civil Strife*, Princeton University Press, Princeton, 1964.

Richard Falk, 'Introduction', in Richard Falk, ed, *The International Law of Civil Wars*, Johns Hopkins Press, Baltimore, 1971.

Toyin Falola, *History of Nigeria*, Greenwood Press, Westport, 1999.

James Farrant, 'The Gaza Flotilla Incident and the Modern Law of Blockade' (2013) 66:3 *Naval War College Review* 81.

Charles Fenwick, 'Piracy in the Caribbean' (1961) 55 *American Journal of International Law* 426.

William Finlason, *Commentaries upon Martial Law with Special Reference to its Regulation and Restraint*, Stevens & Sons, London, 1867.

William Finlason, *A Review of the Authorities as to the Repression of Riot or Rebellion: With Special Reference to Criminal or Civil Liability*, Stevens & Sons, London, 1868.

Edwin Brown Firmage, 'Summary and Interpretation', in Richard Falk, ed, *The International Law of Civil War*, Johns Hopkins Press, Baltimore, 1971.

Arnold Fraleigh, 'The Algerian Revolution as a Case Study in International Law', in Richard Falk, ed, *The International Law of Civil Wars*, Johns Hopkins Press, Baltimore, 1971.

Thomas Franck, '"To Define and Punish Piracies"—The Lesson of the Santa Maria: A Comment' (1961) 36 *New York University Law Review* 839.

Thomas Frank and Nigel Rodley, 'Legitimacy and Legal Rights of Revolutionary Movements with Special Reference to the Peoples' Revolutionary Government of South Viet Nam' (1970) 45 *New York University Law Review* 679.

Eugene Fryer, 'Applicability of International Law to Internal Armed Conflicts: Old Problems, Current Endeavors' (1977) 11:3 *International Lawyer* 567.

Tom Gal, 'Territorial Control by Armed Groups and the Regulation of Access to Humanitarian Assistance' (2017) 50:1 *Israel Law Review* 25.

Boaz Ganor, 'Identifying the Enemy in Counterterrorism Operations—A Comparison of the Bush and Obama Administrations' (2014) 90 *International Law Studies* 341.

James Gathii, 'Kenya's Piracy Prosecutions' (2010) 104:3 *American Journal of International Law* 416.

Robin Geiβ and Michael Siegrist, 'Has the Armed Conflict in Afghanistan Affected the Rules on the Conduct of Hostilities?' (2011) 93:881 *International Review of the Red Cross* 11.

Raoul Ghent, 'The Charge of Piracy in the Spanish Civil War' (1938) 32 *American Journal of International Law* 253.

Edward Gibbs, *England and South Africa*, Longmans, Green & Co, London, 1889.

Alexander Gillespie, *A History of the Laws of War: Volume I—The Customs and Laws of War with Regards to Combatants and Captives*, Hart, Oxford, 2011.

Juan Carlos Gomez, 'Twenty-First Century Challenges: The Use of Military Forces to Combat Criminal Threats' (2011) 88 *International Law Studies* 279.

Robert W Gomulkiewicz, 'International Law Governing Aid to Opposition Groups in Civil War: Resurrecting the Standards of Belligerency' (1988) 63 *Washington Law Review* 43.

Ryan Goodman, 'The Power to Kill or Capture Enemy Combatants' (2013) 24:3 *European Journal of International Law* 819.

Ryan Goodman, 'Authorization versus Regulation of Detention in Non-International Armed Conflicts' (2015) 91 *International Law Studies* 155.

Thomas Grant, 'Defining Statehood: The Montevideo Convention and Its Discontents' (1999) 37 *Columbia Journal of Transnational Law* 403.

Thomas Grassey, 'Some Perspectives on Revolution' (1980) 62 *International Law Studies* 66.

Christine Gray, 'Bosnia and Herzegovina: Civil War or Inter-State Conflict? Characterization and Consequences' (1997) 67 *British Yearbook of International Law* 155.

Leslie Green, 'The Santa Maria: Rebels or Pirates' (1961) 37 *British Yearbook of International Law* 496.

Leslie Green, *International Law Through the Cases* (4th Edition), Carswell, Toronto, 1978.

Leslie Green, 'Low-Intensity Conflict and the Law' (1997) 3 *ILSA Journal of International and Comparative Law* 493.

Stephen Greenblatt, 'Murdering Peasants: Status, Genre, and the Representation of Rebellion' (1983) 1:1 *Representations* 1.

Stephen Greenblatt, *The Swerve: How the Renaissance Began*, Vintage Books, London, 2011.

Eldon Van Cleef Greenberg, 'Law and the Conduct of the Algerian Revolution' (1970) 11 *Harvard International Law Journal* 37.

Alan Greene, 'Defining Terrorism: One Size Fits All?' (2017) 66:2 *International and Comparative Law Quarterly* 411.

Charles Gregory, 'Doctrine of Continuous Voyage' (1910–1911) 24:3 *Harvard Law Review* 167.

Constantin von der Groeben, 'Criminal Responsibility of German Soldiers in Afghanistan: The Case of Colonel Klein' (2010) 11 *German Law Journal* 469.

Hugo Grotius, *On the Law of War and Peace* (5th Edition, 1646), edited and annotated by Stephen Neff, Cambridge University Press, Cambridge, 2012.

Douglas Guilfoyle, 'The Mavi Marmara Incident and Blockade in Armed Conflict' (2011) 81 *British Yearbook of International Law* 171.

Douglas Guilfoyle, 'Prosecuting Somali Pirates: A Critical Evaluation of the Options' (2012) 10:4 *Journal of International Criminal Justice* 76.

Green Hackworth, *Digest of International Law: Vol 2*, US Government Printing Office, Washington, DC, 1940–1944.

Sam Foster Halabi, 'Traditions of Belligerent Recognition: The Libyan Intervention in Historical and Theoretical Context' (2012) 27:2 *American University International Law Review* 321.

William Hall, *A Treatise on International Law* (3rd Edition), Clarendon Press, Oxford, 1890.

HW Halleck, *International Law; Or Rules Regulating the Intercourse of States in Peace and War*, van Nostrand, New York, 1861.

Neil Hanson, *The Confident Hope of a Miracle*, Corgi Books, London, 2003.

Vernon Harcourt, 'The Rights and Duties of Neutrals in Time of War: Part I' (1866) 9 *Journal of the Royal United Service Institution* 313.

Vernon Harcourt, 'The Rights and Duties of Neutrals in Time of War: Part II' (1866) 9 *Journal of the Royal United Services Institution* 329.

Vernon Harcourt, *Letters by Historicus on Some Questions of International Law*, MacMillan and Co, London, 1863 (Kraus Reprint Co, New York, 1971).

Thomas Harris, *The Trent Affair, Including a Review of English and American Relations at the Beginning of the Civil War*, Bobbs-Merrill Co, Indianapolis, 1896.

Pierre Hauck and Sven Peterke, 'Organised Crime and Gang Violence in National and International Law' (2010) 92:878 *International Review of the Red Cross* 407.

Jennifer Hazen, 'Understanding Gangs as Armed Groups' (2010) 92:878 *International Review of the Red Cross* 369.

Wolff Heintschel von Heinegg and Peter Dreist, 'The 2009 Kunduz Air Attack: The Decision of the Federal Prosecutor-General on the Dismissal of Criminal Proceedings Against Members of the German Armed Forces' (2010) 53 *German Yearbook of International Law* 833.

Wolff Heintschel von Heinegg, 'Methods and Means of Naval Warfare in Non-International Armed Conflicts' (2012) 88 *International Law Studies* 211.

Ian Henderson, 'Civilian Intelligence Agencies and the Use of Armed Drones' (2010) 13 *Yearbook of International Humanitarian Law* 133.

Ian Henderson and Bryan Cavanagh, 'Military Members Claiming Self-Defence during Armed Conflict: Often Misguided and Unhelpful', in Jadranka Petrovic, ed, *Accountability for Violations in International Humanitarian Law: Essays in Honour of Tim McCormack*, Routledge, Abingdon, 2016.

Elisabeth Henn, 'The Development of German Jurisprudence on Individual Compensation for Victims of Armed Conflicts: The Kunduz Case' (2014) 12:3 *Journal of International Criminal Justice* 615.

Amos Hershey, 'The Recognition of Cuban Belligerency' (1896) *Annals of the American Academy* 450.

Amos Hershey, 'The Venezuelan Affair in the Light of International Law' (May 1903) *The American Law Register* 249.

Amos Hershey, *The Essentials of International Public Law and Organization* (Revised Edition), Macmillan, New York, 1939.

Rosalyn Higgins, 'International Law and Civil Conflict', in Evan Luard, ed, *The International Regulation of Civil Wars*, Thames & Hudson, London, 1972.

JL Hilton, 'Theodor Mommsen and the Liberal Opposition to British Imperialism at the Time of the Second South African War of Independence (1899–1902)' (2014) 6:1 *Classical Receptions Journal* 48.

Duncan Hollis, 'Accountability in Chechnya—Addressing Internal Matters with Legal and Political International Norms' (1995) 36 *Boston College Law Review* 793.

Fred Hopkins, 'For Flag and Profit: The Life of Commodore John Daniel Danels of Baltimore' (1985) 80:4 *Maryland Historical Magazine* 392.

Fred Hopkins, 'For Freedom and Profit: Baltimore Privateers in the Wars of South American Independence' (2008) XVIII:3–4 *The Northern Mariner*, 93.

Charles Cheney Hyde, *International Law Chiefly as Interpreted and Applied by The United States: Volume I*, Little, Brown and Co, Boston, 1922.

David Ijalaye, 'Was "Biafra" at Any Time a State in International Law?' (1971) 65:3 *American Journal of International Law* 551.

Phillip Jessup, 'Force under a Modern Law of Nations' (1947) 25 *Foreign Affairs* 90.

Phillip Jessup, 'Should International Law Recognise an Intermediate Status between Peace and War?' (1954) 48 *American Journal of International Law* 98.

Philip Jessup, *A Modern Law of Nations: An Introduction*, Archon Books, Hamden, 1968.

DHN Johnson, 'Piracy in Modern International Law' (1953) 43 *Transactions of the Grotius Society* 63.

Howard Jones, *Blue and Gray Diplomacy: A History of Union and Confederate Foreign Relations*, University of North Carolina Press, Chapel Hill, 2010.

'Judicial Decisions: House of Lords, *Government of Republic of Spain v. SS Arantzazu Mendi*, February 23, 1939' (1939) 33:3 *American Journal of International Law* 583.

William Kaufmann, *British Policy and the Independence of Latin America, 1804–1828*, Yale University Press, New Haven, 1951.

Keesing's Record of World Events: Volume 13 (1967), Issue No. 6 (June).

Keesing's Record of World Events: Volume 14 (1968), Issue No. 12 (December).

Joshua Kelly, 'Re Civilian Casualty Court Martial: Prosecuting Breaches of International Humanitarian Law Using the Australian Military Justice System' (2013) 37:2 *Melbourne University Law Review* 342.

James Kent, *Kent's Commentary on International Law* (2nd Edition, J. Abdy, ed), Deighton Bell, Cambridge, 1878.

Daoud Khairallah, *Insurrection under International Law with Emphasis on the Rights and Duties of Insurgents*, Lebanese University, Beirut, 1973.

Donald deKieffer and David Hartquist, 'Transkei: A Legitimate Birth' (1977–1978) 13 *New England Law Review* 428.

Charles King, 'Revolutionary War, Guerrilla Warfare, and International Law' (1971–1972) 4 *Case Western Reserve Journal of International Law* 91.

Jann Kleffner, 'The Applicability of International Humanitarian Law to Organized Armed Groups' (2011) 93:882 *International Review of the Red Cross* 443.

Baron SA Korff, 'The Ninth International Red Cross Conference' (1912) 6:4 *American Journal of International Law* 858.

James Kraska, 'Rule Selection in the Case of Israel's Naval Blockade of Gaza: Law of Naval Warfare or Law of the Sea?' (2010) 13 *Yearbook of International Humanitarian Law* 367.

Michel Krauss, 'Internal Conflicts and Foreign States: In Search of the State of the Law' (1978–1979) 5 *Yale Studies in World Public Order* 173.

Claus Kreβ and Frederic Megret, 'The Regulation of Non-International Armed Conflicts: Can a Privilege of Belligerency Be Envisioned in the Law of Non-International Armed Conflicts?' (2015) 96:893 *International Review of the Red Cross* 29.

John Kutolowski, 'Mid-Victorian Public Opinion, Polish Propaganda, and the Uprising of 1863' (1969) 8:2 *Journal of British Studies* 86.

Pieter Kuyper, 'Recognition: Netherlands Theory and State Practice', in HF van Panhuys et al, eds, *International Law in The Netherlands: Volume I*, TMC Asser, The Hague, 1978.

John Laband, 'Burying the Union Jack: British Loyalists in the Transvaal during the First Anglo-Boer War, 1880–1881' (2004) 4:1 *History of Intellectual Culture* 1.

John Laband, *The Transvaal Rebellion: The First Boer War, 1880–1881*, Pearson Longman, Harlow, 2005.

Andrew Lambert, *Admirals*, Faber and Faber, London, 2008.

Walter Laqueur, *Guerrilla Warfare: A Historical and Critical Study*, Transaction Publishers, New Brunswick, 1976.

Elihu Lauterpacht, 'The Legal Irrelevance of the "State of War"' (1968) 62 *Proceedings of the American Society of International Law at Its Annual Meeting (1921–1969)* 58.

Hersch Lauterpacht, 'Revolutionary Activities by Private Persons Against Foreign States' (1928) 22:1 *American Journal of International Law* 105.

Hersch Lauterpacht, *Recognition in International Law*, Cambridge University Press, Cambridge, 1947.

TJ Lawrence, *The Principles of International Law*, Macmillan, London, 1900.

Julia Leikin, '"The Prostitution of the Russian Flag": Privateers in Russian Admiralty Courts, 1787–98' (2017) 35:4 *Law and History Review* 1049.

David Letts and Rob McLaughlin, 'Law of Naval Warfare', in Rain Liivoja and Tim McCormack, eds, *Routledge Handbook of the Law of Armed Conflict*, Routledge, Abingdon, 2016.

Yair Lootsteen, 'The Concept of Belligerency in International Law' (2000) 166 *Military Law Review* 109.

James Lorimer, *The Institutes of the Law of Nations*, Blackwood and Sons, London, 1883.

Evan Luard, 'Civil Conflicts in Modern International Relations', in Evan Luard, ed, *The International Regulation of Civil Wars*, New York University Press, New York, 1972.

Evan Luard, 'Conclusions', in Evan Luard, ed, *The International Regulation of Civil Wars*, New York University Press, New York, 1972.

Lucan, *The Civil War: Books I–X (Pharsalia)*, I.1-8 (Trans. J D McDuff), William Heinemann, London, 1928.

Martin Luther, *Against the Robbing and Murdering Hordes of Peasants*, May 1525.

Campbell McLachlan, *Foreign Relations Law*, Cambridge University Press, Cambridge, 2014.

Rob McLaughlin, 'The Legal Regime Applicable to Use of Lethal Force When Operating under a United Nations Security Council Chapter VII Mandate Authorising "All Necessary Means"' (2007) 12:3 *Journal of Conflict and Security Law* 389.

Rob McLaughlin, 'The Use of Lethal Force by Military Forces on Law Enforcement Operations—Is There a "Lawful Authority"?' (2009) 37:3 *Federal Law Review* 441.

Rob McLaughlin, 'Legal-Policy Considerations and Conflict Characterisation at the Threshold between Law Enforcement and Non-International Armed Conflict' (2012) 13:1 *Melbourne Journal of International Law* 94.

Rob McLaughlin and Dale Stephens, 'International Humanitarian Law in the Maritime Context: Characterization in Judicial and Quasi-Judicial Contexts', in Derek Jinks, Jackson Maogoto, and Solon Solomon, eds, *Applying International Humanitarian Law in Judicial and Quasi-Judicial Bodies*, TMC Asser Press, The Hague, 2014.

Rob McLaughlin, 'The Law Applicable to Naval Mine Warfare in a Non-International Armed Conflict' (2014) 90 *International Law Studies* 475.

Arnold McNair, 'The Law Relating to the Civil War in Spain' (1937) 53 *The Law Quarterly Review* 471.

Arnold McNair, *International Law Opinions: Selected and Annotated*, Cambridge University Press, Cambridge, 1956.

Arnold McNair and Arthur Watts, *The Legal Effects of War*, Cambridge University Press, Cambridge, 1966.

Vidya Dhar Mahajan, *Public International Law* (5th Edition), Eastern Book Co, Lucknow, 1974.

Alfred Thayer Mahan, 'The Merits of the Transvaal Dispute' (1900) 170:520 *The North American Review* 312.

Thomas Maissen, 'The 1848 Conflicts and their Significance in Swiss Historiography', in Michael Butler et al, eds, *The Making of Modern Switzerland, 1848–1998*, St Martin's Press, London, 2000.

Dennis Mandsager, Alan Cole, Phillip Drew, and Rob McLaughlin, *Sanremo Handbook on Rules of Engagement*, International Institute of Humanitarian Law, San Remo, 2009.

Shula Marks and Stanley Trapido, 'Lord Milner and the South African State' (1979) 8 *History Workshop* 50.

Georg von Martens, *The Law of Nations*, 4th Edition translated and published by William Cobbett, London, 1829.

Konstantinos Mastorodimos, 'Belligerency Recognition: Past, Present and Future' (2014) 29 *Connecticut Journal of International Law* 301.

Samuel Menefee, 'Piracy, Terrorism, and the Insurgent Passenger: A Historical and Legal Perspective', in Natalino Ronzitti, ed, *Maritime Terrorism and International Law*, Martinus Nijhof, The Hague, 1990.

Theodor Meron, *Human Rights in Internal Strife: Their International Protection*, Grotius Publications, Cambridge, 1987.

Theodor Meron, *Henry's Wars and Shakespeare's Laws: Perspectives on the Laws of War in the Latter Middle Ages*, Clarendon Press, Oxford, 1993.

Erik Midelfort, 'The Revolution of 1525? Recent Studies of the Peasants' War' (1978) 11:2 *Central European History* 189.

Marko Milanovic and Vidan Hadzi-Vidanovic, 'A Taxonomy of Armed Conflict', in *Research Handbook on International Conflict and Security Law*, in Nigel White and Christian Henderson, eds, Edward Elgar, Cheltenham, 2013.

Lindsay Moir, 'The Historical Development of the Application of Humanitarian Law in Non-International Armed Conflicts to 1949' (1998) 47 *International and Comparative Law Quarterly* 337.

Lindsay Moir, *The Law of Internal Armed Conflict*, Cambridge University Press, Cambridge, 2002.

John Bassett Moore, *A Digest of International Law: Volume I*, US Government Printing Office, Washington, DC, 1906.

John Norton Moore, 'The Control of Foreign Intervention in Internal Conflict' (1969) 9:2 *Virginia Journal of International Law* 5.

John Norton Moore, 'Legal Standards for Intervention in Internal Conflicts' (1983) 13 *Georgia Journal of International and Comparative Law* 191.

Orby Mootham, 'The Doctrine of Continuous Voyage, 1756–1815' (1927) 8 *British Yearbook of International Law* 62.

Madeline Morris, 'Terrorism: The Politics of Prosecution' (2005) 5:2 *Chicago Journal of International Law* 406.

Martin Murphy, 'Suppression of Piracy and Maritime Terrorism: A Suitable Role for a Navy?' (2007) 60:3 *Naval War College Review* 23.

Darragh Murray, *Human Rights Obligations of Non-State Armed Groups*, Bloomsbury, London, 2016.

Bill Nasson, 'The Jameson Raid of Its Day' (2006) 47:2 *The Journal of African History* 335.

Stephen Neff, *War and the Law of Nations: A General History*, Cambridge University Press, Cambridge, 2005.

Fred K Nielsen, 'Insurgency and Maritime Law' (1937) 31 *American Society of International Law Proceedings* 144.

Timo Noetzel, 'The German Politics of War: Kunduz and the War in Afghanistan' (2011) 87:2 *International Affairs* 397.

Lester Nurick and Roger Barrett, 'Legality of Guerrilla Forces under the Laws of War' (1946) 40 *American Journal of International Law* 563.

DP O'Connell, *The Influence of Law on Sea Power*, Naval Institute Press, Annapolis, 1975.

Aidan O'Hara, 'Judge Charles Daly and the New York Irish in the Era of the Civil War', in Arthur H Mitchell, ed, *Fighting Irish in the American Civil War and the Invasion of Mexico: Essays*, McFarland and Co, Jefferson, 2017.

Vernon O'Rourke, 'Recognition of Belligerency and the Spanish War' (1937) 31:3 *American Journal of International Law* 398.

Heiko Oberman, 'The Gospel of Social Unrest: 450 Years after the So-Called "German Peasants' War" of 1525' (1976) 69 *Harvard Theological Review* 103.

Roscoe Oglesby, *Internal War and the Search for Normative Order*, Martinus Nijhof, The Hague, 1971.

Jens Ohlin, 'The Combatant's Privilege in Asymmetric and Covert Conflicts' (2015) 40 *Yale Journal of International Law* 337.

Chris Okeke, *Controversial Subjects of Contemporary International Law*, Rotterdam University Press, Rotterdam, 1974.

Lassa Oppenheim, *International Law—A Treatise: Volume II Disputes, War and Neutrality*, Longmans, Green and Co, London, 1906.

Lassa Oppenheim, *International Law. A Treatise 6th Edition: Volume 2 Disputes, War and Neutrality* (Hersch Lauterpacht, ed), Longmans, London, 1944.

Lassa Openheim, *International Law. A Treatise 7th Edition Volume 1 Peace* (Hersch Lauterpacht, ed), Longmans, London, 1948.

Lassa Oppenheim, *International Law. A Treatise 7th Edition: Volume 2 Disputes, War and Neutrality* (Hersch Lauterpacht, ed), Longmans, London, 1952.

Laurence Orzell, 'A "Favourable Interval": The Polish Insurrection in Civil War Diplomacy, 1863' (1978) 24:4 *Civil War History* 332.

Bruce Oswald, 'The Harmonization Project: Improving Compliance with the Law of War in Non- International Armed Conflicts' (2014) 53 *Columbia Journal of Transnational Law* 105.

Norman Padelford, 'Foreign Shipping During the Spanish Civil War' (1938) 32:2 *American Journal of International Law* 264.

Norman Padelford, *International Law and Diplomacy in the Spanish Civil Strife*, Macmillan, New York, 1939.

Tamsin Paige, 'Piracy and Universal Jurisdiction' (2013) 12 *Macquarie Law Journal* 131.

Stanley Palmer, 'Review: *The Transvaal Rebellion: The First Boer War, 1880–1881*' (2006) 48:3 *Victorian Studies* 571.

Haro Van Panhuys, 'Aircraft Hijacking and International Law' (1970) 9 *Columbia Journal Transnational Law* 1.

'Part IV—Piracy' (1932) 26 *American Journal of International Law* (Supplement) 743.

Clive Parry (ed), *Law Officers' Opinions to the Foreign Office 1793–1860*, Gregg International, Farnborough, 1973 (97 Vols).

Jordan Paust, Cherif Bassiouni, et al, *International Criminal Law: Cases and Materials* (4th Edition), Carolina Academic Press, Durham, 2013.

Jordan Paust, 'NIAC Nonsense, the Afghan War, and Combatant Immunity' (2015–2016) 44:3 *Georgia Journal of International and Comparative Law* 555.

Jelena Pejic, 'Status of Conflict', in Elizabeth Wilmshurst and Susa Breau, eds), *Perspectives on the ICRC Study on Customary International Humanitarian Law*, Cambridge University Press, Cambridge, 2007.

Jean Pictet, 'The New Geneva Conventions for the Protection of War Victims' (1951) 45 *American Journal of International Law* 462.

George Politakis, *Modern Aspects of the Laws of Naval Warfare and Maritime Neutrality*, Kegan Paul, London, 1988.

Paul A Povlock, 'A Guerrilla War at Sea: The Sri Lankan Civil War' (2011) *Small Wars Journal* (online).

George Prugh, *Law at War: Vietnam 1964–1973*, Department of the Army, Washington, DC, 1975.

Julius Puente, *International Law as Applied to Foreign States*, Burdette Smith, Chicago, 1928.

Christopher Quaye, *Liberation Struggles in International Law*, Temple University Press, Philadelphia, 1991.

David Raby, 'Transatlantic Intrigues: Humberto Delgado, Henrique Galvao and the Portuguese Exiles in Brazil and Morocco' (2004) 3:3 *Portuguese Journal of Social Science* 143.

Sasha Radin, 'The Current Relevance of the Recognition of Belligerency', in Marcel Brus et al, eds, *International Law between Conflict and Peacetime: In Search of the Human Face*, Asser Press, The Hague, 2013.

Walter Rech, 'Rightless Enemies: Schmitt and Lauterpacht on Political Piracy' (2012) 32:2 *Oxford Journal of Legal Studies* 235.

Tyson Reeder, '"Sovereign Lords" and "Dependent Administrators": Artigan Privateers, Atlantic Borderwaters, and State Building in the Early Nineteenth Century' (2016) *Journal of American History* 323.

Enoch Resnick, 'Spain's Reaction to Portugal's Invasion of the Banda Oriental in 1816' (1972) 73:74 *Revista de Historia de America* 131.

'Rights and Duties of Neutral States in Naval and Aerial War' (1939) 33 *American Journal of International Law* (Supplement) 167.

David Roe and Russell Osgood, 'United States Supreme Court February Term 1824' (1974–1975) 84 *Yale Law Journal* 770.

Gabor Rona, 'Is There a Way Out of the Non-International Armed Conflict Dilemma?' (2015) 91 *International Law Studies* 32.

Natalino Ronzitti (ed), *The Law of Naval Warfare: A Collection of Agreements and Documents with Commentaries*, Martinus Nijhof, The Hague, 1988.

Alfred Rubin, 'The Status of Rebels under the Geneva Conventions of 1949' (1972) 21:3 *International and Comparative Law Quarterly* 472.

Alfred Rubin, 'Is Piracy Illegal?' (1976) 70 *American Journal of International Law* 92.

Tom Ruys and Luca Ferro, 'Weathering the Storm: Legality and Legal Implications of the Saudi-Led Military Intervention in Yemen' (2016) 65:1 *International and Comparative Law Quarterly* 61.

Joel Samuels, 'The Full Story of United States v. Smith, America's Most Important Piracy Case' (2012) 1:2 *Penn State Journal of Law and International Affairs* 320.

Deborah Sanders, *Maritime Power in the Black Sea*, Routledge, London, 2016.

Andrew Sanger, 'The Contemporary Law of Blockade and the Gaza Freedom Flotilla' (2010) 13 *Yearbook of International Humanitarian Law* 397.

Soliman M Santos Jr, 'Correspondent's Reports: The Philippines' (2003) 6 *Yearbook of International Humanitarian Law* 561.

Marco Sassoli, 'Query: Is There a Status of "Unlawful Combatant"?' (2006) 80 *International Law Studies* 57.

Michael Schmitt, Charles Garraway, and Yoram Dinstein, *The Manual on the Law of Non-International Armed Conflict with Commentary*, International Institute of Humanitarian Law, San Remo, 2006.

Michael Schmitt, 'The Status of Opposition Fighters in a Non-International Armed Conflict' (2011) 88 *International Law Studies* 119.

Michael Schmitt, 'Wound, Capture, or Kill: A Reply to Ryan Goodman's "The Power to Kill or Capture Enemy Combatants"' (2013) 24:3 *European Journal of International Law* 855.

Michael Schmitt (ed), *Tallinn Manual 2.0 on the International Law Applicable to Cyber Operations*, Cambridge University Press, Cambridge, 2017.

Constantin Schüßler and Yee-Kuang Heng, 'The Bundeswehr and the Kunduz Air Strike 4 September 2009: Germany's Post-Heroic Moment?' (2013) 22:3 *European Security* 355.

Georg Schwarzenberger, 'Jus Pacis Ac Belli' (1943) 37 *American Journal of International Law* 460.

Georg Schwarzenberger, 'Human Rights and Guerrilla Warfare' (1971) 1 *Israel Yearbook on Human Rights* 246.

Haig Silvanie, *Responsibility of States for Acts of Unsuccessful Insurgent Governments*, Columbia University Press, New York, 1939.

Sandesh Sivakumaran, *The Law of Non-International Armed Conflict*, Oxford University Press, Oxford, 2012.

Herbert Smith, *Great Britain and the Law of Nations*, King & Son, London, 1932.

Joseph Smith, 'Britain and the Brazilian Naval Revolt of 1893–4' (1970) 2:2 *Journal of Latin American Studies* 175.

Justin Smith, *The War with Mexico: Volume II*, MacMillan, New York, 1919.

Rhea Smith, 'Book Review: *Santa Maria: My Crusade for Portugal*, by Henrique Galavao' (1962) 42:4 *The Hispanic American Historical Review* 578.

Louis Sohn, 'The Role of the United Nations in Civil Wars' (1963) 57 *Proceedings of the American Society of International Law* 208.

Dawn Steinhoff, 'Talking to the Enemy: State Legitimacy Concerns with Engaging Non-State Armed Groups' (2009) 45 *Texas International Law Journal* 297.

James G Stewart, 'Towards a Single Definition of Armed Conflict in International Humanitarian Law: A Critique of Internationalised Armed Conflict' (2003) 85:850 *International Review of the Red Cross* 313.

Ellery Stowell, *Intervention in International Law*, John Byrne & Co, Washington, DC, 1921.

Keith Surridge, 'Rebellion, Martial Law and British Civil-Military Relations: The War in Cape Colony 1899–1902' (1997) 8:2 *Small Wars and Insurgencies* 35.

Casper Sylvest, '"Our Passion for Legality": International Law and Imperialism in Late Nineteenth-Century Britain' (2008) 34:3 *Review of International Studies* 403.

Felicity Szesnat and Annie Bird, 'Columbia', in Elizabeth Wilmshurst, ed, *International Law and the Classification of Conflicts*, Oxford University Press, Oxford, 2012

Hannis Taylor, *A Treatise on Public International Law*, Callaghan and Co, Chicago, 1901.

Grant Richard Telfer, 'Maritime Insurgency and the Law of the Sea: An Analysis Using the Doctrine of Distress' (1982–1983) 20 *San Diego Law Review* 625.

Ann van Wynen and AJ Thomas Jr, 'International Legal Aspects of the Civil War in Spain', in Richard Falk, ed, *The International Law of Civil War*, Johns Hopkins Press, Baltimore, 1971.

IP Trainin, 'Questions of Guerrilla Warfare in the Law of War' (1946) 40 *American Journal of International Law* 534.

Transvaal Independence Committee, *A Reply to Sir Bartle Frere's Letter to 'The Times', 25 Feb., 1881 and a Letter on the Subject of Alleged Slavery in the Transvaal* (reprinted from 'The Daily News', 23 Feb. 1881) by Geo. P. Moodie, William Ridgway, London, 1881.

Daniel Tretiak, 'China's Vietnam War and its Consequences' (1979) 80 *The China Quarterly* 740.

Robert Tucker, 'The Law of War and Neutrality at Sea' (1955) 50 *International Law Studies* 1.

Emer de Vattel, *The Law of Nations or the Principles of Natural Law* (1758 Edition), Trans. Charles Fenwick (1916), Oceana Publications, New York, 1964.

Ferenc Vali, 'The Santa Maria Case' (1961–1962) 56 *Northwestern University Law Review* 168.

Thomas Walker, *A Manual of Public International Law*, Cambridge University Press, Cambridge, 1895.

Wyndham Walker, 'Recognition of Belligerency and Grant of Belligerent Rights' (1937) 23 *Transactions of the Grotius Society* 177.

Kenneth Watkin, 'Opportunity Lost: Organized Armed Groups and the ICRC Direct Participation in Hostilities Interpretive Guidance' (2009) 42:3 *New York University Journal of International Law and Politics* 641.

Kenneth Watkin, *Fighting at the Legal Boundaries: Controlling Use of Force in Contemporary Conflict*, Oxford University Press, Oxford, 2016.

Charles Webster (ed), *Britain and the Independence of Latin America, 1812–1830: Select Documents from the Foreign Office Archives*, Oxford University Press, London, 1938.

Henryk Wereszycki, 'Great Britain and the Polish Question in 1863' (1935) 50:197 *The English Historical Review* 78.

Francis Wharton, *A Digest of the International Law of the United States*, US Government Printing Office, Washington, DC, 1887.

Henry Wheaton, *Elements of International Law* (1866 Edition, Richard Dana, ed), Oceana, NY, 1964 reprint.

GJ Wheeler, *Foreign Enlistment Act, 1870, 33 & 34 Vict. c. 90.: With Notes of the Leading Cases on This and the American Act*, London, 1896.

Joseph Wieczerzak, 'American Reactions to the Polish Insurrection of 1863' (1965) 22:2 *Polish American Studies* 90.

David Williamson, *The Polish Underground, 1939–1947*, Pen and Sword Books, Yorkshire, 2012.

George Grafton Wilson, 'Insurgency and International Maritime Law' (1907) 1:1 *American Journal of International Law* 46.

Heather Wilson, *International Law and the Use of Force by National Liberation Movements*, Clarendon Press, Oxford, 1990.

Peter Wilson, *Heart of Europe: A History of the Holy Roman Empire*, Belknap Press, Cambridge, MA, 2016.

Robert Wilson, 'Recognition of Insurgency and Belligerency' (1937) 31 *American Society of International Law Proceedings* 136.

Theodore Woolsey, 'The Consequences of Cuban Belligerency' (1892–1896) 5 *Yale Law Journal* 182.

Lester Woolsey, 'Early Cases on the Doctrine of Continuous Voyages' (1910) 4:4 *American Journal of International Law* 823.

Quincy Wright, 'International Law and the American Civil War' (1921–1969) 61 *Proceedings of The American Society of International Law at its Annual Meeting* (27–29 April 1967) 50.

Adam Zamoyski, *Rites of Peace: The Fall of Napoleon and the Congress of Vienna*, Harper Press, London, 2007.

Adam Zamoyski, *Poland: A History*, William Collins, London, 2009.

Liesbeth Zegveld, *The Accountability of Armed Opposition Groups in International Law*, Cambridge University Press, Cambridge, 2002.

Charles Zorgbibe, 'Sources of the Recognition of Belligerent Status' (1977) 17:192 *International Review of the Red Cross* 111.

Michal Zourek, 'Operation MANUEL: When Prague Was a Key Transit Hub for International Terrorism' (2015) 3 *Central European Journal of International and Security Studies* 78.

Simone Zurbuchen, 'Emer de Vattel on the Society of Nations and the Political System of Europe', in Stefan Kadelbach, Thomas Kleinlein, and David Roth-Isigkeit, eds, *System, Order, and International Law: The Early History of International Legal Thought from Machiavelli to Hegel*, Oxford University Press, Oxford, 2017.

Anna van Zwanenberg, 'Interference with Ships on the High Seas' (1961) 10:4 *International and Comparative Law Quarterly* 785.

Cases

The Schooner Exchange v. McFaddon, US 7 Cranch 116 (1812).

US v. Palmer, 16 US 610 (1818).

Divina Pastora, 17 US 52 (1819).

US v. Smith, 18 US 153 (1820).

The Santissima Trinidad and the St Sander, 20 US 283 (1822).

The Gran Para, 20 US 471 (1822).

La Nereyda, 21 US 8 Wheat. 108 (1823).

R v. Tunkoo Mahomed Saad and Others (1840), 2 Ky (Cr 18) (in Clive Parry and J Hopkins, *Commonwealth International Law Cases: Vol I*, Oceana Publications, New York, 1974).

The Magellan Pirates [1853], 1 Sap Ecc & Ad 81 July 26 1853.

The Prize Cases, 2 Black 635 (1862).

Attorney-General v. Sillem and Others (1863), 176 ER 295.

The Chesapeake (1864), Vice-Admiralty Court of New Brunswick (extracted in Norman MacKenzie and Lionel Laing, eds, *Canada and the Law of Nations*, Ryerson Press, Toronto, 1938, pp 528–529).

Hawkins v. Filkins, 24 Ark. 286 (1866).

Mauran v. Insurance Company, 73 US (6 Wall.) 1 (1867).

Thorington v. Smith, 75 US 1 (1868).

The Queen v. James Carlin (ship 'Salvador' (Bahamas)) [1870], UKPC 25.

Planters' Bank v. Union Bank, 83 US 483 (1872).

Williams v. Bruffy, 96 US 176 (1877).

Ford v. Surget, 97 US 594 (1878).

The Ambrose Light, 25 Fed. 408 (1885).

The Three Friends, 166 US 1 (1897).

Warner Barnes and Co v. US, 40 Ct Cl 1, 29 (1904).

Republic of Bolivia v. Indemnity Mutual Marine Assurance Co Ltd (1909), 1 KB 785.

Eastern Carrying Insurance Company v National Benefit Life and Property Insurance Co Ltd (1919), 35 TLR 292.

Curtis and Sons v. Mathews [1919], 1 KB 425.

Luther v. James Sagor and Co [1921], 3 KB 532.

Spanish Government v. The North of England Steamship Company (1938), 54 TLR 852

R v. Frost and Eleven Others (1939), 9 Carrington & Payne 129.

Government of Republic of Spain v. SS Arantzazu Mendi [1939], AC 256.

Shaw Savill & Albion Company Ltd v. The Commonwealth (1940), 66 CLR 344.

The Hostages Trial: Trial of Wilhelm List and Others (1948), United States Military Tribunal, Nuremberg.

Corfu Channel Case, Judgment, (1949) ICJ Reports 4.

The Fjeld (1950), 17 ILR 345.

Luigi Monta of Genoa v. Cechofracht Co Ltd [1956], 2 All ER 769.

Societe Purafina Francaise v. Cie. D'Assurances la Nationale (1962), 44 ILR 439.

Legal Consequences for States of the Continued Presence of South Africa in Namibia (South West Africa) notwithstanding Security Council Resolution 276 (1970), ICJ Advisory Opinion of 21 June 1971.

Nicaragua Case (Merits) (1986), ICJ Rep 14.

Prosecutor v Tadic Case No. IT-94-1-AR72, ICTY, Decision on the Defence Motion for Interlocutory Appeal on Jurisdiction, 2 October 1995.

Hamdan v. Rumsfeld, 548 US 557 (2006).

Nasser Al-Aulaqi v. Barack H Obama, et al, Civil Action No.10-1469 (JDB), District of Columbia District Court, 7 December 2010.

Re Civilian Casualty Court Martial (2011), 259 FLR 208.

Hassan v. UK (Judgment of Grand Chamber), Eur. Ct. H.R. (2014).

Serdar Mohammed v. MOD [2014], EWHC 1369 (QB).

Serdar Mohammed v. MOD [2015], EWCA Civ 843.

Serdar Mohammed v. MOD [2017], UKSC 1 & [2017] UKSC 2.

R v. Alexander Wayne Blackman [2017], EWCA Crim 190.

Select treaties and international instruments

The Webster-Ashburton Treaty. Treaty to Settle and Define the Boundaries between the Territories of the United States and the Possessions of Her Britannic Majesty in North America, for the Final Suppression of the African Slave Trade, and for the Giving Up of Criminals Fugitive from Justice, in Certain Cases, Washington 9 August 1842.

Sand River Convention 1852.

Orange River (Bloemfontein) Convention 1854.

Paris Declaration 1856.

Treaty between United States and Great Britain for the Suppression of the Slave Trade, Washington, DC, 7 April 1862.

Treaty of Washington: Treaty between Her Majesty and the United States of America, Washington, 8 May 1871.

Convention of Pretoria 1881.

London Convention 1884.

Vereeniging Peace Treaty 1902.

Convention IV Respecting the Laws and Customs of War on Land and Its Annex: Regulations Concerning the Laws and Customs of War on Land 1907.

Hague Convention XIII Concerning the Rights and Duties of Neutral Powers in Naval War 1907.

Declaration Concerning the Laws of Naval War ('*London Declaration*') 26 February 1909 (3 *American Journal of International Law* (Supplement) 186).

Inter-American Convention on the Rights and Duties of States in Event of Civil Strife, Havana, 20 February 1928 (134 LNTS 45).

Montevideo Convention on the Rights and Duties of States 1933 [1936], LNTS CLXV No. 3802.

Nyon Agreement, 1937.
Geneva Convention, I 1949.
Geneva Convention, II 1949.
Geneva Convention, III 1949.
Inter-American Treaty of Reciprocal Assistance 1947 (Rio Treaty).
1957 Protocol to The Convention on Duties and Rights of States in the Event of Civil Strife (1928 Havana Convention).
1977 *Additional Protocol I.*
1977 *Additional Protocol II.*
Convention on the Prohibition of the Development, Production, Stockpiling and Use of Chemical Weapons and on Their Destruction, 1993.

News reports

'Details of the Surrender; Reported Change of Crew; the Crew of the Shenandoah', *The New York Times*, 21 November 1865.
'The Annexation of the Transvaal', *The Spectator*, 12 May 1877.
'President Grant on Belligerency', *The Daily Evening Telegraph—Philadelphia*, 25 July 1879.
'The Ambrose Light', *The New York Times*, 8 June 1885.
'Cuba', *The Wichita Daily Eagle*, 7 December 1897.
'War Legislation of the Senate', *The National Tribune*, 30 July 1903.
'British Isolate Falke Filibusters: Trinidad Authorities Forbid Supplying of Venezuelan Rebel Ship at Port of Spain', *New York Times*, 16 August 1929.
'Falke with "Admiral" Stuck at Trinidad: Skipper Tells of Rank Conferred by Venezuelan Rebels and of Flying "Liberation Colors"', *New York Times*, 17 August 1929.
'Venezuelan Rebels Rout Federal Force: Hold Cumana Against Attack of Troops and Plane—Junta Ridicules Falke Report', *New York Times*, 21 August 1929.
'Insurrection Is Not Piracy: Doubts about Right to Intervene', *The Guardian*, 25 January 1961.
'Russia Reaffirms Neutrality', *Civil Georgia*, 16 March 2004.
Kiraz Janicke, 'Venezuelan Legislature Supports Belligerent Status for Colombian Rebels', *Venezuela Analysis*, 19 January 2008.
Chris Krual, 'Chavez Keeps Up Campaign to Get Rebels off Terrorist List', *Los Angeles Times*, 20 January 2008.
'Bolivar's Sword: Venezuela's Recognition of the Colombian Insurgency', *Pravda*, 25 January 2008.
'The FARC Files', *The Economist*, 22 May 2008.
Dan Karpenchuk, 'NATO Troops to Go after Afghan Drug Lords', *ABC*, 7 February 2009.
Walter Jayawardhana, 'Captain Ali, a Ship Carrying Alleged LTTE Cargo Seized by Sri Lanka Navy during the Wee Hours of Thursday', *Lanka Web*, 4 June 2009.
'Georgia: Abkhazia Protests Blockade', *New York Times*, 21 August 2009.
'Russia to Protect Ships Bound to Abkhazia', *Civil Georgia (online)*, 29 August 2009.
'Russian Warns Georgia Against Ship Seizures', *Civil Georgia (online)*, 3 September 2009.
Daniel McLaughlin, 'Georgia to Meet Russians over Abkhazia Sea Blockade', *Irish Times*, 8 September 2009.
Salah Nasrawi, 'Saudi Arabia Imposes Naval Blockade on Coast of Northern Yemen', *The Washington Post*, 11 November 2009.

David Smith, 'Rwandan Soldiers Joined Forces with Congo Rebels, UN Told', *The Guardian*, 4 December 2012.

'Kunduz Bombing: German Court Drops Case Over Civilian Deaths', *Spiegel Online*, 11 December 2013.

Thomas Ruttig, 'The Incident at Coordinate 42S VF 8934 5219: German Court Rejects Claim from Kunduz Air Strike Victims', *Afghanistan Analysts*, 15 December 2013.

Greg Botelho and Saeed Ahmed, 'Saudi-Led Coalition Strikes Rebels in Yemen, Inflaming Tensions in Region', *CNN*, 27 March 2015.

Peter Layton, 'How Sri Lanka Won the War', *The Diplomat*, 9 April 2015.

Mohammad Mukashaf, 'Pakistan Declines Saudi Call for Armed Support in Yemen Fight', *Reuters*, 10 April 2015.

'Yemen Conflict: Aid Effort Begins as Truce Takes Hold', *BBC*, 13 May 2015.

'Judges Quash UK Marine Alexander Blackman's Murder Conviction - Briton Who Killed Injured Taliban Fighter Found Guilty of Manslaughter on Grounds of Diminished Responsibility Instead', *The Guardian*, 15 March 2017.

'Syria War: A Brief Guide to Who's Fighting Whom', *BBC News*, 7 April 2017.

Faysal Itani, 'The End of American Support for Syrian Rebels Was Inevitable', *The Atlantic*, 21 July 2017.

Bethan McKernan, 'Turkish Troops Enter Syria in Major Operation to Support Anti-Assad Rebels', *The Independent*, 9 October 2017.

Bethan McKernan, 'Saudi Arabia Lifts Blockade on Yemen Air and Seaports to Allow in Vital Aid', *The Independent*, 22 November 2017.

'The War the World Ignores', *The Economist*, 2 December 2017.

'From Bad to Worse', *The Economist*, 2 December 2017.

SELECTED GOVERNMENTAL DOCUMENTS AND ARCHIVAL SOURCES

Australia

Australian Defence Doctrine Publication (ADDP) 06.4 *Law of Armed Conflict*, Australian Department of Defence, May 2006.

Columbia

'Columbia: Statement of Government of Columbia regarding the Status of FARC, 16 June 1999' (1999), 2 *Yearbook of International Humanitarian Law* 440.

France

Letter Dated 25 October 1956 from the Representative of France Addressed to the Secretary-General (S/3689).

Israel

Turkel Commission, The Public Commission to Examine the Maritime Incident of 31 May 2010: Part I ('Turkel Report') (2011).

Nigeria

'Operational Code of Conduct for the Nigerian Army', July 1967, in AHM Kirk-Greene, *Crisis and Conflict in Nigeria: A Documentary Sourcebook, 1966–70*, Volume I, Oxford University Press, Oxford, 1971.

United Kingdom

HL Deb 05 March 1833 vol 16 cc196-9.
HC Deb 29 March 1833 vol 16 cc1236-83.
HL Deb 05 February 1863 vol 169 cc8-64.
HC Deb 15 August 1901 vol 99 cc978-1051.
HC Deb 20 January 1902 vol 101 cc324-436.
HC Deb 24 January 1961 vol 633 col 32-35.
HC Deb 27 February 1961 vol 635 cc1196-7.
HC Deb 27 August 1968 vol 769 cc1433-534.
Report of the Committee of Privy Counsellors appointed to inquire into the recruitment of mercenaries, Cmnd. 6569, August 1976 (the 'Diplock Report').
British Foreign Office Policy Document No. 148, dated July 1984 (extracted in (1986), 57 *British Yearbook of International Law* 614).
UK Ministry of Defence, *The Manual of the Law of Armed Conflict*, Oxford University Press, Oxford, 2004.

UK Archives Files

ADM 116/5752
ADM 116/5713
ADM 116/5862
ADM 116/6315
ADM 128/47
CAB/24/264
CAB/24/265
CAB/24/268
CAB 37/63
CAB/66/54/12
CAB/128/42
CAB/128/43
CAB/128/44
CAB/129/139
CAB/129/140
CAB/129/146
CO 137/661
CO 321/62
FO 72/1302
FO 179/585
FO 371/112062
FO 371/120939
FO 371/135884
FO 371/144071
FO 371/160248
FO 371/160249
FO 371/160755
FO 371 - WS 1483/1
FO 371 - WS 1483/6
FO 417/311

FO 800/924
FO 881/43
FO 881/996
FO 881/1012
FO 881/1014
FO 881/1048
FO 881/2068
FO 881/2897
FO 881/4854X
FO 881/5799
FO 881/5799X
FO 954/20B
FO/954/27A
FCO 17/113
FCO 65/780
PREM 11/3472
PRO 30/22/14F
WO 32/7799
WO 32/8122

United States

President James Monroe, *First Annual Message*, 2 December 2 1817.

Proclamation 81—Declaring a Blockade of Ports in Rebellious States, 19 April 1861.

Instructions for the Government of Armies of the United States in the Field (Lieber Code), 24 April 1863.

A Century of Lawmaking for a New Nation: U.S. Congressional Documents and Debates, 1774–1875, US Serial Set, Number 1395 Senate Executive Document 11, 41st Congress, 1st Session.

Office of the Historian, *Papers Relating to the Foreign Relations of the United States, With the Address of the President to Congress December 2, 1913*, US Department of State, Washington, DC.

Office of the Historian, *Foreign Relations of the United States Diplomatic Papers, 1932, The American Republics, Volume V*, US Department of State, Washington, DC.

Cable 893.00/6-2345, Ambassador in China (Hurley) to the Secretary of State, dated 23 June, 1945.

Cable 893.801/6-649, Minister-Counselor of Embassy in China (Clark) to the Secretary of State, dated 6 June 1949.

US Department of State, *United States Relations with China, with Special Reference to the Period 1944-1949*, US Government Printing Office, Washington, DC, 1949.

US Army, *The Law of Land Warfare* (FM 27-10) 18 July 1956 (as amended 15 July 1976).

Office of the Historian, *Foreign Relations of the United States, 1958–1960, Indonesia, Volume XVII*, US Department of State, Washington, DC.

Office of the Historian, *Foreign Relations of the United States, 1961–1963, Volume X, Cuba, January 1961–September 1962*, US Department of State, Washington, DC.

'Memorandum Containing Comments on Fourth Draft of a Department of State—Department of Defense Paper on U.S. Assistance to Revolt in Cuba', 8 June 1963.

Whiteman's Digest of International Law: Volume 4, Department of State Publication 7825, US Government Printing Office, Washington, DC, April 1965.

'H.Res. 1049 (110th): Calling for the Bolivarian Republic of Venezuela to Be Designated a State Sponsor of Terrorism', 13 March 2008.

US Department of Defence Directive series 2311.01E (promulgated December 1998, updated May 2006, and reconfirmed February 2011).

Harold Hongju Koh, 'The Obama Administration and International Law', Speech to the Annual Meeting of the American Society of International Law, Washington, DC, 25 March 2010.

US Army Judge-Advocate General's Legal Centre and School, *Operational Law Handbook 2012*.

US Department of State, *Digest of United States Practice in International Law (2012)*.

'Presidential Policy Guidance: Procedures for Approving Direct Action Against Terrorist Targets Located Outside the United States and Areas of Active Hostilities, 23 May 2013' (2017) 56 *International Legal Materials* 1212.

Remarks by President Barak Obama at the National Defence University, 23 May 2013.

US Department of Defence Law of War Manual, June 2015.

US Navy, Marine Corps, and Coast Guard, NWP 1-14M. *Commander's Handbook on the Law of Naval Operations* (2017).

Venezuela

'Resolution and Reality: H.Res 1049', Venezuelan Embassy, Washington, DC, 2008.

Vietnam

'Application of Geneva Conventions in Viet-Nam: Letter of Democratic Republic Of Viet-Nam' (1966) 5 *International Legal Materials* 124

Peoples Republic of China

'Foreign Ministry Note to Britain: New China News Agency, Peking, 22 June 1957' (Document 18-3), in Jerome Cohen and Hungdah Chiu, *People's China and International Law: A Documentary Study, Volume I*, Princeton University Press, Princeton, 1974, pp 595–596.

UN and Associated Documents

Report of the League of Nations Committee of Experts (1927), League of Nations Document C.196.M.70.1927.V.

Committee of Experts for the Progressive Codification of International Law, 'Report to the Council of the League of Nations on the Questions which Appear Ripe for International Regulation' (1928) 22:1 *American Journal of International Law* (Supplement) 4.

Resolutions of The Diplomatic Conference, 75 U.N.T.S. 21 August 12, 1949.

UN General Assembly Resolution 2395 (XXIII) *Question of Territories under Portuguese Administration*, 29 November 1968.

UN General Assembly Resolution 2396 (XXIII) (A/7348), 2 December 1968.

Secretary-General's Report on Respect For Human Rights In Armed Conflicts (UN Doc A/ 8052, 18 September 1970).

Report of the Secretary-General's Panel of Experts on accountability in Sri Lanka, 31 March 2011.

Geoffrey Palmer, Alvaro Uribe, et al, *Report of the Secretary-General's Panel of Inquiry on the 31 May 2010 Flotilla Incident ('Palmer-Uribe Report')* (2011).

United Nations Assistance Mission in Afghanistan / Afghanistan Independent Human Rights Commission, *Afghanistan Annual Report 2010: Protection of Civilians in Armed Conflict*, March 2011.

United Nations Assistance Mission in Afghanistan / Afghanistan Independent Human Rights Commission, *Afghanistan Mid-Year Report on Protection of Civilians in Armed Conflict: 2012.*

UNSCR 2140, Yemen, 26 February 2014.

ICC Office of the Prosecutor, *Situation on Registered Vessels of Comoros, Greece and Cambodia: Article 53(1) Report (6 November 2014) ('ICC OTP Mavi Marmara Report').*

'Identical letters dated 26 March 2015 from the Permanent Representative of Qatar to the United Nations addressed to the Secretary-General and the President of the Security Council' (S/2015/217), 27 March 2015.

UNSCR 2342, Yemen, 23 February 2017.

NATO documents

COMISAF 06 July 2009 Tactical Memorandum (as amended 30 November 2011).

NATO Legal Adviser, Letters to Judge Kirsch of the UN International Commission of Inquiry on Libya, 23 January 2012, and 15 February 2012.

ICRC documents

Final Record of The Diplomatic Conference of Geneva of 1949 Vol II-B.

Jean Pictet (ed), *Geneva Convention for the Amelioration of the Condition of the Wounded and Sick in Armed Forces in the Field: Commentary*, ICRC, Geneva, 1952.

ICRC, *Report on Reaffirmation and Development of the Laws and Customs of War Applicable in Armed Conflicts: Submitted by the ICRC for the 21st International Conference of the Red Cross*, Istanbul, 1969, Geneva, 1969.

Official Records of the Diplomatic Conference on the Reaffirmation and Development of International Humanitarian Law Applicable in Armed Conflicts, Geneva, 1974–1977.

Yves Sandoz, Christophe Swinarski, and Bruno Zimmermann (eds), *Commentary on The Additional Protocols of 8 June 1977 to The Geneva Conventions of 12 August 1949*, ICRC, Geneva, 1987.

Jean-Marie Henckaerts and Louise Doswald-Beck, *Customary International Humanitarian Law*, ICRC/Cambridge University Press, Geneva/Cambridge, 2005.

Nils Melzer, *Interpretive Guidance on the Notion of Direct Participation in Hostilities under International Humanitarian Law*, ICRC, Geneva, 2009.

ICRC, *Commentary on the First Geneva Convention*, Cambridge University Press, Cambridge, 2016.

ICRC, *Commentary on the Second Geneva Convention*, ICRC, Geneva, 2017.

Other documents, reports, and sources

David Bederman, 'Privateering', *Max Planck Encyclopedia of Public International Law*, at http://opil.ouplaw.com/view/10.1093/law:epil/9780199231690/law-9780199231690-e382?rskey=g5gbiW&result=3&prd=OPIL

Pascal Bongard, 'Engaging Armed Non-State Actors on Humanitarian Norms: Reflections on Geneva Call's Experience' (2013) 58 *Humanitarian Exchange Magazine.*

Patrick Browning, *The Gran Para: The Delicate Dance of South American Privateering from Baltimore*, JD Thesis, University of Maryland, 22 January 2015.

Geneva Call, *Engaging with Armed Non-State Actors in the Broader Middle East on the Protection of Civilians*, Conference Report, Broumana, Lebanon, 30–31 March 2012.

Robert Campbell, *Neutral Rights and Obligations in the Anglo-Boer War*, Johns Hopkins University Press, Baltimore, 1908.

Civil War Facts: 1861–1865, at https://www.nps.gov/civilwar/facts.htm

European Council on Foreign Relations, 'Mapping the Yemen Conflict', 2017.

PK Ghosh, 'Maritime Security Challenges in South Asia and the Indian Ocean: Response Strategies', paper delivered at the Centre for Strategic and International Studies/America-Pacific Sealanes Security Institute, *Conference on Maritime Security in Asia*, 18–20 January 2004.

Constantin von der Groben, 'German Federal Prosecutor Terminates Investigation Against German Soldiers with Respect to NATO Airstrike in Afghanistan', *EJIL Talk*, 29 April 2010, at http://www.ejiltalk.org/german-federal-prosecutor-terminates-investigation-against-german-soldiers-with-respect-to-nato-air-strike-in-afghanistan/

Kevin Heller, 'The Civil War and the Blockade of Gaza (a Response to Posner)', *Opinio Juris*, 4 June 2010, at http://opiniojuris.org/2010/06/04/eric-posners-incomplete-editorial-on-the-blockade-of-gaza/

Institute of International Law, 'Resolution on Rights and Duties of Foreign Powers as Regards the Established and Recognized Governments in Case of Insurrection', Neuchatel meeting, 8 September 1900, in James Brown Scott, ed, *Resolutions of the Institute of International Law*, Oxford University Press, Oxford, 1916.

Institute of International Law, 'Regulations Respecting the Responsibility of States by Reason of Damages Suffered by Aliens in Case of Riot, Insurrection or Civil War' (adopted 10 September 1900), in James Brown Scott, ed, *Resolutions of The Institute of International Law*, Oxford University Press, Oxford, 1916.

Institut de Droit International, *The Application of International Humanitarian Law and Fundamental Human Rights, in Armed Conflicts in which Non-State Entities are Parties* (Resolution adopted at the Berlin session, 25 August 1999).

Institute for National Security and Counterterrorism (INSCT), *Libya In Conflict: Mapping The Libyan Armed Conflict* (2012).

Quinta Jurecic, 'The Lieber Code' (23 July 2015) *Lawfare*, at https://www.lawfareblog.com/throwback-thursday-lieber-code

Eugene Kontorovich, 'International Legal Responses to Piracy off the Coast of Somalia' (2009) 13:2 *ASIL Insights*, at https://www.asil.org/insights/volume/13/issue/2/international-legal-responses-piracy-coast-somalia

Eugene Kontorovich, 'Iran's Relief Ship and the Blockade of Yemen', *Opinio Juris*, 11 May 2015, at http://opiniojuris.org/2015/05/11/guest-post-irans-relief-ship-and-the-blockade-of-yemen/

Angana Kotokey, 'Pakistan's Neutrality on Yemen Crisis: A Domestic Compulsion', Centre for Studies in International Relations and Development, 22 August 2015, at http://csird.org.in/wp-content/uploads/2017/02/Pakistan.pdf.

Rob McLaughlin, 'Common Article 2 as a Paradigmatically Challenging Threshold for the Application of IHL', *ILA Reporter*, 11 November 2016, at http://ilareporter.org.au/2016/11/common-article-2-as-a-paradigmatically-challenging-threshold-for-the-application-of-ihl-rob-mclaughlin/

Manual on the Laws of Naval War, Oxford University Press, Oxford, 1913.

Marko Milanovic, 'What Exactly Internationalises an Internal Armed Conflict?', *EJIL Talk*, 7 May 2010, at http://www.ejiltalk.org/what-exactly-internationalizes-an-internal-armed-conflict/

North of England P&I Association, 'Loss Prevention: Yemen Information Sheet', April 2015.

Office of the Historian, 'The Trent Affair, 1861', *US Department of State*, at https://history.state.gov/milestones/1861-1865/trent-affair

James Renwick and Gregory Treverton, 'The Challenges of Trying Terrorists as Criminals', *RAND Centre for Global Risk and Security*, 2008.

Philippe Sands, Andrew Clapham, and Blinne Ni Ghralaign, 'The Lawfulness of the Authorisation by The United Kingdom of Weapons and Related Items for Export to Saudi Arabia in the Context of Saudi Arabia's Military Intervention in Yemen', 11 December 2015.

Soliman M Santos Jr, *Evolution of the Armed Conflict on the Communist Front* (background paper submitted to the Human Development Network Foundation, Inc. for the Philippine Human Development Report 2005).

STRATFOR Worldview, 'In Yemen, Anti-Houthi Operations Confront Forceful Opposition', 25 August 2015.

Kenneth Watkin, 'Warriors without rights? Combatants, Unprivileged Belligerents, and the Struggle over Legitimacy' (2005) *Program on Humanitarian Policy and Conflict Research.*

Diane Webber, 'Hassan v. United Kingdom: A New Approach to Security Detention in Armed Conflict?', *ASIL Insights*, 2 April 2015, at http://www.asil.org/insights/volume/19/issue/7/hassan-v-united-kingdom-new-approach-security-detention-armed-conflict#_edn1

Jan Wouters and Sten Verhoeven, 'Desuetudo', *Max Planck Encyclopedia of Public International Law*, at http://opil.ouplaw.com/view/10.1093/law:epil/9780199231690/law-9780199231690-e1027?prd=EPIL

Index

For the benefit of digital users, indexed terms that span two pages (e.g., 52–53) may, on occasion, appear on only one of those pages.